Alan Bold was born in [ ] university and worked as a journalist. A well known poet, critic, biographer and anthologist, he was 1989 Scottish Writer of the Year, winning the prestigious McVitie's Prize for *MacDiarmid*, his acclaimed biography of the poet Hugh MacDiarmid with whom he was associated for many years.

The author of numerous books of criticism, he is a regular reviewer for the *Glasgow Herald* and a contributor to the *Sunday Times*. He has published many books of poetry, including *To Find the New* and *In This Corner*, and has edited several anthologies, such as *The Penguin Book of Socialist Verse*, the *Cambridge Book of English Verse 1939–75* and *Making Love: The Picador Book of Erotic Verse*. He is also the author of two collections of short stories and one novel, *East is West*, published in 1991.

Best known as a writer, he has long been active as a visual artist. His pictures have been bought by the Scottish National Gallery of Modern Art, the Scottish Arts Council and the National Library of Scotland, and he has had one-man exhibitions in galleries throughout the UK and overseas.

An authority on Burns's life and work, he is the author of *A Burns Companion* (1991) and a pictorial profile, *Robert Burns* (1992). He has also exhibited paintings on Burnsian themes in galleries in Dumfries and in Burns's native Ayrshire.

Alan Bold, who has worked as a full-time writer and artist since 1966, lives in rural Fife. He is currently working on a major new critical biography of Robert Burns to be published for the bicentenary of the poet's death in 1996.

BOOKS BY ALAN BOLD

POETRY
Society Inebrious
The Voyage
To Find the New
A Perpetual Motion Machine
Penguin Modern Poets 15 (with
 Brathwaite and Morgan)
The State of the Nation
The Auld Symie
He Will Be Greatly Missed
A Century of People
A Pint of Bitter
Scotland, Yes
This Fine Day
A Celtic Quintet (with Bellany)
In This Corner: Selected Poems
 1963–83
Haven (with Bellany)
Summoned by Knox
Homage to MacDiarmid (with
 Bellany)
Bright Lights Blaze Out (with Owen
 and O'Callaghan)

FICTION
Hammer and Thistle: Stories (with
 Morrison)
The Edge of the Wood: Stories
East Is West: A Novel

NONFICTION
Thom Gunn & Ted Hughes
George Mackay Brown
The Ballad
The Sensual Scot
Modern Scottish Literature
MacDiarmid: The Terrible Crystal
True Characters (with Giddings)
The Book of Rotters (with Giddings)
Longman Dictionary of Poets
Muriel Spark

Who Was Really Who in Fiction
 (with Giddings)
Scotland: A Literary Guide
MacDiarmid: A Critical Biography
An Open Book: Critical Essays
A Burns Companion

AS EDITOR
The Penguin Book of Socialist Verse
The Martial Muse: Seven Centuries
 of War Poetry
Cambridge Book of English Verse
 1939–75
Making Love: The Picador Book of
 Erotic Verse
The Bawdy Beautiful: The Sphere
 Book of Improper Verse
Mounts of Venus: The Picador Book
 of Erotic Prose
Drink To Me Only: The Prose (and
 Cons) of Drinking
Smollett: Author of the First
 Distinction
The Sexual Dimension in Literature
A Scottish Poetry Book
Scott: The Long-Forgotten Melody
Byron: Wrath and Rhyme
The Thistle Rises: A MacDiarmid
 Miscellany
MacDiarmid: Aesthetics in Scotland
The Letters of Hugh MacDiarmid
The Poetry of Motion
Muriel Spark: An Odd Capacity for
 Vision
Harold Pinter: You Never Heard
 Such Silence
Auden: The Far Interior
A Second Scottish Poetry Book
Scottish Quotations
The Quest for le Carré
Dylan Thomas: Craft or Sullen Art

RHYMER RAB

An Anthology of Poems and Prose

ROBERT BURNS

EDITED BY ALAN BOLD

BLACK SWAN

RHYMER RAB:
AN ANTHOLOGY OF POEMS AND PROSE BY ROBERT BURNS
A BLACK SWAN BOOK: 0 552 99526 6

First publication in Great Britain

PRINTING HISTORY
Black Swan edition published 1993

This anthology copyright © Alan Bold 1993

The right of Alan Bold to be identified as the editor of this work
has been asserted in accordance with sections 77 and 78 of the
Copyright Designs and Patents Act 1988.

Conditions of Sale

1. This book is sold subject to the condition that it shall not, by
way of trade or otherwise, be lent, re-sold, hired out or otherwise
circulated in any form of binding or cover other than that in which it is
published and without a similar condition including this condition being
imposed on the subsequent purchaser.

2. This book is sold subject to the Standard Conditions of Sale of
Net Books and may not be re-sold in the UK below the net price
fixed by the publishers for the book.

Set in 10/11 pt Monotype Bembo by
Phoenix Typesetting, Ilkley, West Yorkshire

Black Swan Books are published by Transworld Publishers Ltd,
61–63 Uxbridge Road, London W5 5SA,
in Australia by Transworld Publishers (Australia) Pty Ltd,
15–25 Helles Avenue, Moorebank, NSW 2170
and New Zealand by Transworld Publishers (NZ) Ltd,
3 William Pickering Drive, Albany, Auckland.

Reproduced, printed and bound in Britain by
Cox & Wyman Ltd, Reading, Berks.

CONTENTS

PART TWO: PROSE

PREFACE

This anthology contains fifty-one of Burns's finest poems and songs, fifty of his most revealing letters as well as the Autobiographical Letter by way of Prologue. Also included are extracts from the two Commonplace Books and the two tourist Journals, the Preface to the Kilmarnock edition, the Dedication to the first Edinburgh edition, and a little-known story by way of Epilogue. By way of clarifying content and context, I have provided a topographical note on Burns Country, a Chronology, a Who's Who and a glossary of all Scots words used in the book. My editorial intention is to indicate the extraordinary artistic, emotional and intellectual range of Robert Burns.

Both parts of the book are arranged chronologically (so far as a reliable chronology can be established). Some songs and poems of Burns chose themselves ('It was upon a Lammas night' and 'Tam o' Shanter' for example); others are included as outstanding examples of his artistry ('The Jolly Beggars') or as significant in the story of Burns ('My father was a farmer'). The prose, likewise, represents both Burns the superlative literary stylist and Burns the compulsive commentator on his life and times.

Obviously, in a selection from a prolific writer, some popular favourites must be omitted and this applies especially to the songs. I have settled for songs that read well as lyrics. For those who wish to hear the songs sung well, an ambitious attempt to record all songs associated with Burns is in progress as *The Songs of Robert Burns*, researched by Serge Hovey (1920–89) and sung by Jean Redpath, and available on records and cassettes from Philo/Rounder Records, Cambridge, Massachusetts, and Greentrax Records, Edinburgh.

I am currently writing, for the same publisher, a critical biography of Burns. As the planet spins towards a new century, there is a need to reassess the importance of a poet who has remained popular for more than 200 years and looks more certain than most writers to feature prominently in the future. This anthology is part of the reassessment; the biography will attempt to tell the whole story.

A.B.

ACKNOWLEDGEMENTS

I would like to thank James A. Mackay for his kind permission to use texts from his editions, both authorised by the Burns Federation, of *The Complete Works of Robert Burns* (Ayr: Alloway Publishing, 1986, rev. 1990) and *The Complete Letters of Robert Burns* (Ayr: Alloway Publishing, 1987). I am similarly grateful to Raymond Lamont Brown for his permission to use texts from his editions of *Robert Burns' Common Place Book* (Wakefield: S.R. Publishers, 1969), *Robert Burns's Tour of the Borders 5 May – 1 June 1787* (Ipswich: The Boydell Press, 1972), and *Robert Burns's Tours of the Highlands and Stirlingshire 1787* (Ipswich: The Boydell Press, 1978). References to James Kinsley's three-volume edition of *The Poems and Songs of Robert Burns* (1968) are by kind permission of Oxford University Press.

My thanks, too, to John Saddler, editor at Black Swan, for commissioning this anthology and encouraging me during my work on it; and to Duncan McAra for copy-editing the text.

A.B.

ABBREVIATIONS

Several abbreviations are used in the Introduction and Chronology and headnotes to songs and poems:

CH *Robert Burns: The Critical Heritage*, ed. Donald A. Low (London, 1974).

ch-w *The Life and Works of Robert Burns*, ed. Robert Chambers, rev. William Wallace (4 vols., Edinburgh, 1896).

CL *The Complete Letters of Robert Burns*, ed. James A. Mackay (Ayr, 1987).

CURRIE *The Works of Robert Burns*, ed. James Currie (2nd edn., 4 vols., London, 1801).

CW *The Complete Works of Robert Burns*, ed. James A. Mackay (2nd edn., Ayr, 1990).

H-H *The Poetry of Robert Burns*, ed. W.E. Henley & T.F. Henderson (4 vols., Edinburgh, 1896).

KINSLEY *The Poems and Songs of Robert Burns*, ed. James Kinsley (3 vols., Oxford, 1968).

MMC *The Merry Muses of Caledonia; A Collection of Favourite Scots Songs, Ancient and Modern; Selected for use of the Crochallan Fencibles* (c. 1800).

NSS *Notes on Scottish Song by Robert Burns*, ed. J.C. Dick (London, 1908); reproduced in 1991 reprint of SMM (see below).

SC *A Select Collection of Original Scotish Airs for The Voice*, ed. George Thomson (8 vols., Edinburgh, 1793–1818).

SMM *The Scots Musical Museum*, ed. James Johnson (6 vols., Edinburgh, 1787–1803); reprinted with Introduction by Donald A. Low (2 vols., Aldershot, 1991).

SNYDER *The Life of Robert Burns*, by F.B. Snyder (1932; reprinted Hamden, Conn., 1968).

EDITIONS OF *POEMS, CHIEFLY IN THE SCOTTISH DIALECT*

Three editions of *Poems, Chiefly in the Scottish Dialect* were approved by Burns:

KILMARNOCK EDITION: Printed by John Wilson of Kilmarnock, it appeared in late July 1786, probably 31 July, in an edition of 612 copies, selling at three shillings a copy. Burns estimated he earned, after expenses, around £20 from the Kilmarnock edition.

FIRST EDINBURGH EDITION: Published by William Creech and printed by William Smellie, it appeared on 17 April 1787 in an edition of 3000 copies, selling at five shillings to 1500 subscribers, six shillings to others. It contained all the poems from the Kilmarnock edition (except three epitaphs) as well as twenty-two new pieces including 'Death and Doctor Hornbook', 'The Brigs of Ayr', 'Address to the Unco Guid' and 'To a Haggis'. The frontispiece portrait is a copper engraving by John Beugo from a portrait in oil painted by Alexander Nasmyth. Burns earned around £450 from the first Edinburgh edition, including 100 guineas for the sale of his copyright to Creech.

SECOND EDINBURGH EDITION: Published by William Creech, in two volumes, on 16 February 1793. It declared itself 'The second edition considerably enlarged', the nineteen previously uncollected poems including 'Tam o' Shanter'. Having sold his copyright to Creech, Burns had to content himself with twenty complimentary copies of the second Edinburgh edition which was reprinted in 1794.

THE BURNS COUNTRY

Ostensibly the topographical story of Burns is a tale of two Scottish counties, Ayrshire and Dumfriesshire, as well as four Scottish tours of 1787 and two Galloway tours of 1793–4. Poetically it is essentially about Ayrshire. In the first Commonplace Book (see p.239) Burns declared his ambition to be the bard of Ayrshire and he was always associated with the area. Henry Mackenzie's influential essay in the *Lounger* (9 Dec. 1786) acclaimed 'an Ayrshire Ploughman' (CH, 68); Thomas Stewart's edition of 1801 collected *Poems ascribed to Robert Burns, the Ayrshire Bard*.

Burns lived most of his life in Ayrshire and first left the county when he was twenty-seven and on his way to fame, if not fortune, in Edinburgh in November 1786. All the poems and songs in the Kilmarnock edition were composed in Ayrshire and his best-known poem 'Tam o' Shanter', though written on his Dumfriesshire farm of Ellisland, refers back to Ayrshire.

A maritime county in the south-west of Scotland, Ayrshire is bounded on the west by the Firth of Clyde and North Channel. Alexander Webster's *An Account of the Number of People in Scotland*, compiled four years before Burns was born, estimated the population of Ayrshire as 59,009 from a total Scottish population of 1,265,380. In 1755 Ayr, the county capital, had a population of 2964. Ayrshire is the 'well-known land' of 'The Vision', Ayr the 'ancient borough' of that poem. Burns describes Ayr in 'The Brigs of Ayr' and celebrates it in 'Tam o' Shanter' as 'Auld Ayr, wham ne'er a town surpasses,/For honest men and bonie lasses'.

Alloway, where Burns was born in a cottage (preserved with an adjoining museum) close to Kirk Alloway (300 yards north of the river Doon), is a hamlet just over two miles south of Ayr. In Ayrshire Burns lived in the Alloway cottage, built by his father, from 1759 to 1766; at Mount Oliphant farm (2½ miles south-east of Ayr) from 1766 to 1777; at Lochlea farm (2½ miles north-east of Tarbolton) from 1777 to 1784; at Mossgiel farm (1½ miles north-west of Mauchline) from 1784 to 1786 (he transferred his share in Mossgiel to his brother Gilbert in 1786 though he made return visits until 1788).

Burns honoured the old division of Ayrshire into three areas defined by rivers: Cunninghame, north of the river Irvine; Kyle, between the Irvine and the Doon; and Carrick, south of the Doon. His poems assume a familiarity with these areas. He called himself a lad 'born in

Kyle' (see p.206) because Alloway was in the central area. He said his
father was 'a farmer upon the Carrick border' (see p.105) since Mount
Oliphant farm is so located in Kyle. He has one of the Jolly Beggars,
gathered in Poosie-Nansie's tavern in Mauchline, say 'I met my old boy
in a Cunningham Fair' (see p.152) to establish an itinerant existence.

Ayrshire has almost eighty miles of coastline and during the years
he spent in the county Burns was never far away from water, often
enjoying spectacular views of the Firth of Clyde. In 'The Vision' he
notes how 'rivers in the sea were lost' (see p.143) and specifies the
rivers Doon, Irvine ('well-fed Irwine') and Ayr. In 'The Brigs of
Ayr' he mentions the Coil (a stream that rises north of Dalmellington
and, after a run of fourteen miles, falls into the river Ayr, four miles
east of the town); Garpal Water (a tributary of river Ayr, one mile
south-west of Muirkirk); Greenock Water (tributary of the river Ayr,
joining it four miles west of Muirkirk); the Lugar (river flowing $12\frac{1}{2}$
miles north-west to the river Ayr).

That Burns knew much of Ayrshire intimately is evident from topographical references scattered through his work. Catrine, catalogued
in 'The Brigs of Ayr' as the country home of Dugald Stewart, is a small
town $2\frac{1}{2}$ miles south-east of Mauchline. Cumnock (of the Cumnock
Hills in 'Death and Doctor Hornbook') is a town on the river Lugar,
sixteen miles east of Ayr. Glenbuck ('The Brigs of Ayr') is a village
$3\frac{1}{2}$ miles north-east of Muirkirk which is itself twenty-three miles
east-north-east of Ayr and cited in the first 'Epistle to J. Lapraik'.
More minute local allusions were meaningful to Burns: the Willie's
mill of 'Death and Doctor Hornbook' was the home of miller William
Muir, on the eastern edge of Tarbolton.

Burns was well placed to explore Ayrshire. Agnes Broun, his mother,
was raised and married in Maybole (eight miles south-south-west
of Ayr), the old capital of Carrick. In the summer of 1772 Burns
attended the parish school in Dalrymple (four miles south-east of
Ayr) on the Kyle border with Carrick. He spent the summer of 1775
at Kirkoswald (four miles south-west of Maybole), a coastal village in Carrick, and there met some of the characters supposedly
recreated in 'Tam o' Shanter'. In 1781–2 he learned the business
of flax-dressing in Irvine (ten miles north of Ayr), Cunningham.
His first volume of verse was printed in Kilmarnock (eleven miles
north-north-east of Ayr), Cunningham.

After going to Edinburgh, Burns made four tours of Scotland
in 1787: the Border tour with Robert Ainslie, 5 May–1 June; the
solo tour of the West Highlands in late June; the Highland tour with
William Nicol, 25 August–16 September; the Stirlingshire tour

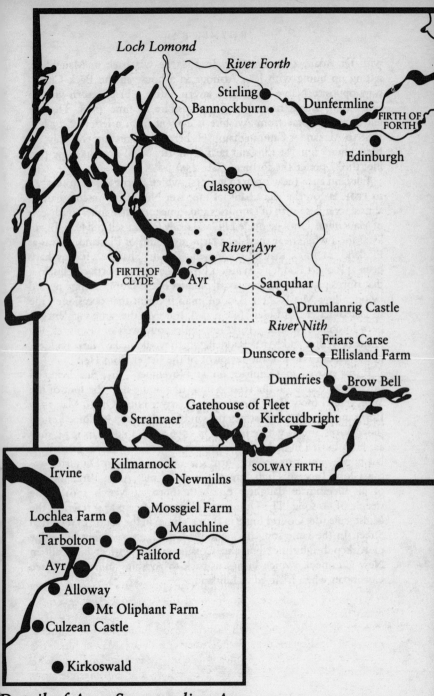

Detail of Area Surrounding Ayr

with Dr Adair, 4–20 October. In 1788 he was back in Mauchline, setting up home with Jean Armour in a house in the Back Causeway, opposite Nanse Tinnock's tavern. After a brief return visit to Edinburgh, Burns moved to Dumfriesshire in June 1788. That he felt displaced away from Ayrshire is evident from a letter of 27 July 1788 to Alexander Cunningham: 'Hitherto my direction was only "at Mauchline" but "at Ellisland near Dumfries" will now likewise find me; tho' I prefer the former.' (CL, 455)

Ellisland farm (now open to visitors), which Burns leased from 1788 to 1791, lay on the right bank of the river Nith, in Dunscore parish; almost six miles north of Dumfries and some forty-five miles south-east of Mauchline. Until he made Ellisland ready for himself and Jean, Burns lived for a while near the Isle, a farm just south of Ellisland. It was at Ellisland, in 1790, that he composed 'Tam o' Shanter'. It may have been at Robert Riddell's mansion Friars' Carse, just north of Ellisland, that Burns made the biggest social blunder of the Dumfriesshire period by offending Mrs Robert Riddell in an incident that occasioned the so-called 'letter from Hell' (see p.325); however the same incident has been located at Woodley Park, four miles southwest of Dumfries, the home of Walter and Maria Riddell, which would make Maria Riddell, not Elizabeth Riddell, the recipient of the 'letter from Hell'.

Burns moved to Dumfries on 11 November 1791, first living in three small rooms on the second floor of a house near the foot of the Wee Vennel (now Bank Street) near the river Nith. On 19 May 1793 Burns moved into a two-storey red sandstone house in Millbrae Vennel (now Burns Street) where he died in 1796 and Jean died in 1834: they are both buried in St Michael's churchyard, a few minutes from their last home, now a museum. Burns's favourite tavern in Dumfries was the Globe Inn, 56 High Street, where he met Anne Park, mother of his illegitimate daughter Elizabeth (born 22 March 1791). The steeple of his song 'The Dumfries Volunteers' (see p.234) refers to the Midsteeple (the Court House in Burns's time) in the centre of the High Street. In the same song he mentions Criffel, a prominent hill-ridge in Kirkcudbrightshire; but also Corsincon, a 1547-feet-high hill in New Cumnock, which brings us back to Ayrshire: Burns could see Corsincon when he lived at Ellisland.

CHRONOLOGY

1757
On 15 December, William Burnes (1721–84) marries Agnes Broun (1732–1820) in Maybole and moves with her into the two-roomed clay thatched cottage he has built on land leased in Alloway.

1759
Robert Burns (Ayrshire spelling of surname), the first of seven children, is born on 25 January in his parents' cottage.

1760
Gilbert Burns born 28 September. Other children are: Agnes (1762–1834), Annabella (1764–1832), William (1767–90), John (1769–85), Isabella (1771–1858).

1765
William Burnes and four neighbours hire, turn about, the services of schoolmaster John Murdoch (1747–1824) who recalls: 'Gilbert always appeared to me to possess a more lively imagination and to be more of the wit, than Robert.' (Currie I, 89)

1766
William Burnes rents the seventy-acre hilltop farm of Mount Oliphant, two miles south-east of Alloway: 'almost the very poorest soil I know of in a state of cultivation' (Gilbert Burns, Currie I, 69).

1768
Murdoch leaves Alloway and William Burnes takes personal charge of his sons' education.

1769
William Fergusson, William Burnes's landlord at Mount Oliphant, dies on 7 November. 'My father's generous Master died; the farm proved a ruinous bargain; and, to clench the curse, we fell into the hands of a Factor who sat .or the picture I have drawn for one in my Tale of two dogs.' (CL, 250)

1772
Robert and Gilbert attend Dalrymple parish school, week about, during the summer quarter. Burns reads Richardson's *Pamela*. On Mount Oliphant farm, Robert 'at the age of thirteen, assisted in

threshing the crop of corn' (Gilbert Burns, Currie I, 69). Murdoch, now teaching English in Ayr, sends Robert and Gilbert the poetic works of Pope.

1773

With an interruption to help with the harvest at Mount Oliphant, Robert is sent to Ayr for three weeks to lodge with Murdoch and study grammar, French and a little Latin. According to Gilbert, Burns is 'considered as a sort of prodigy' at French (Currie I, 66).

1774

At Mount Oliphant, Burns 'at fifteen was the principal labourer on the farm, for we had no hired servant, male or female' (Gilbert Burns, Currie I, 69). Working in the harvest with Nelly Kilpatrick, Burns 'first committed the sin of RHYME' (CL, 250), writing the song 'O, once I lov'd a bonie lass'.

1775

In the summer Burns studies mathematics under Hugh Rodger at Kirkoswald; he is distracted from his studies by Peggy Thomson. He reads Shenstone and Thomson.

1777

At Whitsun, William Burnes moves from Mount Oliphant to Lochlea farm, Tarbolton, renting 130 swampy acres for £130 per year from David McLure. During the Lochlea period Burns reads widely, studying Locke's *An Essay concerning Human Understanding* and the songs collected in Allan Ramsay's *The Tea-Table Miscellany*.

1779

Burns joins a country-dancing school in Tarbolton: 'My father had an unaccountable antipathy against these meetings; and my going was, what to this hour I repent, in absolute defiance of his commands.' (CL, 251–2)

1780

Robert, Gilbert and five friends form the Tarbolton Bachelors' Club on 11 November; at the first meeting, Burns is elected president for the night.

1781

William Burnes in dispute with David McLure. Burns becomes a Freemason, entered an apprentice in Lodge St David, Tarbolton, on 4 July. Burns makes romantic overtures to Alison Begbie but is rejected; goes to Irvine to learn the business of flax-dressing.

1782

On 1 January, the Irvine flax-dressing shop 'by the drunken carelessness
of my Partner's wife, took fire and was burnt to ashes; and left me like
a true Poet, not worth sixpence' (CL, 254). Burns returns to Lochlea
in March; on 24 September the dispute between William Burnes
and McLure is referred to arbiters.

1783

In April Burns begins his first Commonplace Book. On 17 May a
warrant of sequestration is operated against William Burnes who, on
25 August, makes his first appeal to the Court of Session, Edinburgh.
As a precaution against ruin, Robert and Gilbert Burns arrange to rent,
for £90 per year from Gavin Hamilton, the 180-acre upland farm of
Mossgiel, in the parish of Mauchline.

1784

On 27 January the Court of Session upholds William Burnes who
dies on 13 February: 'When my father died, his all went among the
rapacious hell-hounds that growl in the kennel of justice' (CL, 254).
Burns and the family move into Mossgiel in March: now familiar with
the Scots poems of Robert Fergusson, Burns 'now began to be known
in the neighbourhood as a maker of rhymes' (CL, 255). Meets Jean,
daughter of Mauchline mason James Armour.

1785

On 22 May, the poet's illegitimate daughter by Betty Paton, is born.
In October Burns's youngest brother, John, dies.

1786

Burns signs a paper attesting his marriage to Jean whose father is
appalled on hearing of her pregnancy: 'He was in the greatest distress,
and fainted away.' (Gilbert Burns, Currie I, 75) Burns plans to emigrate
to Jamaica to make enough money to support a family: 'As he had not
sufficient money to pay for his passage [Gavin] Hamilton advised him
to publish his poems in the mean time by subscription, as a likely way
of getting a little money to provide him more liberally in necessaries
for Jamaica.' (Gilbert Burns, Currie I, 76) On 3 April Burns sends
Proposals for publishing by subscription 'Scotch Poems' to Kilmarnock
printer John Wilson who publishes the Proposals on 14 April, the day
James Armour has the marriage attestation mutilated. Burns embarks
on his affair with Mary Campbell and on 14 May the couple meet
at Failford and plan to marry and emigrate together. On 25 June,
Burns agrees to stand three Sundays in Mauchline kirk for rebuke

so he can obtain a certificate pronouncing him a free bachelor; on
22 July he transfers his share in Mossgiel to Gilbert; on 30 July he
writes to John Richmond: 'Armour has got a warrant to throw me
in jail till I find security for an enormous sum . . . I am wandering
from one friend's house to another' (CL, 78). The Kilmarnock edition
of *Poems, Chiefly in the Scottish Dialect* appears on 31 July. On 6 August
Burns and Jean make their last public penitential appearance in kirk.
Burns postpones his Jamaican voyage on 1 September, and on Sunday,
3 September, is at Mossgiel when told Jean has given birth to twins.
On 4 September (in a letter that is passed to Burns) Thomas Blacklock
praises the Kilmarnock edition and suggests an enlarged edition: 'a letter
from Dr Blacklock to a friend of mine overthrew all my schemes by
rousing my poetic ambition' (CL, 256). Burns sets out, on a borrowed
pony, for Edinburgh on 27 November: on 14 December, William
Creech issues subscription bills for the first Edinburgh edition of
Poems, Chiefly in the Scottish Dialect.

1787

On 14 January, Burns is considering a proposal from Patrick Miller
to lease a farm near Dumfries: 'I dare say he means to favour me,
yet he may give me, in his opinion, an advantageous bargain that
may ruin me' (CL, 100). On 17 April the first Edinburgh edition
is published; on 23 April Burns sells his copyright to Creech for
100 guineas. From 5 May to 1 June Burns tours the Borders with
Robert Ainslie; before the end of June he tours the West Highlands
alone; from 25 August to 16 September he tours the Highlands with
William Nicol; from 4 to 20 October he tours Stirlingshire with Dr
James Adair. Back in Edinburgh, Burns hears of the death of his
infant daughter Jean and, on 4 December, meets Mrs McLehose.
Three days later he dislocates his knee in a fall from a carriage and,
thus immobilised, begins his celebrated correspondence with Mrs
McLehose, the 'Clarinda' to his 'Sylvander'.

1788

On 7 January, Burns asks Robert Graham of Fintry to be his patron
in securing an appointment in the Excise. Burns leaves Edinburgh
and on 23 February is back in Mossgiel: writing to Mrs McLehose,
he condemns Jean, now in an advanced state of pregnancy: 'I am
disgusted with her; I cannot endure her! . . . I have done with
her, and she with me.' (CL, 399.) On 3 March Jean gives birth to
twin girls both of whom die before the end of the month. Back in
Edinburgh, Burns meets Patrick Miller on 18 March and signs the

lease on Ellisland, a farm on the banks of the river Nith, six miles north-west of Dumfries. Back in Mauchline he is moved by Jean's misery: 'I found a once much-loved and still much lov'd Female, literally & truly cast out to the mercy of the naked elements.' (CL, 147–8) By April, Burns is married to Jean, and living in a rented room in the Back Causeway, Mauchline. After a course of Excise instruction at Mauchline, Burns goes to Ellisland on 11 June. On 14 July, Burns receives his Excise commission. In November, Jenny Clow bears Burns a son in Edinburgh.

1789

Burns goes to Edinburgh (16 February) to settle accounts with Creech and deal with Jenny Clow's writ (settled 27 February). In the summer Burns meets Captain Francis Grose at Friars' Carse, Robert Riddell's home near Ellisland. On 18 August, Francis Wallace Burns is born. On 1 September Burns begins work as an Excise officer at an annual salary of £50. Riding up to forty miles a day in all weathers as an Exciseman exhausts Burns who writes on 13 December: 'For now near three weeks I have been so ill with a nervous head-ach, that I have been obliged to give up for a time my Excise-books, being scarce able to life my head, much less to ride once a week over ten muir Parishes.' (CL, 181)

1790

On 27 January, Burns is listed as eligible for promotion to Examiner or Supervisor of Excise. In February he writes to Mrs McLehose: 'I have, indeed, been ill, Madam, this whole winter. An incessant headache, depression of spirits, and all the truly miserable consequences of a deranged nervous system, have made dreadful havoc of my health and peace.' (CL, 406.) On 24 July, the month Burns is transferred to the Dumfries Third Division of Excise, his younger brother William dies in London. Burns completes 'Tam o' Shanter' and sends copy to Grose on 1 December.

1791

Towards the end of January Burns is injured in fall with horse. On 31 March, Anne Park, barmaid of the Globe Inn, Dumfries, gives birth to Burns's daughter Elizabeth; on 9 April, Jean gives birth to the poet's son William Nicol Burns. Burns's crops are auctioned at Ellisland on 25 August and on 10 September he formally renounces the Ellisland lease. He moves on 11 November to a second-floor apartment in the Wee Vennel (now Bank Street), Dumfries. From 29 November to 11 December, Burns is in Edinburgh, meeting Mrs

McLehose for the last time on 6 December; on 27 December he sends her 'Ae Fond Kiss' from Dumfries.

1792
In February, Burns is promoted to the Dumfries Port Division of Excise, compact enough to be covered on foot: his salary rises to £70 a year with the possibility of an additional £20 in perquisites. On 29 February Burns and other Excisemen capture the smuggling schooner *Rosamond* in the Solway Firth below Dumfries (he subsequently purchases four carronades at the sale of the seized vessel and sends them to revolutionary government in France). On 10 April, Burns is made an honorary member of the Royal Company of Archers. Elizabeth Riddell Burns born on 21 November. On 6 December, Burns writes to Mrs Dunlop about political unrest in Dumfries: 'in our Theatre here, "God save the king" has met with some groans and hisses, while Ça ira [the French revolutionary song] has been repeatedly called for' (CL, 202). Before the end of December an informer denounces Burns, to the Excise Board, as being 'head of a disaffected party' (CL, 436).

1793
On 5 January, Burns defends his political position in a letter to Robert Graham of Fintry, protesting that he honours the British Constitution and has become disillusioned with revolutionary France: 'I was her enthusiastic votary at the beginning of the business. – When she came to shew her old avidity for conquest, in annexing Savoy, &c. to her dominions, & invading the rights of Holland, I altered my sentiments.' (CL, 437) Burns keeps his Excise job. The second Edinburgh edition of *Poems, Chiefly in the Scottish Dialect* is published by William Creech on 16 February: a two-volume edition 'greatly enlarged with New Poems', including 'Tam o' Shanter'. On 19 May, Burns moves into a two-storey sandstone house in Millbrae Vennel (now Burns Street). From 30 July to 2 August, Burns tours Galloway with John Syme. Probably before the year ends (a precise date is impossible) Burns makes the biggest social blunder of his Dumfriesshire days: either at Friars' Carse (just north of Ellisland) he offends Elizabeth Riddell; or at Woodley Park (four miles south-west of Dumfries) he offends Maria Riddell. The offence is supposedly a simulation of the Rape of the Sabines (H-H II, 420), hence his 'letter from Hell' (see p.325).

1794
From 25 to 28 June, Burns and Syme make their second Galloway tour. On 12 August, James Glencairn Burns is born. On 22 December, Burns is appointed Acting Supervisor of Excise, Dumfries.

1795

At the beginning of the year Burns is in a revolutionary mood: early in January he sends George Thomson 'A Man's a Man for a' That'; on 12 January he writes to Mrs Dunlop (who is outraged by the remark) describing the executions of Louis XVI and Marie Antoinette as 'the deserved fate of . . . a perjured Blockhead & an unprincipled Prostitute' (CL, 214). Nevertheless, on 31 January Burns and some leading citizens of Dumfries petition the War Office for authority to organize the Dumfries Volunteers for whom he writes a patriotic song (see p.234). . Elizabeth Riddell Burns, the poet's only legitimate daughter to survive infancy, dies at the age of three, in September: 'I had scarcely began to recover from that shock, when became myself the victim of a most severe Rheumatic fever' (CL, 215).

1796

In January, Burns is seriously ill and psychologically distressed over his position in Dumfries: 'here, we have actual famine . . . Many days my family and hundreds of other families, are absolutely without one grain of meal; as money cannot purchase it.' (CL, 215) There are Meal Riots in Dumfries from 12 to 14 March. From 3 to 17 July, Burns is at Brow, a hamlet on the shores of the Solway Firth, seeking a cure for his condition in sea-bathing. On 7 July he writes, to Alexander Cunningham, 'Alas! my friend, I fear the voice of the Bard will soon be heard among you no more! . . . these last three months I have been tortured with an excruciating rheumatism, which has reduced me to nearly the last stage. – You actually would not know me if you saw me.' (CL, 473) On 12 July, he asks George Thomson for five pounds to settle an account with a 'cruel scoundrel of a Haberdasher [who] has commenced a process & will infallibly put me into jail' (CL, 679); Thomson sends the money on 14 July. On 18 July Burns returns to Dumfries where he dies, at home, on 21 July: on the day of his funeral, 25 July, his son Maxwell is born.

2 3 0 1 . 9 6
0 9 . 1 5
№ 0 0 2 4
· 2 0 0
· 2 0 0 4

...K (1765–1802): Son of an Ayr doctor ...p, Adair studied medicine at Edinburgh ... companion on the Stirlingshire tour of ...11 November 1789 Adair married Gavin ...arlotte Hamilton.

AIKE..., ...–1807): 'The Cotter's Saturday Night' is dedicated to A... ...icitor in Ayr where he met Burns around 1783. He champione... ...rns's poetry and secured 145 subscribers for the Kilmarnock edition. In the summer of 1785, Aiken successfully defended Gavin Hamilton before the Presbytery of Ayr against charges preferred by the Kirk Session of Mauchline. Burns briefly fell out with Aiken as the solicitor was probably responsible for mutilating Burns's promissory note to Jean Armour, but soon resumed friendly relations.

AINSLIE, ROBERT (1766–1838): Burns's companion on the first part of his Border tour of 5 May–1 June 1787 was born at Berrywell, near Duns, and was studying law in Edinburgh when he met the poet early in 1787. Burns introduced his friend to Mrs McLehose and on 3 March 1788 sent Ainslie the infamous 'horse litter' letter from Mauchline about Jean Armour (see p.298). Ainslie became a Writer to the Signet in 1789, married in 1798, and gradually became a pillar of Edinburgh society, serving as a kirk elder and writing two religious pamphlets.

ANDERSON, DR ROBERT (1750–1830): Ten when his father died, Anderson was educated in his native Carnwarth and at Edinburgh University where he studied theology then switched to medicine. Settling as a married man in Edinburgh, he abandoned medicine for literature, compiling *A Complete Edition of the Poets of Great Britain* and editing *The Works of John Moore, M.D.* Anderson met Burns in Edinburgh.

ARMOUR, JAMES (d.1798): A prosperous master mason and contractor in Mauchline, James Armour was hostile to Burns and opposed to marriage between his pregnant daughter and the poet in 1786.

ARMOUR, JEAN (1767–1834): Burns met Jean, daughter of James Armour, in Mauchline after settling at Mossgiel in 1784. He signed a document attesting his marriage to Jean; in March 1786, James

Armour fainted on hearing his daughter was pregnant by Burns (she gave birth to twins on 3 September, the boy surviving, the girl dying in infancy) and had Burns's marriage attestation mutilated. Burns contemplated emigration to Jamaica and turned his affections to another girl, 'Highland Mary' Campbell. A literary celebrity when he saw Jean in the summer of 1787, with the 'usual consequences' (CL, 149) – she gave birth to twin girls on 3 March 1788 – Burns married her around April 1788. Evidently Jean was a tolerant woman ('Our Robbie should have had twa wives,' she supposedly said after taking in his illegitimate daughter by Anne Park) and a devoted wife.

ARNOT, JOHN (c.1738-c. 1789): Transcribing his letter to Arnot (see p.269) in the Glenriddell Manuscript, Burns called him 'one of the most accomplished of the sons of men that I ever met with – John Arnot of Dalquatswood in Ayrshire – alas! had he been equally prudent!' (CL, 107) Arnot subscribed to the first Edinburgh edition and died possibly in financial disgrace.

AULD, WALTER: A Dumfries saddler who took delivery of parcels.

AULD, REVD WILLIAM (1709–91): Educated at the universities of Edinburgh, Glasgow and Leyden, he was ordained Minister of Mauchline in 1742. An Auld Licht ('old light' and rigidly Calvinist) minister, he publicly rebuked Burns and Jean Armour for 'the sin of fornication' in 1786.

BAILLIE, LESLEY (d.1843): Daughter of Robert Baillie of Mayfield, Ayrshire, she met Burns in August 1792 and inspired 'O, saw ye bonie Lesley' (SC, 1798), assuredly not one of his best songs though he enjoyed it for its associations with its heroine. He never again saw Lesley Baillie who married Robert Cumming of Logie in 1799.

BALLANTINE, JOHN (1743–1812): As Dean of Guild in Ayr, merchant and banker Ballantine supported the building of the New Brig and was the dedicatee of 'The Brigs of Ayr'. In 1787 Ballantine became Provost of Ayr and remained ready to advance Burns's interests.

BEGBIE, ALISON: In his Autobiographical Letter, Burns refers to being jilted (around 1781) by a girl traditionally identified as Alison Begbie, a Galston farmer's daughter who worked as a servant in a house near the river Cessnock. She may have been the Mary Morrison of the celebrated song (see p.104).

edition, Blacklock looked forward to an enlarged
Burns, it was Blacklock's letter that persuaded him to abandon his plans
to emigrate to Jamaica and seek his poetic fortune in Edinburgh.

BLAIR, REVD DR HUGH (1718–1800): A kinsman of Robert Blair,
author of *The Grave* (a poem well known to Burns), Hugh Blair was
educated at Edinburgh University which, in 1762, appointed him
Professor of Rhetoric and Belles-Lettres, a position he combined with
his work as senior minister of the High Kirk of St Giles. Blair was
one of Scotland's most influential men of letters (he encouraged James
Macpherson in his Ossianic adventure) and his open admiration of
Burns advanced the poet's reputation in Edinburgh. On Blair's advice,
Burns omitted 'The Jolly Beggars' (and another poem, 'The Prophet
and God's Complaint', now lost) from the first Edinburgh edition. His
abilities are assessed in the second Commonplace Book (see p.250).

BRICE, DAVID: Mauchline born, Brice became a shoemaker in
Glasgow.

BROUN, AGNES (1732–1820): The poet's mother was the eldest child
of Carrick farmer Gilbert Broun. Ten when her mother died and 12
when her father remarried, she went to live with a grandmother at
Maybole where she met William Burnes and married him on 15
December 1757. In Burns's childhood Agnes sang Scottish songs and
ballads but, unlike her husband, had no appreciation of books. After
her husband's death she lived mainly with the poet's brother and died
at Gilbert's home, Grant's Brae, East Lothian.

BROWN, CLOCKIE: A Mauchline clockmaker and friend of Burns.

BROWN, CAPTAIN RICHARD (1753–1833): Brown was born in Irvine
where Burns met him in 1781–2 while learning the trade of flax-
dressing. Burns was enormously impressed by the young seaman and
describes his friendship with him at length in the Autobiographical
Letter. Burns told Brown it was his praise that 'encouraged me to
endeavour at the character of a Poet' (CL, 418).

BUCHAN, ELSPETH (1738–91): Leader of the Buchanites, a religious sect, Mrs Buchan was invited to Irvine by the Revd Hugh White and stayed for about two years; in 1784, she was attacked by a mob and officially expelled from Irvine by magistrates. Burns describes the Buchanites in a letter of 3 August 1784 (see p.267).

BURNES, ROBERT (1719–89): Burns's uncle Robert left Kincardine-shire with his brother William Burnes and eventually settled in Stewarton, Ayrshire, where the poet visited him.

BURNES, WILLIAM (1721–84): The poet's father William Burnes (the 'e' was omitted in the Ayrshire spelling) was born at Clochnahill farm in the parish of Dunnottar, Kincardineshire, the third son of Robert Burnes and Isabella Keith. Burnes worked as a gardener in Edinburgh, then Ayrshire. In 1756 he leased land in Alloway and built on it a thatched two-roomed clay cottage, 'the auld clay biggin' of 'The Vision' and the home to which he took Agnes Broun after marrying her on 15 December 1757. Despite the difficulties he encountered in farming (Mount Oliphant, 1766–77; Lochlea from 1777 until his death) Burnes attempted to provide an education for his children. His last years at Lochlea were made miserable because of a legal dispute with his landlord David McLure. He was buried in Alloway churchyard and is portrayed by Burns as the pious patriarch of 'The Cotter's Saturday Night'.

BURNESS, JAMES (1750–1837): First cousin of Burns, and a lawyer in Montrose.

BURNS, GILBERT (1760–1827): The poet's brother (born 28 Sept. 1760 at the Alloway cottage), Gilbert shared Robert's upbringing and education. With their father in difficulties over Lochlea farm, Robert and Gilbert arranged to become partners in Mossgiel farm to which they moved in March 1784. On 22 July 1786 Robert transferred his share of Mossgiel to Gilbert who brought up the poet's illegitimate daughter Elizabeth Paton.

BURNS, WILLIAM (1767–90): Youngest brother of the poet, William Burns was apprenticed to a saddler in Longtown, moved to Newcastle, then settled in London as journeyman saddler with William T. Barber in the Strand. He died in London and Burns covered the costs incurred by his illness (a fever) and funeral.

CAMERON, MAY: An Edinburgh servant girl who gave birth to a child by Burns and had a writ served on him; he was freed from the writ on 15 August 1787.

CAMPBELL, MARY (1763–86): In 1786, with Jean Armour pregnant and Burns repudiated by her family, the poet contemplated emigrating to Jamaica and turned his attention to Mary Campbell, a Coilsfield dairymaid (born in Auchamore, by Dunoon, the daughter of a seaman) who had previously been a nursemaid in Gavin Hamilton's Mauchline house. On 14 May 1786 Burns and Mary met at Failford and made a matrimonial gesture by exchanging bibles (the two-volume Bible Burns gave Mary is in the Alloway Cottage Museum). The scene is recreated in the song 'Will ye go to the Indies, My Mary' (see p.191). Burns claimed that Mary died 'at Greenock, where . . . she was seized with a malignant fever' (NSS, 72). She remains the subject of much speculation.

CHARTERIS, FRANCIS (1749–1808): The 36th Grand Master-Mason of Scotland, 1786–7, Charteris subscribed for four copies of the first Edinburgh edition: he is referred to as 'Charters' in a letter of Burns (see p.278).

CLARK, SAMUEL (1769–1814): Born in Dumfries where, like his father, he worked as a solicitor, Samuel Clark jun., was a boozing crony of Burns. One Saturday night in January 1794, Clark was present when Burns, during the war with revolutionary France, gave a provocative toast that almost led to a duel with one Captain Dods (see p.327).

CLARKE, JAMES (c.1761–1825): Appointed master of Moffat Grammar School in 1786, he sought friendship and financial assistance from the poet. In 1794 he was appointed master of the Burgh School at Forfar.

CLEGHORN, ROBERT (d.1789): Born in Corstorphine, on the outskirts of Edinburgh, Cleghorn was a farmer (at Saughton Mills, where Burns often visited him when in Edinburgh) and a member of the Crochallan Fencibles, the Edinburgh convivial club that welcomed Burns to its company. To Cleghorn, Burns sent some of the bawdy poems later collected in The Merry Muses.

CLOW, JENNY: While Burns was conducting his epistolary affair with 'Clarinda' in Edinburgh, he had a sexual affair with Jenny who, in November 1788, bore him a son. It seems that, like May Cameron, Jenny served Burns with a writ: a letter of 6 January 1789 to Ainslie explains: 'I must again trouble you to find & secure for me a direction where to find Jenny Clow, for a main part of my business in Edinburgh is to settle that matter with her, & free her hand of the process.' (CL, 337) In November 1791, Burns had a letter from 'Clarinda' telling him that Jenny was apparently close to death; Burns asked her to get a porter to take Jenny five shillings.

CORBET, WILLIAM (1755–1811): A senior officer in the Excise: Supervisor-General at Stirling, 1786–7; Acting Supervisor-General at Edinburgh, 1789–91, a post he then held permanently until 1797 when he became Collector of the Excise at Glasgow.

CREECH, WILLIAM (1745–1815): When Burns arrived in Edinburgh in 1786, the Earl of Glencairn introduced him to parsimonious publisher-bookseller Creech who conducted his business in his shop in the centre of the High Street. The first Edinburgh edition was published by Creech who bought the copyright for 100 guineas which meant he could issue new editions for his own profit: a second Edinburgh edition was published by Creech, in February 1793, in two volumes and 'greatly enlarged with New Poems', one of which was 'Tom o' Shanter'. Creech was slow to pay Burns money due to him on the first Edinburgh edition and also delayed paying the 100 guineas he owed the poet.

CRUICKSHANK, WILLIAM (d.1795): A graduate of Edinburgh University, Cruickshank became (in 1770) Rector of the Burgh School in the Canongate and (in 1772) Latin master at the city's High School. Introduced to Cruickshank by William Nicol, Burns lived with the Cruickshank family in 2 St James's Square, Edinburgh, from October 1787 to February 1788.

CUNNINGHAM, ALEXANDER (c.1763–1812): Eldest son of James Cunningham of Hyndhope and nephew of the historian William Robertson, Cunningham practised law in Edinburgh where Burns met him. The two men became close friends and Cunningham was the main fundraiser for the poet's widow and orphans.

CUNNINGHAM, JAMES, 14TH EARL OF GLENCAIRN (1749–91): After the death of Glencairn (30 Jan. 1791), Burns described him as 'the Patron from whom all my fame & good fortune took its rise' (CL, 262)

and 'my best Friend, my first and dearest Patron & Benefactor; the man
to whom I owe all that I am & have!' (CL, 506) When Burns came
to Edinburgh in 1786 he was warmly welcomed by Glencairn who
invited him to his home and introduced him to his friends, including publisher William Creech. Glencairn and his mother subscribed
for twenty-four copies of the first Edinburgh edition and Glencairn
encouraged the members of the Caledonian Hunt to subscribe for
100 copies (see p.276). When Burns decided to enter the Excise he
approached Glencairn who used his influence on the poet's behalf. In honour of his friend, Burns named his fourth son (born 12
Aug. 1794) James Glencairn Burns.

DALRYMPLE, JAMES (c.1752–95):   Son of Charles Dalrymple of
Ayr, in 1750 James Dalrymple married the heiress to the estate of
Orangefield, Ayrshire, and succeeded to the estate in 1785. He subscribed for ten copies of the Kilmarnock edition, put the poet in
touch with the Earl of Glencairn in Edinburgh, and on 7 December 1786 introduced Burns at a meeting of Canongate Kilwinning
Lodge of Freemasons. Bankrupt in 1791, Dalrymple had to dispose
of Orangefield shortly before his death.

DAVIDSON, BETTY: Widow of a cousin of Agnes Broun, Betty
Davidson often stayed with the Burns family at Alloway and entertained the infant poet with her old wife's tales and songs. See
the Autobiographical Letter.

DAVIDSON, JOHN (1728–1806):   Traditionally identified as the original of Souter Johnie in 'Tam o' Shanter', Davidson lived at Glenfoot
of Ardlochan, near Douglas Graham's Shanter farm. A cobbler, he
accompanied Graham to Ayr on market days. In 1785 Davidson moved
into the thatched cottage now preserved by the National Trust for
Scotland as Souter Johnie's House, Kirkoswald.

DUNLOP, MRS FRANCES ANNA (1730–1815):   In 1748 Frances Anna
Wallace (eldest daughter of Sir Thomas Wallace of Craigie who
claimed to be a kinsman of the Scottish patriot William Wallace)
married John Dunlop of Dunlop by whom she had thirteen children.
In 1786, doubly distressed by the recent death of her husband and
the financial problems of her son Thomas, she found solace in 'The
Cotter's Saturday Night' (shown to her by a friend) and sent a
messenger to Mossgiel requesting six copies of the Kilmarnock edition
and asking the author to visit Dunlop House. Burns sent her five copies,

all he could spare, and visited Mrs Dunlop in June 1787, February 1788, May 1789, June 1791, and December 1792. During their long and stimulating correspondence she advised Burns to avoid impropriety in his poems and expressed strong disapproval of his political faith in the French Revolution. As she had put the poet in touch with Dr Moore, she was aghast when Burns wrote to her, on 1 January 1795, condemning the reactionary tone of Moore's *Journal during a Residence in France* (1793) and describing the executions of Louis XVI and Marie Antoinette as 'the deserved fate of . . . a perjured Blockhead & an unprincipled Prostitute' (CL, 214). She ignored subsequent letters until Burns wrote to her on 10 July 1796, shortly before his death: 'An illness which has long hung about me in all probability will speedily send me beyond that bourne whence no traveller returns.' (CL, 215) She replied in a letter which was probably one of the last things Burns read on his deathbed.

EGLINTON, 11TH EARL OF, *see* MONTGOMERIE, ARCHIBALD.

ERSKINE, HON. HENRY (1746–1817): Second son of the 10th Earl of Buchan, Erskine was called to the bar in 1768 and chosen Dean of the Faculty of Advocates in 1786, the year he met Burns at a meeting of Canongate Kilwinning Lodge of Freemasons (7 Dec. 1786). He was ousted as Dean of Faculty in January 1796 because he had led opposition to the Sedition Bills then before Parliament.

ERSKINE, JOHN FRANCIS (1741–1825): Erskine – later 27th Earl of Mar and 12th Lord Erskine – never met Burns but offered to come to his assistance in 1793 (see p.322).

FERGUSSON, DR WILLIAM (1709–69): Burns's father worked as gardener at Doonholm House, Alloway, home of Fergusson who leased Mount Oliphant farm to William Burnes in November 1765. Fergusson, a retired London banker, was twice Provost of Ayr, in 1759–61 and 1763–5.

FISHER, WILLIAM (1739–1809): A farmer's son and Mauchline kirk elder, Fisher was the original of Burns's Holy Willie (see p.114). In 1790 the sanctimonious Fisher was rebuked by the Revd Auld for drunkenness; he died in a ditch by the roadside near Mauchline.

FONTENELLE, LOUISA (*c.*1773–99): An actress who made her London debut in 1788, Fontenelle was, in the winter seasons of

1792 and 1793, one of the players at the new Theatre Royal, Dumfries, and much admired by Burns.

GLENCAIRN, EARL OF, *see* CUNNINGHAM, JAMES, 14TH EARL OF GLENCAIRN.

GORDON, JANE, DUCHESS OF GORDON (1746–1812):   Born in Edinburgh, where she grew up as an ostenstatiously obstreperous girl, Jane married Alexander, 4th Duke of Gordon, in 1767. She met Burns shortly after he arrived in Edinburgh in 1786 and was charmed by his character and conversation. Burns visited her at Castle Gordon, just north of Fochabers, on 7 September 1787 (see p.259).

GOW, NEIL (1727–1807):   The celebrated fiddler and composer (whose tunes Burns used in his songwriting) was born at Inver, near Dunkeld. Burns met him on 31 August 1787 at Dunkeld (see p.259).

GRAHAM, DOUGLAS (1738–1811):   Traditionally identified as the original of 'Tam o' Shanter', Graham rented the farm of Shanter, near Kirkoswald, where Burns spent the summer of 1775. As a dealer in malt, Graham would go on market day to Ayr (accompanied by John Davidson). Supposedly these drunken visits were anathema to Graham's wife Helen (née McTaggart) who is thus identified as the Kate of 'Tam o' Shanter'.

GRAHAM OF FINTRY, ROBERT (1749–1815):   On 31 August 1787, during his Highland tour with William Nicol, Burns visited Athole House and met Robert Graham of Fintry, a Commissioner of the Scottish Board of Excise. On 7 January 1788 the poet wrote to Graham asking him to use his influence to secure him a post with the Excise. Graham obliged and Burns described his patron as 'one of the worthiest and most accomplished Gentlemen, not only of this Country, but I will dare to say it, of this Age' (CL, 151). After Burns's political opinions were investigated by the Excise Board in December 1792 he wrote to Graham for assistance (see p.319).

GREENFIELD, REVD WILLIAM (d.1827):   Minister of St Andrew's, Edinburgh, from 1784 until 1787 when he became Hugh Blair's assistant preacher at the High Kirk of St Giles, Greenfield was highly praised by Burns in the second Commonplace Book (see p.250). Burns did not live to see Greenfield's downfall. In 1796 Greenfield became

Moderator of the General Assembly of the Church of Scotland: two
years later, probably because of involvement in some sexual scandal, he
was deposed and excommunicated by the Presbytery of Edinburgh. He
lived subsequently in the north of England under an assumed name.

GREGORY, DR JAMES (1753–1821):   Appointed Professor of Physick
in Edinburgh University in 1776, Gregory was highly regarded by
Burns.

GROSE, CAPTAIN FRANCIS (1731–91):   Born at Greenford, Middle-
sex, the son of a wealthy Swiss merchant, Grose studied art and served
in the Surrey Militia, retiring with the rank of Captain. Having
squandered a family fortune, he pursued his antiquarian interests with
profit: his *Antiquities of England and Wales* was published, in six volumes,
from 1773 to 1787. Burns met him, at Captain Robert Riddell's
home, Friars' Carse, in summer 1789, while Grose was in Scotland
researching his *Antiquities of Scotland* (2 vols., 1789 and 1791). For
Grose's part in the making of 'Tam o' Shanter' see headnote to
the poem and letter on p.311. Grose intended to produce another
antiquarian work on Ireland but died, soon after arriving, of an
apoplectic fit. He is buried near Dublin.

HAMILTON, GAVIN (1751–1805):   Burns dedicated the Kilmarnock
edition to Gavin Hamilton, a lawyer's son who followed in his father's
footsteps, first working in John Hamilton's office then setting up his
own practice in Mauchline. Hamilton met Burns, a fellow freemason,
in autumn 1783 and the poet and his brother Gilbert rented from
Hamilton, for £90 per year, the 118-acre farm of Mossgiel. As a
liberal New Licht member of the kirk, Hamilton fell foul of Mauchline
Kirk Session which, in 1785, accused him of irregular attendance and
failure to uphold family worship, a dispute discussed in the headnote
to 'Holy Willie's Prayer'. According to the Train Manuscript, when
Burns married Jean Armour around April 1788, the private ceremony
was held in Hamilton's office in Mauchline.

HERON, ROBERT (1764–1807):   The Heron condemned in the epistle
'To Dr Blacklock' became the first biographer of Burns. Heron was
born in Creehead, New Galloway; studied at Edinburgh University;
became a licentiate of the Church in 1789; and earned his living as
a writer (his *Journey through the Western Counties of Scotland* appeared
in 1793). He met Burns (at Dr Blacklock's house) in Edinburgh
and later visited him at Ellisland. Heron's 'Original Memoirs of the

Late Robert Burns' was serialised in the *Monthly Magazine and British Register* (Jan.–June 1797) and republished as *A Memoir of the Life of the Late Robert Burns* (1797). Heron acclaimed Burns as a poetic genius and, an assiduous gatherer of gossip from Dumfries, suggested that the poet gradually degenerated into a self-destructive drunk. Ironically, the moralistic Heron spent some of his final years as a debtor in Newgate Prison. He died at St Pancras Hospital, London.

HILL, PETER (1754–1837):   A clerk in Creech's shop when Burns met him in Edinburgh, Hill set up his own bookselling business in 1788 and supplied books to Burns in Dumfriesshire.

JOHNSON, JAMES (*c.*1750–1811):   Probably a native of Ettrick, Johnson settled in Edinburgh, running an engraving shop in the High Street and a music shop in the Lawnmarket. In 1787 he published the first volume (100 songs) of his *The Scots Musical Museum*, an anthology of the words and music of Scottish songs. Burns met Johnson when the first volume was in the press and, agreeing to collaborate on subsequent volumes, contributed around 200 songs (some composed by Burns, others collected or revised).

JOHNSTON, CAPTAIN WILLIAM: An enthusiastic supporter of re-form in Edinburgh, Johnston founded the *Edinburgh Gazetteer* in November 1792 and, soon after, was imprisoned by the authorities. One of the charges against Burns as a supposedly subversive Exciseman was his alleged association with Johnston, (see p.320).

KEMP, REVD DR JOHN (1744–1805):   Mrs McLehose's moralistic confidant, Kemp was minister of the Tolbooth Church, Edinburgh, from 1779 until his death.

KILPATRICK, NELLY (*c.*1760–*c.*1820):   The subject of Burns's first song (see headnote to 'O, once I lov'd a bonie lass'), Nelly was the daughter of a farmer at Parclewan, Dalrymple, Ayrshire.

LAWRIE, ARCHIBALD (1768–1837):   Son of the Revd George Lawrie of Loudon, Ayrshire, Archibald Lawrie was friendly with Burns while a student in Edinburgh. He succeeded his father as Loudon's parish minister in 1799.

LEWARS, JESSY (1778–1855):   Younger daughter of John Lewars, Supervisor of Excise at Dumfries; after her father's death in 1789

Jessy lived with her brother John, a fellow exciseman of Burns, in Millbrae Vennel opposite the poet's home. For her part in the making of 'O, wert thou in the cauld blast' see headnote to the song. After Burns's death, Jessy helped look after his children for a while. She married in 1799 and is buried in St Michael's churchyard, Dumfries, quite close to the poet's grave.

MACKENZIE, HENRY (1745–1831): Burns described Henry Mackenzie's sentimental novel *The Man of Feeling* (1771) as 'a book I prize next to the Bible' (CL, 55) and identified with the lachrymose hero, Harley. Son of an Edinburgh physician, Mackenzie studied law in Edinburgh and London and practised in the Scottish Court of Exchequer. He was editor of the *Mirror* (printed by William Creech) and the *Lounger*. Shown a copy of the Kilmarnock edition by Dugald Stewart, he wrote an unsigned essay on the book in the *Lounger* (9 Dec. 1786) acclaiming Burns as 'this Heaven-taught ploughman' (CH, 70). Burns met Mackenzie shortly after arriving in Edinburgh in 1786.

MACKENZIE, DR JOHN (*c.*1755–1837): An Ayrshire man, Mackenzie studied medicine at Edinburgh University and established a practice in Mauchline. He met Burns, at Lochlea in 1783, when attending the poet's ailing father. Burns's regard for Mackenzie is evident in 'The Holy Fair' where the doctor is personified as Common Sense. When Burns returned to Mauchline in 1788 he rented an upstairs room in Mackenzie's house, in the Back Causeway, for himself and Jean who there gave birth to a second set of twins. The house was acquired by the Burns Federation in 1917 and is preserved as a museum.

MCLAUGHLAN, JAMES: In a note on 'The Twa Brigs', in the first Edinburgh edition, Burns calls McLauchlan, 'A well-known performer of Scottish music on the violin'. A Highlander, McLaughlan came to Ayrshire with a Fencible Regiment and was patronised by Hugh Montgomerie of Coilsfield.

MCLEHOSE, AGNES CRAIG (1758–1841): Burns's 'Clarinda' and the Nancy of 'Ae Fond Kiss', Agnes Craig, the daughter of a Glasgow surgeon, married John McLehose at the age of eighteen; before the birth of her last child (1781) she separated from her husband and returned to her father who died in 1782 whereupon Agnes – Nancy to her friends – moved to General's Entry, Potterrow (house gone). Her ambition to meet Burns, then the literary lion of Edinburgh, was

realized on 4 December 1787 at a tea-party. She invited the poet
to her home but, before he could accept, he dislocated his knee
in a fall from a coach. This enforced passivity led to the celebrated
correspondence between 'Sylvander' and 'Clarinda', Arcadian names
suggested by Nancy and welcomed by Burns (in a letter of 28 Dec.
1787). This epistolary courtship excited Burns who wrote to Richard
Brown (30 Dec. 1787): 'I am at this moment ready to hang myself for
a young Edinburgh widow, who has wit and beauty more murderously
fatal than the assassinating stiletto of the Sicilian Banditti.' (CL, 419)
Learning that Nancy intended to rejoin her now prosperous husband
in Jamaica, Burns went to see her in Edinburgh where, on 6 December
1791 'Clarinda' and 'Sylvander' met for the last time at Lamont's Land.
On 27 December, Burns sent Nancy 'Ae Fond Kiss', the finest of the
ten songs he wrote for her. In February 1792, Nancy sailed for Jamaica
in the hope of a reconciliation with her husband but found, instead, that
he had a black mistress. Returning to Scotland, Nancy corresponded
briefly with Burns and, in her *Journal* (6 Dec. 1831), noted: 'This day
I can never forget. Parted with Burns, in the year 1791, never more
to meet in this world. Oh, may we meet in Heaven!'

MCLURE, DAVID: A merchant in Ayr, he was William Burnes's
landlord for Lochlea farm, Tarbolton, charging an annual rent of
£1 per acre for 130 swampy acres. It was an oral agreement and
eventually McLure, desperately short of cash, demanded arrears of
rent. A warrant of sequestration was operated in 1783 against William
Burnes who took his case to the Edinburgh Court of Session which,
in January 1784, upheld him; less than a month after the court decision,
Burnes died. McLure later became a merchant in Liverpool.

MILLER, PATRICK (1731–1815): Burns's landlord at Ellisland was born
in Glasgow. After working as a sailor he set up as a banker in Edinburgh,
becoming a director of the Bank of Scotland in 1767. He bought the
estate of Dalswinton, in the Nith valley near Dumfries, in 1785 and
attempted to improve his run-down property through agricultural
experiments (he also attempted innovations in steam navigation).
Discovering, in December 1786, that Miller was the giver of a gift of
ten guineas, Burns met his admirer. On 14 January 1787 he cautiously
considered Miller's offer to rent him a farm on Dalswinton estate,
noting 'Mr Miller is no Judge of land; and though I dare say he means
to favour me, yet he may give me, in his opinion, an advantageous
bargain that may ruin me.' (CL, 100) Burns eventually decided to
strike a bargain with Miller in March 1788: he was to pay an annual

rent of £50 for the first three years, thereafter £70 annually; Miller
provided £300 for the building of a farmhouse and the fencing of
the fields. Burns's doubts about the viability of Ellisland farm were
confirmed by the first harvest and on 11 January 1790 he wrote to
his brother Gilbert: 'This Farm has undone my enjoyment of myself.
– It is a ruinous affair on all hands. – But let it go to hell! I'll fight
it out and be off with it.' (CL, 358) After some acerbic exchanges,
Burns sold the lease of Ellisland to Miller whom the poet cursed for
his 'meddling vanity' (CL, 320).

MITCHELL, JOHN (1731–1806):   A farmer's son who first studied for
the ministry, Mitchell became Collector of Excise at Dumfries in 1788.
The following year Burns, armed with a letter of introduction from
Robert Graham of Fintry, presented himself to Mitchell who, in
August, indicated that Burns would be appointed to the Excise. In
a letter (9 Dec. 1789) to Graham of Fintry, Burns acknowledged 'the
generous friendship of Mr Mitchel my Collector' (CL, 431). When
the poet's political opinions were investigated by the Excise Board in
December 1792, Mitchell spoke up in Burns's favour.

MONTGOMERIE, ARCHIBALD, 11th EARL OF EGLINTON (1726–96):
Lt-Colonel in command of the 77th Regiment of Foot, which he
raised in 1757, Montgomerie succeeded to the title in 1769. MP
for Ayrshire for some time, he was chosen as one of the sixteen
Scottish Representative Peers in 1776. He subscribed for forty-two
copies of the first Edinburgh edition.

MOORE, DR JOHN (1729–1802):   For details of the man to whom
Burns addressed his celebrated Autobiographical Letter (2 Aug. 1787)
see headnote to Prologue.

MUIR, ROBERT (1758–88):   Born in Kilmarnock, Muir became a wine
merchant in his father's business. After meeting him in 1786 Burns
became a firm friend of Muir who subscribed for seventy-two copies
of the Kilmarnock edition and forty copies of the first Edinburgh
edition. Writing to Mrs Dunlop (13 Dec. 1789) Burns remembered
Muir as 'the disinterested friend of my early life; the man who rejoiced
to see me, because he loved me & could serve me' (CL, 181).

MURDOCH, JOHN (1747–1824):   A powerful early influence on the
poet, he was hired by William Burnes as tutor to his sons Robert
and Gilbert. Born in Ayr, educated at the local burgh school and

Edinburgh, Murdoch was engaged by Burnes (and four of his neigh-
bours), in May 1765, to teach at Alloway school a few yards from
Burnes's clay cottage. Murdoch instructed Robert and Gilbert in
reading and writing, using several standard texts: the Bible, A. Fisher's
New Grammar, with English Exercise, Arthur Masson's *English Spelling
Book* and Masson's *Collection of Prose and Verse* which contained verse
by Shakespeare, Milton, Dryden, Addison, Thomson, Gray, Akenside,
Shenstone as well as such prosaic models as Mrs Elizabeth Rowe's
Moral Letters. Murdoch left Alloway in 1768 and in 1773, when he
was teaching English in Ayr, Burns spent three weeks with him.
For criticising the Revd William Dalrymple, minister in Ayr and
the man who baptised Burns, Murdoch was (in 1776) dismissed from
his teaching post in Ayr. He lived in London as a shopkeeper who
supplemented his meagre income by teaching French.

NICOL, WILLIAM (1744–97): A tailor's son, born at Dumbretton in
Annan parish, Nicol was educated at Annan Academy and Edinburgh
University. In 1774 he became classics master in the High School of
Edinburgh where he was known as a sadistic schoolteacher. Nicol
accompanied Burns on his Highland tour (25 Aug.–16 Sept. 1787) and
often embarrassed the poet who described him as 'that obstinate Son
of Latin Prose' (CL, 361). Still, the two men remained friends. In 1795
Nicol quarrelled with the Rector of the High School and left to form
his own school which, appropriately enough, died when he did.

NIMMO, ERSKINE: It was at Miss Nimmo's Edinburgh house, on the
first floor of a tenement in Allison Square, that Burns first met Agnes
McLehose on 4 December 1787.

PATON, ELIZABETH: The subject of 'My girl she's airy', Elizabeth
Paton was a servant girl at Lochlea. After his father's death, in February
1784, Burns felt free to consummate his relationship with her when he
moved to Mossgiel and she returned to her home at Largieside. She
gave birth to the poet's first illegitimate child, Elizabeth, on 22 May
1785.

POOSIE NANSIE: Wife of George Gibson and owner of Poosie-
Nansie's Tavern, at the corner of Loudon Street and the Cowgate in
Mauchline, Agnes Gibson was the landlady on the evening described
in 'The Jolly Beggars'. On account of her speed at running errands,
Poosie Nansie's dimwitted daughter was known as 'Racer Jess' and
is mentioned in 'The Holy Fair'.

RICHMOND, JOHN (1765–1846): A lawyer's clerk in Gavin Hamilton's office, he was Burns's closest friend during his first year in
Mauchline and, subsequently, the recipient of some of his most
revealing letters. Richmond shared Burns's love of convivial and
female company; he, too, was a fornicator disciplined by Mauchline
Kirk Session. Richmond moved to Edinburgh in 1785 and, at the close
of the following year, Burns arrived in the city and stayed in the room
his friend rented in Baxter's Close, Lawnmarket. In August 1787 Burns
again stayed with Richmond (for two days) in Edinburgh. Richmond
eventually went back to Mauchline and married Janet Surgeoner, with
whom he had been cited by Mauchline Kirk Session.

RIDDELL, ELIZABETH KENNEDY (d.1801): Daughter of Walter
Kennedy, Elizabeth married Robert Riddell of Glenriddell in 1784.
Burns thought enough of her to name his daughter, born on 21
November 1792, Elizabeth Riddell Burns. He soon had reason to
regret his friendship for after the incident referred to in the 'letter
from Hell' (see p.325) she broke with Burns. It may have been at
Friars' Carse, the Riddell mansion north of Ellisland, that the incident
occurred and it may have been Elizabeth to whom Burns wrote this
letter though Maria Riddell has also been identified as the recipient.

RIDDELL, MARIA BANKS WOODLEY (1772–1808): Born and raised
in England, in 1788 Maria went with her father (Governor of the
Leeward Islands) to the West Indies where she met and (in 1790)
married Walter Riddell – younger brother of Robert Riddell and a
widower who had inherited his wife's sugar estates. In 1792 Walter
put down a deposit on the estate of Goldielea, four miles south-west of
Dumfries, and renamed it Woodley Park in honour of his wife. Before
she moved into Woodley Park, Maria asked Burns to introduce her to
William Smellie who was pleased to publish her *Voyages to the Madeira
and Leeward and Caribbee Islands* (1792). She also wrote poems which
Burns pronounced 'always correct, & often elegant [and] much beyond
the common run of the Lady Poetesses of the day' (CL, 597). Greatly
attracted to Maria, Burns was wounded when she broke with him after
the so-called Sabine Rape incident referred to in the 'letter from Hell'
(see p.325). It has generally been assumed that Maria was the recipient
of this letter (H-H II, 420) though its mention of 'Your husband' has
caused confusion since Walter Riddell was absent from Scotland from
(around) June 1793 to April 1794 while in the West Indies. In 1795
Burns and Maria were reconciled. After his death, she wrote a fine
tribute to him in the Dumfries *Weekly Journal* (Aug. 1796).

RIDDELL, CAPTAIN ROBERT (1735–94):   Eldest son of Walter Riddell of Glenriddell (in Glencairn parish, Dumfriesshire) he was educated at Dumfries and at the universities of St Andrews and Edinburgh. Joining the Royal Scots, he was promoted to Captain in 1771. He retired in 1782 – settling in Friars' Carse (north of Ellisland) on the Glenriddell estate – and two years later married Elizabeth Kennedy. On moving into Ellisland in 1788, Burns became friendly with his neighbour Riddell. It was for Riddell that Burns prepared (in 1791) the Glenriddell Manuscript, two calf-bound volumes, one of verse, the other of letters. Only the volume of verse was given to Riddell for the two men fell out after the so-called Sabine Rape incident and the 'letter from Hell' (see p.325). Whether or not the Sabine scenario occurred at Friar's Carse, Elizabeth Riddell was unforgiving and Riddell died on 20 April 1794, a few months after the incident.

RODGER, HUGH (1726–96):   In the summer of 1775, Burns went to Kirkoswald to study mathematics under Rodger, the parish school master.

SIBBALD, JAMES (1745–1803):   Son of a Roxburgh farmer, Sibbald set up his bookselling business in Parliament Close, Edinburgh, and in 1783 founded the monthly Edinburgh Magazine which in October 1786, in the earliest review of the Kilmarnock edition, described Burns as 'a striking example of native genius bursting through the obscurity of poverty' (CH, 64). When Patrick Miller left a gift of ten guineas for Burns (see p.276) he entrusted it to Sibbald.

SMELLIE, WILLIAM (1740–95):   Printer of the first Edinburgh edition, Smellie, son of a stonemason, was born in Edinburgh and attended classes at the university while serving his apprenticeship as a printer. He became the first editor of the Encyclopaedia Britannica in 1771, co-founded the Edinburgh Magazine in 1773, and translated Buffon's Natural History (six vols., 1780–1). He also founded the Crochallan Fencibles, a convivial club which met in Anchor Close (off the High Street) where Smellie's office was also located. Smellie introduced Burns to the Crochallan Fencibles in 1787 and, as the poet's printer, entertained him in his office where Burns corrected his proofs on a stool which came to be known as Burns's Stool.

SMITH, JAMES (1765–c.1823): Smith and John Richmond were Burns's closest drinking cronies in Mauchline. Son of a Mauchline merchant who died when Smith was ten, he was raised by a strict stepfather. He ran a draper's shop close to Nanse Tinnock's tavern in Mauchline, subsequently going into partnership with a calico printer in Linlithgow, then emigrating to Jamaica where he died.

STEWART, PROFESSOR DUGALD (1753–1828):   Professor of Moral Philosophy at Edinburgh University from 1785 until his retirement in 1810, Dugald Stewart was, for Burns, 'the most perfect character I ever saw' (see p.251). He first met Burns, on 23 October 1786, when the poet dined at his country house in Catrine, near Mauchline (see headnote to 'Extempore Verses on Dining with Lord Daer'). When Stewart returned to Edinburgh, for the university term, he took a copy of the Kilmarnock edition to Henry Mackenzie who reviewed the volume enthusiastically in the *Lounger*. Stewart subsequently entertained and encouraged Burns in Edinburgh where he was a prominent advocate of Scottish Common Sense Philosophy.

SYME, JOHN (1755–1831):   After a spell in the Army, Syme became a Writer to the Signet in Dumfries. He inherited his father's Kirkcudbrightshire estate but, with the collapse of the Ayr Bank in 1773, had to leave the estate. In 1791, becoming Collector of Stamps for the District, he settled in Dumfries: Burns's three-room apartment in the Wee Vennel (now Bank Street) was located on the floor above Syme's office. Burns visited Syme at his villa at Ryedale, on the west side of the Nith, and the two men became close friends who twice toured Galloway together (30 July–2 Aug. 1793 and 25–28 June 1794). Syme visited Burns at Brow on 15 July 1796 and was appalled at the poet's condition; after his friend's death Syme helped to organize his funeral and raise funds for his family.

TENNANT, JOHN (1760–1853):   John Tennant jun. was the second son of John Tennant of Glenconner by his second wife. He was unsuccessful in his ventures as shipbuilder and distiller and eventually settled on the farm of Auchenbay, Ochiltree.

TENNANT OF GLENCONNER, JOHN (1725–1810):   When Burns lived in Alloway, Tennant was a neighbour at Laigh Corton farm; he may have been the John Tennant who witnessed Burns's baptism. Factor to the Countess of Glencairn for eleven years, Tennant rented the farm of Glenconner, a mile west of Ochiltree. When Burns was offered the lease of Ellisland, he took Tennant to look over the farm and accepted his advice that it was a viable proposition.

THOMSON, GEORGE (1757–1851):   Born at Limekilns, Dunfermline, Thomson was the son of the local schoolmaster. He studied law and, in 1780, was appointed clerk – subsequently Chief Clerk – to the Board of Trustees for the Encouragement of Art & Manufacture in Scotland. A skilled violinist, he pursued his musical passions as a performer (favouring the violin quartets of Pleyel) and as a collector of Scottish songs. In September 1792 he wrote to Burns, asking him to write some 25 songs for melodies arranged by Pleyel: for Burns's reply, see p.317. When the first part of Thomson's *A Select Collection of Scotish Airs* appeared in June 1793, with twenty-five songs by Burns, Thomson sent the poet a copy plus a £5 note. Burns objected to this 'pecuniary parcel' (CL, 631) as an insult to his integrity and asked Thomson not to repeat the insult. Delighted, however, by the quality of Thomson's production, Burns continued to supply songs – more than seventy in all – until shortly before his death. Sometimes Thomson altered songs without consulting the poet and in the case of 'Scots Wha Hae' he rejected Burns's preference for the air 'Hey, tutti, tatie' and substituted the tune 'Lewie Gordon'. For Burns's last letter to Thomson, see p.329.

THOMSON, PEGGY: When Burns went to Kirkoswald, in 1775, to study mathematics under Hugh Rodger, he was distracted by a young woman he describes in the Autobiographical Letter as 'a charming Fillette'. This was Peggy Thomson. After she married, Burns presented her with a copy of the Kilmarnock edition inscribed with lines in honour of 'an old Sweetheart'.

TINNOCK, NANSE: Nanse Tinnock's ale-house, in the Back Causeway overlooking Mauchline kirk, was where revellers refreshed themselves during 'The Holy Fair'. According to Gilbert Burns (*Poetical Works of Robert Burns*, 1823) Nanse denied that the poet was a regular toper in her tavern: 'she shook her head, and said, he scarcely ever had spent a shilling in her house'.

URBANI, PIETRO (1749–1861):   After studying music in his native Milan, Urbani settled in Glasgow, in 1780, then in Edinburgh, in 1784. His *Selection of Scots Songs* (1792–4) was ridiculed by his rival George Thomson. Burns met Urbani in 1793 and sent him 'A red red Rose', first published in Urbani's anthology in 1794.

WHITEFOORD, SIR JOHN (1734–1803):   An Ayrshire laird and (in 1782) Master of St James's Masonic Lodge, Tarbolton. After selling his

Ballochmyle estate in 1785 he moved to Edinburgh. He suggested that Burns should invest the money he made on his poems in the stocking of a small farm, advice the poet accepted.

WILLIAMSON, DAVID (1766–1824):   Shortly before he died, Burns was frantic because he owed money, on a Dumfries Volunteer uniform, to a 'cruel scoundrel of a Haberdasher' (see p.329). David Williamson was the culprit.

WILSON, JOHN (1759–1821):   Printer of the Kilmarnock edition, Wilson ran his workshop in the attic of a building entered from Star Inn Close, on the north side of Waterloo Street, Kilmarnock. The shop is long gone but the site can be seen in a modern shopping mall named after Burns. In 1803 Wilson co-founded (with his brother Peter) the *Ayr Advertiser*, Ayrshire's first newspaper.

WILSON, JOHN (c.1751–1839):   A parish schoolmaster in Tarbolton, Wilson was the original of Burns's Hornbook, see headnote to 'Death and Doctor Hornbook'.

INTRODUCTION

Two days after Robert Burns died, at the age of thirty-seven at home in Dumfries on 21 July 1796, an obituary appeared in the *Edinburgh Evening Courant*:

> On the 21st inst. died at Dumfries, after a lingering illness, the celebrated ROBERT BURNS. His poetical compositions, distinguished equally by the force of native humour, by the warmth and the tenderness of passion, and by the glowing touches of a descriptive pencil, will remain a lasting monument of the vigour and the versatility of a mind guided only by the lights of nature and the inspirations of genius. The public, to whose amusement he has so largely contributed, will learn with regret, that his extraordinary endowments were accompanied with frailties which rendered them useless to himself and his family.[1]

In the first biography of Burns, *A Memoir of the Life of the Late Robert Burns* (1797) by Robert Heron who knew the poet personally, the combination of genius and moral decline was made more explicit: 'that exalted mind' was, by Heron's account, finally destroyed in Dumfries where 'his dissipation became still more deeply habitual'.[2]

In the first collected edition, *The Works of Robert Burns* (1800) by Dr James Currie who only once met the poet, the case against Burns as a self-destructive genius was concluded:

> Perpetually stimulated by alcohol in one or other of its various forms [Burns] fled from himself into society, often of the lowest kind . . . He who suffers the pollution of inebriation, how shall he escape other pollution? But let us refrain from the mention of errors over which delicacy and humanity draw the veil. (Currie I, 214–15)

Not every reader was convinced by Currie's portrait of the poet as a fallen man. Wordsworth, in *A Letter to a Friend of Robert Burns* (1816), wrote:

> I well remember the acute sorrow with which, by my own fire-side, I first perused Dr Currie's Narrative . . . Here, said I, being moved beyond what it would become me to express, here is a revolting account of a man of exquisite

genius, and confessedly of many high moral qualities, sunk
into the lower depths of vice and misery! But the painful
story, notwithstanding its minuteness, is incomplete, – in
essentials it is deficient; so that the most attentive and
sagacious reader cannot explain how a mind, so well established by knowledge, fell – and continued to fall, without
power to prevent or retard its own ruin. (CH, 280–1)

Wordsworth composed poetic tributes to Burns and mourned the
man in the seventh stanza of 'Resolution and Independence' (1802)
as 'Him who walked in glory and in joy/Following his plough, along
the mountain side'.

Coleridge, in an epistle to Charles Lamb ('To a Friend', 1796)
expressed his indignation over Burns wasting his creative time by
discharging his tedious and tiring duties as an Exciseman: 'They
snatch'd him from the sickle and the plough –/To gauge ale-firkins.'
Keats, who visited Burns Cottage in 1818, wrote a sonnet on the
occasion. In America, Longfellow wrote a poem on Burns ('Robert
Burns', in *Harper's New Monthly Magazine*, Aug. 1880). For the Boston
celebration of the centenary of the birth of Burns, Whittier wrote 'The
Memory of Burns' which was recited, in Whittier's absence, by Ralph
Waldo Emerson. The penultimate stanza calls for forgiveness for one
portrayed as an imperfect human being but a perfect poet:

> To-day be every fault forgiven
>   Of him in whom we joy!
> We take, with thanks, the gold of Heaven
>   And leave the earth's alloy.
> Be ours his music as of spring,
>   His sweetness as of flowers,
> The songs the bard himself might sing
>   In holier ears than ours.

Despite the *Edinburgh Evening Courant* and Heron and Currie, then,
Burns was treated with respect, not revulsion, after his death. Statues
of him were erected all over the place: in London, Albany, Barre,
Chicago, Denver, Milwaukee, San Franscisco, Fredericton, Toronto,
Adelaide, Ballarat, Melbourne, Sydney, Dunedin to say nothing of
Scotland where there are Burns statues in every self-respecting city
and town.

Today Burns remains one of the most popular writers in the world,
a man whose witty and poignant poems and whose heartbreakingly
beautiful songs seem personally directed at each of his admirers. He

could (as he claimed in the first 'Epistle to J. Lapraik') 'touch the heart', tug at the emotions as in 'To a Mouse':

> The best-laid schemes o' mice an' men
>   Gang aft agley,
> An' lea'e us nought but grief an' pain,
>   For promis'd joy!

From those lines countless readers have extracted a meaningful maxim and John Steinbeck the title of a novella.[3] Admired in the United States, revered in Russia, translated into the major languages of the world, Burns crosses boundaries and cuts through classes. Princes praise him (the future George IV was one of the subscribers for the Burns Monument in Alloway), Presidents sing his songs ('Auld lang syne' at the White House), working men and women carry a torch for Burns in pubs and clubs.

None of his literary contemporaries achieved the immediacy of Burns; even Blake is trapped in his time, obscuring his vision with Swedenborgian symbolism (by contrast Burns's freemasonic allusions are never arcane for 'A man's a man for a' that'). At his best Burns apparently transcends his time, today still singing or speaking with the familiarity of a close friend. It is, of course, an illusion, a triumph of artistry. Burns was very much a product of his period. Born a farmer's son the year before George III was crowned king of Great Britain, he was seventeen when Congress carried the American Declaration of Independence, twenty-four when William Pitt (a man his own age) became Prime Minister of Great Britain, thirty when French Revolutionaries sacked the Bastille. All these events profoundly affected his life and work.

Poetically, Burns emerged at a propitious time in Scotland. His Kilmarnock edition came out forty years after the catastrophe of Culloden, the defeat of the Scottish clans by the Hanoverian Duke of Cumberland. Scotland needed an eloquent national voice and Burns provided it so successfully that he was, albeit posthumously, virtually recognized as royalty in his native land. The most enduring icon in Scotland is not the head of a monarch but the face of Burns as featured on everything from shortbread tins to the Clydesdale Bank £5 note. It is a case of The Kingdom is Dead, Long Live the King – King Robert who declared 'The honest man, though e'er sae poor,/Is king o' men for a' that.'

In Scotland, Burns has become a symbol of nationhood. He is treated as Scottish saviour, his birthplace cottage immaculately preserved as a shrine complete with the bed in which he was supposedly born; the

adjoining museum exhibiting relics such as the family Bible of William
Burnes (the same 'big ha'-Bible' cited in 'The Cotter's Saturday
Night'), a hair-bracelet and lock of Jean Armour's hair, the poet's
'gilt-headed Wangee rod' (CL, 192). As a poet he is often worshipped
uncritically as the one-and-only, the be-all-and-end-all and not only at
the annual Burns Suppers over whisky and haggis. The Scottish author
James Barke, by no means an unintelligent man, put it like this:

> Just as there can be no greater musician than Beethoven,
> there can be no greater poet than Burns. Before either can
> be surpassed, a new race will have to be born – a different
> and greater species than the *homo sapiens* hitherto known
> to history.[4]

That statement has nothing to do with logic, everything to do with the
blind faith of love for a man every reader thinks he or she knows. Barke
wrote a five-novel sequence on the life of Burns, *The Immortal Memory*
(1946–54), which he proudly proclaimed as 'unashamedly romantic
and idealistic'.[5] He could have added the epithet 'sentimental' for
Barke's fictional Burns is more of a saint than a sinner. Like Burns
Cottage, Barke's Burns is whitewashed.

It would be easy to ridicule this love of Burns as irresponsibly
escapist but for the fact that it is a faith that sustains many people.
Tom Sutherland, a Stirlingshire-born American citizen, spent more
than six years as a hostage in Beirut before his release in 1991.
Returning to Scotland for a Burns Supper in January 1992 he acknowledged he overcame the torment of his captivity through his
passion for the poems and songs of Burns.

> The line that would sustain me was 'My Love is Like a
> Red, Red Rose' . . . Burns was something that I would
> occupy my mind with. We didn't have newspapers, so
> I turned to Burns's poetry and tried to reconstruct as
> many verses as possible in my mind. Holy Willie's Prayer,
> Ode to a Mouse were favourites.[6]

Burns is many things to many people but most of those who express an admiration for him find it impossible to separate his poetry
from his compelling personality.

Roleplaying

When he died Burns was a poor man in a warring world immeasurably
enriched by his artistry. During his lifetime, he was much misunder-
stood though his own relish for playing a part was one reason for
this. In the Preface to the Kilmarnock edition of his *Poems, Chiefly*

in the Scottish Dialect (1786) he projected himself as an ill-educated toiler: lacking 'the advantages of learned art', burdened by 'the toil and fatigues of a laborious life', he asked his readers to 'make every allowance for Education and Circumstances of Life' (see p.246). Yet this was a man who had studied the philosophy of Locke and Adam Smith and Thomas Reid; the fiction of Sterne and Richardson and Smollett; the poetry of Milton and Pope and Thomson. The self-styled 'simple Bardie' ('The Author's Earnest Cry and Prayer') was an exceptionally erudite individual.

Taking their cue from the Kilmarnock edition, however, the early critics acclaimed him as an inspired but intellectually limited peasant: to the *Edinburgh Magazine* 'a common ploughman' offering 'the exertions of untutored fancy' (CH, 64); to the *Edinburgh Evening Courant* 'a common farmer' whose 'sentiments would do honour to a much more enlightened scholar' (CH, 65); to Henry Mackenzie, in the *Lounger,* 'this Heaven-taught ploughman' (CH, 70). Burns's roleplaying was a conscious strategy for survival as Robert Anderson, who met the poet in Edinburgh, observed:

> It was, I know, a part of the machinery, as he called it, of his poetical character to pass for an illiterate ploughman who wrote from pure inspiration. When I pointed out some evident traces of poetical imitation in his verses, privately, he readily acknowledged his obligations, and even admitted the advantages he enjoyed in poetical composition from the *copia verborum*, the command of phraseology, which the knowledge and use of the English and Scottish dialects afforded him; but in company he did not suffer his pretensions to pure inspiration to be challenged, and it was seldom done where it might be supposed to affect the success of the subscription for his *Poems* . . . (Kinsley, 1538).

Burns had long relished his roleplaying. In Tarbolton, a friend observed, Burns 'wore the only tied hair in the parish' (Ch-W I, 68) and the poet said of himself: 'That feeling heart but acts a part–/'Tis rakish art in Rob Mossgiel' (see p.114).

It is worth dwelling further on this roleplaying as it affected the perception of the poet as well as the man. Burns's favourite novel, so he frequently said, was Henry Mackenzie's *The Man of Feeling* (1771): a book, Burns claimed, 'I prize next to the Bible' (CL, 55). Hero of Mackenzie's novel is the lachrymose Harley, a hypersensitive soul who bursts into tears at every opportunity. That Burns to some extent modelled himself on Harley is evident in an early letter Burns

wrote to his father (see p.263). 'As for this world,' Burns exclaimed, 'I
despair of ever making a figure in it – I am not formed for the bustle
of the busy nor the flutter of the Gay'. 'This world,' exclaims Harley,
'was a scene in which I never much delighted. I was not formed for
the bustle of the busy, nor the dissipation of the gay.'[7]

Literary influence is one thing, substituting roleplaying for reality
another. Consider, however, Sir Walter Scott's memory of meeting
Burns in Edinburgh during the winter of 1786–7 when Scott was
fifteen:

> The only thing I remember which was remarkable in
> Burns' manner, was the effect produced upon him by a
> print of Bunbury's, representing a soldier lying dead in
> the snow, his dog sitting in misery on the one side, on the
> other his widow, with a child in her arms . . . Burns seemed
> much affected by the print, or rather the ideas which it sug-
> gested to his mind. He actually shed tears. (CH, 261–2)

That sounds suspiciously like Burns acting the part of Harley in order
to establish himself as the peasant equivalent of a Man of Feeling for
an assembled company including Dugald Stewart, the philosopher.
Stewart became accustomed to seeing Burns in tears on their walks
together on the Braid Hills: 'I repeated to him many passages of English
poetry, with which he was unacquainted, and have more than once
witnessed the tears of admiration and rapture, with which he heard
them.' (Currie I, 142.) Stewart also noted that Burns dressed for the
part he played in Edinburgh: 'he always wore boots; and, when on
more than usual ceremony, buck-skin breeches' (Currie I, 138). Burns
also wore the buff and blue colours of the Whigs.

Like many others who met Burns, Stewart valued the poet's conversation about his verse:

> Nothing perhaps was more remarkable among his various
> attainments, than the fluency, and precision, and original-
> ity of his language, when he spoke in company; more
> particularly as he aimed at purity in his turn of expression,
> and avoided more successfully than most Scotchmen, the
> peculiarities of Scottish phraseology. (Currie I, 137)

Compare that to the insistence of Burns's wife, Jean Armour, that he
'never spoke English, but spoke very correct Scotch'.[8] But Stewart's remarks on Burns's speech are revealing. The Scotland into which Burns
was born was obsessed about its identity, having surrendered its parliamentary independence in 1707 and having endured the defeat of the

Scottish clans at Culloden. Scotland had been reduced to a mere region – North Britain, essentially an outpost of England. In the aftermath of Culloden, Highland dress and bagpipe-playing were proscribed.

Highly acclaimed works in Scotland after the parliamentary Union were in English. John Home, author of the five-act verse drama *Douglas* (1756), was (according to an enthusiastic member of the audience) the Scottish Shakespeare. William Wilkie, whose *The Epigoniad* (1757) was admired by David Hume, was supposedly the Scottish Homer. James Macpherson's Ossianic improvisations were accepted as genuine translations from the Gaelic by Hugh Blair who hailed them as examples of the Scottish Sublime.[9] By contrast Robert Fergusson, whose Scots poems were collected in 1773, was largely ignored by the Scottish literary establishment and died, at the age of twenty-four in the Edinburgh Bedlam. Burns bitterly observed in an epistle 'To William Simson':

> O Fergusson! thy glorious parts
> Ill-suited law's dry, musty, arts!
> My curse upon your whunstane hearts,
>   Ye E'nbrugh gentry!
> The tythe o' what ye waste at cartes
>   Wad stow'd his pantry!

Burns frequently acknowledged his poetic debt to Fergusson ('By far my elder Brother in the muse' he wrote below the frontispiece portrait in the 1782 edition of Fergusson's *Poems*) and, not long after arriving in Edinburgh, he arranged for a tombstone to be erected on Fergusson's unmarked grave in Canongate churchyard (see pp.282 & 314).

Stylistically, the influence of Fergusson on Burns is immense. Burns relied heavily on the six-line Standard Habbie stanza as did Fergusson (and Ramsay before him); he used Ramsay's simplified form of the nine-line Christis Kirk stanza, as adapted by Fergusson, in 'The Holy Fair' which is modelled on Fergusson's 'Leith Races'. 'Scotch Drink' is modelled on Fergusson's 'Caller Water', 'The Cotter's Saturday Night' on Fergusson's 'The Farmer's Ingle' and so on. When Burns first read Fergusson is uncertain. The Autobiographical Letter implies that Burns read Fergusson in Irvine but the second edition of Fergusson's *Poems* was not published until after May 1782 and Burns left Irvine in March of that year (poetic evidence suggests that Burns became familiar with Fergusson's work in 1783).

By harping on his humble birth and lack of formal education, Burns avoided the fate of Fergusson who had little promotional expertise, flaunted his university education and frequently caused offence to the establishment by his obstreperous life and work: his comment on Mackenzie's *The Man of Feeling* was a comical poem 'The Sow of Feeling'. Burns certainly enjoyed boozing in Edinburgh, joining the Crochallan Fencibles, a convivial club that met in Dawney Douglas's tavern in Anchor Close (near William Smellie's printing shop) and for whom he collected the bawdy poems printed as *The Merry Muses*. But he behaved himself impeccably with sober members of the literary establishment. Dugald Stewart noted 'I should have concluded in favor of his habits of sobriety, from all of him that ever fell under my own observation.' (Currie I, 1411.) That Stewart had to be approached in habits of sobriety is shown by a remark of Henry Mackenzie: 'Dugald Stewart, who first introduced [Burns] to me, told me latterly that his conduct and manners had become so degraded that decent persons could hardly take any notice of him.'[10]

Drink

On the subject of drink, so eloquently eulogised in 'Scotch Drink' (on whisky) and a letter of 1787 to Archibald Lawrie (on port, see p.288) and 'Go, fetch to me a pint of wine', various comments are contradictory. Heron and Currie were convinced that Burns drank himself to death. Gilbert Burns disagreed, claiming that such poems as 'Scotch Drink' were written by the roleplaying Burns:

> [Burns] assumed a poetic character very different from the real character of the man at that time . . . At the time when many of these rhapsodies respecting drinking and drunkenness were composed, and first published, few people were less addicted to drinking than our poet.[11]

Jean Armour insisted that Burns 'never drank by himself at home [and in coMpany drank] chiefly rum and gin; very little whisky was used'.[12] The epistolary evidence tells a different tale.

'I am miserably fou' (CL, 309) Burns wrote to Peter Hill on 17 May 1787; 'occasional hard drinking is the devil to me' (CL, 203) he wrote to Mrs Dunlop on 31 December 1792. These two statements, from the poet's own parched lips as it were, speak volumes for a drinking problem that has been distorted by dogma since the death of Burns. Burns was haunted by hangovers and given to sporadic, rather than regular, drinking. However, commentators have rarely been willing to let the subject rest in peace though the poet's friends took his boozing in their stride as they followed in his bootsteps. Writing to Currie about the Galloway tour he made with Burns in July–August 1793, John Syme recalled 'We got utterly wet, and to revenge ourselves

Burns insisted at Gatehouse, on our getting utterly drunk.' (Kinsley, 1420.) Had he anticipated his posthumous reputation as a toper, Burns might have extended the session, insisting that he and Syme (like Tam o' Shanter and Souter Johnie) got 'fou for weeks thegither'.

Every year, on 25 January, the birthday of Burns is celebrated, in Scotland and internationally, with Burns Suppers at which haggis and copious amounts of whisky are consumed. The haggis, of course, honours Burns's enthusiastic 'To a Haggis'. The whisky, equally obviously, endorses the sentiments Burns expressed in 'Scotch Drink' and other poems. That Burns drank heavily on occasions is beyond doubt and the habit is a familiar enough occupational hazard for poets, one that does not normally trouble readers of poetry unduly. Admirers of the Welsh poet Dylan Thomas or the American poet John Berryman do not expend energy in denying that their hero got drunk or was alcoholically inclined. Burns, however, is seen as a spiritual saviour thus prompting moralistic comment on the subject of spirits. Despite the epistolary and (often reliable) anecdotal evidence to the contrary, Snyder asserted that Burns 'was never a drunkard' (Snyder, 435). Other Burnsians have said much the same, dismissing as malicious gossip 'the legend of Burns the drunkard'.[13] Unable to accept that their hero might have been as keen on drink as his fellow countrymen, Burnsians seem as convinced as Currie that insobriety is a sin.

Burns himself was more philosophical about drink. His Autobiographical Letter spins stories about tippling in taverns. Writing to Samuel Clark he saw no contradiction between drinking and decency though, on this occasion, he was too hungover to clarify his own condition:

> I recollect something of a drunken promise yesternight
> to breakfast with you this morning. – I am sorry that
> it is impossible . . . Some of our folks about the Excise
> Office, Edinburgh, had and perhaps still have conceived
> a prejudice against me as being a drunken dissipated
> character. – I might be all this, you know, & yet be an
> honest fellow, but you know that I am an honest fellow
> and am nothing of this. (CL, 702)

The 'drunken promise' is typical of the heavy tippler, confident in his cups but diffident as the morning-after dawns.

There is no evidence to suggest that Burns was habitually drunk from morning to night on a daily basis. Josiah Walker, an admirer, spent two days with Burns in Dumfries in November 1795 and recalled a visit to the Globe Inn:

When it began to grow late, he shewed no disposition
to retire, but called for fresh supplies of liquor, with a
freedom which might be excusable, as we were in an
inn, and no condition had been distinctly made, though
it might easily have been inferred, had the inference been
welcome, that he was to consider himself as our guest;
nor was it till he saw us worn out, that he departed,
about three in the morning . . . He, on this occasion,
drank freely without being intoxicated, a circumstance
from which I concluded, not only that his constitution
was still unbroken, but that he was not addicted to solitary
cordials; for if he had tasted liquor in the morning, he must
have easily yielded to the excess of the evening.[14]

Drunken promises and drunken nights at the Globe Inn: it fits a definite
pattern.

From all the evidence available, it looks as if Burns conforms to the
behavioural pattern of the bout-alcoholic who can do without drink for
sustained periods and then depend on it for days on end. He certainly
suffered from the guilt-edged insecurity of the bout-alcoholic, as
his letters make clear. Towards the end of 1791 he wrote to Bob
Ainslie about 'the horrors of penitence, regret, remorse, head-ache,
nausea, and all the rest of the damned hounds of hell, that beset
a poor wretch, who has been guilty of the sin of drunkenness'
(CL, 339). In March 1793 he apologized for his behaviour the night
before in a letter to John McMurdo:

I believe last night that my old enemy, the Devil, taking
the advantage of my being in drink (he well knows he has
no chance with me in my sober hours) tempted me to be
a little turbulent. – You have too much humanity to heed
the maniac ravings of a poor wretch whom the powers of
Hell, & the potency of Port, beset at the same time. (CL,
494)

His notorious 'letter from Hell' (see p.325) expresses alarm at the
behavioural changes wrought by drink. Bout-alcoholism, with its
euphoric self-indulgence dissolving into remorse as the bout shakily
ends, is often associated with manic-depressive behaviour which, in
turn, is often found in highly creative individuals. Poets, with their
bouts of intense creativity and their bouts of despair, are understandably
prone to bout-alcoholism and Burns was definitely a bout-writer
producing the poems of the Kilmarnock edition in a fury of creativity,

writing songs for Johnson and Thomson in bursts. Burns's remark that 'occasional hard drinking is the devil to me' (CL, 203) is a classic confession of bout-alcoholism.

Maria Riddell, who knew Burns well, acknowledged his heavy drinking and refused to 'undertake to be the apologist of the irregularities even of a man of genius' (Currie I, 256). Almost two centuries after the death of Burns it is even less necessary to apologize for a poet who enjoyed drinking but dreaded the mornings after. 'Scotch Drink' makes his position clear. In his enthusiasm for drink, as in his attitude to poetry, he was a follower of Fergusson who, in 'Caller Water' (the model for 'Scotch Drink', remember) produced a Standard Habbie stanza on the subject:

> The fuddlin' Bardies now-a-days
> Rin *maukin*-mad in Bacchus' praise,
> And limp and stoiter thro' their lays
> > *Anacreontic,*
> While each his sea of wine displays
> > As big's the Pontic.

Burns put it more succinctly when he called for a pint of wine (see p.212).

Scots and English

As richly versed in the Scots language as Fergusson, Burns succeeded, to some extent, in overcoming the obstacles of prejudice that prevailed in the pro-English linguistic climate after 1707. Conditioned by what we now call culture-shock after being absorbed into the Union, several prominent literary Scots became ashamed of their Scottishness. On 8 February 1759, about a week after the birth of Burns, David Hume wrote to congratulate William Robertson on his *History of Scotland* (1759) and to point out, incidentally, that Robertson had committed the sin of Scotticism:

> The Word *Interference* is Scotch: The *Whole Nobles* is the same; the English never use the whole but to a Singular; as the *whole Body of Nobility*. I beseech you change the Word *Nobles*, nine places in ten, for Nobility, Peers, Barons, Great men, Chieftains.[15]

Twenty years later James Beattie, a poet and philosopher Burns admired, brought out his *Scoticisms, Arranged in Alphabetical Order, Designed to Correct Improprieties of Speech in Writing*. Though Ramsay and Fergusson wrote Scots verse, the English language was in the ascendant in Scotland. St:11, Burns reckoned the English could tolerate a measure of Scots in his songs: 'A small sprinkling of Scoticisms, is no objection to an English reader.' (CL, 642.)

Typical of the reaction to Burns's Scots poems was a letter, of 1 February 1787 from the 11th Earl of Buchan, commending the 'little doric pieces of yours in our provincial dialect' (CL, 266). Burns was advised to write in English by men such as Dr John Moore, to whom the poet addressed his Autobiographical Letter. On 23 May 1787, Moore wrote to Burns:

> It is evident that you already possess a great variety of expression and command of the English language, you ought therefore to deal more sparingly, for the future, in the provincial dialect – why should you, by using *that*, limit the number of your admirers to those who understand the Scottish, when you can extend it to all persons of taste who understand the English language? (Currie II, 80)

Burns was used to such criticism. The *Monthly Review* of December 1786 had regretted that his poems were 'written in some measure in an unknown tongue, which must deprive most of our Readers of the pleasure they would otherwise naturally create' (CH, 72). The *English Review* (Feb. 1787) lamented that Burns's 'provincial dialect confines his beauties to one half of the island' (CH, 78). The *General Magazine* (1787) thought the use of Scots in the poems 'must necessarily confine their beauties to a small circle of readers' (CH, 89).

Yet Burns produced poetry of genius only in Scots and the passing years confirmed to him that this was so. Writing to George Thomson (19 Oct. 1794), Burns confessed 'I have not that command of the [English] language that I have of my native tongue. – In fact, I think that my ideas are more barren in English than in Scottish.' (CL, 660) By then Burns had seen three editions of his poems published and surely reflected, on reading them, that his English efforts were pastiches of favourite English poets whereas his poems 'chiefly in the Scottish dialect' were masterful. Using the language of Pope, Shenstone and Gray he was bound to come off second best. Quoting some of Burns's English verse, Matthew Arnold remarked: 'By his English poetry Burns in general belongs to the eighteenth century, and has little importance for us.'[16] This judgement of one poet by another is just. Remarkably, Burns achieved recognition by casting his finest work in a national language in a state of atrophy. Scots, like English a dialect of Anglo-Saxon, had developed as an indigenous and eloquently expressive language in Scotland and, by the first half of the sixteenth

century, had acquired 'its full status as a national speech adequate for all
the demands laid on it, for poetry, for literary and official prose, public
records and the ordinary business transactions of life'.[17] However, Scots
began to be undermined by the triumph of the Protestant Reformation
in 1560. In the absence of a Scots translation of the Bible, the Reformers
adopted a translation completed in 1560 by English refugees in Geneva.
This had profound linguistic consequences. The word of God, the
sacred logos, was uttered in English. Scots began to be perceived as an
inferior language, suitable for everyday conversation and comic verse
but lacking the scriptural authority of English.

In 1603 the Scottish and English crowns were both conferred on
James VI & I and with the Union of Crowns the Scottish court
followed the king to London. The king himself began to write
poetry in English and other Scottish poets followed the royal example.
Consecrated by the Geneva Bible and commended by the court,
the king's English was twice-blessed. With the parliamentary Union
of 1707, English became the official language of Scotland (North
Britain) as well as England. Born into a nation reduced to provincial status, Burns looked back in anger and indignation at the
trashing of a great literary tradition. His use of Scots was a defence
of a distinctively Scottish culture.

As the Kilmarnock and Edinburgh editions demonstrated, Burns
used Scots not only for emotional outbursts and descriptive 'manners-
painting' ('The Vision') but for ecclesiastical satire ('The Holy Fair'),
social comment ('The Twa Dogs'), folksy-philosophical reflection ('To
a Mouse'), graveyard humour ('Death and Doctor Hornbook') and
matters of morality ('Address to the Unco Guid'). For all his roleplaying
as a poetic primitive, Burns took his Scots work seriously, denying that
the use of dialect alone automatically produced poetry. Writing to Mrs
Dunlop in 1789 he complained 'my success has encouraged such a shoal
of ill-spawned monsters to crawl into public notice under the title of
Scots Poets, that the very term, Scots Poetry, borders on the burlesque'
(CL, 169). The Scots-writing Scottish poet had to use the language
inventively, not rest passively on the linguistic laurels of the past.

Burns was enough of a product of his period to assume English
affectations: his professed admiration for Shenstone, his polished epistolary style, his ability to hold his own as a conversationalist in
polite company – Scott thought his conversation 'expressed perfect
self-confidence, without the slightest presumption' (CH, 262). As a
Scots poet, however, he presumed to renew tradition in a startling
way, applying his art to a bewildering variety of subjects. Writing
in Scots he managed, by great artistry, to simulate a conversational

tone that sounded anything but artificial. Not so in English. All poetic
language is, by definition, artificial but, for Burns, Augustan English
was excruciatingly artificial – indeed alien – as a literary medium.

Burns's poems in English are, by general consent, his poorest productions. The Kilmarnock edition has poems that alternate Augustan
English with Scots, most effectively in 'The Cotter's Saturday Night'
where the first English stanza is in deliberate contrast to Scots stanzas
that follow. Shortly after he arrived in Edinburgh, Burns composed
an 'Address to Edinburgh' which duly appeared in the first Edinburgh
edition. Here Burns might have risen racily to the occasion. After all,
he was worldly enough to observe what went on in the capital with
'bucks strutting, ladies flaring, blackguards sculking, whores leering'
(CL, 81) and he knew 'Auld Reikie' by his favourite Fergusson with
its portrait of a doleful doxy lingering by a lamp-post: 'Stands she that
beauty lang had kend,/Whoredom her trade, and vice her end'. Alas,
Burns was unable to emulate Fergusson on this occasion, beginning
his poem by apostrophising 'Edina! Scotia's darling seat!'

Whereas the Scots poems of the Kilmarnock edition had vividly
explored the landscape of Ayrshire in unforgettably energetic language, this English poem praises the capital unconvincingly. Here is
Burns's tribute to Edinburgh Castle:

> There, watching high the least alarms,
>   Thy rough, rude fortress gleams afar;
> Like some bold vet'ran, grey in arms,
>   And mark'd with many a seamy scar:
>   The pond'rous wall and massy bar,
> Grim-rising o'er the rugged rock,
>   Have oft withstood assailing war,
> And oft repell'd th'invader's shock.

It is pedestrian verse constructed around clichés, a far cry from
Fergusson, a fall from the linguistic grace of the Kilmarnock edition.

Burns had no problem writing English prose and could occasionally
impress in English verse when he used the language unpretentiously as
in 'Lines on Stirling' (see p.207) but eighteenth-century English poetic
diction was unsuited to Burns's artistic talent and temperament. He
could imitate English poets but such derivative pieces make no advance
on the originals and are notable only as a contrast to those Scots poems
in which Burns imaginatively raised the Scots dialect to a new lexical
level. Writing in English, Burns was a performer; entertaining in his
English prose, ill at ease in his English verse. Writing in Scots, a native
language competing for attention with English, he was a natural; or

managed to sound like one by articulating his ideas and emotions with verbal virtuosity. Burns knew that Scots was no naïve alternative to English, but a language tested by oral tradition, examined by Ramsay and Fergusson. And yet, if he had been formed only by his father, Burns might have been only another Scottish poet writing in English.

Education and Oral Tradition

In 1765, William Burnes engaged John Murdoch to teach his sons Robert and Gilbert the basic elements of English. Murdoch was not an ideal choice of teacher. As his own letters show, he was pedantic and pompous, his description of William Burnes's clay cottage as 'the argillaceous fabric' (Currie I, 87) typical of his turn of phrase. His judgement that 'Robert's ear, in particular, was remarkably dull' (Currie I, 89) says more about his lack of musical appreciation than Burns's limitations, given the irresistible evidence of the great songs. Similarly, his opinion that Gilbert was more witty and imaginative than Robert shows how erroneously Murdoch could assess the potential of his pupils for Gilbert's own writing is solemn rather than scintillating.

However, Murdoch discharged his duties competently in the boring business of 'dividing words into syllables by rule, spelling without book, parsing sentences' (Currie I, 88). Encouraged by William Burnes, he trained Robert and Gilbert to memorise hymns and poems. Well pleased with the result, he then trained them to paraphrase poems:

> As soon as they were capable of it, I taught them to turn verse into its natural prose order; sometimes to substitute synonimous expressions for poetical words, and to supply all the ellipses. These, you know, are the means of knowing that the pupil understands his author. These are excellent helps to the arrangement of words in sentences, as well as to a variety of expression. (Currie I, 88–9)

Murdoch had few textbooks to teach his pupils. The Bible, of course, was basic to life in school as well as at home. Other textbooks were *New Grammar, with English Exercise* by A. Fisher (actually one Mrs Slack of Newcastle); a standard spelling book, probably Masson's *English Spelling Book*; and, most important for Burns, Masson's *Collection of Prose and Verse*.

Arthur Masson's *A Collection of Prose and Verse, from the Best English Authors, For the Use of Schools* (reprinted in 1767) was an edifying anthology of verse and prose. Poems included Pope's eclogue 'The Messiah', Thomas Parnell's moral narrative 'The Hermit', Addison's long 'Letter to Lord Halifax', David Mallet's mock-antique ballad

'William and Margaret', an anonymous poem 'The Horn Book' ('by
a gentleman in his old age'), Dryden's 'Alexander's Feast', Shenstone's
'Pastoral Ballad'; and extracts from Thomson's *The Seasons*, Milton's
Paradise Lost and Shakespeare's plays ('All the world's a stage', 'To be
or not to be'). Prose included extracts from Mrs Elizabeth Rowe's
Moral Letters and these had a lasting impact on Burns's epistolary style.
Masson's anthology was entirely in English.

In 1772 Murdoch, then teaching English in Ayr, sent Burns the
poetic works of Pope. When Burns went to Kirkoswald in 1775,
to learn mathematics, he took time out to read the poetic works
of Shenstone whose elegies he thought 'divine' (see p.246). Between
them, William Burnes and Murdoch made Burns 'an excellent English
scholar' (CL, 249). Murdoch approved of William Burnes's own
attempts to do what so many of his self-styled social superiors had
done since the Union of 1707; that is, speak English like a gentleman.
Eulogising the character of William Burnes, Murdoch wrote: 'He
spoke the English language with more propriety (both with respect
to diction and pronunciation) than any man I ever knew, with no
greater advantages.' (Currie I, 95) That was a supreme compliment
from one imitative Englishman to another.

Fortunately, there was another influence on Burns. In his earliest
years Burns owed his consciousness of Scottish culture not to his
English-speaking father, not to the English-teaching Murdoch, but
to his ballad-singing mother. At the height of his fame Burns was
aware that the traditional vitality of his verse was a tribute to his
mother. Dugald Stewart observed:

> His memory was uncommonly retentive, at least for
> poetry, of which he recited to me frequently long
> compositions with the most minute accuracy. They
> were chiefly ballads, and other pieces in our Scottish
> dialect; great part of them (he told me) he had learned
> in his childhood, from his mother, who delighted in
> such recitations, and whose poetical taste, rude as it
> probably was, gave, it is presumable, the first direction
> to her son's genius. (Currie I, 143–4)

Much has been written in honour of the poet's father, much less in
appreciation of his mother.

Agnes Broun was a small, shapely woman with pale red hair and dark
eyes, 'extremely active and industrious – naturally cheerful'.[18] Like her
husband, she was familiar with the hard life of the Scottish farmer for
her father was a farmer at Craigenton, Kirkoswald. The only form of

education she received was in Kirkoswald where a weaver, who had
a few such pupils by him as he worked at the loom, taught her bits
of the Bible but not how to write. Ten when her mother died, she
was twelve when her father remarried and sent her to Maybole to
live with her grandmother. In Maybole she became housekeeper to her
paternal uncle William Brown, a widower mentioned by Burns in a
letter (16 Aug. 1788) to Mrs Dunlop:

> I had an old Grand uncle with whom my Mother lived
> a while in her girlish years; the good old man, for such
> he was, was long blind ere he died, during which time
> his most voluptuous enjoyment was to sit down & cry
> while my Mother would sing the simple old song of
> The Life & Age of Man. (CL, 153)

As cited by Burns (CL, 153) the song began:

> 'Twas in the sixteenth hunder year
>   Of God & fifty three
> Frae Christ was born that bought us dear,
>   As Writings testifie   (l264)

Not one of the best songs in Agnes's repertoire but Burns's tribute to
the emotional power of his mother's singing is important.

Little is known of Agnes Broun but much can be made of her
singing. It is certain she sang traditional ballads as well as songs. Her
daughter Isabella testified: 'She sang very well, and had a never-failing
store of old ballads and songs, on which her poetical son must have fed
in his boyhood.'[19] Nonliterate – Isabella said that Agnes 'was never
able even to write her own name'[20] – she was alive to the oral
tradition. Before the ballads began to be collected and scrutinised
by scholars in the eighteenth century, they were transmitted – and
transmuted – by word of mouth. In a fundamental sense, the ballads
were old wives' tales, passing from mother to daughter, perpetuated
by women. In John Barbour's fourteenth-century vernacular epic The
Brus there is a reference to a ballad: 'Young women quhen thai
will play,/Syng it amang thaim ilka day.' In Act II of Shakespeare's
Twelfth Night, the Duke requests an old song: 'The spinsters and the
knitters in the sun,/And the free maids, that weave their thread
with bones,/Do use to chant it.'

Invariably, when a ballad has been collected from tradition, the
source has been female.[21] Agnes Broun was a ballad-singer and
tradition-bearer who gave birth to a poet she raised on Scottish
songs and ballads. William Burnes, with his educational aspirations,
s,

and Agnes Broun with her oral inheritance: their marriage was also
the union of English affectation and Scottish folk tradition. All his life
Burns was to feel the tension of two traditions but he had the best of
both worlds in being familiar with both booklore and folklore.

In 'There was a lad', composed when he was basking in the critical
success of his poems, Burns seems to be celebrating himself but, on
closer inspection, the song is a celebration of the Scottish folk. The
blast of January wind is a gift to the bard, a gust of the spirit of Scotland.
This notion is implied in the four final stanzas spoken by the gossip
– an old wife, the kind of woman central to the oral traditions of
Scotland, such as Betty Davidson, fondly remembered by Burns in
the Autobiographical Letter (see p.89). The prophecies about Robin
are prophecies emerging from the same source that sang the ballads
of Scotland and told the traditional tales. Giving the gossip a larger
dimension than that of one woman strengthens the line 'He'll be a
credit till us a' ': that is, he will be a credit to the Scottish folk, not
simply to one palm-reading onlooker.

Similarly, the last two stanzas link Burns not only to a few women
but to the glory of womankind – 'our kin', as the gossip calls her
sex. The gossip's discussion of Robin's sexuality is both spellbinding
('But sure as three times three mak nine' sounds like a spell) and
specific: for him the women will keep their legs apart ('aspar') for
penetration. Burns is thus seen as a force capable of revitalising the
Scottish folk. What sounds like an innocent song has distinctive
national connotations when considered in the context of the folk
tradition. From infancy, then, Burns listened to songs and ballads
known by his mother and tales told by Betty Davidson in Alloway.
It was in 1765 that the Burnes family left Alloway for the relative
isolation of Mount Oliphant farm. Burns spent his first seven years
in the 'auld clay biggin' and appropriately so; seven is a magical
number in the traditional ballads.

In some ways William Burnes, with his reverence for education and
his patriarchal piety (see the portrait of the father in 'The Cotter's
Saturday Night') was an oppressive influence on Burns. He disapproved
of Burns attending a dancing-class in Tarbolton, he constantly appealed
to virtue, he spoke in sermons whereas his wife sang songs. In his
dying days William Burnes told his daughter Isabella, twelve at the
time, to 'walk in virtue's paths, and shun every vice'.[22] After William
Burnes died, at Lochlea on 13 February 1784, Burns produced an
epitaph in English, a poor performance that ends with a quotation
from Goldsmith's *The Deserted Village*: 'For ev'n his failings lean'd
to Virtue's side.' It was only after his father died that Burns was

able to have the creative time of his life, producing Scots poems of genius and enjoying sex with Elizabeth Paton who became pregnant in the autumn of 1784 ('The Fornicator' suggests she was the first woman he slept with). As long as William Burnes was alive, Robert Burns had to pay lip service to virtue and religion and a' that went against the grain of his natural gifts.

Religion

According to the Westminster Confession (accepted by the Scottish parliament in 1643, and again in 1690, as the doctrine of the Church of Scotland) only the 'Elect', as chosen by God, are redeemed by Christ: theoretically, therefore, good works are irrelevant since all children of the sinner Adam are depraved from birth. Scottish theologians of the eighteenth century constantly reiterated this claim. For example, Thomas Boston's *Human Nature in its Fourfold State* (1720) asserted that 'even the new-born babe [is] a child of hell'.[23] Burns, an avid reader of theological works, described Boston's book as 'stupid' (CL, 260) and 'trash' (CL, 318). The absurd antinomianism of Boston and likeminded ministers lies behind Holy Willie's appeal to a God who 'Sends ane to Heaven an' ten to Hell'.

The doctrine of the 'Elect', derived from Calvin's belief in predestination, was not accepted uncritically throughout eighteenth-century Scotland. Far from representing a unified House of God, the Presbyterian kirk of Burns's day was a house divided and subdivided. The Patronage Act of 1712, giving lay patrons the right to present ministers to vacant parishes, was held to violate the Act of Security (1707) and eventually led to a secession, in 1732, when an Act of Assembly gave the power of election to heritors and elders whenever the patron did not exercise his right. A further secession occurred in 1747 over the Burgher's Oath (requiring holders of public office to affirm the Presbyterian religion) and the Anti-Burghers established synods separate from those of the Burghers. Yet another secession resulted from the issue of civil compulsion in religious affairs: the minority, holding the Solemn League and Covenant as a sacred obligation, comprised the Original Burghers, or 'Auld Lichts' (old lights); the majority, wishing to modify Presbyterian commitment to the Covenant, comprised the 'New Lichts'.

Burns spent a great deal of energy in Ayrshire, where the Auld Licht burned brightly, querying 'Calvinism with so much heat and indiscretion that I raised a hue and cry of heresy against me' (CL, 250). His attitude led him to embrace a body of thought formed by the notion of love. When he rejoiced in religion, he qualified his feelings:

'We can no more live without Religion, than we can live without air; but give me the Religion of Sentiment and Reason.' (CL, 191.) In theory as well as practice Burns was inclined to value natural and artistic creation more than arid doctrines of divine Creation.

His father – who watched the one-day-old Burns being baptised by the liberal minister of Ayr, the Revd William Dalrymple – would have found his advocacy of 'Sentiment and Reason' provocative in its anti-authoritarian implications but might have tolerated, in his milder moods, the preference for delight over dogma. William Burnes was relatively liberal in his approach to religion and did not confine his family to the repressive Calvinist doctrines of the Auld Licht of Ayrshire. In the little leisure time he enjoyed at Mount Oliphant farm, William Burnes compiled *A Manual of Religious Belief, in a Dialogue Between Father and Son* – 'transcribed, with grammatical corrections, by John Murdoch, teacher' and subsequently published in Kilmarnock in 1875. It is a seminal source of the poet's theological suppositions.

Commentators agree that the *Manual* amounts to a liberal critique of Calvinist orthodoxy: it is 'definitely not Calvinistic' (Snyder, 53). After a little preamble, the Manual invokes the argument from design to affirm the existence of God 'for nothing can make itself; and this fabrick of Nature demonstrates its Creator to be possessed of all possible perfection' (Ch-W I, 455). Acknowledging original sin, Burnes argues that fear of the Devil should be controlled by a personal faith that overcomes evil. Burnes then cites scripture to prove the revelation of God and, when the questioning son of the dialogue doubts his capacity to live up to the perfection of God and thus be 'justified', Burnes defines the glory of the Christian religion as its tolerance of human imperfections. Faith, says this father, 'is a firm persuasion of the Divine mission of our Lord Jesus Christ' (Ch-W I, 457) and repentance is to be achieved through the exercise of the intelligence above the animal instincts:

> I not only mean [by repentance] a sorrowing for sin, but a labouring to see the malignant nature of it; as setting nature at variance with herself, by placing the animal part before the rational, and thereby putting ourselves on a level with the brute beasts, the consequence of which will be an intenstine war in the human frame, until the rational part be entirely weakened, which is spiritual death, which in the nature of the thing renders us unfit for the society of God's spiritual kingdom, and to see the beauty of holiness. On the contrary, setting

> the rational part above the animal, though it promote
> a war in the human frame, every conflict and victory
> affords us grateful reflection, and tends to compose the
> mind more and more, not to the utter destruction of
> the animal part, but to the real and true enjoyment of
> them, by placing Nature in the order that its Creator
> designed it, which, in the natural consequences of the
> thing, promotes Spiritual Life, and renders us more and
> more fit for Christ's spiritual kingdom; and not only so,
> but gives to animal life pleasure and joy that we never
> could have had without it. (Ch-W I, 458)

In other words, the rational individual is able to relish his animal
instincts whereas the human brute has no way of putting such pleasure
in an appropriately human context. Robert Burns certainly grew into a
man who applied this text to his own instincts – a letter of 1788 refers
to 'a great unknown Being who could have no other end in giving
[the individual] existence but to make him happy' (CL, 90) – though
not without 'an intestine war' in his human frame.

In the Autobiographical Letter, Burns refers to the 'idiot piety' of his
childhood and little wonder considering the emphasis his father placed
on religion. William Burnes not only relied on the Bible but brought
many theological works before his children (see the Autobiographical
Letter for a list of some of these books). Following the death of his
father, Burns went beyond theological theory and gained practical, and
painful, experience of parochial Scottish Calvinism in action, especially
during his Mossgiel period when he was part of Mauchline parish.

The Mauchline Burns knew was dominated by kirk politics and disputed by the evangelical Auld Lichts and the tolerant New Lichts.
Rigidly Calvinistic, and faithful to the Westminster Confession,
the Auld Lichts believed in preordained damnation or salvation
so worshipped a vindictively selective God who punished sinners
in a blazing hellfire: 'A vast, unbottom'd, boundless pit,/Fill'd fou
o' lowin brunstane' ('The Holy Fair'). The moderate New Lichts
regarded religion with 'carnal wit an' sense' ('The Holy Fair') and
held that a merciful God would reward good deeds, thus modifying
the deterministic doctrine of the 'Elect'.

Burns, like his friend Gavin Hamilton, was temperamentally drawn
to the New Lichts, partly as a result of his father's critique of Calvinist
fundamentalism and partly as a consequence of his common sense and
sense of humour. He particularly deplored the power of the Kirk
Session, a council of kirk elders taking their cue from the minister. In

Mauchline the Kirk Session, presided over by the Revd William Auld, publicly rebuked Burns for fornication and accused Gavin Hamilton of failing to keep the Presbyterian faith. Burns's great ecclesiastical satires ('Holy Willie's Prayer', 'The Holy Fair') make his position clear: he detested the hypocrisy of Calvinism and looked on the Auld Lichts as inimical to the concept of a benign God.

Since Burns fell foul of the kirk's way with sexual offenders, it is worth recalling the punitive power of the Kirk Session. For dealing with fornicators it retained the 'cutty-stool', the stool of repentance, as described in R.H. Cromek's *Remains of Nithsdale and Galloway Song* (1810):

> This stool of terror was fashioned like an arm-chair, and was raised on a pedestal, nearly two foot higher than the other seats, directly fronting the pulpit. [Arrayed 'in the black sack-cloth gown of fornication', the culprit] stood three Sundays successively, his face uncovered, and the awful scourge of unpardoning divinity hung over him. The women stood here in the same accoutrements, and were denied the privilege of a veil. (Kinsley, 1038)

As a result of his affair with Elizabeth Paton, Burns sat on the cutty-stool in 1785, though not in Mauchline (see 'The Fornicator'). The following year, as a result of his affair with Jean Armour, he had to make three penitential appearances in Mauchline kirk though (he wrote to John Richmond on 9 July 1786) 'I am indulged so far as to appear in my own seat' (CL, 77). On 6 August 1786, after their third penitential appearance, Burns and Jean had to listen as the Revd Auld publicly condemned them for their sins:

> You appear there to be rebuked, and at the same time making profession of repentence for the sin of fornication. The frequency of this sin is just matter of lamentation among Christians, and affords just ground of deep humili-ation to the guilty persons themselves . . . Beware of returning to your sin as some of you have done, like the dog to its vomit, or like the sow that is washed to her wallowing in the mire. (Snyder, 126)

Burns had good reason to remember the quotation (2 Peter 2: 22) with which Auld ended his rebuke and it turns up, incongruously in relation to his failure as a farmer, in his Autobiographical Letter: 'I returned "Like the dog to his vomit, and the sow that was washed to her wallowing in the mire"'.

Under the influence of Enlightenment ideals and his reading of
philosophical works, Burns developed as a Deist though did not wish
to make a dogma of Deism, observing 'I hate a Man that wishes to
be a Deist, but I fear, every fair, unprejudiced Enquirer must in some
degree be a Sceptic.' (CL, 459) Brought up on a demanding land and
in a divided society, Burns used his own intelligence, informed by
ideas in philosophical fashion, when he associated himself with 'the
Religion of God & Nature; the Religion that exalts, that ennobles man'
(CL, 208). The most compelling evidence for his Deism, understood
as a natural religion devoid of doctrinal superstition, is in his art.
An 'Elegy on Captain Matthew Henderson', for example, sends the
subject not to some theological heaven but to a universal infinity
among the 'twinkling starnies', a vision of a wonderfully complex
cosmos beyond dogma and doctrine.

Philosophy

As a result of the obsequious Preface to the Kilmarnock edition
and Henry Mackenzie's description of the poet as a 'Heaven-taught
ploughman' (CH, 70) Burns was seen, by his early audience, as
a primitive peasant able, by some miracle, to produce poetry. An
unsigned notice in the General Magazine and Impartial Review (1787)
summed up the position: 'By general report we learn, that R.B. is a
plough-boy, of small education' (CH, 88). As already noted, by the
time the Kilmarnock edition was published, Burns had read not only
the poetry of Milton and Pope and Shenstone, not only the fiction
of Sterne and Richardson and Smollett, but the philosophy of John
Locke and Thomas Reid and Adam Smith.

The impact of Locke's An Essay concerning Human Understanding
(1689) on Burns was considerable, stimulating his insights into human
nature and reinforcing his critical attitude to the kirk (religious dogma-
tists were disturbed by Locke's argument that reasonable discourse de-
pended on considerable ideas, not obscurantist theological theories).

Burns mentions Locke's Essay in his Autobiographical Letter and,
writing to Mrs McLehose in January 1788, refers to 'the Great and
likewise Good Mr Locke, Author of the famous essay on the human
understanding' (CL, 386). Burns surely delighted in Locke's appeal to
individual observation, his advice to remain open to natural experience
rather than relying on dogma. Locke argued that the mind knows
nothing but what it receives from without; knowledge is founded on
observation which the mind rearranges. Endorsing empirical science
(in particular the achievement of Newton), with its basis in observation
and experiment, Locke rejected the arrogant appeal to innate ideas (of

God or anything else). Reacting against scholastic essentialism, Locke distinguished between the real (and unknown) essence of an object and its nominal essence, accessible to observation.

It was a philosophy attractive to a poet of Burns's inquisitive outlook. Indeed, Locke (in 'The Epistle to the Reader') encouraged the individual to follow his own intellectual quest as an end in itself:

> For the Understanding, like the Eye, judging of Objects only by its own Sight, cannot but be pleased with what it discovers, having less regret for what has scaped it, because it is unknown. Thus he who has raised himself above the Alms-Basket, and not content to live lazily on scraps of begg'd opinions, sets his own Thoughts on work, to find and follow Truth, will (whatever he lights on) not miss the Hunter's Satisfaction; every moment of his pursuit will reward his pains with some Delight, and he will have reason to think his time not ill spent, even when he cannot boast of any great Acquisition.[24]

Burns avoided 'scraps of begg'd opinions' on which the self-righteous relied.

Never a systematic student of philosophy, Burns nevertheless showed a shrewd appreciation of those philosophers who confirmed what he concluded intuitively. By turns radical, reformist and revolutionary in politics, he was liberal in philosophy; as well as gaining an understanding of Lockean liberalism he was able, in the early summer of 1789, to enthuse over Adam Smith's *Wealth of Nations* (1776) with its emphasis on natural liberty and insistence that productivity take priority over pedigree, thus putting the gentry in their place. The Scottish intellectual climate of his time was enlightened and Burns, though raised in a farming community, expanded his intellect through reading to embrace the body of thought that stood for the Enlightenment.

In his first Commonplace Book, Burns praises Adam Smith's *The Theory of Moral Sentiments* (1759), a collection of lectures influenced by the empiricist Francis Hutcheson who had taught Smith at Glasgow University and whose *Inquiry Into the Origins of Our Ideas of Beauty and Virtue* (1725) associated moral judgement with an apprehension of virtue as a pleasure. Smith considered that happiness was quantitative and endorsed Hutcheson's sentimental view of morality. The argument of *Morals Sentiments* is based on Smith's sympathy principle:

> How selfish soever man may be supposed, there are evi-
> dently some principles in his nature, which interest him in

the fortune of others, and render their happiness necessary
to him. Of this kind is pity or compassion, the emotion
which we feel for the misery of others, when we either see
it, or are made to conceive it in a very lively manner.[25]

Burns was one of the most compassionate of poets, easily moved by
the misery of others. In praise of Smith, he wrote: 'I entirely agree
with that judicious philosopher Mr Smith in his excellent Theory of
Moral Sentiments, that Remorse is the most painful sentiment that
can embitter the human bosom' (see p.240).

By 1786 Burns was familiar with Thomas Reid's *An Inquiry Into
The Human Mind, on the Principles of Common Sense* (1764), the fundamental text of Scottish Common Sense philosophy. Reid makes
his position clear in his Dedication to Lord Deskfoord. Acknowledging that he was startled by the sceptical argument of Hume's
A Treatise of Human Nature (1738), Reid traced Hume's hypothesis
back to the ancient philosophers:

> The hypothesis I mean is, That nothing is perceived but
> what is in the mind which perceives it: That we do not
> really perceive things that are external, but only certain
> images and pictures of them imprinted upon the mind,
> which are called *impressions* and *ideas*.
>
>   If this be true; supposing certain impressions and ideas to
> exist presently in my mind, I cannot, from their existence,
> infer the existence of any thing else; my impressions and
> ideas are the only existences of which I can have any
> knowledge or conception: and they are such fleeting
> and transitory beings, that they can have no existence
> at all, any longer than I am conscious of them. So that,
> upon this hypothesis, the whole universe about me, bodies
> and spirits, sun, moon, stars, and earth, friends and re-
> lations, all things without exception, which I imagined
> to have a permanent existence whether I thought of
> them or not, vanish at once . . . [26]

Reid misrepresented Hume by reducing his subtle arguments to
absurdity.

  After chapters on the operation of the five senses ('Of Smelling',
'Of Tasting', 'Of Hearing', 'Of Touch', 'Of Seeing') Reid came to
a smugly comfortable conclusion:

> When I perceive a tree before me, my faculty of seeing
> gives me not only a notion or simple apprehension of

the tree, but a belief of its existence, and of its figure, distance, and magnitude; and this judgement or belief is not got by comparing ideas, it is included in the
very nature of the perception . . . They [that is, 'original and natural judgements'] make up what is called *the
common sense of mankind*; and what is manifestly contrary to any of those first principles, is what we call
absurd. The strength of them is *good sense*, which is often found in those who are not acute in reasoning. A
remarkable deviation from them, arising from a disorder
in the constitution, is what we call *lunacy*; as when a
man believes that he is made of glass. When a man
suffers himself to be reasoned out of the principles of
common sense, by metaphysical arguments, we may call
this *metaphysical lunacy*; which differs from the other species
of the distemper in this, that it is not continued, but
intermittent: it is apt to seize the patient in solitary and
speculative moments; but when he enters into society,
Common Sense recovers her authority.[27]

Of Reid, Dugald Stewart wrote:

Dr Reid, who first called the Ideal Theory in question,
offers no argument to prove that the material world exists; but considers our belief in it as an ultimate fact in
our nature. It rests on the same foundation with our
belief of the reality of our sensations, which no man has
disputed.[28]

More to the point, Burns wrote of the Common Sense philosophers:
'To common sense they now appeal –/What wives and wabsters see
and feel!' ('Letter to James Tennant of Glenconner').

Still, Burns allied himself with the Common Sense philosophy and
genuinely admired Dugald Stewart (see p.251) who was, in turn, an
admirer (and biographer) of Thomas Reid. Stewart's introduction to
his *Outlines of Moral Philosophy* (1793) gives some indication of his
approach:

The ultimate object of philosophical inquiry is the same
which every man of plain understanding proposes to himself, when he remarks the events which fall under his
observation with a view to the future regulation of his
conduct. The more knowledge of this kind we acquire, the
better can we accommodate our plans to the established

order of things, and avail ourselves of natural Powers and
Agents for accomplishing our purposes.[29]

If, as is likely, Stewart expressed such notions in conversation with
Burns, the effect would have been encouraging to a poet who aspired
to address 'every man of plain understanding'.

Burns also admired James Beattie, not only as a poet but as a
Common Sense philosopher (he was Professor of Moral Philosophy
at Aberdeen University). Beattie, in his *Essay on the Nature and Immutability of Truth* (1770), had attempted to refute Hume's scepticism.
Burns praised Beattie in 'The Vision' for his verse and for his attack on
Hume the sceptic. According to Gilbert Burns, in the Mount Oliphant
period Burns 'remained unacquainted . . . with Hume' (Currie I, 65),
which suggests he subsequently read Scotland's greatest philosopher.
Though Hume had been dead for a decade when Burns arrived in
Edinburgh, the sceptic was still a dangerous subject to discuss, still
widely regarded as the atheistic scourge of God-fearing folk. Though
he never openly praised Hume as philosopher, the work of Burns is
in accord with Hume's naturalism.

In his Conclusion to Book I of *A Treatise of Human Nature*, Hume
declared 'Human Nature is the only science of man; and yet has been
hitherto the most neglected.'[30] In Section I, Part IV of Book I of the
Treatise, Hume said:

> Nature, by an absolute and uncontrollable necessity, has
> determined us to judge as well as to breathe and feel;
> nor can we any more forbear viewing certain objects in a
> stronger and fuller light, upon account of their customary
> connection with a present impression, than we can hinder
> ourselves from thinking, as long as we are awake, or
> seeing the surrounding bodies, when we turn our eyes
> towards them in broad sunshine . . . It is happy, therefore,
> that nature breaks the force of all sceptical arguments
> in time, and keeps them from having any considerable
> influence on the understanding.[31]

This appeal to nature is as compelling as that of Rousseau, Hume's
hostile friend. It is difficult to believe that Burns did not approve
of Hume – the enemy of dogma, the empirical successor to Locke,
the admirer of nature, the friend of Adam Smith and Dr Blacklock
(to whom Hume transferred his salary as librarian of the Advocates'
Library) – even though direct evidence is elusive. It was not politic
for Burns to celebrate the sceptic.

Politics

In a letter (28 Feb. 1793) to his publisher William Creech, Burns drew
a distinction between 'Great Folks whom I respect [and] Little Folks
whom I love' (CL, 307). In fact there were very few aristocratic Great
Folks he genuinely admired (with obvious exceptions such as the Earl
of Glencairn); for example, he described the 4th Duke of Queensberry
ironically as a 'Great Man' and accurately as 'a flaming Zealot [with]
a character of which one cannot speak with patience' (CL, 432). In
the same letter (of 9 Dec. 1789 to Graham of Fintry) he described
himself as 'too little a man to have any political attachments' (CL,
432). Contemporary party politics, indeed, he saw as a game played
by the great at the expense of the poor. His political opinions sought
wider horizons than those displayed in Ayrshire or Dumfriesshire.

Gilbert Burns supposed his brother had 'a particular jealousy of
people who were richer than himself, or who had more consequence in
life' (Currie I, 71). 'Jealousy' is a misleading word here. Burns resented
the rich, despised them for the way they exploited the poor as he makes
clear in 'The Twa Dogs'. Though on occasion he was obliged to toady
to his self-styled social superiors, he believed profoundly, as letters as
well as poems demonstrate, that an impoverished tenant-farmer was
as worthy as any aristocrat up to and including a king. His egalitarian
ideas were hardly original, but he prized them as the most encouraging
part of the political options of his time.

In *Common Sense* (1776) Tom Paine had written 'Of more worth
is one honest man to society and in the sight of God, than all the
crowned ruffians that ever lived.'[32] Burns likewise believed 'The
honest man, tho e'er sae poor,/Is king o men for a' that' (see p.233).
Though he had, periodically, to conceal his opinions and compromise
for the sake of his career, his revolutionary faith in the common people
was consistent. His vision of an international republic presumed an
informed majority, not 'a rabble' (CL, 436), an 'uninformed mob'
(CL, 691), a 'Swinish Multitude' (CL, 215); what Milton, one of
his favourite poets, called 'A miscellaneous rabble, who extol/Things
vulgar' (*Paradise Regained*, III.lines 50–1). The honest man in whom
Burns believed was made in his own image.

Growing up in a period when egalitarian ideals were being applied
internationally, Burns was seventeen when, on 4 July 1776, the Con-
tinental Congress carried the American Declaration of Independence.
Jefferson's prose (Franklin substituted 'self-evident' for Jefferson's
'sacred and undeniable') sharply stated a position Burns shared:

We hold these truths to be self-evident, that all men are

created equal; that they are endowed by their Creator
with certain unalienable rights; that among these are life,
liberty, and the pursuit of happiness. That, to secure these
rights, governments are instituted among men, deriving
their just powers from the consent of the governed; that,
whenever any form of government becomes destructive
of these ends, it is the right of the people to alter or
to abolish it, and to institute a new government, lay-
ing its foundation on such principles, and organizing its
powers in such form, as to them shall seem most likely to
effect their safety and happiness.

This defence of natural rights, encouraging the pursuit of happiness
and recognizing the supremacy of 'the people', animates Burns's
poetry and prose. For him, as for the American revolutionaries, a
meaningful life was synonymous with liberty: 'Liberty's a glorious
feast' Burns sang in 'The Jolly Beggars'.

In the context of domestic politics, Burns was a Scottish patriot who
bitterly regretted the loss of Scottish independence that resulted from
the parliamentary union of 1707: 'what are all the boasted advantages
which my Country reaps from a certain union, that can counterbalance
the annihilation of her Independance, & even her very Name!' (CL,
185) The spectacle of Scotland reduced to the regional status of North
Britain infuriated him as he made clear by describing the Scottish
commissioners, who sold out Scotland in 1707, as 'a parcel of rogues
in a nation' ('Such a parcel of rogues in a nation'). Looking back, he
found his heroes in Wallace and Bruce, the great Scots of the Wars of
Independence (1296–1328) he saluted in 'Scots, Wha Hae'. However,
Burns was not being merely nostalgic in that song which also expressed
his interest in revolutionary politics.

His most colourful gesture of support for revolutionary France
occurred in 1792: in February he and other Excisemen captured the
smuggling brig *Rosamond*, in the Solway Firth below Dumfries; then,
at a sale of the seized vessel, he purchased four carronades which he
dispatched to the French (according to Sir Walter Scott the carronades
were intercepted by the Customs at Dover). Burns was friendly to
France which was not yet the official enemy of his country.

Internal events in 'North Britain', however, were worrying the
government. In July 1792 the Friends of the People was established
in Scotland as a radical reformist movement largely organized by a
young lawyer, Thomas Muir of Huntershill, who had close contacts
with revolutionary France. Like Muir, Burns read Thomas Paine's

Rights of Man, published in 1791–2 in two parts available at twopence each (a poem of November 1792, 'The Rights of Woman', notes 'even children lisp The Rights of Man'). Some sections of Paine must have delighted Burns by reinforcing his own faith in the common people:

> The aristocracy are not the farmers who work the land,
> and raise the produce, but are the mere consumers of the
> rent; and when compared with the active world are the
> drones, a seraglio of males, who neither collect the honey
> nor form the hive, but exist only for lazy enjoyment.[33]

It was subversive stuff, so much so that one of the charges later hurled at Thomas Muir was that he had used his premises for passing *Rights of Man* to his friends.

In September 1792 the French National Convention declared France a republic and the British government's hatred of native radicals and foreign revolutionaries reached hysterical proportions. Captain William Johnston, a radical reformist, founded the *Edinburgh Gazetteer* in November 1792 and was subsequently imprisoned for editing the newspaper (as was his editorial successor). Burns, who had met Johnston in Edinburgh, subscribed to the *Edinburgh Gazetteer* on 13 November 1792, encouraging Johnston to 'Lay bare, with undaunted heart & steady hand, that horrid mass of corruption called Politics & State-Craft!' (see p.319).

The reactionary Tory government of Pitt had reason to be nervous of developments in Scotland. Even in Dumfries there was an upsurge of revolutionary unrest, as Burns explained to Mrs Dunlop on 6 December: 'in our Theatre here, "God save the king" has meet with with some groans & hisses, while Ça ira [the French revolutionary song] has been repeatedly called for' (CL, 202). Before the month was out, an informer had told the Excise Board that Burns was the 'head of a disaffected party' (CL, 436) in Dumfries and he was 'accused to the Board of Excise of being a Republican' (CL, 689). John Mitchell, Collector of Excise, was instructed by the Board to investigate the poet's political position.

Himself hysterical with worry over possible political repercussions of the investigation, Burns wrote for help to his influential friend Robert Graham of Fintry, a Commissioner of the Scottish Board of Excise, on 5 January 1793. The letter was an apostatic statement, a diplomatic retreat from principles Burns held dear (see p.319). Burns had increasingly to hide his political views from his superiors since he was an Exciseman who had taken oaths of allegiance to the government. As he told Mrs Dunlop he was a '*Placeman*' (CL, 202).

In February 1793, the French Republic declared war on Britain and the government increased its attempts to suppress the Friends of the People. Thomas Muir was arrested, and it was at the end of August – coinciding with Muir's trial – that Burns sent 'Scots, Wha Hae' in a letter to George Thomson. In a postscript he referred, pointedly, to 'that glorious struggle for Freedom, associated with the glowing ideas of some other struggles of the same nature, *not quite so ancient*' (CL, 639). In that context, Burns undoubtedly regarded his song as having contemporary radical relevance as well as celebrating Bruce's victory at Bannockburn (see p.229).

Muir was sentenced to fourteen years' transportation for seditiously inciting the Scottish people to rise up and oppose the government. In his speech from the dock (a speech subsequently included in the curriculum in schoolrooms in the American republic) Muir declared: 'Gentlemen, from my infancy to this moment I have devoted myself to the cause of the people. It is a good cause – it shall ultimately prevail – it shall finally triumph.'[34] One month later another Scottish radical, Thomas Palmer – accused of writing and printing seditious literature – was sentenced to seven years' transportation. Openly to declare radical and republican principles in that climate was now suicidally stupid and Burns was never that. He was mindful of the fate of the two radicals, as witness the lines in a Popean parody ('Epistle from Esopus to Maria') written in the winter of 1794–5 but not published in the poet's lifetime (the 'Woolwich hulks' are transportation ships):

> The shrinking Bard adown the alley skulks,
> And dreads a meeting worse than Woolwich hulks,
> Though here, his heresies in Church and State
> Might well award him Muir and Palmer's fate.

That fate was no fantasy in a North Britain ruled by a London government determined to suppress 'the Reform, or . . . Republican spirit' (CL, 202), as Burns well knew.

The poet's opinion of the executions of Louis XVI and Marie Antoinette was conveyed in a letter (12 Jan. 1795) to Mrs Dunlop. Commenting on the reactionary tone of Dr John Moore's *Journal during a Residence in France* (1793) Burns wrote:

> Entre nous, you know my Politics: & I cannot approve of the honest Doctor's whining over the deserved fate of a certain pair of Personages. – What is there in the delivering over a perjured Blockhead & an unprincipled Prostitute into the hands of the hangman that it should arrest for a

moment, attention, in an eventful hour . . . (CL, 214)

Not only did this outrage Mrs Dunlop and, indirectly, end Dr Moore's
friendship with Burns but it has continued to irk Burnsians, one of
whom moralised:

> At the time his letter was written, Burns's remarks of-
> fended the recipient; since then, they have saddened those
> upholders of the liberal values who are admirers of Burns's
> work. For words like these, justifying political murder,
> have become all too familiar in recent years.[35]

Despite the Burnsians, Burns knew what he believed.

On 31 January 1795 Burns became a founder member of the
Dumfries Volunteers for whom he wrote a pointedly patriotic song
(see p.234). To Snyder, 'The Dumfries Volunteers' demonstrates that
Burns 'was heartily on the side of King and Country' (Snyder, 372).
The evidence suggests otherwise. At the beginning of the year, as
stated, Burns had expressed a hostile opinion of the late French royal
family in his letter to Mrs Dunlop. The same month as that letter,
January, he had sent George Thomson his most revolutionary song,
'Is there for honest poverty', unequivocally affirming his republican
faith and ridiculing the pretensions of the aristocracy.

'The Dumfries Volunteers' does oppose the imposition of the will
of one country on another but its moral message amounts to no more
than an insistence on providing British answers for British problems.
Moreover, the last stanza is open to ironic interpretation and can be
read as a criticism of the tyrant and the throne, rather than the two
wretches. Note also that Burns does not say that the radical *should*
hang, but that he 'Shall hang' and that he ends by giving the last word
to the common people. Having been in trouble with the Excise on
account of his political sympathies, Burns had sound pragmatic reasons
for making gestures of loyalty in a period of hysterical hatred for the
French. Hugh MacDiarmid suggested (*Glasgow Herald*, 14 Mar. 1967)
that Burns joined the Dumfries Volunteers as part of a republican plan
to infiltrate the ranks of the soldiery. Given Burns's political principles,
it is not an absurd idea; given his official position and desire to protect
himself and his family, it is highly improbable.

Two years before the French Revolution, Burns told Mrs Dunlop
'I set as little by kings, lords, clergy, critics, &c. as all these respectable
Gentry do by my Bardship.' (CL, 136) Unfortunately for the public
assertion of his principles, he lived during a turbulent time and was
forced by necessity to assume a sycophantic role in order to escape

the most vicious attentions of 'these respectable Gentry'. Politically he was a child of the American Revolution – devoted to 'life, liberty, and the pursuit of happiness' – who matured in a country where it was not politic to state that similar ideals inspired the French Revolution. The 'glorious feast' of liberty was not something a poetic Exciseman could openly enjoy in North Britain.

Craft and Art

The best-known works of Burns – 'To a Mouse', the verse epistles, the songs, 'Tam o' Shanter' – give an impression of a poet who, however revolutionary in politics, was conservative in technique; was content with the Standard Habbie stanza, the quatrain and the octosyllabic couplet. The impression of metrical caution is misleading, based on an inadequate knowledge of the poetry. In his long poem *To Circumjack Cencrastus* (1930), Hugh MacDiarmid described Burns as 'That Langfellow in a' but leid' (that Longfellow in all but song), not only polemically undervaluing Burns's verse but underestimating the significance of song-culture.

Certainly there are pedestrian passages in the English poems but Burns, at his best, was a technically accomplished and adventurous poet. For example, while many of his couplets are self-contained (like those of Pope, one of his favourite poets) and many of his rhymes end a line with the finality of a full-stop, he could use enjambement imaginatively, as in 'The Twa Dogs' (see p.176). In the same poem there is a pararyhme as effective as anything by Wilfred Owen: 'I see how folk live that hae riches;/But surely poor-folk maun be wretches!'

That Burns thought carefully about technique is evident in his comments, in the first Commonplace Book, on the metrical irregularity of Scottish songs (see p.243). One of the hallmarks of his genius is his ability to use metrical forms with a conversational tone and a musical fluency, just as the great ballad-singers of the oral tradition did. Burns collected ballads and (like Sir Walter Scott after him) tinkered with the texts he had transcribed. 'John Barleycorn', included in the first Edinburgh edition, appeared with a note acknowledging 'This is partly composed on the plan of an old song known by the same name.' 'Tam Lin', a ballad communicated by Burns to *The Scots Musical Museum*, had a text retouched by the poet, a man intimately aware of ballad techniques. Those techniques inform even the most subjective of his songs.

For his Scots poems, Burns experimented with various options available to him. His use of the Christis Kirk stanza (in, for example, 'The Holy Fair' and the seventh recitativo of 'The Jolly Beggars') was influenced by Allan Ramsay who, in his *Poems* (1721), added two

cantos to the poem 'Christis Kirk on the Green' (then attributed to
James I) and used the stanzaic pattern *abababab̄c*, that is two quatrains
with an abbreviated last line. Like Fergusson, Burns took poetic
liberties with the stanzaic pattern.

Again through Ramsay, Burns learned the tricks of the Cherrie
and the Slae stanza. Alexander Montgomerie's poem 'The Cherrie and
the Slae' (1597) was included in James Watson's *Choice Collection
of Comic and Serious Scots Poems* (1706–11) and in Ramsay's *Ever
Green* (1724). Burns used the fourteen-line stanza imaginatively in
the first recitativo of 'The Jolly Beggars'. As for the six-line Standard
Habbie stanza, which deserves to be renamed the Standard Rabbie
stanza since Burns used it so brilliantly and so frequently, Burns got
the measure of this from several sources including Fergusson who
followed the example of Ramsay, who first named it 'Standard Habby'
in honour of its use by Robert Sempill of Beltrees in the seventeenth
century comic elegy 'The Life and Death of Habbie Simpson'. As
Burns used it the stanza could be sublime or ridiculous or both, so
great was his skill with the form.

In 'The Cotter's Saturday Night', a mixture of Scots and English,
Burns used the Spenserian stanza (as did Fergusson in 'The Farmer's
Ingle', the model for Burns's poem). Going further back than Fergusson
or Spenser, Burns used the medieval catalogue – think of the catalogue
of local heroes in 'The Vision', the catalogue of ministers in 'The Holy
Fair', the catalogue of diabolic relics in 'Tam o' Shanter'. The tradition
of the medieval catalogue was renewed by Dunbar in 'Lament for the
Makars', a poem Burns knew from Ramsay's anthology *Ever Green*
(where it has the title 'On the Uncertainty of Life and Fear of
Death, or a Lament for the Loss of the Poets'). Dunbar, ballads
from the oral tradition, the Scots revivalist poems of Ramsay and
Fergusson: from such sources Burns evolved his own distinctively
conversational-cum-confidential tone, simulating the sound of a man
talking – singing – to those in tune with that tradition.

From an early age Burns was an avid reader of songbooks including
Ramsay's *The Tea-Table Miscellany* (see p.91). By his adolescence he was
familiar with traditional songs and printed songbooks. Later he took
an informed interest in the technique of songwriting, describing John
Aikin, author of *Essays on Song-Writing* (1772), as 'A great critic' (CL,
669) in a letter of 1795 to George Thomson.

The Kilmarnock edition contains only a sprinkling of songs, including the splendid 'It was upon a Lammas night', but the volume
was specifically entitled *Poems, Chiefly in the Scottish Dialect* which
explains the omissions. In the last nine years of his life Burns's creative

energies were almost entirely devoted to songwriting: beginning in 1787 he wrote some 200 songs for Johnson's *The Scots Musical Museum*; and, beginning in 1792, he wrote around seventy songs for George Thomson's *A Select Collection of Original Scotish Airs*. To this prolific output can be added other songs and ballads Burns wrote throughout his life. Indeed his first composition (see p.103) was prompted by a tune sung by Nelly Kilpatrick.

While his verbal virtuosity is not in doubt, it is not known for sure how much Burns knew about musical technique. He could certainly play the fiddle to some extent. Jean Armour said that her husband could ' "step a tune" rudely on the fiddle, but was no player'.[36] Isabella Burns said her brother 'could read music, either written or printed' but 'never saw anyone dance to his music [since he] had not arrived at such perfection in his fiddle-playing'.[37] Commenting on a collection of Highland airs to Johnson, Burns said 'I have had an able Fiddler two days already on it' (CL, 294) which suggests he did not have much faith in his own fiddling. Directing Johnson to alterations in an Argyllshire air, Burns exhibited an understanding of musical notation:

> The alterations are: in the fourth bar of the first and third strains, which are to be the tune, instead of the crotchet C, and the quavers G and E, at the beginning of the bar make an entire minim in E, I mean E, the lowest line.[38]

This contradicts Burns's statement, to Thomson, that 'my pretensions to musical taste, are merely a few of Nature's instincts, untaught & untutored by Art' (CL, 638). He was not musically illiterate.

Burns's most celebrated statement on his songwriting is contained in a letter of September 1793 to Thomson:

> untill I am compleat master of a tune, in my own singing, (such as it is) I never can compose for it. – My way is: I consider the poetic Sentiment, correspondent to my idea of the musical expression; then chuse my theme, begin one Stanza; when that is composed, which is generally the most difficult part of the business, I walk out, sit down now & then, look out for objects in Nature around me that are in unison or harmony with the cogitations of my fancy & workings of my bosom; humming every now & then the air with the verses I have framed: when I feel my Muse beginning to jade, I retire to the solitary fireside of my study, & there commit my effusions to paper; swinging, at intervals, on the hind-legs of my

elbow-chair, by way of calling forth my own critical
strictures, as my pen goes on. (CL, 643)

The reference to a natural harmony is particularly relevant to Burns's
songs.

Occasionally, Burns felt it necessary to defend his musical taste, as
he did in a letter (Sept. 1794) to Thomson:

I am sensible that my taste in Music must be inelegant
& vulgar, because people of undisputed & cultivated taste
can find no merit in many of my favorite tunes. – Still,
because I am cheaply pleased, is that any reason why I
should deny myself that pleasure? (CL, 656)

The rhetorical question answers itself just as surely as Burns's songs
speak volumes for his genius as a songwriter.

As we know from a letter (16 Sept. 1792) to Thomson (see p.318),
Burns would not accept any payment for the songs he composed,
collected or revised. And, as the last letters reveal, he spent some of
his dying days worrying about money, at least his lack of it. Burns's
basic salary on becoming an exciseman was £50 a year; compare that
with the pension of £200 a year given by the Pitt government to the
Southampton-born songwriter Charles Dibdin. Burns's fellow-Scots
gave him an abundance of advice but expected him to fend for himself
financially. To repeat the Coleridge quotation: 'They snatch'd him
from the sickle and the plough –/To gauge ale-firkins.'

It is doubly ironical that Burns missed meeting two of the most
influential Scots of his time. Adam Smith, who subscribed for four
copies of the first Edinburgh edition, was Commissioner for Customs
for Scotland (a sinecure paying £600 a year) when Burns arrived
in Edinburgh in 1786. Mrs Dunlop wrote to Burns on 29 March
1787:

Indeed, first when your Book [the Kilmarnock Edition]
reached Edr., Mr Smith, Commissioner of the Customs,
suggested a thing which he thought might be procured,
and which he said was just what he would have wished
for himself had he been in narrow circumstances – being
a Salt Officer. Their income is from £30 to £40, their
duty easie, independent, and free from that odium or
oppression attached to the Excise . . . He was one of
those first held your name forcibly to the public at Edr.
when very few had seen your book, and my son told me
was the person he heard take the most interest in your

future prospects, wishing to procure you leisure to write,
which he said was all you wanted to insure your figure
and fortune. He lately complained that he had asked it,
but could not get a sight of you.[39]

Mrs Dunlop asked Burns to call on Smith but, alas, as Burns explained
on 15 April 1787: 'Dr Smith was just gone to London the morning
before I received your letter to him.' (CL, 136.) Suffering from a
chronic obstruction of the bowel, Smith had headed south to see his
surgeon. Nothing more was heard of the matter.

On 13 November 1788, Burns wrote a letter to Bruce Campbell,
cousin and agent of James Boswell who (since the death of his father
in 1782) was Laird of Auchinleck, an estate near Mauchline. Enclosing
some poems, Burns told Campbell:

Should they procure me the honor of being introduced
to Mr Boswell, I shall think they have great merit [since]
to have been acquainted with such a man as Mr Boswell,
I would hand down to my Posterity as one of the honors
of their Ancestor. (CL, 489)

Boswell received Burns's letter and wrote on it: 'Mr Robert Burns
the Poet expressing very high sentiments of me.' (CL, 489.) But
Boswell made no attempt to contact Burns and instead went on to
write his great *Life of Johnson* (1791). A meeting between Burns and
Boswell would have been an eighteenth-century event since Bozzy
was – could afford to be – more of a boozer and womaniser than
Burns.

It was only after Burns's death in 1796 that Scotland really woke
up to his importance: erecting statues and monuments in his honour,
holding Burns Suppers, making him the central icon in a tourist
industry. Burnsian Bardolators revere a sanctified image of Burns
more than they read him. Hugh MacDiarmid, the greatest Scottish poet since Burns,[40] wrote in *A Drunk Man Looks at the Thistle*
(1926):

No' wan in fifty kens a wurd Burns wrote
But misapplied is a'body's property,
And gin there was his like alive the day
They'd be the last a kennin' haund to gi'e.

It is the intention of this anthology to change all that, to make the poetry and prose of a major artist accessible in a single volume that displays Burns at his marvellous best.

1   *Edinburgh Evening Courant*, 23 July 1796, p.3.

2   Robert Heron, *A Memoir of the Life of the Late Robert Burns* (Edinburgh, 1797); rept. in Hans Hecht, *Robert Burns: The Man and his Work* (1936; rept. Ayr, 1981), p.276.

3   John Steinbeck, *Of Mice and Men* (1937).

4   James Barke (ed.), *Poems and Songs of Robert Burns* (Glasgow, 1960), pp.10–11.

5   James Barke, *The Well of the Silent Harp* (Glasgow, 1954), p.6. The separate novels in Barke's sequence are *The Wind that Shakes the Barley* (1946), *The Song in the Green Thorn Tree* (1947), *The Wonder of All the Gay World* (1949), *The Crest of the Broken Wave* (1953), *The Well of the Silent Harp* (1954).

6   *Stirling Observer*, 17 Jan. 1992, p.7.

7   Henry Mackenzie, *The Man of Feeling* ed. Brian Vickers (London, 1967), pp.127–8.

8   P. Hately Waddell (ed.), *Life and Works of Burns* (Glasgow, 1867), Appendix, p.xxv.

9   Fiona Stafford, *The Sublime Savage: James Macpherson and the Poems of Ossian* (Edinburgh, 1988), p.173. Blair, in his *Lectures*, wrote: 'The works of Ossian . . . abound with examples of the Sublime.'

10 Harold William Thompson, *A Scottish Man of Feeling* (London, 1931), pp.230–1.

11 Gilbert Burns (ed.), *Poetical Works of Robert Burns* (2 vols., London, 1822), 'Character of the Author by his brother Gilbert Burns', p.xx.

12 P. Hately Waddell (ed.), Appendix, p.xxiii.

13 Maurice Lindsay, *The Burns Encyclopedia* (3rd edn., London, 1980), p.129.

14 Robert T. Fitzhugh, *Robert Burns: The Man and the Poet* (London, 1971), pp.360–1.

15 Raymond Klibansky & Ernest C. Mossner (eds.), *New Letters of David Hume* (Oxford, 1954), p.51.

16 Matthew Arnold, 'The Study of Poetry' in *Essays in Criticism: Second Series* (1888). See *Matthew Arnold: Selected Prose* ed. P.J. Keating (Harmondsworth, 1970), p.360.

17 David Murison, *The Guid Scots Tongue* (Edinburgh, 1977), p.5.

18 Robert Chambers (ed.), *The Life and Works of Robert Burns* (4 vols., Edinburgh, 1851), Vol.1, p.339.

19 Ibid.

20 Ibid., p.338.

21 The best-known ballad-singer was Mrs Brown of Falkland who learned her repertoire from her mother, her nurse, her aunt. She preserved 133 ballads, with variations, and all of them were canonised by Child. See Alan Bold, *The Ballad* (London, 1979), pp.15–18.

22   Robert Chambers (ed.), Vol.I, p.82.

23   David Daiches, *God and the Poets* (Oxford, 1984), p.134.

24   John Locke, *An Essay concerning Human Understanding* ed. Peter H. Nidditch (Oxford, 1975), p.6.

25   Robert L. Heilbroner (ed.), *The Essential Adam Smith* (Oxford, 1986), p.65.

26   Thomas Reid, *An Inquiry Into the Human Mind, on the Principles of Common Sense* (Dublin, 1764), pp.v–vi.

27   Ibid., pp.312–13.

28   Sir William Hamilton (ed.), *The Collected Works of Dugald Stewart* (10 vols., Edinburgh, 1854–8), Vol.II, p.19.

29   Ibid., Vol.II, p.6.

30   David Hume, *A Treatise of Human Nature* (1739–40; rept. with introd. by A.D. Linsday, 2 vols., London, 1959), Vol.I, p.257.

31   Ibid., Vol.I, pp.179 & 182.

32   Thomas Paine, *Common Sense* ed. Isaac Kramnick (Harmondsworth, 1976), p.81.

33   Thomas Paine, *Rights of Man* ed. Eric Foner (Harmondsworth, 1985), p.227.

34   P. Berresford Ellis & Seamus Mac a' Ghobhainn, *The Scottish Insurrection of 1820* (London, 1970), p.64.

35   Maurice Lindsay, *The Burns Encyclopedia*, p.244. Lindsay was doubtless thinking of the revolutionary rhetorical question in the title poem of Hugh MacDiarmid's *First Hymn to Lenin* (1931): 'What maitters 't wha we kill/To lessen that foulest murder than deprives/Maist men o' real lives?'

36   P. Hately Waddell (ed.), *Life and Works of Burns*, Appendix, p.xxiii.

37   J.C. Ewing, 'Mrs Begg's Reminiscences of Burns the Fiddler', *Burns Chronicle* (1948), p.36.

38   Robert T. Fitzhugh, *Robert Burns: The Man and the Poet*, p.312.

39   Maurice Lindsay, p.337.

40   For an assessment of the achievement of MacDiarmid, see Alan Bold, *MacDiarmid* (London, 1988; rept. London, 1990).

PROLOGUE

THE AUTOBIOGRAPHICAL LETTER

After a solo tour of the West Highlands, during which he was bruised in a fall with his mare Jenny Geddes, Burns was back at Mossgiel at the beginning of July 1787. In a sustained period of reflection he composed for Dr John Moore an autobiographical letter that remains the main source for reconstructions of the poet's life. The original is in the British Library, London.

Moore (1729–1802) was a minister's son who studied medicine at Glasgow University. After making an impression on the Duchess of Hamilton, he was invited to accompany her son, Douglas, Duke of Hamilton, on a Grand Tour of Europe. On his return in 1778 he settled in London then published *A View of Society and Manners in France, Switzerland, and Germany* (1779) which Burns greatly enjoyed for its humour. In 1786 Moore published his novel *Zeluco*, a sensational critical and commercial success.

Moore read the Kilmarnock edition and subscribed for four copies of the first Edinburgh edition. Flattered by the attentions of a celebrated writer, Burns was anxious to impress his countryman which is why the autobiographical letter was sent to Moore rather than another. Subsequently, Burns deplored the anti-revolutionary tone of Moore's *Journal during a Residence in France* (1793).

Text: CL, 248–56.

Mauchline, 2nd August 1787

Sir

For some months past I have been rambling over the country, partly on account of some little business I have to settle in various places; but of late I have been confined with some lingering complaints originating as I take it in the stomach. – To divert my spirits a little this miserable fog of Ennui, I have taken a whim to give you a history of MYSELF. – My name has made a small noise in the country; you have done me the honor to interest yourself very warmly in my behalf; and I think a faithful account of, what character of a man I am, and how I came by that character, may perhaps amuse you in an idle moment. – I will give you an honest narrative, though I know it will be at the expence of frequently being laughted at; for I assure you, Sir, I have, like Solomon whose character, excepting the trifling affair of WISDOM, I sometimes think I resemble, I have, I say, like him 'Turned my eyes to behold Madness and Folly;"[1] and like him too, frequently shaken hands with their intoxicating friendship. – In the very polite letter Miss Williams[2] did me the honor to write me, she tells me you have got a complaint in your eyes. – I pray to God that it may be removed; for considering that lady and you are my common friends, you will probably employ her to read this letter; and then goodnight to that esteem with which she was pleased to honor the Scotch Bard. – After you have perused these pages, should you think them trifling and impertinent, I only beg leave to tell you that the poor Author wrote them under some very twitching qualms of conscience, that, perhaps he was doing what he ought not to do: a predicament he has more than once been in before. –

I have not the most distant pretensions to what the pyecoated guardians of escutcheons call, A Gentleman. – When at Edinburgh last winter, I got acquainted in the Herald's Office, and looking through that granary of Honors I there found almost every name in the kingdom; but for me.

> ' – My ancient but ignoble blood
> Has crept thro' Scoundrels ever since the flood' –[3]

Gules, Purpure, Argent, &c. quite disowned me. – My Fathers rented land of the noble Keiths of Marshal, and had the honor to share their fate. – I do not use the word, Honor, with any reference to Political principles; loyal and disloyal I take to be merely relative terms in that ancient and formidable court known in this Country by the name of CLUB-LAW. – Those who dare welcome Ruin and shake hands with Infamy for what they sincerely believe to be the cause of their God or their King – 'Brutus and Cassius are honorable men.' – [4] I mention this circumstance because it threw my father on the world at large; where after many years' wanderings and sojournings, he pickt up a pretty large quantity of Observation and Experience, to which I am indebted for most of my little pretensions to wisdom. – I have met with few who understood 'Men, their manners and their ways'[5] equal to him; but stubborn, ungainly Integrity, and headlong, ungovernable Irrascibility are disqualifying circumstances: consequently I was born a very poor man's son. – For the first six or seven years of my life, my father was gardiner to a worthy gentleman[6] of small estate in the neighbourhood of Ayr. – Had my father continued in that situation, I must have marched off to be one of the little underlings about a farm-house; but it was his dearest wish and prayer to have it in his power to keep his children under his own eye till they could discern between good and evil; so with the assistance of his generous Master my father ventured on a small farm[7] in his estate. – At these years I was by no means a favorite with any body. – I was a good deal noted for a retentive memory, a stubborn, sturdy something in my disposition, and an enthusiastic, idiot – I say idiot piety, because I was then but a child. – Though I cost the schoolmaster[8] some thrashings, I made an excellent English scholar, and against the years of ten or eleven, I was absolutely a Critic in substantives, verbs and particles. – In my infant and boyish days too, I owed much to an old Maid of my Mother's,[9] remarkable for her ignorance, credulity and superstition. – She had, I suppose, the largest collection in the county of tales and songs concerning devils, ghosts, fairies, brownies, witches, warlocks, spunkies, kelpies, elf candles, dead-lights, wraiths, apparitions, cantraips, giants, inchanted towers, dragons and other trumpery. – This cultivated the latent seeds of Poesy; but had so strong an effect on my imagination, that to this hour, in my nocturnal rambles, I sometimes keep a sharp look-out in suspicious places; and though nobody can be more sceptical in these matters than I, yet it often takes an effort of Philosophy to shake off these idle terrors. – The earliest thing of Composition that I recollect taking pleasure in was, The vision of Mirza[10] and a hymn of Addison's beginning – 'How are Thy servants blest, O Lord!' I particularly remember one half-stanza which was music to my boyish ear –

'For though in dreadful whirls we hung,
'High on the broken wave' –

I met with these pieces in Masson's English Collection, one of my school-books. – [11] The two first books I ever read in private, and which gave me more pleasure than any two books I ever read again, were, the life of Hannibal and the history of Sir William Wallace. – [12] Hannibal gave my young ideas such a turn that I used to strut in raptures up and down after the recruiting drum and bagpipe, and wish myself tall enough to be a soldier; while the story of Wallace poured a Scotish prejudice in my veins which will boil along there till the flood-gates of life shut in eternal rest. – Polemical divinity about this time was putting the country half-mad; and I, ambitious of shining in conversation parties on sundays between sermons, funerals, &c. used in a few years more to puzzle Calvinism with so much heat and indiscretion that I raised a hue and cry of heresy against me which has not ceased to this hour. –

My vicinity to Ayr was of great advantage to me. – My social disposition, when not checked by some modification of spited pride, like our catechism definition of Infinitude, was 'without bounds or limits.' – I formed many connections with other Youngkers who possessed superiour advantages; the youngling Actors who were busy with the rehearsal of PARTS in which they were shortly to appear on that STAGE where, Alas! I was destined to druge behind the SCENES. It is not commonly at these green years that the young Noblesse and Gentry have a just sense of the immense distance between them and their ragged Playfellows. – It takes a few dashes into the world to give the young Great man that proper, decent, unnoticing disregard for the poor, insignificant, stupid devils, the mechanics and peasantry around him; who perhaps were born in the same village. – My young Superiours never insulted the clouterly appearance of my ploughboy carcase, the two extremes of which were often exposed to all the inclemencies of all the seasons. – They would give me stray volumes of books; among them, even then, I could pick up some observations; and ONE, whose heart I am sure not even the MUNNY BEGUM´S scenes have tainted, helped me to a little French. – Parting with these, my young friends and benefactors, as they dropped off for the east or west Indies, was often to me a sore affliction; but I was soon called to more serious evils. – My father's generous Master died; the farm proved a ruinous bargain; and, to clench the curse, we fell into the hands of a Factor who sat for the picture I have drawn of one in my Tale of two dogs. – My father was advanced in life when he married; I was the eldest of seven children; and he, worn out by early hardship, was unfit for labour. – My father's spirit was soon irritated, but not easily broken. – There was a freedom in his lease in two years more, and to weather these two years we retrenched expences. – We lived very poorly; I was a dextrous Ploughman for my years; and the next eldest to me was a brother,[13] who could drive the plough very well and help me to thrash. – A Novel-Writer might perhaps have viewed these scenes with some satisfaction, but so did not I: My indignation yet boils at the recollection of the scoundrel tyrant's insolent, threatening epistles, which used to set us all in tears. –

This kind of life, the chearless gloom of a hermit with the unceasing moil of a galley-slave, brought me to my sixteenth year; a little before which period I first committed the sin of RHYME. – You know our country custom of coupling a man and woman together as Partners in the labors of Harvest. – In my fifteenth autumn, my Partner was a bewitching creature[14] who just counted an autumn less. – My scarcity of English denies me the power of doing her justice in that language; but you know the Scotch idiom, She was a bonie, sweet, sonsie lass. – In short, she altogether unwittingly to herself, initiated me in a certain delicious Passion, which in spite of acid Disappointment, gin-horse

Prudence and bookworm Philosophy, I hold to be the first of human joys, our dearest pleasure here below. – How she caught the contagion I can't say; you medical folks talk much of infection by breathing the same air, the touch, &c. but I never expressly told her that I loved her. – Indeed I did not well know myself, why I liked so much to loiter behind with her, when returning in the evening from our labors; why the tones of her voice made my heartstrings thrill like an Eolian harp; and particularly, why my pulse beat such a furious ratann when I looked and fingered over her hand, to pick out the nettle-stings and thistles. – Among her other love-inspiring qualifications, she sung sweetly; and 'twas her favorite reel[15] to which I attempted giving an embodied vehicle in rhyme. – I was not so presumtive as to imagine that I could make verses like printed ones, composed by men who had Greek and Latin; but my girl sung a song which was said to be composed by a small country laird's son, on one of his father's maids, with whom he was in love; and I saw no reason why I might not rhyme as well as he, for excepting smearing sheep and casting peats, his father living in the moors, he had no more Scholarcraft than I had. –

Thus with me began Love and Poesy: which at times have been my only, and till within this last twelvemonth have been my highest enjoyment. – My father struggled on till he reached the freedom in his lease, when he entered on a larger farm[16] about ten miles farther in the country. – The nature of the bargain was such as to throw a little ready money in his hand at the commencement, otherwise the affair would have been impractible. – For four years we lived comfortably here; but a lawsuit between him and his Landlord[17] commencing, after three years tossing and whirling in the vortex of Litigation, my father was just saved from absorption in a jail by phthistical consumption, which after two years promises, kindly stept in and snatch'd him away – 'To where the wicked cease from troubling, and where the weary be at rest.' – [18]

It is during this climacterick that my little story is most eventful. – I was, at the beginning of this period, perhaps the most ungainly, aukward being in the parish. – No Solitaire was less acquainted with the ways of the world. – My knowledge of ancient story was gathered from Salmon's and Guthrie's geographical grammars; my knowledge of modern manners, and of literature and criticism, I got from the Spectator. – These, with Pope's works, some plays of Shakespear, Tull and Dickson on Agriculture, The Pantheon, Locke's Essay on the human understanding, Stackhouse's history of the bible, Justice's British Gardiner's directory, Boyle's lectures, Allan Ramsay's works, Taylor's scripture doctrine of original sin, a select Collection of English songs, and Hervey's meditations had been the extent of my reading.[19]

– The Collection of Songs was my vade mecum. – I pored over them, driving my cart or walking to labor, song by song, verse by verse; carefully noting the true tender or sublime from affectation and fustian. – I am convinced I owe much to this for my critic-craft such as it is. –

In my seventeenth year, to give my manners a brush, I went to a country dancing school. – [20] My father had an unaccountable antipathy against these meetings; and my going was, what to this hour I repent, in absolute defiance of his commands. – My father, as I said before, was the sport of strong passions: from that instance of rebellion he took a kind of dislike to me, which, I believe was one cause of that dissipation which marked my future years. – I only say, Dissipation, comparative with the strictness and sobriety of Presbyterean country life; for though the will-o'-wisp meteors of thoughtless Whim were almost the sole lights of my path, yet early ingrained Piety and Virtue never failed to point me out the line of Innocence. – The great misfortune of my life was, never to have AN AIM. – I had felt early some stirrings of Ambition, but they were the blind gropings of Homer's Cyclops round the walls of his cave: I saw my father's situation entailed on me perpetual labor. – The only two doors by which I could enter the fields of fortune were, the most niggardly economy, or the little chicaning art of bargain-making: the first is so contracted an aperture, I never could squeeze myself into it; the last, I always hated the contamination of the threshold. – Thus, abandoned of aim or view in life; with a strong appetite for sociability, as well from native hilarity as from a pride of observation and remark; a constitutional hypochondriac taint which made me fly solitude; add to all these incentives to social life, my reputation for bookish knowledge, a certain wild, logical talent, and a strength of thought something like the rudiments of good sense, made me generally a welcome guest; so 'tis no great wonder that always 'where two or three were met together, there was I in the midst of them.'[21] – But far beyond all the other impulses of my heart was, un penchant á l'adorable moitiée du genre humain. – My heart was compleatly tinder, and was eternally lighted up by some Goddess or other; and like every warfare in this world, I was sometimes crowned with success, and sometimes mortified with defeat. – At the plough, scythe or reap-hook I feared no competitor, and set Want at defiance: and as I never cared farther for my labors than while I was in actual exercise, I spent the evening in the way after my own heart. – A country lad rarely carries on an amour without an assisting confident. – I possessed a curiosity, zeal and intrepid dexterity in these matters which recommended me a proper Second in duels of that kind; and I dare say, I felt as much pleasure at being in the secret of half the armours in the parish, as ever did Premier at knowing the intrigues of half the courts of Europe. –

The very goosefeather in my hand seems instinctively to know the well-worn path of my imagination, the favorite theme of my song; and is with difficulty restrained from giving you a couple of paragraphs on the amours of my Compeers, the humble Inmates of the farm-house and cottage; but the grave sons of Science, Ambition or Avarice baptize these things by the name of Follies. – To the sons and daughters of labor and poverty they are matters of the most serious nature: to them, the ardent hope, the stolen interview, the tender farewell, are the greatest and most delicious part of their enjoyments. –

Another circumstance in my life which made very considerable alterations in my mind and manners was, I spent my seventeenth[22] summer on a smuggling coast a good distance from home at a noted school,[23] to learn Mensuration, Surveying, Dialling, &c. in which I made a pretty good progress. – But I made greater progress in the knowledge of mankind. – The contraband trade was at that time very successful; scenes of swaggering riot and roaring dissipation were as yet new to me; and I was no enemy to social life. – Here, though I learned to look unconcernedly on a large tavern-bill, and mix without fear in a drunken squabble, yet I went on with a high hand in my Geometry; till the sun entered Virgo, a month which is always a carnival in my bosom, a charming Fillette[24] who lived next door to the school overset my Trigonometry and set me off in a tangent from the sphere of my studies. – I struggled on with my Sines and Co-sines for a few days more; but stepping out to the garden one charming noon, to take the sun's altitude, I met with my Angel,

> —'Like Proserpine gathering flowers,
> 'Herself a fairer flower' – [25]

It was vain to think of doing any more good at school. – The remaining week I staid, I did nothing but craze the faculties of my soul about her, or steal out to meet with her; and the two last nights of my stay in the country, had sleep been a mortal sin, I was innocent. –

I returned home very considerably improved. – My reading was enlarged with the very important addition of Thomson's and Shenstone's works; I had seen mankind in a new phasis; and I engaged several of my schoolfellows to keep up a literary correspondence with me. – This last helped me much on in composition. – I had met with a collection of letters by the Wits of Queen Ann's reign, and I pored over them most devoutly. – I kept copies of any of my own letters that pleased me, and a comparison between them and the composition of most of my correspondents flattered my vanity. – I carried this whim so far that though I had not three farthings worth of business in the world, yet every post brought me as many letters as if I had been a broad, plodding son of Day-book & Ledger. –

My life flowed on much in the same tenor till my twenty third year. – Vive l'amour et vive la bagatelle, were my sole principles of action. – The addition of two more Authors to my library gave me great pleasure; Sterne and Mckenzie. – Tristram Shandy and the Man of Feeling were my bosom favorites. – Poesy was still a darling walk for my mind, but 'twas only the humour of the hour. – I had usually half a dozen or more pieces on hand; I took up one or other as it suited the momentary tone of this mind, and dismissed it as it bordered on fatigue. – My Passions when once they were lighted up, raged like so many devils, till they got vent in rhyme; and then conning over my verses, like a spell, soothed all into quiet. – None of the rhymes of those days are in print, except, Winter, a dirge, the eldest of my printed pieces; The death of Poor Mailie, John Barleycorn, And songs first, second and third: song second was the ebullition of that passion which ended the forementioned school-business. –

My twenty third year was to me an important era. – Partly thro' whim, and partly that I wished to set about doing something in life, I joined with a flax-dresser in a neighbouring town[26] to learn his trade and carry on the business of manufacturing and retailing flax. – This turned out a sadly unlucky affair. – My Partner was a scoundrel of the first water who made money by the mystery of thieving; and to finish the whole, while we were given a welcoming carousal to the New year, our shop, by the drunken carelessness of my Partner's wife, took fire and was burnt to ashes; and left me like a true Poet, not worth sixpence. – I was obliged to give up business; the clouds of misfortune were gathering thick round my father's head, the darkest of which was, he was visibly far gone in a consumption; and to crown all, a belle-fille[27] whom I adored and who had pledged her soul to meet me in the field of matrimony, jilted me with peculiar circumstances of mortification. – The finishing evil that brought up the rear of this infernal file was my hypochondriac complaint being irritated to such a degree, that for three months I was in diseased state of body and mind, scarcely to be envied by the hopeless wretches who have just got their mittimus, 'Depart from me, ye Cursed.'[28] –

From this adventure I learned something of a town-life. But the principal thing which gave my mind a turn was, I formed a bosom-friendship with a young fellow,[29] the first created being I had ever seen, but a hapless son of misfortune. – He was the son of a plain mechanic; but a great Man in the neighbourhood taking him under his patronage gave him a genteel education with a view to bettering his situation in life. – The Patron dieing just as he was ready to launch forth into the world, the poor fellow in despair went to sea; where after a variety of good and bad fortune, a little before I was acquainted with him, he had been set ashore by an American Privateer on the wild coast of Connaught, stript of every thing. – I cannot quit this poor fellow's story without adding that he is at this moment Captain of a large westindiaman belonging to the Thames. –

This gentleman's mind was fraught with courage, independance, Magnanimity, and every noble, manly virtue. – I loved him, I admired him, to a degree of enthusiasm; and I strove to imitate him. – In some measure I succeeded: I had the pride before, but he taught it to flow in proper channels. – His knowledge of the world was vastly superior to mine, and I was all attention to learn – He was the only man I ever saw who was a greater fool than myself when WOMAN was the presiding star; but he spoke of a certain fashionable failing with levity, which hitherto I had regarded with horror. – Here his friendship did me a mischief; and the consequence was, that soon after I resumed the plough, I wrote the WELCOME inclosed.[30] – My reading was only encreased by two stray volumes of Pamela, and one of Ferdinand Count Fathom, which gave me some idea of Novels. – Rhyme, except some religious pieces which are in print, I had given up; but meeting with Fergusson's Scotch Poems,[31] I strung anew my wildly-sounding, rustic lyre with emulating vigour. – When my father died, his all went among the rapacious hell-hounds that growl in the kennel of justice; but we made a shift to scrape a little money in the family amongst us, with which, to keep us together, my brother and I took a neighbouring farm. – [32] My brother wanted my harebrained imagination as well as my social and amorous madness, but in good sense and every sober qualification he was far my superiour. –

I entered on this farm with a full resolution, 'Come, go to, I will be wise!'[33] – I read farming books; I calculated crops; I attended markets; and in short, in spite of 'The devil, the world and the flesh,' I believe I would have been a wise man; but the first year from unfortunately buying in bad seed, the second from a late harvest, we lost half of both our crops: this overset all my wisdom, and I returned 'Like the dog to his vomit, and the sow that was washed to her wallowing in the mire – '.[34]

I now began to be known in the neighbourhood as a maker of rhymes. – The first of my poetic offspring that saw the light was a burlesque lamentation on a quarrel between two reverend Calvinists,[35] both of them dramatis personae in my Holy Fair. – I had an idea myself that the piece had some merit; but to prevent the worst, I gave a copy of it to a friend who was very fond of these things, and told him I could not guess who was the Author of it, but that I thought it pretty clever. – With a certain side of both clergy and laity it met with a roar of applause. – Holy Willie's Prayer next made its appearance, and alarmed the kirk-Session so much that they held three several meetings to look over their holy artillery, if any of it was pointed against profane Rhymers. – Unluckily for me, my idle wanderings led me, on another side, point blank within the reach of their heaviest metal. – This is the unfortunate story alluded to in my printed poem, The Lament. – [36] 'Twas a shocking affair, which I cannot yet bear to recollect; and had very nearly given me one or two of the principal qualifications for the place among those who have lost the chart and mistake the reckoning of Rationality. – I gave up my part of the farm to my brother, as in truth it was only nominally mine; and made what little preparation was in my power for Jamaica. Before leaving my native country for ever, I resolved to publish my Poems. – [37] I weighed my productions as impartially as in my power; I thought they had merit; and 'twas a delicious idea that I would be called a clever fellow, even though it should never reach my ears a poor Negro-driver, or perhaps a victim to that inhospitable clime gone to the world of Spirits. – I can truly say that pauvre Inconnu as I then was, I had pretty nearly as high an idea of myself and my works as I have at this moment. – It is ever my opinion that the great, unhappy mistakes and blunders, both in a rational and religious point of view, of which we see thousands daily guilty, are owing to their ignorance, or mistaken notions of themselves. – To know myself had been all along my constant study. – I weighed myself alone; I balanced myself with others; I watched every means of information how much ground I occupied both as a Man and as a Poet: I studied assiduously Nature's DESIGN where she seem'd to have intended the various LIGHTS and SHADES in my character. – I was pretty sure my Poems would meet with some applause; but at the worst, the roar of the Atlantic would deafen the voice of Censure, and the novelty of west-Indian scenes make me forget Neglect. –

I threw off six hundred copies, of which I had got subscriptions for about three hundred and fifty. – My vanity was highly gratified by the reception I met with from the Publick; besides pocketing, all expences deducted, near twenty pounds. – This last came very seasonable, as I was about to indent myself for want of money to pay my freight. So soon as I was master of nine guineas, the price of wafting me to the torrid zone, I bespoke a passage in the very first ship that was to sail, for

'Hungry ruin had me in the wind' – [38]

I had for some time been sculking from covert to covert under all the terrors of a Jail; as some ill-advised, ungrateful people had uncoupled the merciless legal pack at my heels. – I had taken the last farewel of my few friends, my chest was on the road to Greenock; I had composed my last song I should ever measure in Caledonia, 'The gloomy night is gathering fast,' when a letter from Dr. Blacklock[39] to a friend of mine overthrew all my schemes by rousing my poetic ambition. – The Doctor belonged to a set of Critics for whose applause I had not even dared to hope. – His idea that I would meet with every encouragement for a second edition fired me so much that away I posted to Edinburgh without a single acquaintance in town, or a single letter of introduction in my pocket. – The baneful Star that had so long shed its blasting influence in my Zenith, for once made a revolution to the Nadir; and the providential care of a good God placed me under the patronage of one of his noblest creatures, the Earl of Glencairn: 'Oublie moi, Grand Dieu, si jamais je l'oublie!' –

I need relate no farther. – At Edinburgh I was in a new world: I mingled among many classes of men, but all of them new to me; and I was all attention 'to catch the manners living as they rise.' – [40]

You can now, Sir, form a pretty near guess what sort of a Wight he is whom for some time you have honored with your correspondence. – That Fancy & Whim, keen Sensibility and riotous Passions may still make him zig-zag in his future path of life, is far from being improbable; but come what will, I shall answer for him the most determinate integrity and honor; and though his evil star should again blaze in his meridian with tenfold more direful influence, he may reluctantly tax Friendship with Pity but no more. –

My most respectful Compliments to Miss Williams. – Her very elegant and friendly letter I cannot answer at present, as my presence is requisite in Edinburgh, and I set off tomorrow. –

If you will oblidge me so highly and do me so much honor as now and then to drop me a letter, Please direct to me at Mauchline, Ayrshire. –

I have the honor to be, Sir
your ever grateful humble servant
Robt Burns

1   Ecclesiastes 2:12. 'And I turned myself to behold wisdom, and madness, and folly . . . '
2   Helen Maria Williams (1762–1827), English writer and amanuensis to Moore.
3   Pope, *An Essay on Man*, IV, 211.

4   Shakespeare, *Julius Caesar*, Act III, sc.2.

5   Pope, *January and May*, line 157.

6   Dr William Fergusson of Doonholm, who died 7 Nov. 1769, aged
      sixty. Provost of Ayr 1759–61, 1763–5.

7   Mount Oliphant farm, two miles south-east of Alloway, which William
      Burnes rented from 1766 to 1777.

8   John Murdoch (1747–1824) who taught Burns in Alloway 1765–8; and
      in Ayr, 1773.

9   Betty Davidson, widow of a cousin of Burns's mother and a familiar
      figure in the Alloway cottage.

10   Addison's allegory 'Human life and eternity: the vision of Mirzah'
      (*Spectator* 159, 1 Sept. 1711) was included in Arthur Masson's *A Collection
      of Prose and Verse* (2nd edn., 1767). The Vision of Mirzah sees life as a
      bridge over which multitudes move.

11   See note 10.

12   The book on Hannibal cannot be identified. The history of Wallace was
      Blind Harry's *Wallace* as abridged and Anglicised by William Hamilton
      of Gilbertfield in *A New Edition of the Life and Heroick Actions of the
      Renown'd Sir William Wallace* (1722).

13   Gilbert Burns (1760–1827).

14   Nelly Kilpatrick (1760–1820), the subject of Burns's first song (see
      p.103).

15   In the first Commonplace Book, Burns's lyric is matched to the tune
      'I am a man unmarried'.

16   Lochlea farm, Tarbolton parish, rented by William Burnes from 1777
      until his death in 1784.

17   David McLure.

18   Job 3:17. 'There the wicked cease *from* troubling; and there the weary
      be at rest.'

19   Burn's reading list includes Thomas Salmon, *A New Geographical and
      Historical Grammar*; William Guthrie, *A New Geographical, Historical
      and Commercial Grammar*; Jethro Tull, *The Horse-Hoing Husbandry: or
      an Essay on the Principles of Tillage and Vegetation*; Adam Dickson, *A
      Treatise on Agriculture*; Andrew Tooke, *Pantheon*; John Locke, *An Essay
      concerning Human Understanding*; Thomas Stackhouse, *A New History of
      the Holy Bible*; James Justice, *British Gardner's Directory*; William Derham,
      Physico-Theology and *Astro-Theology* (these two being the 'Boyle's lec-
      tures' mentioned by Burns); John Taylor, *Scripture Doctrine of Original
      Sin*; James Hervey, *Meditations among the Tombs*. The first collection
      of English songs prized by Burns was Allan Ramsay's popular *The
      Tea-Table Miscellany*; he later owned a collection called *The Lark*
      (1765).

20   Burns has misdated this incident: the country dancing school was in
      Tarbolton, 1779, when Burns was twenty.

21   Matthew 18:20. 'For where two or three are gathered together in my
      name, there am I in the midst of them.'

22 'seventeenth' deleted and 'nineteenth or twentieth' substituted in another hand.

23 Hugh Rodger's school, Kirkoswald, where Burns studied in the summer of 1775.

24 Peggy Thomson.

25 Milton, *Paradise Lost*, Book IV, lines 269–70: 'where Prosperine gathering flowers/Herself a fairer Flower'.

26 Irvine, fifteen miles north of Ayr, where Burns went in 1781 to learn the business of flax-dressing.

27 Alison Begbie, a Galston farmer's daughter who, when courted by Burns, worked as a servant in a house near the river Cessnock.

28 Matthew 26:41. 'Then shall he say also unto them on the left hand, Depart from me, ye cursed, into everlasting fire, prepared for the devil and his angels.'

29 Richard Brown (1753–1833) who subsequently married and settled in Port Glasgow. Of Burns's reference to the sailor's sexual experience, Brown said: 'When I first knew Burns he had nothing to learn in that respect.' (H–H IV, 251.)

30 'A Poet's Welcome to his Love-Begotten Daughter' (see p.130) addressed to Burns's illegitimate daughter by Elizabeth Paton: Elizabeth, born 22 May 1785.

31 Burns owned a copy of the second edition of Robert Fergusson's *Poems* (1782), published after he left Irvine.

32 Mossgiel, near Mauchline, which Burns and his brother Gilbert moved into in March 1784.

33 Ecclesiastes 7: 23. 'All this have I proved by wisdom: I said, I will be wise; but it *was* far from me.'

34 2 Peter 2: 22. 'The dog *is* turned to his own vomit again; and the sow that was washed to her wallowing in the mire.'

35 The Revd Alexander Moodie and the Revd John Russell, two Auld Licht ministers mentioned in 'The Holy Fair', are featured as the antagonists in 'The Twa Herds: or, The Holy Tulzie' – an account of their doctrinal squabble.

36 'The Lament', included in the Kilmarnock edition, deals with Burns's despair at his treatment following his affair with Jean Armour: on learning, in 1786, that his daughter was pregnant by Burns, James Armour repudiated the poet and had his marriage attestation mutilated.

37 Kilmarnock edition.

38 Not identified.

39 Dr Thomas Blacklock's letter (4 Sept. 1786) was written to the Revd George Lawrie who sent it to Gavin Hamilton, who gave it to Burns.

40 Pope, *An Essay on Man*, I, 14. 'And catch the manners living as they rise.'

PART ONE

SONGS AND POEMS

O, ONCE I LOV'D A BONIE LASS

Burns's first song was composed in autumn 1774 after he had been partnered, in the Mount Oliphant harvest, with Nelly Kilpatrick: 'Thus with me began Love and Poesy' (CL, 251).
Text: H–H III, 197–8.

O, ONCE I lov'd a bonie lass,
    Ay, and I love her still!
And whilst that virtue warms my breast,
    I'll love my handsome Nell.

As bonie lasses I hae seen,
    And monie full as braw,
But for a modest gracefu' mien
    The like I never saw.

A bonie lass, I will confess,
    Is pleasant to the e'e;
But without some better qualities
    She's no a lass for me.

But Nelly's looks are blythe and sweet,
    And, what is best of a',
Her reputation is complete
    And fair without a flaw.

She dresses ay sae clean and neat,
    Both decent and genteel;
And then there's something in her gait
    Gars onie dress look weel.

A gaudy dress and gentle air
    May slightly touch the heart;
But it's innocence and modesty
    That polishes the dart.

'Tis this in Nelly pleases me,
    'Tis this enchants my soul;
For absolutely in my breast
    She reigns without controul.

MARY MORRISON

**Burns described the song as 'one of my juvenile works . . . I do
not think it very remarkable, either for its merits or demerits'
(CL, 623). The identity of the heroine remains a mystery: a
Mary Morrison buried in Mauchline churchyard (she died of
consumption in 1791) was twelve years younger than Burns
so an unlikely heroine of an early song. More plausibly Alison
Begbie, the girl who rejected Burns's romantic overtures in
1781, has been associated with the song, Burns changing the
name to suit the tune ('Duncan Davison'). It was published
by Currie (1800) and in SC (1818).**

Text: H–H III, 286–7.

> O Mary, at thy window be!
>   It is the wish'd, the trysted hour.
> Those smiles and glances let me see,
>   That make the miser's treasure poor.
>   How blythely wad I bide the stoure,
> A weary slave frae sun to sun,
>   Could I the rich reward secure—
> The lovely Mary Morison!
>
> Yestreen, when to the trembling string
>   The dance gaed thro' the lighted ha',
> To thee my fancy took its wing,
>   I sat, but neither heard or saw:
>   Tho' this was fair, and that was braw,
> And yon the toast of a' the town,
>   I sigh'd and said amang them a':—
> 'Ye are na Mary Morison!'
>
> O Mary, canst thou wreck his peace
>   Wha for thy sake wad gladly die?
> Or canst thou break that heart of his
>   Whase only faut is loving thee?
>   If love for love thou wilt na gie,
> At least be pity to me shown:
>   A thought ungentle canna be
> The thought o' Mary Morison.

MY FATHER WAS A FARMER

**Collected in R.H. Cromek's *Reliques of Robert Burns* (1808), this
was first entered in the first Commonplace Book in April 1784,
matched to the tune 'The weaver and his shuttle O' with
the note: 'The following Song is a wild Rhapsody miserably
deficient in versification, but, as the sentiments are the genuine
feelings of my heart, for that reason I have a particular reason in
conning it over.' Kinsley thinks it composed 'perhaps as early
as 1782' (Kinsley, 1015). Carrick is the area of Ayrshire south
of the river Doon; Mount Oliphant farm, in Kyle, was close to
Carrick.**
    Text: H–H IV, 8.

    My father was a farmer upon the Carrick border, O,
    And carefully he bred me in decency and order, O.
    He bade me act a manly part, though I had ne'er a
        farthing, O,
    For without an honest, manly heart no man was worth
        regarding, O.

    Then out into the world my course I did deter-
        mine, O:
    Tho' to be rich was not my wish, yet to be great was
        charming, O.
    My talents they were not the worst, nor yet my
        education, O—
    Resolv'd was I at least to try to mend my situa-
        tion, O.

    In many a way and vain essay I courted Fortune's
        favour, O:
    Some cause unseen still stept between to frustrate
        each endeavour, O.
    Sometimes by foes I was o'erpower'd, sometimes by
        friends forsaken, O,
    And when my hope was at the top, I still was worst
        mistaken, O.

    Then sore harass'd, and tir'd at last with Fortune's
        vain delusion, O,

I dropt my schemes like idle dreams, and came to
    this conclusion, O:—
The past was bad, and the future hid; its good or ill
    untrièd, O,
But the present hour was in my pow'r, and so I
    would enjoy it, O.

No help, nor hope, nor view had I, nor person to
    befriend me, O;
So I must toil, and sweat, and broil, and labour to
    sustain me, O!
To plough and sow, to reap and mow, my father bred
    me early, O:
For one, he said, to labour bred was a match for
    Fortune fairly, O.

Thus all obscure, unknown, and poor, thro' life I'm
    doom'd to wander, O,
Till down my weary bones I lay in everlasting
    slumber, O.
No view nor care, but shun whate'er might breed
    me pain or sorrow, O,
I live to-day as well's I may, regardless of to-
    morrow, O!

But, cheerful still, I am as well as a monarch in a
    palace, O,
Tho' Fortune's frown still hunts me down, with all
    her wonted malice, O:
I make indeed my daily bread, but ne'er can make
    it farther, O,
But, as daily bread is all I need, I do not much
    regard her, O.

When sometimes by my labour I earn a little
    money, O,
Some unforeseen misfortune comes gen'rally upon
    me, O:
Mischance, mistake, or by neglect, or my good-
    natur'd folly, O—
But, come what will, I've sworn it still, I'll ne'er
    be melancholy, O.

All you who follow wealth and power with unremit-
    ting ardour, O,
The more in this you look for bliss, you leave your
    view the farther, O.
Had you the wealth Potosi boasts, or nations to
    adore you, O,
A cheerful, honest-hearted clown I will prefer before
    you, O!

THE DEATH AND DYING WORDS OF POOR MAILIE, THE AUTHOR'S ONLY PET YOWE, AN UNCO MOURNFU' TALE.

Written at Lochlea, possibly 1783; it was entered in the first Commonplace Book in June 1785 and first published in the Kilmarnock edition. Citing this as one of the few poems his brother composed before 1784, Gilbert Burns explained:

> The circumstances of the poor sheep were pretty much as he has described them. He had, partly by way of frolic, bought a ewe and two lambs from a neighbour, and she was tethered in a field adjoining the house at Lochlie. He and I were going out, with our teams, and our two younger brothers to drive for us, at mid-day; when Hugh Wilson, a curious-looking awkward boy, clad in plaiding, came to us with much anxiety in his face, with the information that the ewe had entangled herself in the tether, and was lying in the ditch. Robert was much tickled with *Huoc*'s appearance and postures on the occasion. Poor Maillie was set to rights, and when we returned from the plough in the evening, he repeated to me her *Death and dying Words* pretty much in the way they now stand. (Currie III, 380)

It is 'Burns's first significant essay in Scots' (Kinsley, 1018).

Burns's apparently spontaneous production was tempered by tradition. The mode of the mock elegy ostensibly uttered by a Scots-speaking animal goes back to 1706 and 'The Last Dying Words of Bonnie Heck, a Famous Grey-hound in the Shire of Fife' by William Hamilton of Gilbertfield: Hamilton uses the Standard Habbie stanza, Burns (surprisingly given the precedent and his subsequent expertise with the Standard Habbie)

uses couplets, mainly iambic tetrameter. Some of the couplets
have echoes of Fergusson: compare 'As Mailie, an her lambs
thegither,/Was àe day nibblin on the tether' with Fergusson's
'In sun-shine, and in weety weather,/Our thrawart lot we bure
thegither' ('Mutual Complaint of Plainstanes and Causey').

Text: H–H I, 53–6.

> As Mailie, an' her lambs thegither,
> Was ae day nibblin on the tether,
> Upon her cloot she coost a hitch,
> An' owre she warsl'd in the ditch:
> There, groanin, dying, she did lie,
> When Hughoc he cam doytin by.
>
> Wi' glowrin een, an' lifted han's
> Poor Hughoc like a statue stan's;
> He saw her days were near-hand ended,
> But, wae's my heart! he could na mend it!
> He gapèd wide, but naething spak.
> At length poor Mailie silence brak:—
>
> 'O thou, whase lamentable face
> Appears to mourn my woefu' case!
> My dying words attentive hear,
> An' bear them to my Master dear.
>
> 'Tell him, if e'er again he keep
> As muckle gear as buy a sheep—
> O, bid him never tie them mair,
> Wi' wicked strings o' hemp or hair!
> But ca' them out to park or hill,
> An' let them wander at their will:
> So may his flock increase, an' grow
> To scores o' lambs, an' packs o' woo'!
>
> 'Tell him, he was a Master kin',
> An' ay was guid to me an' mine;
> An' now my dying charge I gie him,
> My helpless lambs, I trust them wi' him.
>
> 'O, bid him save their harmless lives,
> Frae dogs, an' tods, an' butchers' knives!

But gie them guid cow-milk their fill,
　Till they be fit to fend themsel;
An' tent them duly, e'en an' morn,
Wi' teats o' hay an' ripps o' corn.

　'An' may they never learn the gaets,
Of ither vile, wanrestfu' pets—
To slink thro' slaps, an' reave an' steal,
At stacks o' pease, or stocks o' kail!
So may they, like their great forbears,
For monie a year come thro' the sheers:
So wives will gie them bits o' bread,
An' bairns greet for them when they're dead.

　'My poor toop-lamb, my son an' heir,
O, bid him breed him up wi' care!
An' if he live to be a beast,
To pit some havins in his breast!
An' warn him—what I winna name—
To stay content wi' yowes at hame;
An' no to rin an' wear his cloots,
Like other menseless, graceless brutes.

　'An' niest, my yowie, silly thing;
Gude keep thee frae a tether string!
O, may thou ne'er forgather up,
Wi' onie blastit, moorland toop;
But ay keep mind to moop an' mell,
Wi' sheep o' credit like thysel!

　'And now, my bairns, wi' my last breath,
I lea'e my blessin wi' you baith:
An' when you think upo' your mither,
Mind to be kind to ane anither.

　'Now, honest Hughoc, dinna fail,
To tell my master a' my tale;
An' bid him burn this cursed tether,
An' for thy pains thou'se get my blether.'

　This said, poor Mailie turn'd her head,
An' clos'd her een amang the dead!

GREEN GROW THE RASHES: A FRAGMENT

Copied into the first Commonplace Book in August 1784, it was included in the first Edinburgh edition and in SMM (1787). Pope stated, in *An Essay on Man*, 'An honest man's the noblest work of God' (which Burns quoted in 'A Cotter's Saturday Night'); feminists might note the closing quatrain of this song offers an alternative ideal.

Text: H–H I, 251–2.

CHORUS
Green grow the rashes, O;
Green grow the rashes, O;
The sweetest hours that e'er I spend,
Are spent among the lasses, O.

THERE'S nought but care on ev'ry han',
   In every hour that passes, O:
What signifies the life o' man,
   An' 'twere na for the lasses, O.

The war'ly race may riches chase,
   An' riches still may fly them, O;
An' tho' at last they catch them fast,
   Their hearts can ne'er enjoy them, O.

But gie me a cannie hour at e'en,
   My arms about my dearie, O,
An' war'ly cares an' war'ly men
   May a' gae tapsalteerie, O!

For you sae douce, ye sneer at this;
   Ye're nought but senseless asses, O:
The wisest man the warl' e'er saw,
   He dearly lov'd the lasses, O.

Auld Nature swears, the lovely dears
   Her noblest work she classes, O:
Her prentice han' she try'd on man,
   An' then she made the lasses, O.

CHORUS

Green grow the rashes, O;
Green grow the rashes, O;
The sweetest hours that e'er I spend,
Are spent among the lasses, O.

IT WAS UPON A LAMMAS NIGHT

Included in the Kilmarnock edition, matched to the traditional tune 'Corn rigs are bonie' which was popularised in Allan Ramsay's 'My Patie is a Lover Gay' (the closing song of *The Gentle Shepherd*, 1725). The honour of being Annie was claimed by Anne Rankine whose father farmed Adamhill, near Lochlea. She told a tale of meeting Burns and saying how surprised she was at seeing herself praised in print, whereupon the poet remarked: 'O ay, I was just wanting to give you a cast among the lave' (Ch-W I, 98). A likely story, indicating that in later life Anne Rankine wanted to bask in the reflected glory of Burns. Kinsley dates the poem 'among the pieces written before [Burns's] twenty-third year (1782)' (Kinsley, 1010), this on the basis of a reference in the Autobiographical Letter to song 'first', 'It was upon a Lammas night' being the first song in the Kilmarnock edition. However Burns was imprecise about dates in the Autobiographical Letter and the passion of the song suggests the poem dates from Lammas (1 August, autumn quarter-day in Scotland) 1784 and refers to his affair with Elizabeth Paton: the illegitimate child of the affair, baby Elizabeth (born 22 May 1785), was conceived in August 1784. For obvious reasons, Burns would have been coy about identifying Paton as the heroine of this song of seduction. The name Annie not only protected Paton but supplied the necessary rhyme.

Text: H–H I, 180–1.

IT was upon a Lammas night,
  When corn rigs are bonie,
Beneath the moon's unclouded light,
  I held awa to Annie;
The time flew by, wi' tentless heed;
  Till, 'tween the late and early,

Wi' sma' persuasion she agreed
  To see me thro' the barley.
      Corn rigs, an' barley rigs,
        An' corn rigs are bonie:
      I'll ne'er forget that happy night,
        Amang the rigs wi' Annie.

The sky was blue, the wind was still,
  The moon was shining clearly;
I set her down, wi' right good will,
  Amang the rigs o' barley:
I ken't her heart was a' my ain;
  I lov'd her most sincerely;
I kiss'd her owre and owre again,
  Amang the rigs o' barley.

I lock'd her in my fond embrace;
  Her heart was beating rarely:
My blessings on that happy place,
  Amang the rigs o' barley!
But by the moon and stars so bright,
  That shone that hour so clearly!
She ay shall bless that happy night
  Amang the rigs o' barley.

I hae been blythe wi' comrades dear;
  I hae been merry drinking;
I hae been joyfu' gath'rin gear;
  I hae been happy thinking:
But a' the pleasures e'er I saw,
  Tho' three times doubl'd fairly—
That happy night was worth them a',
  Amang the rigs o' barley.
      Corn rigs, an' barley rigs,
        An' corn rigs are bonie:
      I'll ne'er forget that happy night,
        Amang the rigs wi' Annie.

MY GIRL SHE'S AIRY

Entered in the first Commonplace Book in September 1784, matched to the tune 'Black Joke' (a euphemism for the female genitalia) and sent to Robert Ainslie in a letter of 29 July 1787, the song celebrates Elizabeth Paton with whom Burns had an affair in 1784.

Text: CW, 82.

> My girl she's airy, she's buxom and gay;
> Her breath is as sweet as the blossoms in May;
> A touch of her lips it ravishes quite.
> She's always good natur'd, good humour'd and free;
> She dances, she glances, she smiles with a glee;
> Her eyes are the lightenings of joy and delight;
> Her slender neck, her handsome waist,
> Her hair well buckled, her stays well lac'd,
> Her taper white leg with an et, and a, c,
> For her a, b, e, d, and her c, u, n, t,
> And oh, for the joys of a long winter night!!!

O, LEAVE NOVELS

Collected by Currie in 1800 (matched to the tune 'Donald Blue') and included in SMM (1803) the song was 'written probably in 1784–5 before the affair with Jean Armour absorbed Burns's attentions' (Kinsley, 1033). After celebrating the seductive power of popular novels (Fielding's *Tom Jones*, Richardson's *Sir Charles Grandison*) Burns acknowledges his relish for roleplaying: 'That feeling heart but acts a part'.

Text: H–H IV, 11.

> O, LEAVE novéls, ye Mauchline belles—
> Ye're safer at your spinning-wheel!
> Such witching books are baited hooks
> For rakish rooks like Rob Mossgiel.
>
> Your fine *Tom Jones* and *Grandisons*
> They make your youthful fancies reel!

They heat your brains, and fire your veins,
   And then you're prey for Rob Mossgiel.

Beware a tongue that's smoothly hung,
   A heart that warmly seems to feel!
That feeling heart but acts a part—
   'Tis rakish art in Rob Mossgiel.

The frank address, the soft caress
   Are worse than poisoned darts of steel:
The frank address and politesse
   Are all finesse in Rob Mossgiel.

HOLY WILLIE'S PRAYER

Written early in 1785, the savagely satirical Prayer was considered too provocative for Burns to publish as his own work. It
appeared anonymously as a pamphlet of 1789, posthumously
as Burns's work in a Glasgow pamphlet of 1799, was omitted
from Currie's edition of 1800, then printed in Thomas Stewart's
Poems ascribed to Robert Burns, the Ayrshire Bard (1801).
   Holy Willie was William Fisher (1737–1809), an elder of
Mauchline kirk and a member of the Kirk Session. At Fisher's instigation the Kirk Session took action against Gavin
Hamilton in August 1784, accusing him of absences from the
kirk and neglect of family worship. Hamilton appealed to the
Presbytery of Ayr which, in January 1785, found in his favour
(in July, Mauchline Kirk Session gave Hamilton a certificate
freeing him from censure); for Burns, this was a triumph of
commonsense over sanctimonious nonsense and he celebrated
by circulating his poem in manuscript in Mauchline. It is a
dramatic monologue in the Standard Habbie stanza, beginning with a statement of the Calvinist doctrine of preordained
damnation or salvation. For the Glenriddell Manuscript, Burns
provided an explanatory Argument:

> Holy Willie was a rather oldish batchelor Elder in
> the parish of Mauchline, and much and justly famed
> for that polemical chattering which ends in tippling
> Orthodoxy, and for that Spiritualized Bawdry which
> refines to Liquorish Devotion. – In a Sessional
> process with a gentleman in Mauchline, a Mr Gavin

Hamilton, Holy Willie, and his priest, father Auld,
after full hearing in the Presbytry of Ayr, came
off but second best; owing partly to the oratorical
powers of Mr Robt Aiken, Mr Hamilton's Counsel; but chiefly to Mr Hamilton's being one of the
most irreproachable and truly respectable characters
in the country. – On losing his Process, the Muse
overheard him at his devotions as follows—

Text: H–H II, 25–30.

And send the godly in a pet to pray. POPE

O THOU that in the Heavens does dwell,
Wha, as it pleases best Thysel,
Sends ane to Heaven an' ten to Hell
    A' for Thy glory,
And no for onie guid or ill
    They've done before Thee!

I bless and praise Thy matchless might,
When thousands Thou hast left in night,
That I am here before Thy sight,
    For gifts an' grace
A burning and a shining light
    To a' this place.

What was I, or my generation,
That I should get sic exaltation?
I, wha deserv'd most just damnation
    For broken laws
Sax thousand years ere my creation,
    Thro' Adam's cause!

When from my mither's womb I fell,
Thou might hae plung'd me deep in hell
To gnash my gooms, and weep, and wail
    In burning lakes,
Whare damnèd devils roar and yell,
    Chain'd to their stakes.

Yet I am here, a chosen sample,
To show Thy grace is great and ample:

I'm here a pillar o' Thy temple,
   Strong as a rock,
A guide, a buckler, and example
   To a' Thy flock!

But yet, O Lord! confess I must:
At times I'm fash'd wi' fleshly lust;
An' sometimes, too, in warldly trust,
   Vile self gets in;
But Thou remembers we are dust,
   Defiled wi' sin.

O Lord! yestreen, Thou kens, wi' Meg—
Thy pardon I sincerely beg—
O, may't ne'er be a living plague
   To my dishonour!
An' I'll ne'er lift a lawless leg
   Again upon her.

Besides, I farther maun avow—
Wi' Leezie's lass, three times, I trow—
But, Lord, that Friday I was fou,
   When I cam near her,
Or else, Thou kens, Thy servant true
   Wad never steer her.

Maybe Thou lets this fleshly thorn
Buffet Thy servant e'en and morn,
Lest he owre proud and high should turn
   That he's sae gifted:
If sae, Thy han' maun e'en be borne
   Until Thou lift it.

Lord, bless Thy chosen in this place,
For here Thou has a chosen race!
But God confound their stubborn face
   An' blast their name,
Wha bring Thy elders to disagrace
   An' open shame!

Lord, mind Gau'n Hamilton's deserts:
He drinks, an' swears, an' plays at cartes,

Yet has sae monie takin arts
        Wi' great and sma',
Frae God's ain Priest the people's hearts
        He steals awa.

And when we chasten'd him therefore,
Thou kens how he bred sic a splore,
And set the warld in a roar
        O' laughin at us:
Curse Thou his basket and his store,
        Kail an' potatoes!

Lord, hear my earnest cry and pray'r
Against that Presbyt'ry of Ayr!
Thy strong right hand, Lord, mak it bare
        Upo' their heads!
Lord, visit them, an' dinna spare,
        For their misdeeds!

O Lord, my God! that glib-tongu'd Aiken,
My vera heart and flesh are quakin
To think how we stood sweatin, shakin,
        An' pish'd wi' dread,
While he, wi' hinging lip an' snakin,
        Held up his head.

Lord, in Thy day o' vengeance try him!
Lord, visit him wha did employ him!
And pass not in Thy mercy by them,
        Nor hear their pray'r,
But for Thy people's sake destroy them,
        An' dinna spare!

But, Lord, remember me and mine
Wi' mercies temporal and divine,
That I for grace an' gear may shine
        Excell'd by nane!
And a' the glory shall be Thine—
        Amen, Amen!

DEATH AND DOCTOR HORNBOOK. A
TRUE STORY

A hornbook was a pedagogic aid (a sheet of paper, mounted on
wood and covered with a protective sheet of horn, displaying
the alphabet, digits, the Lord's Prayer and rules of spelling)
and Burns wrote the poem after hearing a tedious speech
by the Tarbolton schoolteacher John Wilson (c.1751–1839).
Dating the satire early 1785 Gilbert Burns explained:

> The Schoolmaster of Tarbolton parish, to eke up
> the scanty subsistence allowed to that useful class of
> men, had set up a shop of grocery goods. Having
> accidentally fallen in with some medical books, and
> become most hobby-horsically attached to the study
> of medicine, he had added the sale of a few medicines
> to his little trade. He had got a shop-bill printed, at
> the bottom of which, overlooking his own incapacity,
> he had advertised, that 'Advice would be given in
> common disorders at the shop gratis.' Robert was
> at a mason-meeting in Tarbolton, when the *Dominie*
> unfortunately made too ostentatious a display of his
> medical skill. As he parted in the evening from this
> mixture of pedantry and physics, at the place where he
> describes his meeting with Death, one of those floating
> ideas of apparition he mentions in his letter to Dr
> Moore, crossed his mind; this set him to work for the
> rest of the way home. These circumstances he related
> when he repeated the verses to me next afternoon, as
> I was holding the plough and he was letting the water
> off the field beside me. (Currie III, 382)

Lockhart's biography of Burns claimed the satire quickly ruined
the reputation of the real 'Doctor Hornbook' but Wilson remained in Tarbolton until 1792 when parishioners successfully
petitioned against him as an incompetent schoolmaster.

Burns himself considered the poem 'too trifling and prolix
to publish' (CL, 97) but Hugh Blair persuaded him to include
it in the first Edinburgh edition where Burns footnoted the
reference to Buchan, in the fourteenth stanza, as 'Buchan's Domestic Medecine': William Buchan's *Domestic Medecine* (1769)
was essential reading for rural healers.

Text: H–H I, 191–200.

SOME books are lies frae end to end,
And some great lies were never penn'd:
Ev'n ministers, they hae been kend,
                    In holy rapture,
A rousing whid at times to vend,
                    And nail't wi' Scripture.

But this that I am gaun to tell,
Which lately on a night befel,
Is just as true's the Deil's in hell
                    Or Dublin city:
That e'er he nearer comes oursel
                    'S a muckle pity!

The clachan yill had made me canty,
I was na fou, but just had plenty:
I stacher'd whyles, but yet took tent ay
                    To free the ditches;
An' hillocks, stanes, an' bushes, kend ay
                    Frae ghaists an' witches.

The rising moon began to glowr
The distant Cumnock Hills out-owre:
To count her horns, wi' a' my pow'r
                    I set mysel;
But whether she had three or four,
                    I cou'd na tell.

I was come round about the hill,
And todlin down on Willie's mill,
Setting my staff wi' a' my skill
                    To keep me sicker;
Tho' leeward whyles, against my will,
                    I took a bicker.

I there wi' *Something* does forgather,
That pat me in an eerie swither;
An awfu' scythe, out-owre ae shouther.
                    Clear-dangling, hang;
A three-tae'd leister on the ither
                    Lay, large an' lang.

Its stature seem'd lang Scotch ells twa;
The queerest shape that e'er I saw,
For fient a wame it had ava;
        And then its shanks,
They were as thin, as sharp an' sma'
        As cheeks o' branks.

'Guid-een,' quo' I; 'Friend! hae ye been
   mawin,
When ither folk are busy sawin?'
It seem'd to mak a kind o' stan',
        But naething spak.
At length, says I: 'Friend! whare ye gaun?
        Will ye go back?'

It spak right howe: 'My name is Death,
But be na' fley'd.' Quoth I: 'Guid faith,
Ye're may be come to stap my breath;
        But tent me, billie:
I red ye weel, take care o' skaith,
        See, there's a gully!'

'Gudeman,' quo' he, 'put up your whittle,
I'm no design'd to try its mettle;
But if I did, I wad be kittle
        To be mislear'd:
I wad na mind it, no that spittle
        Out-owre my beard.'

'Weel, weel!' says I, 'a bargain be't;
Come, gie's your hand, an' say we're gree't;
We'll ease our shanks, an' tak a seat:
        Come, gie's your news:
This while ye hae been monie a gate,
        At monie a house.'

'Ay, ay!' quo' he, an' shook his head,
'It's e'en a lang, lang time indeed
Sin' I began to nick the thread
        An' choke the breath:
Folk maun do something for their bread,
        An' sae maun Death.

'Sax thousand years are near-hand fled
Sin' I was to the butching bred,
An' monie a scheme in vain's been laid
                    To stap or scar me;
Till ane Hornbook's ta'en up the trade,
                    And faith! he'll waur me.

'Ye ken Jock Hornbook i' the clachan?
Deil mak his king's-hood in a spleuchan!—
He's grown sae weel acquaint wi' *Buchan*
                    And ither chaps,
The weans haud out their fingers laughin,
                    An' pouk my hips.

'See, here's a scythe, an' there's a dart,
They hae pierc'd monie a gallant heart;
But Doctor Hornbook wi' his art
                    An' cursed skill,
Has made them baith no worth a fart,
                    Damn'd haet they'll kill!

' 'Twas but yestreen, nae father gane,
I threw a noble throw at ane;
Wi' less, I'm sure, I've hundreds slain;
                    But Deil-ma-care!
It just played dirl on the bane,
                    But did nae mair.

'Hornbook was by wi' ready art,
An' had sae fortify'd the part,
That when I lookèd to my dart,
                    It was sae blunt,
Fient haet o't wad hae pierc'd the heart
                    Of a kail-runt.

'I drew my scythe in sic a fury,
I near-hand cowpit wi' my hurry,
But yet the bauld Apothecary
                    Withstood the shock:
I might as weel hae try'd a quarry
                    O' hard whin-rock.

'Ev'n them he canna get attended,
Altho' their face he ne'er had kend it,
Just shit in a kail-blade an' send it,
      As soon's he smells 't,
Baith their disease and what will mend it,
      At once he tells 't.

'And then a' doctor's saws and whittles
Of a' dimensions, shapes, an' mettles,
A' kinds o' boxes, mugs, and bottles,
      He's sure to hae;
Their Latin names as fast he rattles
      As A B C.

'Calces o' fossils, earth, and trees;
True *sal-marinum* o' the seas;
The *farina* of beans an' pease,
      He has't in plenty;
Aqua-fontis, what you please,
      He can content ye.

'Forbye some new, uncommon weapons,
Urinus spiritus of capons;
Or mite-horn shavings, filings, scrapings,
      Distill'd *per se*;
Sal-alkali o' midge-tail-clippings,
      And monie mae.'

'Waes me for Johnie Ged's Hole now,'
Quoth I, 'if that thae news be true!
His braw calf-ward whare gowans grew
      Sae white and bonie,
Nae doubt they'll rive it wi' the plew:
      They'll ruin Johnie!'

The creature grain'd an eldritch laugh,
And says: 'Ye nedna yoke the pleugh,
Kirkyards will soon be till'd eneugh,
      Tak ye nae fear:
They'll a' be trench'd wi' monie a sheugh
      In twa-three year.

'Whare I kill'd ane, a fair strae death
By loss o' blood or want o' breath,
This night I'm free to tak my aith,
   That Hornbook's skill
Has clad a score i' their last claith
   By drap an' pill.

'An honest wabster to his trade,
Whase wife's twa nieves were scarce weel-
 bred,
Gat tippence-worth to mend her head,
   When it was sair;
The wife slade cannie to her bed,
   But ne'er spak mair.

'A countra laird had taen the batts,
Or some curmurring in his guts,
His only son for Hornbook sets,
   An' pays him well:
The lad, for twa guid gimmer-pets,
   Was laird himsel.

'A bonie lass—ye kend her name—
Some ill-brewn drink had hov'd her wame;
She trusts hersel, to hide the shame,
   In Hornbook's care;
Horn sent her aff to her lang hame
   To hide it there.

'That's just a swatch o' Hornbook's way;
Thus goes he on from day to day,
Thus does he poison, kill, an' slay,
   An's weel paid for 't;
Yet stops me o' my lawfu' prey
   Wi' his damn'd dirt:

'But, hark! I'll tell you of a plot,
Tho' dinna ye be speakin o't:
I'll nail the self-conceited sot,
   As dead's a herrin;
Niest time we meet, I'll wad a groat,
   He gets his fairin!'

> But just as he began to tell,
> The auld kirk-hammer strak the bell
> Some wee short hour ayont the twal,
>   Which raised us baith:
> I took the way that pleas'd mysel,
>   And sae did Death.

EPISTLE TO J. LAPRAIK, AN OLD SCOTCH BARD

**Burns wrote three verse epistles in the Standard Habbie meas-
ure to John Lapraik: the first, dated 1 April 1785 and printed
in the Kilmarnock edition, is the finest and contains the poet's
creative credo. After explaining that the word 'rocking' derived
from 'rock' (distaff on which women spun) and came to mean
a social gathering, Gilbert Burns commented:**

> It was at one of these *rockings* at our house, when we
> had twelve or fifteen young people with their *rocks*,
> that Lapraik's song, beginning – 'When I upon thy
> bosom lean,' was sung, and we were informed who
> was the author. Upon this Robert wrote his first
> epistle to Lapraik . . .(Currie III, 383)

**Lapraik's song, first published in the *Weekly Magazine* (1773),
was improved by Burns for SMM (1790). Ruined by the failure
of the Ayr Bank in 1773, Lapraik (1727–1807), was forced to
sell Dalfram farm, Muirkirk (nine miles from Mauchline) but
continued to live in Muirkirk parish. He was imprisoned briefly
for debt in 1785; in an attempt to emulate Burns's success,
Lapraik published *Poems on Several Occasions* in 1788.**

**Fasteneen, in the poem, is Shrove Tuesday evening; Beattie
is poet and philosopher James Beattie; Allan is Allan Ramsay.**
Text: H–H I, 155–61.

> WHILE briers an' woodbines budding green,
> And paitricks scraichin loud at e'en,
> An' morning poussie whiddin seen,
>   Inspire my Muse,
> This freedom, in an unknown frien'
>   I pray excuse.

On Fasten-e'en we had a rockin,
To ca' the crack and weave our stockin;
And there was muckle fun and jokin,
   Ye need na doubt;
At length we had a hearty yokin,
   At 'sang about.'

There was ae sang, amang the rest,
Aboon them a' it pleas'd me best,
That some kind husband had addrest
   To some sweet wife:
It thirl'd the heart-strings thro' the breast,
   A' to the life.

I've scarce heard ought describ'd sae weel,
What gen'rous, manly bosoms feel;
Thought I, 'Can this be Pope or Steele,
   Or Beattie's wark?'
They tald me 'twas an odd kind chiel
   About Muirkirk.

It pat me fidgin-fain to hear 't,
An' sae about him there I spier 't;
Then a' that kent him round declar'd
   He had ingine;
That nane excell'd it, few cam near't,
   It was sae fine:

That, set him to a pint of ale,
An' either douce or merry tale,
Or rhymes an' songs he'd made himsel,
   Or witty catches,
'Tween Inverness an' Teviotdale,
   He had few matches.

Then up I gat, an' swoor an aith,
Tho' I should pawn my pleugh an' graith,
Or die a cadger pownie's death,
   At some dyke-back,
A pint an' gill I'd gie them baith,
   To hear your crack.

But, first an' foremost, I should tell,
Amaist as soon as I could spell,
I to the crambo-jingle fell;
                    Tho' rude an' rough—
Yet crooning to a body's sel,
                    Does weel eneugh.

I am nae poet, in a sense;
But just a rhymer like by chance,
An' hae to learning nae pretence;
                    Yet, what the matter?
Whene'er my Muse does on me glance,
                    I jingle at her.

Your critic-folk may cock their nose,
And say, 'How can you e'er propose,
You wha ken hardly verse frae prose,
                    To mak a sang?'
But, by your leaves, my learned foes,
                    Ye're maybe wrang.

What's a' your jargon o' your Schools,
Your Latin names for horns an' stools?
If honest Nature made you fools,
                    What sairs your grammers?
Ye'd better taen up spades and shools,
                    Or knappin-hammers.

A set o' dull, conceited hashes
Confuse their brains in college-classes,
They gang in stirks, and come out asses,
                    Plain truth to speak;
An' syne they think to climb Parnassus
                    By dint o' Greek!

Gie me ae spark o' Nature's fire,
That's a' the learning I desire;
Then, tho' I drudge thro' dub an' mire
                    At pleugh or cart,
My Muse, tho' hamely in attire,
                    May touch the heart.

O for a spunk o' Allan's glee,
Or Fergusson's, the bauld an' slee,
Or bright Lapraik's, my friend to be,
            If I can hit it!
That would be lear eneugh for me,
            If I could get it.

Now, sir, if ye hae friends enow,
Tho' real friends I b'lieve are few;
Yet, if your catalogue be fow,
            I'se no insist:
But, gif ye want ae friend that's true,
            I'm on your list.

I winna blaw about mysel,
As ill I like my fauts to tell;
But friends, an' folks that wish me well,
            They sometimes roose me;
Tho', I maun own, as monie still
            As far abuse me.

There's ae wee faut they whyles lay to me,
I like the lasses—Gude forgie me!
For monie a plack they wheedle frae me
            At dance or fair;
Maybe some ither thing they gie me,
            They weel can spare.

But Mauchline Race or Mauchline Fair,
I should be proud to meet you there:
We'se gie ae night's discharge to care,
            If we forgather;
And hae a swap o' rhymin-ware
            Wi' ane anither.

The four-gill chap, we'se gar him clatter,
An' kirsen him wi' reekin water;
Syne we'll sit down an' tak our whitter,
            To cheer our heart;
An' faith, we 'se be acquainted better
            Before we part.

Awa ye selfish, warly race,
Wha think that havins, sense, an' grace,
Ev'n love an' friendship should give place
                    To Catch-the-Plack!
I dinna like to see your face,
                    Nor hear your crack.

But ye whom social pleasure charms,
Whose hearts the tide of kindness warms,
Who hold your being on the terms,
                    'Each aid the others,'
Come to my bowl, come to my arms,
                    My friends, my brothers!

But, to conclude my lang epistle,
As my auld pen's worn to the grissle,
Twa lines frae you wad gar me fissle,
                    Who am most fervent,
While I can either sing or whistle,
                    Your friend and servant.

THE FORNICATOR

Collected (first four stanzas only) in MMC, this song (matched to the tune 'Clout the cauldron') dates from 1785 when Burns and the pregnant Elizabeth ('Betsey') Paton did penance, as fornicators, in kirk – presumably in Tarbolton since she came from Largieside. Both the MMC version of the song, and a manuscript (transcript of Burns's untraced holograph), specify a son and Burns's child by Betsey was Elizabeth (born 22 May 1785). So either the song was composed before May in anticipation of a son; or Burns simply needed a boy for his internal rhyme.
   Text: CW, 113–14.

Ye jovial boys who love the joys,
    The blissful joys of Lovers;
Yet dare avow with dauntless brow,
    When th' bony lass discovers;
I pray draw near and lend an ear,
    And welcome in a Frater,

For I've lately been on quarantine,
   A proven Fornicator.

Before the Congregation wide
   I pass'd the muster fairly,
My handsome Betsey by my side,
   We gat our ditty rarely;
But my downcast eye by chance did spy
   What made my lips to water,
Those limbs so clean where I, between,
   Commenc'd a Fornicator.

With rueful face and signs of grace
   I pay'd the buttock-hire,
The night was dark and thro the park
   I could not but convoy her;
A parting kiss, what could I less,
   My vows began to scatter,
My Betsey fell—lal de dal lal lal,
   I am a Fornicator.

But for her sake this vow I make,
   And solemnly I swear it,
That while I own a single crown,
   She's welcome for to share it;
And my roguish boy his Mother's joy,
   And the darling of his Pater,
For him I boast my pains and cost,
   Although a Fornicator.

Ye wenching blades whose hireling jades
   Have tipt you off blue-boram,
I tell ye plain, I do disdain
   To rank you in the Quorum;
But a bony lass upon the grass
   To teach her esse Mater,
And no reward but for regard,
   O that's a Fornicator.

Your warlike Kings and Heros bold,
   Great Captains and Commanders;

Your mighty Cèsars fam'd of old,
  And Conquering Alexanders;
In fields they fought and laurels bought
  And bulwarks strong did batter,
But still they grac'd our noble list
  And ranked Fornicator!!!

A POET'S WELCOME TO HIS LOVE-BEGOTTEN DAUGHTER;
THE FIRST INSTANCE THAT ENTITLED HIM TO THE VENERABLE APPELATION OF FATHER—

Included in the Glenriddell Manuscript and published (in part) in Thomas Stewart's *Poems ascribed to Robert Burns, the Ayrshire Bard* (1801), the poem is an affectionate address to Burns's illegitimate daughter by Elizabeth Paton: Elizabeth, born 22 May 1785.
   Text: H–H II, 37–9.

THOU's welcome, wean! Mishanter fa' me,
If thoughts o' thee or yet thy mammie
Shall ever daunton me or awe me,
     My sweet, wee lady,
Or if I blush when thou shalt ca' me
     Tyta or daddie!

What tho' they ca' me fornicator,
An' tease my name in kintra clatter?
The mair they talk, I'm kend the better;
     E'en let them clash!
An auld wife's tongue's a feckless matter
     To gie ane fash.

Welcome, my bonie, sweet, wee dochter!
Tho' ye come here a wee unsought for,
And tho' your comin I hae fought for
     Baith kirk and queir;
Yet, by my faith, ye're no unwrought for—
     That I shall swear!

Sweet fruit o' monie a merry dint,
My funny toil is no a' tint:

Tho' thou cam to the warl' asklent,
        Which fools may scoff at,
In my last plack thy part's be in't
        The better half o't.

Tho' I should be the waur bestead,
Thou 's be as braw and bienly clad,
And thy young years as nicely bred
        Wi' education,
As onie brat o' wedlock's bed
        In a' thy station.

Wee image o' my bonie Betty,
As fatherly I kiss and daut thee,
As dear and near my heart I set thee,
        Wi' as guid will,
As a' the priests had seen me get thee
        That's out o' Hell.

Gude grant that thou may ay inherit
Thy mither's looks an' gracefu' merit,
An' thy poor, worthless daddie's spirit
        Without his failins!
'Twill please me mair to see thee heir it
        Than stocket mailins.

And if thou be what I wad hae thee,
An' tak the counsel I shall gie thee,
I'll never rue my trouble wi' thee—
        The cost nor shame o't—
But be a loving father to thee,
        And brag the name o't.

THE HOLY FAIR

A note by Burns on the manuscript of the poem in the Kilmarnock Monument Museum reads 'Composed in 1785'. It is likely the poem was written during, or shortly after, August 1785 since the Mauchline Communion was held annually on the second Sunday in August. First published in the Kilmarnock edition.

Holy fairs were an integral part of eighteenth-century Scotland and Mauchline's holy fair conformed to a well-established pattern which, in practice, was chaotic. In 1785 Mauchline had around 400 communicant church members but for the annual communion service – the Sunday climax to days of celebration – more than thrice that number came to receive the sacrament, arriving from within and without the parish and refreshing themselves at Nanse Tinnock's tavern by the churchyard. Since the church could not accommodate such a press of people, a tent was set up on church grounds and rival preachers addressed the crowd. For those present, the occasion was an entertainment with religious overtones. Gilbert Burns commented: 'The farcical scene the poet there describes was often a favourite field of his observation, and the most of the incidents he mentions had actually passed before his eyes.' (Currie III, 385.)

Burns borrowed the Christis Kirk stanza as used by Fergusson in 'Hallow-Fair' and 'Leith Races' – following a rhyme-scheme of *ababcdcde* with the short last line (the tag, or tail) always ending in 'day'. In 'Leith Races' Fergusson meets Mirth who becomes his companion (his 'mate') during a humorous day. Burns, aiming for ecclesiastical satire rather than urban amusement, meets not one but 'Three hizzies': Fun (the equivalent of Fergusson's Mirth) who introduces him to Superstition and Hypocrisy, obligatory presences at Mauchline Holy Fair.

Not only is the poem rooted in the landscape of Mauchline, but local characters are involved in the action (ecclesiastical names were indicated by asterisks in the Kilmarnock edition): 'Racer Jess' (Janet Gibson, dimwitted daughter of Poosie Nansie); the Revd Alexander Moodie (Auld Licht minister of Riccarton); the Revd George Smith (New Licht minister of Galston); the Revd William Peebles (Auld Licht clerk of the Ayr Presbytery); the Revd Alexander Miller (a man seeking the security of an Auld Licht parish); and the Revd John Russell (Auld Licht minister of the High Church in Kilmarnock). 'Common-sense' (sixteenth stanza) is a personification of Burns's friend Dr John Mackenzie.

The satire suggests that Calvinism, with its vision of a cruelly selective God who sends preordained sinners to 'A vast, unbottom'd boundless pit,/Fill'd fou o' lowin brunstane', brings no comfort to the common people who turn instead to the consolations of drink and the saving grace of sex.

Text: H–H I, 36–47.

A robe of seeming truth and trust
  Hid crafty observation;
And secret hung, with poison'd crust,
  The dirk of defamation:
A mask that like the gorget show'd,
  Dye-varying on the pigeon;
And for a mantle large and broad,
  He wrapt him in Religion.

                        HYPOCRICY À-LA MODE

UPON a simmer Sunday morn,
  When Nature's face is fair,
I walkéd forth to view the corn,
  An' snuff the caller air.
The rising sun, owre Galston Muirs,
  Wi' glorious light was glintin;
The hares were hirplin down the furs,
  The lav'rocks they were chantin
                        Fu' sweet that day.

As lightsomely I glowr'd abroad,
  To see a scene sae gay,
Three hizzies, early at the road,
  Cam skelpin up the way.
Twa had manteeles o' dolefu' black,
  But ane wi' lyart lining;
The third, that gaed a wee a-back,
  Was in the fashion shining
                        Fu' gay that day.

The twa appear'd like sisters twin,
  In feature, form, an' claes;
Their visage wither'd, lang an' thin,
  An' sour as onie slaes:
The third cam up, hap-step-an'-lowp,
  As light as onie lambie,
An' wi' a curchie low did stoop,
  As soon as e'er she saw me,
                        Fu' kind that day.

Wi' bonnet aff, quoth I, 'Sweet lass,
   I think ye seem to ken me;
I'm sure I've seen that bonie face,
   But yet I canna name ye.'
Quo' she, an' laughin as she spak,
   An' taks me by the han's,
'Ye, for my sake, hae gi'en the feck
   Of a' the Ten Comman's
                A screed some day.

'My name is Fun—your cronie dear,
   The nearest friend ye hae;
An' this is Superstition here,
   An' that's Hypocrisy.
I'm gaun to Mauchline Holy Fair,
   To spend an hour in daffin:
Gin ye'll go there, yon runkl'd pair,
   We will get famous laughin
                At them this day.'

Quoth I, 'Wi' a' my heart, I'll do 't;
   I'll get my Sunday's sark on,
An' meet you on the holy spot;
   Faith, we'se hae fine remarkin!'
Then I gaed hame at crowdie-time,
   An' soon I made me ready;
For roads were clad, frae side to side,
   Wi' monie a wearie body,
                In droves that day.

Here farmers gash, in riding graith,
   Gaed hoddin by their cotters;
There swankies young, in braw braid-claith,
   Are springin owre the gutters.
The lasses, skelpin barefit, thrang,
   In silks an' scarlets glitter;
Wi' sweet-milk cheese, in monie a whang,
   An' farls, bak'd wi' butter,
                Fu' crump that day.

When by the plate we set our nose,
   Weel heapèd up wi' ha' pence,
A greedy glowr black-bonnet throws,
   An' we maun draw our tippence.
Then in we go to see the show:
   On ev'ry side they're gath'rin;
Some carryin dails, some chairs an' stools,
   An' some are busy bleth'rin
                Right loud that day.

Here stands a shed to fend the show'rs,
   An' screen our countra gentry;
There Racer Jess, an' twa-three whores,
   Are blinkin at the entry.
Here sits a raw o' tittlin jads,
   Wi' heavin breasts an' bare neck;
An' there a batch o' wabster lads,
Blackguardin frae Kilmarnock,
                For fun this day.

Here some are thinkin on their sins,
   An' some upo' their claes;
Ane curses feet that fyl'd his shins,
   Anither sighs an' prays:
On this hand sits a chosen swatch,
   Wi' screw'd-up, grace-proud faces;
On that a set o' chaps, at watch,
   Thrang winkin on the lasses
                To chairs that day.

O happy is that man an' blest!
   Nae wonder that it pride him!
Whase ain dear lass, that he likes best,
   Comes clinkin down beside him!
Wi' arm repos'd on the chair back,
   He sweetly does compose him;
Which, by degrees, slips round her neck,
   An's loof upon her bosom,
                Unkend that day.

Now a' the congregation o'er
   Is silent expectation;
For Moodie speels the holy door,
   Wi' tidings o' damnation:
Should Hornie, as in ancient days,
   'Mang sons o' God present him;
The vera sight o' Moodie's face
    To 's ain het hame had sent him
              Wi' fright that day.

Hear how he clears the points o' Faith
   Wi' rattlin and thumpin!
Now meekly calm, now wild in wrath,
   He's stampin, an' he's jumpin!
His lengthen'd chin, his turn'd-up snout,
   His eldritch squeel an' gestures,
O how they fire the heart devout—
   Like cantharidian plaisters
              On sic a day.

But hark! the tent has chang'd its voice;
   There's peace an' rest nae langer;
For a' the real judges rise,
   They canna sit for anger:
Smith opens out his cauld harangues,
   On practice and on morals;
An' aff the godly pour in thrangs,
   To gie the jars an' barrels
             A lift that day.

What signifies his barren shine,
   Of moral pow'rs an' reason?
His English style, an' gesture fine
   Are a' clean out o' season.
Like Socrates or Antonine,
   Or some auld pagan heathen,
The moral man he does define,
   But ne'er a word o' faith in
            That's right that day.

In guid time comes an antidote
   Against sic poison'd nostrum;
For Peebles, frae the water-fit,
   Ascends the holy rostrum:
See, up he's got the word o' God,
   An' meek an' mim has view'd it,
While Common-sense has taen the road,
   An' aff, an' up the Cowgate
                    Fast, fast that day.

Wee Miller niest, the guard relieves,
   An' orthodoxy raibles,
Tho' in his heart he weel believes,
   An' thinks it auld wives' fables:
But faith! the birkie wants a manse:
   So, cannilie he hums them;
Altho' his carnal wit an' sense
   Like hafflins-wise o'ercomes him
                    At times that day.

Now butt an' ben the change-house fills,
   Wi' yill-caup commentators;
Here's crying out for bakes an' gills,
   An' there the pint-stowp clatters;
While thick an' thrang, an' loud an' lang,
   Wi' logic an' wi' Scripture,
They raise a din, that in the end
   Is like to breed a rupture
                    O' wrath that day.

Leeze me on drink! it gies us mair
   Than either school or college;
It kindles wit, it waukens lear,
   It pangs us fou o' knowledge:
Be't whisky-gill or penny wheep,
   Or onie stronger potion,
It never fails, on drinkin deep,
   To kittle up our notion,
                    By night or day.

The lads an' lasses, blythely bent
   To mind baith saul an' body,
Sit round the table, weel content,
   An' steer about the toddy:
On this ane's dress, an' that ane's leuk,
   They're makin observations;
While some are cozie i' the neuk,
   An' formin assignations
                To meet some day.

But now the Lord's ain trumpet touts,
   Till a' the hills are rairin,
And echoes back return the shouts;
   Black Russell is na spairin:
His piercin words, like Highlan' swords,
   Divide the joints an' marrow;
His talk o' Hell, whare devils dwell,
   Our verra 'sauls does harrow'
                Wi' fright that day!

A vast, unbottom'd, boundless pit,
   Fill'd fou o' lowin brunstane,
Whase ragin flame, an' scorchin heat,
   Wad melt the hardest whun-stane!
The half-asleep start up wi' fear,
   An' think they hear it roarin;
When presently it does appear,
   'Twas but some neebor snorin
                Asleep that day.

'Twad be owre lang a tale to tell,
   How monie stories past;
An' how they crouded to the yill,
   When they were a' dismist;
How drink gaed round, in cogs an' caups,
   Amang the furms an' benches;
An' cheese an' bread, frae women's laps,
   Was dealt about in lunches,
                An' dawds that day.

In comes a gawsie, gash guidwife,
   An' sits down by the fire,
Syne draws her kebbuck an' her knife;
   The lasses they are shyer:
The auld guidmen, about the grace,
   Frae side to side they bother;
Till some ane by his bonnet lays,
   An' gies them't, like a tether,
               Fu' lang that day.

Waesucks! for him that gets nae lass,
   Or lasses that hae naething!
Sma' need has he to say a grace,
   Or melvie his braw claithing!
O wives, be mindfu', ance yoursel,
   How bonie lads ye wanted;
An' dinna for a kebbuck-heel
   Let lasses be affronted
              On sic a day!

Now Clinkumbell, wi' rattlin tow,
   Begins to jow an' croon;
Some swagger hame the best they dow,
   Some wait the afternoon.
At slaps the billies halt a blink,
   Till lasses strip their shoon:
Wi' faith an' hope, an' love an' drink,
   They're a' in famous tune
             For crack that day.

How monie hearts this day converts
   O' sinners and o' lasses!
Their hearts o' stane, gin night, are gane
   As saft as onie flesh is:
There's some are fou o' love divine;
   There's some are fou o' brandy;
An' monie jobs that day begin,
   May end in houghmagandie
             Some ither day.

THE VISION

Kinsley plausibly dates the poem to 'after August 1785' (Kinsley, 1702); it was first published in the Kilmarnock edition then, with seven additional stanzas (the last seven of Duan First), in the first Edinburgh edition. The division into two Duans derives from James Macpherson's use of the term in his 'Cath-loda' (an Ossianic improvisation in three Duans). Amusingly, the Kilmarnock text, finalised when Burns was estranged from Jean Armour, compares Coila's shapely leg to that of Elizabeth Paton: 'And such a *leg*! my BESS, I ween,/Could only peer it'; in the first Edinburgh edition this has become: 'And such a leg! my bonie Jean/Could only peer it'. In pursuit of his ambition to impress as an Ayrshire bard, Burns names his muse Coila after Kyle, his native area of Ayrshire; Burns derived the notion of Coila from James Beattie's use of the muse Scota in his vernacular poem 'To Mr Alexander Ross at Lochlee' (1768).

Kinsley worries over the precise 'auld clay biggin' cited by Burns, since 'Burns's setting is more like the house at Lochlie, where he lived until 1784, than Mossgiel' (Kinsley, 1075). However, as Burns is giving a visionary, not documentary, account of his past he is evidently recalling the Alloway clay cottage where he was born and where the muse claimed him at his 'natal hour'.

As for the Ayrshire heroes honoured by Burns, 'His Country's Saviour' is William Wallace, executed by Edward I in 1305; 'Bold Richardton', Adam Wallace of Riccarton; 'The chief, on Sark', John Wallace of Craigie; 'he whom ruthless fates expel', Mrs Dunlop's eldest son Sir Thomas Wallace who was forced to sell his Craigie estate in 1783; 'a martial race', the Montgomeries of Coilsfield; 'an aged Judge', Alexander Boswell, Lord of Justiciary and father of James Boswell; 'The learned Sire, and Son', Professor Matthew Stewart and his son Professor Dugald Stewart; 'Brydon's brave ward', Colonel William Fullarton, ward of Patrick Brydone; 'Dempster', George Dempster, Whig MP for Forfar Burghs. 'Beattie' is James Beattie, author of *The Minstrel* (1771, 1774), whose *Essay on the Nature and Immutability of Truth* (1770) was an attack on 'The sceptic' David Hume.

Text: H–H, 74–87.

DUAN FIRST

THE sun had clos'd the winter day,
The curlers quat their roaring play,
And hunger'd maukin taen her way,
   To kail-yards green,
While faithless snaws ilk step betray
   Whare she has been.

The thresher's weary flingin-tree,
The lee-lang day had tired me;
And when the day had clos'd his e'e,
   Far i' the west,
Ben i' the spence, right pensivelie,
   I gaed to rest.

There, lanely by the ingle-cheek,
I sat and ey'd the spewing reek,
That fill'd, wi' hoast-provoking smeek,
   The auld clay biggin;
An' heard the restless rattons squeak
   About the riggin.

All in this mottie, misty clime,
I backward mus'd on wasted time:
How I had spent my youthfu' prime,
   An' done naething,
But stringing blethers up in rhyme,
   For fools to sing.

Had I to guid advice but harkit,
I might, by this, hae led a market,
Or strutted in a bank and clarkit
   My cash-account:
While here, half-mad, half-fed, half-sarkit,
   Is a' th' amount.

I started, mutt'ring 'Blockhead! coof!'
An' heav'd on high my waukit loof,
To swear by a' yon starry roof,
   Or some rash aith,
That I henceforth would be rhyme-proof
   Till my last breath—

When click! the string the snick did draw;
And jee! the door gaed to the wa';
And by my ingle-lowe I saw,
                    Now bleezin bright,
A tight, outlandish hizzie, braw,
                    Come full in sight.

Ye need na doubt, I held my whisht;
The infant aith, half-form'd, was crusht;
I glowr'd as eerie's I'd been dusht,
                    In some wild glen;
When sweet, like modest Worth, she blusht,
                    And stepped ben.

Green, slender, leaf-clad holly-boughs
Were twisted, gracefu', round her brows;
I took her for some Scottish Muse,
                    By that same token;
And come to stop those reckless vows,
                    Would soon been broken.

A 'hair-brain'd, sentimental trace'
Was strongly markèd in her face;
A wildly-witty, rustic grace
                    Shone full upon her;
Her eye, ev'n turn'd on empty space,
                    Beam'd keen with honor.

Down flow'd her robe, a tartan sheen,
Till half a leg was scrimply seen;
And such a leg! my bonie Jean
                    Could only peer it;
Sae straught, sae taper, tight an' clean
                    Nane else came near it.

Her mantle large, of greenish hue,
My gazing wonder chiefly drew;
Deep lights and shades, bold-mingling, threw
                    A lustre grand;
And seem'd, to my astonish'd view,
                    A well-known land.

Here, rivers in the sea were lost;
There, mountains to the skies were toss't;
Here, tumbling billows mark'd the coast
              With surging foam;
There, distant shone Art's lofty boast,
              The lordly dome.

Here, Doon pour'd down his far-fetch'd floods;
There, well-fed Irwine stately thuds:
Auld hermit Ayr staw thro' his woods,
              On to the shore;
And many a lesser torrent scuds
              With seeming roar.

Low, in a sandy valley spread,
An ancient borough rear'd her head;
Still, as in Scottish story read,
              She boasts a race
To ev'ry nobler virtue bred,
              And polish'd grace.

By stately tow'r, or palace fair,
Or ruins pendent in the air,
Bold stems of heroes, here and there,
              I could discern;
Some seem'd to muse, some seem'd to dare,
              With feature stern.

My heart did glowing transport feel,
To see a race heroic wheel,
And brandish round the deep-dyed steel
              In sturdy blows;
While, back-recoiling, seem'd to reel
              Their suthron foes.

His Country's Saviour, mark him well!
Bold Richardton's heroic swell;
The chief, on Sark who glorious fell
              In high command;
And he whom ruthless fates expel
              His native land.

There, where a sceptr'd Pictish shade
Stalk'd round his ashes lowly laid,
I mark'd a martial race, pourtray'd
            In colours strong:
Bold, soldier-featur'd, undismay'd,
                They strode along.

Thro' many a wild, romantic grove,
Near many a hermit-fancied cove
(Fit haunts for friendship or for love
            In musing mood),
An aged Judge, I saw him rove,
                Dispensing good.

With deep-struck, reverential awe,
The learned Sire and Son I saw:
To Nature's God, and Nature's law,
            They gave their lore;
This, all its source and end to draw,
                That, to adore.

Brydon's brave ward I well could spy,
Beneath old Scotia's smiling eye;
Who call'd on Fame, low standing by,
            To hand him on,
Where many a patriot-name on high,
                And hero shone.

DUAN SECOND
With musing-deep, astonish'd stare,
I view'd the heavenly-seeming Fair;
A whisp'ring throb did witness bear
            Of kindred sweet,
When with an elder sister's air
                She did me greet.

'All hail! my own inspirèd Bard!
In me thy native Muse regard!
Nor longer mourn thy fate is hard,
            Thus poorly low!
I come to give thee such reward,
                As we bestow.

'Know, the great Genius of this land
Has many a light aerial band,
Who, all beneath his high command,
        Harmoniously,
As arts or arms they understand,
        Their labors ply.

'They Scotia's race among them share:
Some fire the soldier on to dare;
Some rouse the patriot up to bare
        Corruption's heart;
Some teach the bard—a darling care—
        The tuneful art.

' 'Mong swelling floods of reeking gore,
They, ardent, kindling spirits pour;
Or, 'mid the venal Senate's roar,
        They, sightless, stand,
To mend the honest patriot-lore,
        And grace the hand.

'And when the bard, or hoary sage,
Charm or instruct the future age,
They bind the wild poetic rage
        In energy;
Or point the inconclusive page
        Full on the eye.

'Hence, Fullarton, the brave and young;
Hence, Dempster's zeal-inspirèd tongue;
Hence, sweet, harmonious Beattie sung
        His *Minstrel* lays,
Or tore, with noble ardour stung,
        The sceptic's bays.

'To lower orders are assign'd
The humbler ranks of human-kind,
The rustic bard, the laboring hind,
        The artisan;
All chuse, as various they're inclin'd,
        The various man.

'When yellow waves the heavy grain,
The threat'ning storm some strongly rein,
Some teach to meliorate the plain,
                    With tillage-skill;
And some instruct the shepherd-train,
                    Blythe o'er the hill.

'Some hint the lover's harmless wile;
Some grace the maiden's artless smile;
Some soothe the laborer's weary toil
                    For humble gains,
And make his cottage-scenes beguile
                    His cares and pains.

'Some, bounded to a district-space,
Explore at large man's infant race,
To mark the embryotic trace
                    Of rustic bard;
And careful note each opening grace,
                    A guide and guard.

'Of these am I—Coila my name:
And this district as mine I claim,
Where once the Campbells, chiefs of fame,
                    Held ruling pow'r:
I mark'd thy embryo-tuneful flame,
                    Thy natal hour.

'With future hope I oft would gaze,
Fond, on thy little early ways:
Thy rudely caroll'd, chiming phrase,
                    In uncouth rhymes;
Fir'd at the simple, artless lays
                    Of other times.

'I saw thee seek the sounding shore,
Delighted with the dashing roar;
Or when the North his fleecy store
                    Drove thro' the sky,
I saw grim Nature's visage hoar
                    Struck thy young eye.

'Or when the deep green-mantled earth
Warm cherish'd ev'ry flow'ret's birth,
And joy and music pouring forth
    In ev'ry grove;
I saw thee eye the gen'ral mirth
    With boundless love.

'When ripen'd fields and azure skies
Call'd forth the reapers' rustling noise,
I saw thee leave their ev'ning joys,
    And lonely stalk,
To vent thy bosom's swelling rise,
    In pensive walk.

'When youthful Love, warm-blushing, strong,
Keen-shivering, shot thy nerves along,
Those accents grateful to thy tongue,
    Th' adorèd *Name*,
I taught thee how to pour in song
    To soothe thy flame.

'I saw thy pulse's maddening play,
Wild-send thee Pleasure's devious way,
Misled by Fancy's meteor-ray,
    By passion driven;
But yet the light that led astray
    Was light from Heaven.

'I taught thy manners-painting strains
The loves, the ways of simple swains,
Till now, o'er all my wide domains
    Thy fame extends;
And some, the pride of Coila's plains,
    Become thy friends.

'Thou canst not learn, nor can I show,
To paint with Thomson's landscape glow;
Or wake the bosom-melting throe
    With Shenstone's art;
Or pour, with Gray, the moving flow
    Warm on the heart.

'Yet, all beneath th' unrivall'd rose,
The lowly daisy sweetly blows;
Tho' large the forest's monarch throws
      His army-shade,
Yet green the juicy hawthorn grows
      Adown the glade.

'Then never murmur nor repine;
Strive in thy humble sphere to shine;
And trust me, not Potosi's mine,
      Nor king's regard,
Can give a bliss o'ermatching thine,
      A rustic Bard.

'To give my counsels all in one:
Thy tuneful flame still careful fan;
Preserve the dignity of Man,
      With soul erect;
And trust the Universal Plan
      Will all protect.

'And wear though *this*'—She solemn said,
And bound the holly round my head:
The polish'd leaves and berries red
      Did rustling play;
And, like a passing thought, she fled
      In light away.

THE JOLLY BEGGARS (LOVE AND LIBERTY – A CANTATA)

Composed before November 1785 when John Richmond left Ayrshire for Edinburgh since, according to Richmond, it was prompted by a visit he, James Smith and Burns made to Poosie Nansie's tavern, Mauchline: seeing a convivial company of beggars, Burns was 'greatly amused' and had the sequence drafted after 'a few days' (Ch–W I, 244). Burns planned to publish 'Love and Liberty – A Cantata' (the title used in his holograph) in the first Edinburgh edition of 1787 but was persuaded against its inclusion by Hugh Blair who commented:

> The Whole of What is called the Cantata, the Songs
> of the Beggars and their Doxies, with the Grace at
> the end of them, are altogether unfit in my opinion
> for publication. They are by much too licentious;
> and fall below the dignity which Mr Burns possesses
> in the rest of his poems & would rather degrade
> them. (CH, 82)

It was first published by Thomas Stewart as *The Jolly Beggars: or Tatterdemallions. A Cantata* (1799) and included in Stewart's edition of *Poems ascribed to Robert Burns, the Ayrshire Bard* (1801).

Matthew Arnold preferred the Cantata to 'Tam o' Shanter': 'It has a breadth, truth, and power which makes the famous scene in Auerbach's cellar, of Goethe's *Faust*, seem artificial and tame beside it, and which are only matched by Shakespeare and Aristophanes.' ('The Study of Poetry', in *Essays in Criticism, Second Series*, 1888.) Though there were various precedents for Burns's presentation of beggars (vernacular songs such as 'The Gaberlunzie Man', Gay's *The Beggar's Opera* which Burns mentions in letters) the Cantata is one of his most distinctive works, ending with the spectacle of the assembled company on their feet with the Bard to join in a song whose revolutionary implications offer an alternative to the drunken condition and limited consciousness of beggars. Technically, the Cantata shows Burns's mastery of metrical forms: Cherrie and the Slae stanza (first recitativo), Standard Habbie stanza (fifth recitativo), Christis Kirk stanza (seventh recitativo).

Some references in the soldier's song require clarification: Abram, the heights of Abraham scaled by General Wolfe before routing the French at Quebec in 1759; Moro, a fortress at Santiago, Cuba, stormed by the British in 1762; Curtis, Admiral Sir Roger Curtis who destroyed the French floating batteries at Gibraltar in 1782; Elliot, General George Elliot who defended Gibraltar. Kilbaigie (tinker's song) was whisky distilled at Kilbagie, near Clackmannan. Dainty Davie (seventh recitativo) refers to the Revd David Williamson whose exploits made his name synonymous with sex.

Text: H–H II, 1–19.

RECITATIVO

When lyart leaves bestrow the yird,
Or, wavering like the bauckie-bird,
　Bedim cauld Boreas' blast;

When hailstanes drive wi' bitter skyte,
And infant frosts begin to bite,
  In hoary cranreuch drest;
Ae night at e'en a merry core
  O' randie, gangrel bodies
In Poose-Nansie's held the splore,
  To drink their orra duddies:
    Wi' quaffing and laughing
      They ranted an' they sang,
    Wi' jumping an' thumping
      The vera girdle rang.

First, niest the fire, in auld red rags
Ane sat, weel brac'd wi' mealy bags
  And knapsack a' in order;
His doxy lay within his arm;
Wi' usquebae an' blankets warm,
  She blinket on her sodger.
An' ay he gies the tozie drab
  The tither skelpin kiss,
While she held up her greedy gab
  Just like an aumous dish:
    Ilk smack still did crack still
      Like onie cadger's whup;
    Then, swaggering an' staggering,
      He roar'd this ditty up:—

                    AIR

      TUNE: *'Soldier's Joy'*
I am a son of Mars, who have been in many wars,
  And show my cuts and scars wherever I come:
This here was for a wench, and that other in a
    trench
  When welcoming the French at the sound of the
    drum.
                              Lal de daudle, *etc.*

My prenticeship I past, where my leader breath'd
    his last,
  When the bloody die was cast on the heights of
    Abram;

And I servèd out my trade when the gallant game
    was play'd,
  And the Moro low was laid at the sound of the
    drum.

I lastly was with Curtis among the floating batt'ries,
  And there I left for witness an arm and a limb;
Yet let my country need me, with Eliott to head me
  I'd clatter on my stumps at the sound of the
    drum.

And now, tho' I must beg with a wooden arm and
    leg
  And many a tatter'd rag hanging over my bum,
I'm as happy with my wallet, my bottle, and my
    callet
  As when I us'd in scarlet to follow a drum.

What tho' with hoary locks I must stand the
    winter shocks,
  Beneath the woods and rocks oftentimes for a
    home?
When the tother bag I sell, and the tother bottle
    tell,
  I could meet a troop of Hell at the sound of a
    drum.

Lal de daudle, etc.

RECITATIVO

  He ended; and the kebars sheuk
    Aboon the chorus roar;
  While frighted rattons backward leuk,
    An' seek the benmost bore:
  A fairy fiddler frae the neuk,
    He skirl'd out Encore!
  But up arose the martial chuck,
    An' laid the loud uproar:—

AIR
TUNE: *'Sodger Laddie'*

I once was a maid, tho' I cannot tell when,
And still my delight is in proper young men.
Some one of a troop of dragoons was my daddie:
No wonder I'm fond of a sodger laddie!
                              Sing, lal de dal, *etc.*

The first of my loves was a swaggering blade:
To rattle the thundering drum was his trade;
His leg was so tight, and his cheek was so ruddy,
Transported I was with my sodger laddie.

But the godly old chaplain left him in the lurch;
The sword I forsook for the sake of the church;
He riskèd the soul, and I ventur'd the body:
Twas then I prov'd false to my sodger laddie.

Full soon I grew sick of my sanctified sot;
The regiment at large for a husband I got;
From the gilded spontoon to the fife I was
        ready:
I askèd no more but a sodger laddie.

But the Peace it reduc'd me to beg in despair,
Till I met my old boy in a Cunningham Fair;
His rags regimental they flutter'd so gaudy:
My heart it rejoic'd at a sodger laddie.

And now I have liv'd—I know not how long!
But still I can join in a cup and a song;
And whilst with both hands I can hold the glass
        steady,
Here's to thee, my hero, my sodger laddie!
                              Sing, lal de dal, *etc.*

Poor Merry-Andrew in the neuk
    Sat guzzling wi' a tinkler-hizzie;
They mind't na wha the chorus teuk,
    Between themselves they were sae busy.
    At length, wi' drink an' courting dizzy,
He stoiter'd up an' made a face;
    Then turn'd an' laid a smack on Grizzie,
Syne tun'd his pipes wi' grave grimace:—

AIR
TUNE: *'Auld Sir Symon'*
Sir Wisdom 's a fool when he 's fou;
    Sir Knave is a fool in a session:
He's there but a prentice I trow,
    But I am a fool by profession.

My grannie she bought me a beuk,
    An' I held awa to the school:
I fear I my talent misteuk,
    But what will ye hae of a fool?

For drink I wad venture my neck;
    A hizzie's the half of my craft:
But what could ye other expect
    Of ane that's avowedly daft?

I ance was tyed up like a stirk
    For civilly swearing and quaffing;
I ance was abus'd i' the kirk
    For towsing a lass i' my daffin.

Poor Andrew that tumbles for sport
    Let naebody name wi' a jeer:
There's even, I'm tauld, i' the Court
    A tumbler ca'd the Premier.

Observ'd ye yon reverend lad
    Mak faces to tickle the mob?
He rails at our mountebank squad—
    It's rivalship just i' the job!

And now my conclusion I'll tell,
    For faith! I'm confoundedly dry:
The chiel that's a fool for himsel,
    Guid Lord! he's far dafter than I.

RECITATIVO

Then niest outspak a raucle carlin,
Wha kent fu' weel to cleek the sterlin,
For monie a pusie she had hookèd,
An' had in monie a well been doukèd.
Her love had been a Highland laddie,
But weary fa' the waefu' woodie!
Wi' sighs an' sobs she thus began
To wail her braw John Highlandman:—

AIR

TUNE: 'O, An' Ye Were Dead, Guidman'
A Highland lad my love was born,
The lalland laws he held in scorn,
But he still was faithfu' to his clan,
My gallant, braw John Highlandman.

CHORUS

    Sing hey my braw John Highlandman!
    Sing ho my braw John Highlandman!
    There's not a lad in a' the lan'
    Was match for my John Highlandman!

With his philibeg, an' tartan plaid,
An' guid claymore down by his side,
The ladies' hearts he did trepan,
My gallant, braw John Highlandman.

We rangèd a' from Tweed to Spey,
An' liv'd like lords an' ladies gay,
For a lalland face he fearèd none,
My gallant, braw John Highlandman.

They banish'd him beyond the sea,
But ere the bud was on the tree,
Adown my cheeks the pearls ran,
Embracing my John Highlandman.

But, Och! they catch'd him at the last,
And bound him in a dungeon fast.
My curse upon them every one—
They've hang'd my braw John Highland-
    man!

And now a widow I must mourn
The pleasures that will ne'er return;
No comfort but a hearty can
When I think on John Highlandman.

CHORUS

  Sing hey my braw John Highlandman!
  Sing ho my braw John Highlandman!
  There's not a lad in a' the lan'
  Was match for my John Highlandman!

RECITATIVO

A pigmy scraper on a fiddle,
Wha us'd to trystes an' fairs to driddle,
Her strappin limb an' gawsie middle
           (He reach'd nae higher)
Had hol'd his heartie like a riddle,
          An' blawn 't on fire.

Wi' hand on hainch and upward e'e,
He croon'd his gamut, one, two, three,
Then in an *arioso* key
        The wee Apollo
Set off wi' *allegretto* glee
        His *giga* solo:—

AIR

  TUNE: *'Whistle Owre the Lave O't'*
Let me ryke up to dight that tear;
An' go wi' me an' be my dear,
An' then your every care an' fear
  May whistle owre the lave o't.

Chorus

I am a fiddler to my trade,
    An' a' the tunes that e'er I play'd,
The sweetest still to wife or maid
    Was *Whistle Owre the Lave O't.*

At kirns an' weddings we'se be there,
An' O, sae nicely's we will fare!
We'll bowse about till Daddie Care
    Sing *Whistle Owre the Lave O't.*

Sae merrily the banes we'll pyke,
An' sun oursels about the dyke;
An' at our leisure, when ye like,
    We'll— whistle owre the lave o't!

But bless me wi' your heav'n o' charms,
An' while I kittle hair on thairms,
Hunger, cauld, an' a' sic harms
    May whistle owre the lave o't.

Chorus

I am a fiddler to my trade,
    An' a' the tunes that e'er I play'd,
The sweetest still to wife or maid
    Was *Whistle Owre the Lave O't.*

RECITATIVO

Her charms had struck a sturdy caird
    As weel as poor gut-scraper;
He taks the fiddler by the beard,
    An' draws a roosty rapier;
He swoor by a' was swearing worth
    To speet him like a pliver,
Unless he would from that time forth
    Relinquish her for ever.

Wi' ghastly e'e poor Tweedle-Dee
    Upon his hunkers bended,

An' pray'd for grace wi' ruefu' face,
  An' sae the quarrel ended.
But tho' his little heart did grieve
  When round the tinkler prest her,
He feign'd to snirtle in his sleeve
  When thus the caird address'd her:—

AIR

TUNE: *'Clout the Cauldron'*
My bonie lass, I work in brass,
  A tinkler is my station;
I've travell'd round all Christian ground
  In this my occupation;
I've taen the gold, an' been enrolled
  In many a noble squadron;
But vain they search'd when off I march'd
  To go an' clout the cauldron.

Despise that shrimp, that wither'd imp,
  With a' his noise an' cap'rin,
An' take a share wi' those that bear
  The budget and the apron!
And by that stowp, my faith an' houpe!
  And by that dear Kilbaigie!
If e'er ye want, or meet wi' scant,
  May I ne'er weet my craigie!

RECITATIVO
The caird prevail'd: th' unblushing fair
  In his embraces sunk,
Partly wi' love o'ercome sae sair,
  An' partly she was drunk.
Sir Violino, with an air
  That show'd a man o' spunk,
Wish'd unison between the pair,
  An' made the bottle clunk
          To their health that night.

But hurchin Cupid shot a shaft,
  That play'd a dame a shavie:

The fiddler rak'd her fore and aft
   Behint the chicken cavie;
Her lord, a wight of Homer's craft,
   Tho' limpin' wi' the spavie,
He hirpl'd up, an' lap like daft,
   An' shor'd them 'Dainty Davie'
      O' boot that night.

He was a care-defying blade
   As ever Bacchus listed!
Tho' Fortune sair upon him laid,
   His heart, she ever miss'd it.
He had no wish but—to be glad,
   Nor want but—when he thristed,
He hated nought but—to be sad;
   An' thus the Muse suggested
      His sang that night.

AIR

TUNE: *'For A' That, An' A' That'*
I am a Bard, of no regard
   Wi' gentle folks an' a' that,
But Homer-like the glowrin byke,
   Frae town to town I draw that.

CHORUS
For a' that, an' a' that,
   An' twice as muckle's a' that,
I've lost but ane, I've twa behin',
   I've wife eneugh for a' that.

I never drank the Muses' stank,
   Castalia's burn, an' a' that;
But there it streams, an' richly reams—
   My Helicon I ca' that.

Great love I bear to a' the fair,
   Their humble slave an' a' that;
But lordly will, I hold it still
   A mortal sin to thraw that.

In raptures sweet this hour we meet
   Wi' mutual love an' a' that;
But for how lang the flie may stang,
   Let inclination law that!

Their tricks an' craft hae put me daft,
   They've taen me in, an' a' that;
But clear your decks, an' here 's the Sex!
   I like the jads for a' that.

CHORUS

For a' that, an' a' that,
   An' twice as muckle's a' that,
My dearest bluid, to do them guid,
   They 're welcome till 't for a' that!

RECITATIVO

So sung the Bard, and Nansie's wa's
Shook with a thunder of applause,
   Re-echo'd from each mouth!
They toom'd their pocks, they pawn'd their
     duds,
They scarcely left to coor their fuds,
   To quench their lowin drouth.
Then owre again the jovial thrang
   The Poet did request
To lowse his pack, an' wale a sang,
   A ballad o' the best:
     He rising, rejoicing
      Between his twa Deborahs,
     Looks round him, an' found them
      Impatient for the chorus:—

AIR

TUNE: *'Jolly Mortals, Fill Your Glasses'*
See the smoking bowl before us!
   Mark our jovial, ragged ring!
Round and round take up the chorus,
   And in raptures let us sing:

Chorus
A fig for those by law protected!
  Liberty's a glorious feast,
Courts for cowards were erected,
  Churches built to please the priest!

What is title, what is treasure,
  What is reputation's care?
If we lead a life of pleasure,
  'Tis no matter how or where!

With the ready trick and fable
  Round we wander all the day;
And at night in barn or stable
  Hug our doxies on the hay.

Does the train-attended carriage
  Thro' the country lighter rove?
Does the sober bed of marriage
  Witness brighter scenes of love?

Life is all a variorum,
  We regard not how it goes;
Let them prate about decorum,
  Who have character to lose.

Here's to budgets, bags, and wallets!
  Here's to all the wandering train!
Here's our ragged brats and callets!
  One and all, cry out, Amen!

Chorus
A fig for those by law protected!
  Liberty's a glorious feast,
Courts for cowards were erected,
  Churches built to please the priest!

THE COTTER'S SATURDAY NIGHT

Composed during the winter of 1785–6 (the second stanza invokes 'November chill'), listed as complete in Burns's letter (17 Feb. 1786) to John Richmond, it was included in the Kilmarnock edition. Gilbert Burns wrote of the poem:

> Robert had frequently remarked to me that he thought that there was something peculiarly venerable in the phrase, 'Let us worship God,' used by a decent sober head of a family introducing family worship. To this sentiment of the author the world is indebted for the *Cotter's Saturday Night* . . . When Robert had not some pleasure in view in which I was not thought fit to participate, we used frequently to walk together when the weather was favourable, on the Sunday afternoons, (those precious breathing-times to the labouring part of the community) and enjoyed such Sundays as would make one regret to see their number abridged. It was in one of these walks that I first had the pleasure of hearing the author repeat the *Cotter's Saturday Night*. I do not recollect to have read or heard any thing by which I was more highly *electrified*. (Currie III, 384–5)

Written in Spenserian stanzas, like Robert Fergusson's 'The Farmer's Ingle' which influenced it, 'The Cotter's Saturday Night' is an idealistic portrait of a humble Scottish household presided over by a self-righteous patriarch made in the image of the poet's father William Burnes. The tenth stanza has ironic overtones for the informed reader: when Burns wrote those lines he was the father of an illegitimate daughter (Elizabeth Paton, born 22 May 1785). Read in a biographical context, the description of the wretch becomes a subconscious self-portrait, Burns indulging in what Freud called 'projection' by attributing to another an act committed by himself.

Text: H–H I, 106–14.

INSCRIBED TO R. AIKEN, ESQ.

Let not Ambition mock their useful toil,
Their homely joys, and destiny obscure;
Nor Grandeur hear, with a disdainful smile,
The short and simple annals of the poor.

GRAY

My lov'd, my honor'd, much respected friend!
   No mercenary bard his homage pays;
With honest pride, I scorn each selfish end,
   My dearest meed, a friend's esteem and praise:
   To you I sing, in simple Scottish lays,
The lowly train in life's sequester'd scene;
   The native feelings strong, the guileless ways;
What Aiken in a cottage would have been;
Ah! tho' his worth unknown, far happier there
       I ween!

November chill blaws loud wi' angry sugh;
   The short'ning winter-day is near a close;
The miry beasts retreating frae the pleugh;
   The black'ning trains o' craws to their repose:
   The toil-worn Cotter frae his labor goes—
This night his weekly moil is at an end,
   Collects his spades, his mattocks, and his hoes,
Hoping the morn in ease and rest to spend,
And weary, o'er the moor, his course does hame-
       ward bend.

At length his lonely cot appears in view,
   Beneath the shelter of an aged tree;
Th' expectant wee-things, toddlin, stacher through
   To meet their dad, wi' flichterin' noise and glee.
   His wee bit ingle, blinkin bonilie,
His clean hearth-stane, his thrifty wifie's smile,
   The lisping infant, prattling on his knee,
Does a' his weary kiaugh and care beguile,
And makes him quite forget his labor and his toil.

Belyve, the elder bairns come drapping in,
   At service out, amang the farmers roun';
Some ca' the pleugh, some herd, some tentie rin
   A cannie errand to a neebor town:
   Their eldest hope, their Jenny, woman grown,
In youthfu' bloom, love sparkling in her e'e,
   Comes hame; perhaps, to shew a braw new gown,
Or deposite her sair-won penny-fee,
To help her parents dear, if they in hardship be.

With joy unfeign'd, brothers and sisters meet,
   And each for other's welfare kindly spiers:
The social hours, swift-wing'd, unnotic'd fleet;
   Each tells the uncos that he sees or hears.
   The parents partial eye their hopeful years;
Anticipation forward points the view;
   The mother, wi' her needle and her sheers,
Gars auld claes look amaist as weel's the new;
The father mixes a' wi' admonition due.

Their master's and their mistress's command
   The younkers a' are warned to obey;
And mind their labors wi' an eydent hand,
   And ne'er, tho' out o' sight, to jauk or play:
   'And O! be sure to fear the Lord alway,
And mind your duty, duly, morn and night;
   Lest in temptation's path ye gang astray,
Implore His counsel and assisting might:
They never sought in vain that sought the Lord
      aright.'

But hark! a rap comes gently to the door;
   Jenny, wha kens the meaning o' the same,
Tells how a neebor lad came o'er the moor,
   To do some errands, and convoy her hame.
   The wily mother sees the conscious flame
Sparkle in Jenny's e'e, and flush her cheek;
   With heart-struck anxious care, enquires his name,
While Jenny hafflins is afraid to speak;
Weel-pleas'd the mother hears, it 's nae wild, worth-
      less rake.

With kindly welcome, Jenny brings him ben;
A strappin' youth, he takes the mother's eye;
Blythe Jenny sees the visit's no ill taen;
   The father cracks of horses, pleughs, and kye.
   The youngster's artless heart o'erflows wi' joy,
But blate and laithfu', scarce can weel behave;
   The mother, wi' a woman's wiles, can spy
What makes the youth sae bashfu' and sae grave;
Weel-pleas'd to think her bairn's respected like the
      lave.

O happy love! where love like this is found:
  O heart-felt raptures! bliss beyond compare!
I've pacèd much this weary, mortal round,
    And sage experience bids me this declare:—
    'If Heaven a draught of heavenly pleasure spare,
One cordial in this melancholy vale,
    'Tis when a youthful, loving, modest pair,
In other's arms, breathe out the tender tale
Beneath the milk-white thorn that scents the ev'ning
        gale.'

Is there, in human form, that bears a heart,
    A wretch! a villain! lost to love and truth!
That can, with studied, sly, ensnaring art,
    Betray sweet Jenny's unsuspecting youth?
    Curse on his perjur'd arts! dissembling, smooth!
Are honor, virtue, conscience, all exil'd?
    Is there no pity, no relenting ruth,
Points to the parents fondling o'er their child?
Then paints the ruin'd maid, and their distraction
        wild?

But now the supper crowns their simple board,
    The healsome parritch, chief o' Scotia's food;
The soupe their only hawkie does afford,
    That, 'yont the hallan snugly chows her cood;
    The dame brings forth, in complimental mood,
To grace the lad, her weel-hain'd kebbuck, fell;
    And aft he's prest, and aft he ca's it guid;
The frugal wifie, garrulous, will tell,
How 'twas a towmond auld, sin' lint was i' the bell.

The chearfu' supper done, wi' serious face,
    They, round the ingle, form a circle wide;
The sire turns o'er, wi' patriarchal grace,
    The big ha'-Bible, ance his father's pride.
    His bonnet rev'rently is laid aside,
His lyart haffets wearing thin and bare;
    Those strains that once did sweet in Zion glide,
He wales a portion with judicious care,
And 'Let us worship God!' he says, with solemn air.

They chant their artless notes in simple guise,
   They tune their hearts, by far the noblest aim;
Perhaps *Dundee's* wild-warbling measures rise,
   Or plaintive *Martyrs*, worthy of the name;
   Or noble *Elgin* beets the heaven-ward flame,
The sweetest far of Scotia's holy lays:
   Compar'd with these, Italian trills are tame;
The tickl'd ears no heart-felt raptures raise;
Nae unison hae they, with our Creator's praise.

The priest-like father reads the sacred page,
   How Abram was the friend of God on high;
Or, Moses bade eternal warfare wage
   With Amalek's ungracious progeny;
   Or, how the royal Bard did groaning lie
Beneath the stroke of Heaven's avenging ire;
   Or Job's pathetic plaint, and wailing cry;
Or rapt Isaiah's wild, seraphic fire;
Or other holy Seers that tune the sacred lyre.

Perhaps the Christian volume is the theme:
   How guiltless blood for guilty man was shed;
How He, who bore in Heaven the second name,
   Had not on earth whereon to lay His head;
   How His first followers and servants sped;
The precepts sage they wrote to many a land:
   How he, who lone in Patmos banishèd,
Saw in the sun a mighty angel stand,
And heard great Bab'lon's doom pronounc'd by
     Heaven's command.

Then kneeling down to Heaven's Eternal King,
   The saint, the father, and the husband prays:
Hope 'springs exulting on triumphant wing,'
   That thus they all shall meet in future days,
   There, ever bask in uncreated rays,
No more to sigh or shed the bitter tear,
   Together hymning their Creator's praise,
In such society, yet still more dear;
While circling Time moves round in an eternal sphere.

Compar'd with this, how poor Religion's pride,
   In all the pomp of method, and of art;
When men display to congregations wide
   Devotion's ev'ry grace, except the heart
   The Power, incens'd, the pageant will desert,
The pompous strain, the sacerdotal stole;
   But haply, in some cottage far apart,
May hear, well-pleas'd, the language of the soul,
And in His Book of Life the inmates poor enroll.

Then homeward all take off their sev'ral way;
   The youngling cottagers retire to rest:
The parent-pair their secret homage pay,
   And proffer up to Heaven the warm request,
   That He who stills the raven's clam'rous nest,
And decks the lily fair in flow'ry pride,
   Would, in the way His wisdom sees the best,
For them and for their little ones provide;
But, chiefly, in their hearts with Grace Divine pre-
      side.

From scenes like these, old Scotia's grandeur springs,
   That makes her lov'd at home, rever'd abroad:
Princes and lords are but the breath of kings,
   'An honest man's the noblest work of God';
   And certes, in fair Virtue's heavenly road,
The cottage leaves the palace far behind;
   What is a lordling's pomp? a cumbrous load,
Disguising oft the wretch of human kind,
Studied in arts of Hell, in wickedness refin'd!

O Scotia! my dear, my native soil!
   For whom my warmest wish to Heaven is sent!
Long may thy hardy sons of rustic toil
   Be blest with health, and peace, and sweet con-
      tent!
   And O! may Heaven their simple lives prevent
From Luxury's contagion, weak and vile!
   Then, howe'er crowns and coronets be rent,
A virtuous populace may rise the while,
And stand a wall of fire around their much-lov'd
      Isle.

O Thou! who pour'd the patriotic tide,
   That stream'd thro' Wallace's undaunted heart,
Who dar'd to, nobly, stem tyrannic pride,
   Or nobly die, the second glorious part:
   (The patriot's God, peculiarly Thou art,
His friend, inspirer, guardian, and reward!)
   O never, never Scotia's realm desert;
But still the patriot, and the patriot-bard
In bright succession raise, her ornament and guard!

TO A MOUSE,
ON TURNING HER UP IN HER NEST, WITH
THE PLOUGH, NOVEMBER 1785

Written at Mossgiel in November 1785, 'To a Mouse' was composed, according to Gilbert Burns, 'while the author was holding the plough' (Currie III, 383). John Blane, once Burns's gaudsman (goader of the ploughman's team of horses), claimed to have chased after the mouse to kill it, before being admonished by the poet who then became contemplative.

First published in the Kilmarnock edition it has moved countless readers and critics including Snyder who acclaimed it the outstanding achievement in that volume: 'the tragedy of the mouse has become the tragedy of Burns himself, and of all heart-broken folk who review the past with regret, or await the future with misgiving' (Snyder, 181).

Behind what is ostensibly an inspired occasional poem is the tension between philosophical faith and personal insecurity. Informing the address is Burns's Deistic belief in a natural religion, a notion reinforced by his reading of favourite poets such as Thomson and Pope. Subjectively, Burns was in a poignant position in November 1785: the previous year his father had died, a victim of 'the rapacious hell-hounds that growl in the kennel of justice' (see p.95); the previous month his brother John had died at the age of sixteen. Burns had catastrophe on his consciousness.

Text: H–H I, 115–17.

     Wee, sleekit, cowrin, tim'rous beastie,
     O, what a panic 's in thy breastie!

Thou need na start awa sae hasty
                    Wi' bickering brattle!
I wad be laith to rin an' chase thee,
                    Wi' murdering pattle!

I'm truly sorry man's dominion
Has broken Nature's social union,
An' justifies that ill opinion
                    Which makes thee startle
At me, thy poor, earth-born companion
                    An' fellow mortal!

I doubt na, whyles, but thou may thieve;
What then? poor beastie, thou maun live!
A daimen icker in a thrave
                    'S a sma' request;
I'll get a blessin wi' the lave,
                    An' never miss 't!

Thy wee-bit housie, too, in ruin!
Its silly wa's the win's are strewin!
An' naething, now, to big a new ane,
                    O' foggage green!
An' bleak December's win's ensuin,
                    Baith snell an' keen!

Thou saw the fields laid bare an' waste,
An' weary winter comin fast,
An' cozie here, beneath the blast,
                    Thou thought to dwell,
Till crash! the cruel coulter past
                    Out thro' thy cell.

That wee bit heap o' leaves an' stibble,
Has cost thee monie a weary nibble!
Now thou's turned out, for a' thy trouble,
                    But house or hald,
To thole the winter's sleety dribble,
                    An' cranreuch cauld!

But Mousie, thou art no thy lane,
In proving foresight may be vain:
The best-laid schemes o' mice an' men
         Gang aft agley,
An' lea'e us nought but grief an' pain,
         For promis'd joy!

Still thou art blest, compared wi' me!
The present only toucheth thee:
But och! I backward cast my e'e,
         On prospects drear!
An' forward, tho' I canna see,
         I guess an' fear!

TO A LOUSE,
ON SEEING ONE ON A LADY'S BONNET AT CHURCH

Composed towards the end of 1785, a year in which the name of Vincenzo Lunardi (whose balloon flights led to a balloon-shaped bonnet being named in his honour) was celebrated in Scotland, it appeared in the Kilmarnock edition. Comprising eight Standard Habbie stanzas, like its companion 'To a Mouse', the poem is an extraordinary poetic act of empathy with a creature cursed for daring to rise above its humble station in life.

Text: H–H I, 152–4.

HA! whare ye gaun, ye crowlin ferlie?
Your impudence protects you sairly,
I canna say but ye strunt rarely
         Owre gauze and lace,
Tho' faith! I fear ye dine but sparely
         On sic a place.

Ye ugly, creepin, blastit wonner,
Detested, shunn'd by saunt an' sinner,
How daur ye set your fit upon her—
         Sae fine a lady!
Gae somewhere else and seek your dinner
         On some poor body.

Swith! in some beggar's hauffet squattle:
There ye may creep, and sprawl, and sprattle,
Wi' ither kindred, jumping cattle,
                    In shoals and nations;
Whare horn nor bane ne'er daur unsettle
                    Your thick plantations.

Now haud you there! ye're out o' sight,
Below the fatt'rils, snug an' tight;
Na, faith ye yet! ye 'll no be right,
                    Till ye've got on it—
The vera tapmost, tow'ring height
                    O' Miss's bonnet.

My sooth! right bauld ye set your nose out,
As plump an' grey as onie grozet:
O for some rank, mercurial rozet,
                    Or fell, red smeddum,
I'd gie ye sic a hearty dose o 't,
                    Wad dress your droddum.

I wad na been surpris'd to spy
You on an auld wife's flainen toy;
Or aiblins some bit duddie boy,
                    On's wyliecoat;
But Miss's fine Lunardi! fye!
                    How daur ye do 't?

O Jenny, dinna toss your head,
An' set your beauties a' abread!
Ye little ken what cursèd speed
                    The blastie 's makin!
Thae winks an' finger-ends, I dread,
                    Are notice takin.

O wad some Power the giftie gie us
To see oursels as ithers see us!
It wad frae monie a blunder free us,
                    An' foolish notion:
What airs in dress an' gait wad lea'e us,
                    An' ev'n devotion!

SCOTCH DRINK

Influenced by Fergusson's 'Caller Water', also in the Standard
Habbie stanza, 'Scotch Drink' was written at Mossgiel towards
the end of 1785 and included in the Kilmarnock edition.

Ferintosh, in the 19th stanza, is a small Ross-shire village on
the Cromarty Firth. In 1690, to compensate Duncan Forbes of
Culloden for damage done to his estate (including the distilleries at Ferintosh) by Jacobites the previous year, the Scottish
parliament granted him exemption from duty on his distilleries
on payment of a fixed annual sum of 400 merks. In 1785
this privilege was withdrawn and Forbes, unhappy with the
original offer of compensation, took his case to the Scottish
Court of Exchequer which, on 29 November 1785, awarded the
sum of £21,580. Forbes was content but Burns lamented the loss
of the privilege, hence his allusion.

Ironically in view of the condemnation of 'Thae curst horse-
leeches o' th' Excise' (penultimate stanza), Burns wrote to
Robert Aiken (8 Oct. 1786) shortly after the publication of
the poem: 'I have been feeling all the various rotations and
movements within, respecting the excise.' (CL, 93) He was
commissioned an Exciseman on 14 July 1788.

Text: H–H I, 19–25.

> Gie him strong drink until he wink,
>   That's sinking in despair;
> An' liquor guid to fire his bluid,
>   That's prest wi' grief an' care:
> There let him bowse, and deep carouse,
>   Wi' bumpers flowing o'er,
> Till he forgets his loves or debts,
>   An' minds his griefs no more.
>   SOLOMON'S PROVERBS, XXXI. 6, 7

LET other poets raise a frácas
'Bout vines, an' wines, an' drucken Bacchus,
An' crabbit names an' stories wrack us,
                An' grate our lug:
I sing the juice Scotch bear can mak us,
                In glass or jug.

O thou, my Muse! guid auld Scotch drink!
Whether thro' wimplin worms thou jink,
Or, richly brown, ream owre the brink,
       In glorious faem,
Inspire me, till I lisp an' wink,
       To sing thy name!

Let husky wheat the haughs adorn,
An' aits set up their awnie horn,
An' pease an' beans, at e'en or morn,
       Perfume the plain:
Leeze me on thee, John Barleycorn,
       Thou king o' grain!

On thee aft Scotland chows her cood,
In souple scones, the wale o' food!
Or tumbling in the boiling flood
       Wi' kail an' beef;
But when thou pours thy strong heart's blood,
       There thou shines chief.

Food fills the wame, an' keeps us livin;
Tho' life 's a gift no worth receivin,
When heavy-dragg'd wi' pine an' grievin;
       But oil'd by thee,
The wheels o' life gae down-hill, scrievin,
       Wi' rattlin glee.

Thou clears the head o' doited Lear,
Thou cheers the heart o' drooping Care;
Thou strings the nerves o' Labour sair,
       At's weary toil;
Thou ev'n brightens dark Despair
       Wi' gloomy smile.

Aft, clad in massy siller weed,
Wi' gentles thou erects thy head;
Yet, humbly kind in time o' need,
       The poor man's wine:
His wee drap parritch, or his bread,
       Thou kitchens fine.

Thou art the life o' public haunts:
But thee, what were our fairs and rants?
Ev'n godly meetings o' the saunts,
                    By thee inspir'd,
When, gaping, they besiege the tents,
                    Are doubly fir'd.

That merry night we get the corn in,
O sweetly, then, thou reams the horn in!
Or reekin on a New-Year mornin
                    In cog or bicker,
An' just a wee drap sp'ritual burn in,
                    An' gusty sucker!

When Vulcan gies his bellows breath,
An' ploughmen gather wi' their graith,
Or rare! to see thee fizz an' freath
                    I' th' lugget caup!
Then Burnewin comes on like death
                    At ev'ry chaup.

Nae mercy, then, for airn or steel:
The brawnie, bainie, ploughman chiel,
Brings hard owrehip, wi' sturdy wheel,
                    The strong forehammer,
Till block an' studdie ring an' reel,
                    Wi' dinsome clamour.

When skirlin weanies see the light,
Thou maks the gossips clatter bright,
How fumbling cuifs their dearies slight;
                    Wae worth the name!
Nae howdie gets a social night,
                    Or plack frae them.

When neebors anger at a plea,
An' just as wud as wud can be,
How easy can the barley-brie
                    Cement the quarrel!
It's aye the cheapest lawyer's fee,
                    To taste the barrel.

Alake! that e'er my Muse has reason,
To wyte her countrymen wi' treason!
But monie daily weet their weason
        Wi' liquors nice,
An' hardly, in a winter season,
          E'er spier her price.

Wae worth that brandy, burnin trash!
Fell source o' monie a pain an' brash!
Twins monie a poor, doylt, drucken hash,
        O' half his days;
An' sends, beside, auld Scotland's cash
          To her warst faes.

Ye Scots, wha wish auld Scotland well!
Ye chief, to you my tale I tell,
Poor, plackless devils like mysel!
        It set you ill,
Wi' bitter, dearthfu' wines to mell,
          Or foreign gill.

May gravels round his blather wrench,
An' gouts torment him, inch by inch,
Wha twists his gruntle wi' a glunch
        O' sour disdain,
Out owre a glass o' whisky-punch
          Wi' honest men!

O Whisky! soul o' plays an' pranks!
Accept a Bardie's gratefu' thanks!
When wanting thee, what tuneless cranks
        Are my poor verses!
Thou comes—they rattle i' their ranks
          At ither's arses!

Thee, Ferintosh! O sadly lost!
Scotland lament frae coast to coast!
Now colic grips, an' barkin hoast
        May kill us a';
For loyal Forbés' chartered boast
          Is taen awa!

Thae curst horse-leeches o' th' Excise,
Wha mak the whisky stells their prize!
Haud up thy han', Deil! ance, twice, thrice!
    There, seize the blinkers!
An' bake them up in brunstane pies
    For poor damn'd drinkers.

Fortune! if thou'll but gie me still
Hale breeks, a scone, an' whisky gill,
An' rowth o' rhyme to rave at will,
    Tak a' the rest,
An' deal't about as thy blind skill
    Directs thee best.

THE TWA DOGS: A TALE

The first poem in the Kilmarnock edition, 'The Twa Dogs',
was listed as complete in Burns's letter (17 Feb. 1786) to John
Richmond: 'I have likewise compleated my Poem on the dogs,
but have not shown it to the world.' (CL, 76.) From this Kinsley
concludes 'it was planned, and probably in part written, before
Richmond left Ayrshire in November 1785' (Kinsley, 1105).
Gilbert Burns said the poem was 'composed after the resolution
of publishing was nearly taken' (Currie III, 385) which would
date it early 1786. Gilbert also provided an anecdotal origin:

> Robert had had a dog, which he called *Luath*, that
> was a great favourite. The dog had been killed [on
> 12 Feb. 1784] by the wanton cruelty of some person
> the night before my father's death. Robert said to
> me, that he should like to confer such immortality as
> he could bestow upon his old friend *Luath*, and that
> he had a great mind to introduce something into the
> book under the title of *Stanzas to the Memory of a quad-
> ruped Friend*, but this plan was given up for the *Tale* as
> it now stands. *Caesar* was merely the creature of the
> poet's imagination, created for the purpose of hold-
> ing chat with his favourite *Luath*. (Currie III, 385–6)

Luath was named by Burns after one of Fingal's dogs in
James Macpherson's *Fingal* (1762) whose authenticity as a
Gaelic translation had been challenged, hence 'made lang

syne – Lord knows how lang'. King Coil is an allusion to
Kyle, the area of Ayrshire in which Burns was born (see the
muse Coila in 'The Vision').

Burns modelled the poem structurally on Fergusson's 'Mutual Complaint of Plainstanes and Causey, in their Mother-
Tongue', a Scots dialogue in octosyllabic couplets between
Edinburgh pavement and street. The poem, however, is in-
ventive rather than derivative; Fergusson's dialogue (between
inanimate objects, not animals) is fanciful whereas Burns's is
deeply felt, and no previous Scots-speaking poetic animals (in
Henryson's *Moral Fables* or Hamilton of Gilbertfield's 'Bonnie
Heck' for example) have the authority of Caesar. To achieve
psychological subtlety Burns reverses expectations by putting
the case for the poor in the mouth of the rich dog, the poor
dog being conditioned into submission by poverty. Luath's
humility looks back to older animal fables, Caesar's political
bite looks forward to Orwell and *Animal Farm*.

Text: H–H I, 9–19.

'Twas in that place o' Scotland's isle
That bears the name of auld King Coil,
Upon a bonie day in June,
When wearing thro' the afternoon,
Twa dogs, that were na thrang at hame,
Forgathered ance upon a time.

The first I'll name, they ca'd him Cæsar,
Was keepit for 'his Honor's' pleasure:
His hair, his size, his mouth, his lugs,
Shew'd he was nane o' Scotland's dogs;
But whalpit some place far abroad,
Whare sailors gang to fish for cod.

His lockèd, letter'd, braw brass collar
Shew'd him the gentleman an' scholar;
But tho' he was o' high degree,
The fient a pride, nae pride had he;
But wad hae spent an hour caressin,
Ev'n wi' a tinkler-gipsy's messin;
At kirk or market, mill or smiddie,
Nae tawted tyke, tho' e'er sae duddie,
But he wad stan't, as glad to see him,
An' stroan't on stanes an' hillocks wi' him.

The tither was a ploughman's collie,
A rhyming, ranting, raving billie,
Wha for his friend an' comrade had him,
And in his freaks had Luath ca'd him,
After some dog in Highland sang,
Was made lang syne—Lord knows how lang.

He was a gash an' faithfu' tyke,
As ever lap a sheugh or dyke.
His honest, sonsie, baws'nt face
Ay gat him friends in ilka place;
His breast was white, his tousie back
Weel clad wi' coat o' glossy black;
His gawsie tail, wi' upward curl,
Hung owre his hurdies wi' a swirl.

Nae doubt but they were fain o' ither,
And unco pack an' thick thegither;
Wi' social nose whyles snuff'd an' snowkit;
Whyles mice an' moudieworts they howkit;
Whyles scour'd awa' in lang excursion,
An' worry'd ither in diversion;
Till tir'd at last wi' monie a farce,
They sat them down upon their arse,
An' there began a lang digression
About the 'lords o' the creation.'

CAESAR
I've aften wonder'd, honest Luath,
What sort o' life poor dogs like you have;
An' when the gentry's life I saw,
What way poor bodies liv'd ava.

Our laird gets in his rackèd rents,
His coals, his kain, an' a' his stents:
He rises when he likes himsel;
His flunkies answer at the bell;
He ca's his coach; he ca's his horse;
He draws a bonie silken purse,
As lang 's my tail, whare, thro' the steeks,
The yellow letter'd Geordie keeks.

Frae morn to e'en it's nought but toiling,
At baking, roasting, frying, boiling;
An' tho' the gentry first are stechin,
Yet ev'n the ha' folk fill their pechan
Wi' sauce, ragouts, an sic like trashtrie,
That's little short o' downright wastrie:
Our whipper-in, wee, blastit wonner,
Poor, worthless elf, it eats a dinner,
Better than onie tenant-man
His Honor has in a' the lan';
An' what poor cot-folk pit their painch in,
I own it's past my comprehension.

LUATH

Trowth, Cæsar, whyles they're fash't eneugh:
A cotter howkin in a sheugh,
Wi' dirty stanes biggin a dyke,
Baring a quarry, an' sic like;
Himsel, a wife, he thus sustains,
A smytrie o' wee duddie weans,
An' nought but his han' darg to keep
Them right an' tight in thack an' rape.

An' when they meet wi' sair disasters,
Like loss o' health or want o' masters,
Ye maist wad think, a wee touch langer,
An' they maun starve o' cauld and hunger:
But how it comes, I never kend yet,
They're maistly wonderfu' contented;
An' buirdly chiels, an' clever hizzies,
Are bred in sic a way as this is.

CAESAR

But then to see how ye 're negleckit,
How huff'd, an' cuff'd, an' disrespeckit!
Lord man, our gentry care as little
For delvers, ditchers, an' sic cattle;
They gang as saucy by poor folk,
As I wad by a stinking brock.

I've notic'd, on our laird's court-day,
(An' monie a time my heart's been wae),

Poor tenant bodies, scant o' cash,
How they maun thole a factor's snash:
He'll stamp an' threaten, curse an' swear
He'll apprehend them, poind their gear;
While they maun staun', wi' aspect humble,
An' hear it a', an' fear an' tremble!

I see how folk live that hae riches;
But surely poor-folk maun be wretches!

LUATH
They're nae sae wretched 's ane wad think:
Tho' constantly on poortith's brink,
They're sae accustom'd wi' the sight,
The view o 't gies them little fright.

Then chance an' fortune are sae guided,
They're ay in less or mair provided;
An' tho' fatigu'd wi' close employment,
A blink o' rest 's a sweet enjoyment.

The dearest comfort o' their lives,
Their grushie weans an' faithfu' wives;
The prattling things are just their pride,
That sweetens a' their fire-side.

An' whyles twalpennie worth o' nappy
Can mak the bodies unco happy:
They lay aside their private cares,
To mind the Kirk and State affairs;
They'll talk o' patronage an' priests,
Wi' kindling fury i' their breasts,
Or tell what new taxation's comin,
An' ferlie at the folk in Lon'on.

As bleak-fac'd Hallowmass returns,
They get the jovial, ranting kirns,
When rural life, of ev'ry station,
Unite in common recreation;
Love blinks, Wit slaps, an' social Mirth
Forgets there 's Care upo' the earth.

That merry day the year begins,
They bar the door on frosty win's;
The nappy reeks wi' mantling ream,
An' sheds a heart-inspiring steam;
The luntin pipe, an' sneeshin mill,
Are handed round wi' right guid will;
The cantie auld folks crackin crouse,
The young anes ranting thro' the house—
My heart has been sae fain to see them,
That I for joy hae barkit wi' them.

Still it's owre true that ye hae said
Sic game is now owre aften play'd;
There's monie a creditable stock
O' decent, honest, fawsont folk,
Are riven out baith root an' branch,
Some rascal's pridefu' greed to quench,
Wha thinks to knit himsel the faster
In favor wi' some gentle master,
Wha, aiblins thrang a parliamentin',
For Britain's guid his saul indentin'—

CAESAR
Haith, lad, ye little ken about it:
For Britain's guid! guid faith! I doubt it.
Say rather, gaun as Premiers lead him:
An' saying aye or no 's they bid him:
At operas an' plays parading,
Mortgaging, gambling, masquerading:
Or maybe, in a frolic daft,
To Hague or Calais taks a waft,
To mak a tour an' tak a whirl,
To learn *bon ton*, an' see the worl'.

There, at Vienna or Versailles,
He rives his father's auld entails;
Or by Madrid he taks the rout,
To thrum guitars an' fecht wi' nowt;
Or down Italian vista startles,
Whore-hunting amang groves o' myrtles
Then bowses drumlie German-water,

To mak himsel look fair an' fatter,
An' clear the consequential sorrows,
Love-gifts of Carnival signoras.

   For Britain's guid! for her destruction!
Wi' dissipation, feud an' faction.

LUATH
   Hech man! dear sirs! is that the gate
They waste sae monie a braw estate!
Are we sae foughten an' harass'd
For gear ta gang that gate at last?

   O would they stay aback frae courts,
An' please themsels wi' countra sports,
It wad for ev'ry ane be better,
The laird, the tenant, an' the cotter!
For thae frank, rantin, ramblin billies,
Fient haet o' them 's ill-hearted fellows:
Except for breakin o' their timmer,
Or speakin lightly o' their limmer,
Or shootin of a hare or moor-cock,
The ne'er-a-bit they're ill to poor folk.

   But will ye tell me, master Cæsar:
Sure great folk's life's a life o' pleasure?
Nae cauld nor hunger e'er can steer them,
The vera thought o 't need na fear them.

CAESAR
   Lord, man, were ye but whyles whare I am,
The gentles, ye wad ne'er envý 'em!

   It's true, they need na starve or sweat,
Thro' winter's cauld, or simmer's heat;
They've nae sair wark to craze their banes,
An' fill auld-age wi' grips an' granes:
But human bodies are sic fools,
For a' their colleges an' schools,
That when nae real ills perplex them,
They mak enow themsels to vex them;

An' ay the less they hae to sturt them,
In like proportion, less will hurt them.

A countra fellow at the pleugh,
His acre's till'd, he's right eneugh;
A countra girl at her wheel,
Her dizzen's done, she 's unco weel;
But gentlemen, an' ladies warst,
Wi' ev'n down want o' wark are curst:
They loiter, lounging, lank an' lazy;
Tho' deil-haet ails them, yet uneasy:
Their days insipid, dull an' tasteless;
Their nights unquiet, lang an' restless.

An' ev'n their sports, their balls an' races,
Their galloping through public places,
There's sic parade, sic pomp an' art,
The joy can scarcely reach the heart.

The men cast out in party-matches,
Then sowther a' in deep debauches;
Ae night they're mad wi' drink an' whoring,
Niest day their life is past enduring.

The ladies arm-in-arm in clusters,
As great an' gracious a' as sisters;
But hear their absent thoughts o' ither,
They're a' run deils an' jads thegither.
Whyles, owre the wee bit cup an' platie,
They sip the scandal-potion pretty;
Or lee-lang nights, wi' crabbit leuks
Pore owre the devil's pictur'd beuks;
Stake on a chance a farmer's stackyard,
An' cheat like onie unhang'd blackguard.

There's some exceptions, man an' woman;
But this is Gentry's life in common.

By this, the sun was out o' sight,
An' darker gloamin brought the night;
The bum-clock humm'd wi' lazy drone;
The kye stood rowtin i' the loan;

When up they gat, an' shook their lugs,
Rejoic'd they were na *men*, but *dogs*;
An' each took aff his several way,
Resolv'd to meet some ither day.

TO JAMES SMITH

Written early in 1786 when Burns had decided to publish a volume of verse ('To try my fate in guid, black prent') and first published in the Kilmarnock edition, the epistle celebrates Smith who with Burns and John Richmond formed a boozy and bawdy boozy bachelor trio in Mauchline: 'The hairum-scairum, ram-stam boys,/The rattling squad'. Though some of the English stanzas rely on rather feeble personifications, the strongly colloquial Scots stanzas impressively affirm Burns's human presence. 'Where', asked Josiah Walker in his *Account of the Life and Character of Robert Burns* **(1811), 'can we find a more exhilarating enumeration of the enjoyments of youth, contrasted with their successive extinction as age advances, than in "the Epistle to J. S[mith]"?' (CH, 223)**

Dempster, in the epistle, is George Dempster, Whig MP for Forfar Burghs 1761–90 and agricultural improver. William Pitt, Tory Prime Minister from 1783, was born in the same year as Burns who was critical of his contemporary.

Text: H–H I, 59–67.

> *Friendship, mysterious cement of the soul!*
> *Sweet'ner of Life, and solder of Society!*
> *I owe thee much—*
>   BLAIR

Dear Smith, the slee'st, pawkie thief,
That e'er attempted stealth or rief!
Ye surely hae some warlock-breef
                    Owre human hearts;
For ne'er a bosom yet was prief
                    Against your arts.

For me, I swear by sun an' moon,
And ev'ry star that blinks aboon,
Ye 've cost me twenty pair o' shoon,
        Just gaun to see you;
And ev'ry ither pair that's done,
        Mair taen I'm wi' you.

That auld, capricious carlin, Nature,
To mak amends for scrimpit stature,
She 's turn'd you off, a human-creature
        On her first plan;
And in her freaks, on ev'ry feature
        She's wrote the Man.

Just now I've taen the fit o' rhyme,
My barmie noddle's working prime,
My fancy yerkit up sublime,
        Wi' hasty summon:
Hae ye a leisure-moment's time
        To hear what's comin?

Some rhyme a neebor's name to lash;
Some rhyme (vain thought!) for needfu' cash;
Some rhyme to court the countra clash,
        An' raise a din;
For me, an aim I never fash;
        I rhyme for fun.

The star that rules my luckless lot,
Has fated me the russet coat,
An' damn'd my fortune to the groat;
        But, in requit,
Has blest me with a random-shot
        O' countra wit.

This while my notion's taen a sklent,
To try my fate in guid, black prent;
But still the mair I'm that way bent,
        Something cries, 'Hoolie!
I red you, honest man, tak tent!
        Ye'll shaw your folly:

'There's ither poets, much your betters,
Far seen in Greek, deep men o' letters,
Hae thought they had ensur'd their debtors,
        A' future ages;
Now moths deform, in shapeless tatters,
        Their unknown pages.'

Then farewell hopes o' laurel-boughs
To garland my poetic brows!
Henceforth I'll rove where busy ploughs
        Are whistling thrang;
An' teach the lanely heights an' howes
        My rustic sang.

I'll wander on, wi' tentless heed
How never-halting moments speed,
Till Fate shall snap the brittle thread;
        Then, all unknown,
I'll lay me with th' inglorious dead,
        Forgot and gone!

But why o' death begin a tale?
Just now we 're living sound an' hale;
Then top and maintop crowd the sail,
        Heave Care o'er-side!
And large, before Enjoyment's gale,
        Let's tak the tide.

This life, sae far 's I understand,
Is a' enchanted fairy-land,
Where Pleasure is the magic-wand,
        That, wielded right,
Maks hours like minutes, hand in hand,
        Dance by fu' light.

The magic-wand then let us wield;
For, ance that five-an'-forty 's speel'd,
See, crazy, weary, joyless Eild,
        Wi' wrinkl'd face,
Comes hostin, hirplin owre the field,
        Wi' creepin pace.

When ance life's day draws near the gloamin,
Then fareweel vacant, careless roamin;
An' farewell chearfu' tankards foamin,
        An' social noise:
An' fareweel dear, deluding Woman,
          The joy of joys!

O Life! how pleasant, in thy morning,
Young Fancy's rays the hills adorning!
Cold-pausing Caution's lesson scorning,
        We frisk away,
Like school-boys, at th' expected warning,
        To joy an' play.

We wander there, we wander here,
We eye the rose upon the brier,
Unmindful that the thorn is near,
        Among the leaves;
And tho' the puny wound appear,
        Short while it grieves.

Some, lucky, find a flow'ry spot,
For which they never toil'd nor swat;
They drink the sweet and eat the fat,
        But care or pain;
And haply eye the barren hut
        With high disdain.

With steady aim, some Fortune chase;
Keen Hope does ev'ry sinew brace;
Thro' fair, thro' foul, they urge the race,
        And seize the prey:
Then cannie, in some cozie place,
        They close the day.

And others, like your humble servan',
Poor wights! nae rules nor roads observin,
To right or left eternal swervin,
        They zig-zag on;
Till, curst with age, obscure an' starvin,
        They aften groan.

Alas! what bitter toil an' straining—
But truce with peevish, poor complaining!
Is Fortune's fickle *Luna* waning?
        E'en let her gang!
Beneath what light she has remaining,
        Let's sing our sang.

My pen I here fling to the door,
And kneel, ye Pow'rs! and warm implore,
'Tho' I should wander *Terra* o'er,
        In all her climes,
Grant me but this, I ask no more,
        Ay rowth o' rhymes.

'Gie dreeping roasts to countra lairds,
Till icicles hing frae their beards;
Gie fine braw claes to fine life-guards
        And maids of honor;
And yill an' whisky gie to cairds,
        Until they sconner.

'A title, Dempster merits it;
A garter gie to Willie Pitt;
Gie wealth to some be-ledger'd cit,
        In cent. per cent.;
But give me real, sterling wit,
        And I'm content

'While ye are pleas'd to keep me hale,
I'll sit down o'er my scanty meal,
Be 't water-brose or muslin-kail,
        Wi' cheerfu' face,
As lang 's the Muses dinna fail
        To say the grace.'

An anxious e'e I never throws
Behint my lug, or by my nose;
I jouk beneath Misfortune's blows
        As weel's I may;
Sworn foe to sorrow, care, and prose,
        I rhyme away.

O ye douce folk that live by rule,
Grave, tideless-blooded, calm an' cool,
Compar'd wi' you—O fool! fool! fool!
                    How much unlike!
Your hearts are just a standing pool,
                    Your lives a dyke!

Nae hair-brained, sentimental traces
In your unletter'd, nameless faces!
In *arioso* trills and graces
                    Ye never stray;
But *gravissimo*, solemn basses
                    Ye hum away.

Ye are sae grave, nae doubt ye 're wise;
Nae ferly tho ye do despise
The hairum-scairum, ram-stam boys,
                    The rattling squad:
I see ye upward cast your eyes—
                    Ye ken the road!

Whilst I—but I shall haud me there,
Wi' you I'll scarce gang onie where—
Then, Jamie, I shall say nae mair,
                    But quat my sang,
Content wi' you to mak a pair,
                    Whare'er I gang.

POOR MAILIE'S ELEGY

Probably while arranging the contents of the Kilmarnock edition in 1786 Burns wrote a comic elegy, in the Standard Habbie stanza, to accompany 'The Death and Dying Words of Poor Mailie'.
    Text: H–H I, 56–8.

LAMENT in rhyme, lament in prose,
Wi' saut tears tricklin down your nose;
Our Bardie's fate is at a close,
                    Past a' remead!
The last, sad cape-stane of his woes;
                    Poor Mailie's dead!

It 's no the loss of warl's gear,
That could sae bitter draw the tear,
Or mak our Bardie, dowie, wear
                    The mourning weed:
He's lost a friend an' neebor dear
                    In Mailie dead.

Thro' a' the toun she trotted by him;
A lang half-mile she could descry him;
Wi' kindly bleat, when she did spy him,
                    She ran wi' speed:
A friend mair faithfu' ne'er cam nigh him,
                    Than Mailie dead.

I wat she was a sheep o' sense,
An' could behave hersel wi' mense:
I'll say 't, she never brak a fence,
                    Thro' thievish greed.
Our Bardie, lanely, keeps the spence
                    Sin' Mailie's dead.

Or, if he wanders up the howe,
Her livin image in her yowe
Comes bleatin till him, owre the knowe,
                    For bits o' bread;
An' down the briny pearls rowe
                    For Mailie dead.

She was nae get o' moorlan tips,
Wi' tawted ket, an' hairy hips;
For her forbears were brought in ships,
                    Frae 'yont the Tweed;
A bonier fleesh ne'er cross'd the clips
                    Than Mailie's dead.

Wae worth the man wha first did shape
That vile, wanchancie thing—a rape!
It maks guid fellows girn an' gape,
                    Wi' chokin dread;
An' Robin's bonnet wave wi' crape
                    For Mailie dead.

O a' ye bards on bonie Doon!
An' wha on Ayr your chanters tune!
Come, join the melancholious croon
                    O' Robin's reed!
His heart will never get aboon!
                    His Mailie's dead!

WILL YE GO TO THE INDIES, MY MARY

Entered in the second Commonplace Book and collected by
Currie in 1800, this celebration of 'Highland Mary' Campbell
(1763–86) was sent to George Thomson on 27 October 1792 to
suit the tune 'Ewe-Bughts Marion':

> In my very early years, when I was thinking of going
> to the West Indies, I took the following farewell of
> a dear girl . . . You must know, that all my earlier
> love-songs were the breathings of ardent Passion . . .
> (CL, 619)

On the rebound of rejection from Jean Armour, Burns seemingly sought comfort in the arms of Mary from whom he parted
with a promise on 14 May 1786:

> After a pretty long tract of the most ardent recip-
> rocal attachment, we met by appointment, on the
> second Sunday of May, in a sequestered spot by the
> banks of Ayr, where we spent the day in taking a
> farewell, before she should embark for the West
> Highlands, to arrange matters among her friends
> for our projected change of life. (NSS, 72)

The obvious implication of the song is that Burns and Mary
intended to emigrate together to Jamaica.
    Text: H–H IV, 15–16.

WILL ye go to the Indies, my Mary,
　And leave auld Scotia's shore?
Will ye go to the Indies, my Mary,
　Across th' Atlantic roar?

O, sweet grows the lime and the orange,
　And the apple on the pine;
But a' the charms o' the Indies
　Can never equal thine.

I hae sworn by the Heavens to my Mary,
　I hae sworn by the Heavens to be true,
And sae may the Heavens forget me,
　When I forget my vow!

O, plight me your faith, my Mary,
　And plight me your lily-white hand!
O, plight me your faith, my Mary,
　Before I leave Scotia's strand!

We hae plighted our troth, my Mary,
　In mutual affection to join;
And curst be the cause that shall part us!
　The hour and the moment o' time!

ADDRESS TO THE UNCO GUID, OR THE RIGIDLY RIGHTEOUS

First published in the first Edinburgh edition, its absence from the Kilmarnock edition has led to speculation that it was composed after Burns's experience in doing penance for the Armour affair in July–August 1786. Similar sentiments, though, were expressed in the first Commonplace Book in March 1784: 'I say, any man who can thus think, will scan the failings, nay the faults and crimes of mankind around him, with a brother's eye.'

Through his friendship with the Mauchline lawyer Gavin Hamilton, Burns developed an interest in forensic argument and put his knowledge to poetic use in the Address. From the first phrase, 'O ye wha are sae guid yoursel', the poem is confrontational, constructed as a spirited speech for the defence

of common humanity before prejudiced judges representing
the rigidly righteous. By the end of the poem the reader is persuaded that Burns has made his case, that any decently human
verdict on him and his kind must absolve them of guilt.

Text: H–H I, 217–20.

> *My Son, these maxims make a rule,*
>   *An' lump them ay thegither:*
> *The Rigid Righteous is a fool,*
>   *The Rigid Wise anither;*
> *The cleanest corn that e'er was dight*
>   *May hae some pyles o' caff in;*
> *So ne'er a fellow-creature slight*
>   *For random fits o' daffin.*
>
>   SOLOMON (*Eccles.* vii. 16)

O YE, wha are sae guid yoursel,
  Sae pious and sae holy,
Ye've nought to do but mark and tell
  Your neebours' fauts and folly;
Whase life is like a weel-gaun mill,
  Supplied wi' store o' water;
The heapet happer's ebbing still,
  An' still the clap plays clatter!

Hear me, ye venerable core,
  As counsel for poor mortals
That frequent pass douce Wisdom's door
  For glaikit Folly's portals:
I for their thoughtless, careless sakes
  Would here propone defences—
Their donsie tricks, their black mistakes,
  Their failings and mischances.

Ye see your state wi' theirs compared,
  And shudder at the niffer;
But cast a moment's fair regard,
  What makes the mighty differ?
Discount what scant occasion gave;
  That purity ye pride in;
And (what 's aft mair than a' the lave)
  Your better art o' hidin.

Think, when your castigated pulse
   Gies now and then a wallop,
What ragings must his veins convulse,
   That still eternal gallop!
Wi' wind and tide fair i' your tail,
   Right on ye scud your sea-way;
But in the teeth o' baith to sail,
   It maks an unco lee-way.

See Social-life and Glee sit down
   All joyous and unthinking,
Till, quite transmugrify'd, they're grown
   Debauchery and Drinking:
O, would they stay to calculate,
   Th' eternal consequences,
Or—your more dreaded hell to state—
   Damnation of expenses!

Ye high, exalted, virtuous dames,
   Tied up in godly laces,
Before ye gie poor Frailty names,
   Suppose a change o' cases:
A dear-lov'd lad, convenience snug,
   A treach'rous inclination—
But, let me whisper i' your lug,
   Ye're aiblins nae temptation.

Then gently scan your brother man,
   Still gentler sister woman;
Tho' they may gang a kennin wrang,
   To step aside is human:
One point must still be greatly dark,
   The moving *why* they do it;
And just as lamely can ye mark
   How far perhaps they rue it.

Who made the heart, 'tis He alone
   Decidedly can try us:
He knows each chord, its various tone,
   Each spring, its various bias:

Then at the balance let's be mute,
    We never can adjust it;
What 's done we partly may compute,
But know not what 's resisted.

EPITAPH ON A WAG IN MAUCHLINE

**Dated 1786 by Kinsley (Kinsley, 1190) and first printed in
Thomas Stewart's *Poems ascribed to Robert Burns* (1801) the
epitaph alludes to either James Smith or Clockie Brown.**
    Text: H–H II, 268.

Lament him, Mauchline husbands a',
    He aften did assist ye;
For had ye staid hale weeks awa',
    Your wives they ne'er had missed ye!

Ye Mauchline bairns, as on ye pass
    To school in bands thegither,
O, tread ye lightly on his grass—
    Perhaps he was your father!

THE BRIGS OF AYR

**Written in the autumn of 1786 when the construction of the
new bridge of Ayr was underway, the poem was sent to John
Ballantine on 27 September 1786 and published in the first
Edinburgh edition. Ballantine (1743–1812), the dedicatee and
Dean of Guild in Ayr, was prominent in promoting the building
of a new bridge over the Ayr in 1786 as the old bridge, dating
from the fifteenth century, was regarded as unsafe. A design for
the new bridge by Robert Adam was paid for but, according
to local tradition, the mason Alexander Steven, who built
the bridge, worked from his own plans. Interestingly, the
prophecy of the Auld Brig in Burns's poem – 'I'll be a brig
when ye're a shapeless cairn!' – was fulfilled in 1877 when the
New Brig collapsed after flood-damage to the arch at the
south end. It was replaced by the present bridge, 1881–2, and,
in 1910, the Auld Brig was restored.
    References in the poem are clarified as follows: Simpson's,**

inn at the north end of the Auld Brig; Dungeon-Clock, clock on the steeple of Ayr Tolbooth (or town jail) in the Sandgate (building removed in 1826); Wallace Tower, tower at the corner of High Street and Mill Vennel, replaced by present tower in 1834; 'ane Adams', architect Robert Adam; Ducat stream, ancient ford on the river Ayr; Ratton-Key, a quay (now gone) of Ayr harbour; M'Lauchlan, James McLauchlan of Inverary who came to Ayrshire in a fencible regiment; Courage, a tribute to Colonel Hugh Montgomerie, MP for Ayrshire 1784–9; Benevolence, tribute to Mrs Catherine Stewart of Stair; Learning and Worth, tribute to Professor Dugald Stewart who first met Burns in his modest mansion at Catrine.

Text: H-HI, 200–9.

INSCRIBED TO JOHN BALLANTINE, ESQ., AYR

The simple Bard, rough at the rustic plough,
Learning his tuneful trade from ev'ry bough
(The chanting linnet, or the mellow thrush,
Hailing the setting sun, sweet, in the green thorn
    bush;
The soaring lark, the perching red-breast shrill,
Or deep-ton'd plovers grey, wild-whistling o'er the
    hill):
Shall he—nurst in the peasant's lowly shed,
To hardy independence bravely bred,
By early poverty to hardship steel'd,
And train'd to arms in stern misfortune's field—
Shall he be guilty of their hireling crimes,
The servile, mercenary Swiss of rhymes?
Or labour hard the panegyric close,
With all the venal soul of dedicating prose?
No! though his artless strains he rudely sings,
And throws his hand uncouthly o'er the strings,
He glows with all the spirit of the bard,
Fame, honest fame, his great, his dear reward.
Still, if some patron's gen'rous care he trace,
Skill'd in the secret to bestow with grace;
When Ballantine befriends his humble name,
And hands the rustic stranger up to fame,
With heartfelt throes his grateful bosom swells:
The godlike bliss, to give, alone excels.

'Twas when the stacks get on their winter hap,
And thack and rape secure the toil-won crap;
Potatoe-bings are snuggèd up frae skaith
O' coming winter's biting, frosty breath;
The bees, rejoicing o'er their summer toils—
Unnumber'd buds' an' flowers' delicious spoils,
Seal'd up with frugal care in massive waxen piles—
Are doom'd by man, that tyrant o'er the weak,
The death o' devils smoor'd wi' brimstone reek:
The thundering guns are heard on ev'ry side,
The wounded coveys, reeling, scatter wide;
The feather'd field-mates, bound by Nature's tie,
Sires, mothers, children, in one carnage lie:
(What warm, poetic heart but inly bleeds,
And execrates man's savage, ruthless deeds!)
Nae mair the flower in field or meadow springs;
Nae mair the grove with airy concert rings,
Except perhaps the robin's whistling glee,
Proud o' the height o' some bit half-lang tree;
The hoary morns precede the sunny days;
Mild, calm, serene, widespreads the noontide
        blaze,
While thick the gossamour waves wanton in the
        rays.

'Twas in that season, when a simple Bard,
Unknown and poor—simplicity's reward!—
Ae night, within the ancient brugh of Ayr,
By whim inspir'd, or haply prest wi' care,
He left his bed, and took his wayward route,
And down by Simpson's wheel'd the left about
(Whether impell'd by all-directing Fate,
To witness what I after shall narrate;
Or whether, rapt in meditation high,
He wander'd forth, he knew not where nor why):
The drowsy Dungeon-Clock had number'd two,
And Wallace Tower had sworn the fact was true;
The tide-swoln Firth, with sullen-sounding roar,
Through the still night dash'd hoarse along the
        shore;
All else was hush'd as Nature's closèd e'e;
The silent moon shone high o'er tower and tree;

The chilly frost, beneath the silver beam,
Crept, gently-crusting, o'er the glittering stream.

    When, lo! on either hand the list'ning Bard,
The clanging sugh of whistling wings is heard;
Two dusky forms dart thro' the midnight air,
Swift as the gos drives on the wheeling hare;
Ane on th' Auld Brig his airy shape uprears,
The ither flutters o'er the rising piers:
Our warlock rhymer instantly descried
The Sprites that owre the Brigs of Ayr preside.
(That bards are second-sighted is nae joke,
And ken the lingo of the sp'ritual folk;
Fays, spunkies, kelpies, a', they can explain
    them,
And ev'n the vera deils they brawly ken them).
Auld Brig appear'd of ancient Pictish race,
The vera wrinkles Gothic in his face;
He seem'd as he wi' Time had warstl'd lang,
Yet, teughly doure, he bade an unco bang.
New Brig was buskit in a braw new coat,
That he, at Lon'on, frae ane Adams got;
In's hand five taper staves as smooth's a
    bead,
Wi' virls an' whirlygigums at the head.
The Goth was stalking round with anxious
    search,
Spying the time-worn flaws in ev'ry arch.
It chanc'd his new-come neebor took his e'e,
And e'en a vex'd and angry heart had he!
Wi' thieveless sneer to see his modish mien,
He, down the water, gies him this guid-een:—

AULD BRIG
  'I doubt na, frien', ye'll think ye're nae sheep
    shank,
Ance ye were streekit owre frae bank to bank!
But gin ye be a brig as auld as me—
Tho' faith, that date, I doubt, ye'll never see—
There'll be, if that day come, I 'll wad a boddle,
Some fewer whigmeleeries in your noddle.'

NEW BRIG

'Auld Vandal! ye but show your little mense,
Just much about it wi' your scanty sense:
Will your poor, narrow foot-path of a street,
Where twa wheel-barrows tremble when they meet,
Your ruin'd, formless bulk o' stane an' lime,
Compare wi' bonie brigs o' modern time?
There's men of taste would tak the Ducat stream,
Tho' they should cast the vera sark and swim,
E'er they would grate their feelings wi' the view
O' sic an ugly, Gothic hulk as you.'

AULD BRIG

'Conceited gowk! puff'd up wi' windy pride!
This monie a year I 've stood the flood an' tide;
And tho' wi' crazy eild I'm sair forfairn,
I'll be a brig when ye 're a shapeless cairn!
As yet ye little ken about the matter,
But twa-three winters will inform ye better.
When heavy, dark, continued, a'-day rains
Wi' deepening deluges o'erflow the plains;
When from the hills where springs the brawling Coil,
Or stately Lugar's mossy fountains boil,
Or where the Greenock winds his moorland course,
Or haunted Garpal draws his feeble source,
Arous'd by blustering winds an' spotting thowes,
In monie a torrent down the snaw-broo rowes;
While crashing ice, borne on the roaring speat,
Sweeps dams, an' mills, an' brigs, a' to the gate;
And from Glenbuck down to the Ratton-Key
Auld Ayr is just one lengthen'd, tumbling sea—
Then down ye'll hurl (deil nor ye never rise!),
And dash the gumlie jaups up to the pouring skies!
A lesson sadly teaching, to your cost,
That Architecture's noble art is lost!'

NEW BRIG

'Fine architecture, trowth, I needs must say't o't,
The Lord be thankit that we've tint the gate o't!
Gaunt, ghastly, ghaist-alluring edifices,
Hanging with threat'ning jut, like precipices;

O'er-arching, mouldy, gloom-inspiring coves,
Supporting roofs fantastic—stony groves;
Windows and doors in nameless sculptures drest,
With order, symmetry, or taste unblest;
Forms like some bedlam statuary's dream,
The craz'd creations of misguided whim;
Forms might be worshipp'd on the bended knee,
And still the second dread Command be free:
Their likeness is not found on earth, in air, or sea!
Mansions that would disgrace the building taste
Of any mason reptile, bird or beast,
Fit only for a doited monkish race,
Or frosty maids forsworn the dear embrace,
Or cuifs of later times, wha held the notion,
That sullen gloom was sterling true devotion:
Fancies that our guid brugh denies protection,
And soon may they expire, unblest with resur-
     rection!'

AULD BRIG

'O ye, my dear-remember'd, ancient yealings,
Were ye but here to share my wounded feelings!
Ye worthy proveses, an' monie a bailie,
Wha in the paths o' righteousness did toil ay;
Ye dainty deacons, an' ye douce conveeners,
To whom our moderns are but causey cleaners;
Ye godly councils, wha hae blest this town;
Ye godly brethren o' the sacred gown,
Wha meekly gie your hurdies to the smiters;
And (what would now be strange), ye godly
     Writers;
A' ye douce folk I've borne aboon the broo,
Were ye but here, what would ye say or do!
How would your spirits groan in deep vexation
To see each melancholy alteration;
And, agonising, curse the time and place
When ye begat the base degen'rate race!
Nae langer rev'rend men, their country's glory,
In plain braid Scots hold forth a plain, braid story;
Nae langer thrifty citizens, an' douce,
Meet owre a pint or in the council-house:
But staumrel, corky-headed, graceless gentry,

The herryment and ruin of the country;
Men three-parts made by tailors and by barbers,
Wha waste your weel-hain'd gear on damn'd
    New Brigs and harbours!'

NEW BRIG

 'Now haud you there! for faith ye've said enough,
And muckle mair than ye can mak to through.
As for your priesthood, I shall say but little,
Corbies and clergy are a shot right kittle:
But, under favour o' your langer beard,
Abuse o' magistrates might weel be spar'd;
To liken them to your auld-warld squad,
I must needs say, comparisons are odd.
In Ayr, wag-wits nae mair can hae a handle
To mouth 'a Citizen,' a term o' scandal;
Nae mair the council waddles down the street,
In all the pomp of ignorant conceit;
Men wha grew wise priggin owre hops an' raisins,
Or gather'd lib'ral views in bonds and seisins;
If haply Knowledge, on a random tramp,
Had shor'd them with a glimmer of his lamp,
And would to common-sense for once betray'd them,
Plain, dull stupidity stept kindly in to aid them.'

  What farther clish-ma-claver might been said,
What bloody wars, if Sprites had blood to shed,
No man can tell; but, all before their sight,
A fairy train appear'd in order bright:
Adown the glittering stream they featly danc'd;
Bright to the moon their various dresses glanc'd;
They footed o'er the wat'ry glass so neat,
The infant ice scarce bent beneath their feet;
While arts of minstrelsy among them rung,
And soul-ennobling Bards heroic ditties sung.

  O, had M'Lauchlan, thairm-inspiring sage,
Been there to hear this heavenly band engage,
When thro' his dear strathspeys they bore with
    HIghland rage;

Or when they struck old Scotia's melting airs,
The lover's raptured joys or bleeding cares;
How would his Highland lug been nobler fir'd,
And ev'n his matchless hand with finer touch
    inspir'd!
No guess could tell what instrument appear'd,
But all the soul of Music's self was heard;
Harmonious concert rung in every part,
While simple melody pour'd moving on the heart.

  The Genius of the Stream in front appears,
A venerable chief advanc'd in years;
His hoary head with water-lilies crown'd,
His manly leg with garter-tangle bound.
Next came the loveliest pair in all the ring,
Sweet Female Beauty hand in hand with Spring;
Then, crown'd with flow'ry hay, came Rural
    Joy,
And Summer, with his fervid-beaming eye;
All-cheering Plenty, with her flowing horn,
Led yellow Autumn wreath'd with nodding
    corn;
Then Winter's time-bleach'd locks did hoary
    show,
By Hospitality, with cloudless brow.
Next follow'd Courage, with his martial stride,
From where the Feal wild-woody coverts hide;
Benevolence, with mild, benignant air,
A female form, came from the towers of Stair;
Learning and Worth in equal measures trode
From simple Catrine, their long-lov'd abode;
Last, white-rob'd Peace, crown'd with a hazel
    wreath,
To rustic Agriculture did bequeath
The broken, iron instruments of death:
At sight of whom our Sprites forgat their kindling
    wrath.

EXTEMPORE VERSES ON DINING WITH
LORD DAER

Written on 25 October 1786 at Mossgiel two days after a visit
to Dugald Stewart's modest country mansion at Catrine, these
lines were first published as a pamphlet in 1799. Dugald Stewart
('good Stewart') recalled:

> The first time I saw Robert Burns, was on the 23rd
> of October 1786, when he dined at my house in
> Ayrshire, together with our common friend Mr John
> Mackenzie, surgeon in Mauchline, to whom I am
> indebted for the pleasure of his acquaintance . . .
> My excellent and much lamented friend, the late
> Basil, Lord Daer, happened to arrive at Catrine the
> same day, and by the kindness and frankness of his
> manners, left an impression on the mind of the Poet,
> which never was effaced. (Currie I, 133)

Basil William Douglas-Hamilton, Lord Daer (1763–94), was the
second son of the 4th Earl of Selkirk. Libertarian by temperament (he lived to acclaim the French Revolution and died in
France), he was from 1786 manager of the family estates in
Kirkcudbright and Wigtown. 'Scotia's sacred Demosthenes' is
possibly a reference to Dr Hugh Blair.
    Text: H–H II, 49–51.

THIS wot ye all whom it concerns:
I, Rhymer Rab, *alías* Burns,
              October twenty-third,
A ne'er-to-be-forgotten day,
Sae far I sprachl'd up the brae
              I dinner'd wi' a Lord.

I've been at drucken Writers' feasts,
Nay, been bitch-fou 'mang godly Priests—
              Wi' rev'rence be it spoken!—
I 've even join'd the honor'd jorum,
When mighty Squireships o' the Quorum
              Their hydra drouth did sloken.

But wi' a Lord!—stand out my shin!
A Lord, a Peer, an Earl's son!—
   Up higher yet, my bonnet!
An' sic a Lord!—lang Scotch ell twa
Our Peerage he looks o'er them a',
   As I look o'er my sonnet.

But O, for Hogarth's magic pow'r
To show Sir Bardie's willyart glow'r,
   An' how he star'd an' stammer'd,
When, goavin's he'd been led wi' branks,
An' stumpin on his ploughman shanks,
   He in the parlour hammer'd!

To meet good Stewart little pain is,
Or Scotia's sacred Demosthénes:
   Thinks I: 'They are but men'!
But 'Burns'!—'My Lord'!—Good God! I doited,
My knees on ane anither knoited
   As faultering I gaed ben.

I sidling shelter'd in a neuk,
An' at his Lordship staw a leuk,
   Like some portentous omen:
Except good sense and social glee
An' (what surpris'd me) modesty,
   I markèd nought uncommon.

I watch'd the symptoms o' the Great—
The gentle pride, the lordly state,
   The arrogant assuming:
The fient a pride, nae pride had he,
Nor sauce, nor state, that I could see,
   Mair than an honest ploughman!

Then from his Lordship I shall learn
Henceforth to meet with unconcern
   One rank as well's another;
Nae honest, worthy man need care
To meet with noble youthfu' Daer,
   For he but meets a brother.

TO A HAGGIS

**Written in Edinburgh then published in the *Caledonian Mercury*
(19 Dec. 1786) and *Scots Magazine* (Jan. 1787) – 'apparently the
first of his poems to be published in a periodical' (Kinsley,
1221) – it was collected in the first Edinburgh edition. It
is influenced by Fergusson's 'Caller Oysters', also written in
the Standard Habbie stanza. A delicacy in Burns's day, haggis
is now a Scottish national dish, owing its popularity to this
poem which is recited when the haggis is served at annual
Burns Suppers.**
Text: H–H I, 237–9.

> FAIR fa' your honest, sonsie face,
> Great chieftain o' the puddin-race!
> Aboon them a' ye tak your place,
>   Painch, tripe, or thairm:
> Weel are ye wordy of a grace
>   As lang 's my arm.
>
> The groaning trencher there ye fill,
> Your hurdies like a distant hill,
> Your pin wad help to mend a mill
>   In time o' need,
> While thro' your pores the dews distil
>   Like amber bead.
>
> His knife see rustic Labour dight,
> An' cut ye up wi' ready slight,
> Trenching your gushing entrails bright,
>   Like onie ditch;
> And then, O what a glorious sight,
>   Warm-reekin, rich!
>
> Then, horn for horn, they stretch an' strive:
> Deil tak the hindmost, on they drive,
> Till a' their weel-swall'd kytes belyve
>   Are bent like drums;
> Then auld Guidman, maist like to rive,
>   'Bethankit!' hums.

Is there that owre his French *ragout*,
Or *olio* that wad staw a sow,
Or *fricassee* wad mak her spew
        Wi' perfect sconner,
Looks down wi' sneering, scornfu' view
        On sic a dinner?

Poor devil! see him owre his trash,
As feckless as a wither'd rash,
His spindle shank a guid whip-lash.
        His nieve a nit;
Thro' bluidy flood or field to dash,
        O how unfit!

But mark the Rustic, haggis-fed,
The trembling earth resounds his tread,
Clap in his walie nieve a blade,
        He'll make it whissle;
An' legs, an' arms, an' heads will sned
        Like taps o' thrissle.

Ye Pow'rs, wha mak mankind your care,
And dish them out their bill o' fare,
Auld Scotland wants nae skinking ware,
        That jaups in luggies;
But, if ye wish her gratefu' prayer,
        Gie her a Haggis!

THERE WAS A LAD

**Entered in the second Commonplace Book in April 1787,
matched to the tune 'Dainty Davie', this self-congratulatory
lyric was written probably on Burns's birthday in January 1787
when he was basking in the critical success of his poems. It was
published in R.H. Cromek's *Reliques of Robert Burns* (1808). After
naming Kyle, the area of Ayrshire in which Burns was born, the
poem refers to an anecdote confirmed by Gilbert Burns:**

**one very stormy morning, when my brother was
nine or ten days old, a little before day-light a part of**

> the gable fell out, and the rest appeared to shattered,
> that my mother, with the young poet, had to be
> carried through the storm to a neighbour's house,
> where they remained a week till their own dwelling
> was adjusted. (Currie I, 372)

The gossip referred to is probably Betty Davidson, ballad-
singing widow of a cousin of Burns's ballad-singing mother. So
the prophecies about Robin emerge from the same source that
sang the ballads of Scotland and told the tales of folklore.

Text: H–H IV, 13–14.

CHORUS
Robin was a rovin boy,
Rantin, rovin, rantin, rovin,
Robin was a rovin boy,
Rantin, rovin Robin!

THERE was a lad was born in Kyle,
But whatna day o' whatna style,
I doubt it's hardly worth the while
    To be sae nice wi' Robin.

Our monarch's hindmost year but ane
Was five-and-twenty days begun,
'Twas then a blast o' Janwar' win'
    Blew hansel in on Robin.

The gossip keekit in his loof,
Quo' scho:—'Wha lives will see the proof,
This waly boy will be nae coof:
    I think we'll ca' him Robin.

'He'll hae misfortunes great an' sma',
But ay a heart aboon them a'.
He'll be a credit till us a':
    We'll a' be proud o' Robin!

'But sure as three times three mak nine,
I see by ilka score and line,
This chap will dearly like our kin',
    So leeze me on thee, Robin!

'Guid faith,' quo' scho, 'I doubt you, stir,
Ye gar the lasses lie aspar;
But twenty fauts ye may hae waur—
    So blessins on thee, Robin!'

CHORUS
Robin was a rovin boy,
    Rantin, rovin, rantin, rovin,
Robin was a rovin boy,
    Rantin, rovin Robin!

LINES ON STIRLING

**Stirling Palace, part of the Castle complex, was completed
for James V in the 1540s. Burns and William Nicol visited
the Castle on 26 August 1787: seeing the Palace 'unroof'd'
brought out the Jacobite in the poet. The two travellers lodged
at James Wingate's Inn, Quality Street (now the Golden Lion
Hotel, King Street) and apparently the Lines on Stirling were
'afterwards found on the window of their room' (Ch-W II,
156). In the Glenriddell Manuscript Burns introduced the lines
as 'Written by Somebody in the window of an inn at Stirling
on seeing the Royal Palace in ruins'. On 27 January 1788 he told
Mrs McLehose 'I have almost given up the excise idea . . . I have
been question'd like a child about my matters, and blamed and
schooled for my Inscription in Stirling window.' (CL, 390.)**

Here Stewarts once in triumph reign'd,
And laws for Scotland's weal ordain'd;
But now unroof'd their palace stands,
Their sceptre fallen to other hands:
Fallen indeed, and to the earth,
Whence grovelling reptiles take their birth!
The injured Stewart line is gone,
A race outlandish fills their throne:
An idiot race, to honour lost —
Who know them best despise them most.

**According to Allan Cunningham's *The Works of Robert Burns*
(1834) the poet, on being reproved for writing the lines, added
four more. The lines, beginning 'Rash mortal', are not in the**

Glendriddell Manuscript and 'it is not certain they belong with
the other lines' (Kinsley, 1243). The 'old Mansfield' mentioned
by Burns was William Murray, appointed Lord Chief Justice in
1756 and created 1st Earl of Mansfield in 1776:

> Rash mortal, and slanderous poet, thy name
> Shall no longer appear in the records of Fame!
> Dost not know that old Mansfield, who writes like the Bible,
> Says, the more 'tis a truth, Sir, the more 'tis a libel?

Burns's initial Lines on Stirling and a reply to them were published in *Animadversions on some Poets . . . especially R———t B———s*
(1788) by the Revd George Hamilton. Burns must have seen the
reply prior to publication according to a note in the Glenriddell
Manuscript: 'These imprudent lines were answered, very petu-
lantly, by somebody, I believe a Revd Mr Hamilton. – In a
M.S.S. where I met with the answer, I wrote below—'

> With Aesop's lion, Burns says:– 'Sore I feel
> Each other blow: but damn that ass's heel!'

Texts: H–H II, 244–5.

THE BONIE LASS OF ALBANIE

Included in the second Commonplace Book and published
by Robert Chambers in 1852, this song (matched to the tune
'Mary weep no more for me') gives Burns's opinion of the
Hanoverians and was written probably soon after 6 Decem-
ber 1787 when Charlotte, daughter of Prince Charles Edward
Stewart by his mistress Clementina Walkinshaw, was recog-
nized as the Duchess of Albany by the French. The 'town of
fame' is Rothesay, in the Isle of Bute, since the eldest sons of
Scottish kings were Dukes of Rothesay; the 'witless youth' is
Prince George (later George IV); the 'false usurper' is George
II whose third son, the Duke of Cumberland, defeated Prince
Charles Edward at Culloden in 1746.

Text: H–H IV, 22–3.

> My heart is wae, and unco wae,
>   To think upon the raging sea,
> That roars between her gardens green
>   An' the bonie lass of Albanie.

This noble maid's of royal blood,
  That rulèd Albion's kingdoms three;
But O, alas for her bonie face!
  They hae wranged the lass of Albanie.

In the rolling tide of spreading Clyde
  There sits an isle of high degree,
And a town of fame, whose princely name
  Should grace the lass of Albanie.

But there is a youth, a witless youth,
  That fills the place where she should be
We 'll send him o'er to his native shore,
  And bring our ain sweet Albanie!

Alas the day, and woe the day!
  A false usurper wan the gree,
Who now commands the towers and lands,
  The royal right of Albanie.

We'll daily pray, we'll nightly pray,
  On bended knees most fervently,
That the time may come, with pipe and drum
  We'll welcome hame fair Albanie.

GIE THE LASS HER FAIRIN'

From MMC, matched to the tune 'Cauld kail in Aberdeen'.
  Text: CW, 607.

O gie the lass her fairin, lad,
  O gie the lass her fairin,
An something else she'll gie to you,
  That's waly worth the wearin;
Syne coup her o'er amang the creels,
  When ye hae taen your brandy,
The mair she bangs the less she squeels,
  An hey for houghmagandie.

Then gie the lass a fairin, lad,
  O gie the lass her fairin,
An she'll gie you a hairy thing,
  An of it be na sparin;
But coup her o'er amang the creels,
  An bar the door wi baith your heels,
The mair she gets the less she squeels;
  An hey for houghmagandie.

I LOVE MY JEAN

**Included in SMM (1790) and SC (1805), Burns said he composed
the song (matched to the tune 'Miss admiral Gordon's Strath-
spey') 'out of compliment to Mrs Burns . . . during the
honeymoon' (NSS, 46): Burns and Jean Armour were married
by April 1788.**
  Text: H–H III, 56.

Of a' the airts the wind can blaw
  I dearly like the west,
For there the bonie lassie lives,
  The lassie I lo'e best.
There wild woods grow, and rivers row,
  And monie a hill between,
But day and night my fancy's flight
  Is ever wi' my Jean.

I see her in the dewy flowers—
  I see her sweet and fair.
I hear her in the tunefu' birds—
  I hear her charm the air.
There 's not a bonie flower that springs
  By fountain, shaw, or green,
There 's not a bonie bird that sings,
  But minds me o' my Jean.

AULD LANG SYNE

In a letter of 7 December 1788 to Mrs Dunlop, Burns wrote:

> **Apropos, is not the Scots phrase, 'Auld lang syne',**
> **exceedingly expressive. – There is an old song &**
> **tune which has often thrilled thro' my soul . . .**
> **Light be the turf on the breast of the heaven-inspired**
> **Poet who composed this glorious Fragment! There**
> **is more of the fire of native genius in it, than in half**
> **a dozen of modern English Bacchanalians. (CL, 161,**
> **163)**

Burns's song was published in SMM (1796), matched to an old air collected in Playford's _Original Scotch Tunes_ (1700). In SC (1799) it was matched to the tune still sung all over the world in this celebration of companionship.

Burns knew previous versions of the old song: Allan Ramsay's beginning 'Should auld acquaintance be forgot,/Tho' they return with scars'; and John Skinner's 'The Old Minister's Song' beginning 'Should auld acquaintance be forgot,/Or friendship e'er grow cauld'. His version, however, is infinitely superior to these and the song must be regarded as largely, though not all, his own work.

Text: H–H III, 147–9.

CHORUS
For auld lang syne, my dear.
  For auld lang syne,
We'll tak a cup o' kindness yet
  For auld lang syne!

SHOULD auld acquaintance be forgot,
  And never brought to mind?
Should auld acquaintance be forgot,
  And auld lang syne!

And surely ye'll be your pint-stowp,
  And surely I'll be mine,
And we'll tak a cup o' kindness yet
  For auld lang syne!

We twa hae run about the braes,
 And pou'd the gowans fine,
But we've wander'd monie a weary fit
 Sin' auld lang syne.

We twa hae paidl'd in the burn
 Frae morning sun till dine,
But seas between us braid hae roar'd
 Sin' auld lang syne.

And there's a hand, my trusty fiere,
 And gie's a hand o' thine,
And we'll tak a right guid-willie waught
 For auld lang syne!

CHORUS
For auld lang syne, my dear,
 For auld lang syne,
We'll tak a cup o' kindness yet
 For auld lang syne!

GO, FETCH TO ME A PINT O' WINE

Sent to Mrs Dunlop on 7 December 1788 as two 'old Stanzas which please me mightily' (CL, 163) the song appeared anonymously in SMM (1790); but, in a letter of September 1793 to Thomson (to whom he recommended the tune 'Wae's my heart that we should sunder'), Burns described it as 'a song of mine, & I think not a bad one' (CL, 643) and elsewhere observed 'the first half stanza of the song is old, the rest mine' (NSS, 45). Snyder thought the song 'unexcelled by anything [Burns] ever wrote for sheer virtuosity of technique' (Snyder, 350) and it was a favourite of Sean O'Casey who named his play *The Silver Tassie* (1929) after it.
 Text: H–H III, 53–4.

Go, fetch to me a pint o' wine,
 And fill it in a silver tassie,
That I may drink before I go
 A service to my bonie lassie!

The boat rocks at the pier o' Leith,
    Fu' loud the wind blaws frae the Ferry,
The ship rides by the Berwick-Law,
    And I maun leave my bonie Mary.

The trumpets sound, the banners fly,
    The glittering spears are rankèd ready,
The shouts o' war are heard afar,
    The battle closes deep and bloody.
It's not the roar o' sea or shore
    Wad mak me langer wish to tarry,
Nor shouts o' war that 's heard afar:
    It's leaving thee, my bonie Mary!

TO DR BLACKLOCK

Collected by Currie in 1800, this epistle was sent from Ellisland on 21 October 1789 in response to a verse epistle in English from Thomas Blacklock, dated Edinburgh, 24 August 1789. After a diversion expressing irritation at Robert Heron, Burns gives his news: he has become a 'gauger' (he began work as an Exciseman on 1 September 1789 at a salary of £50 a year). He dismisses as spurious any suggestion that he has prostituted his gifts by selling his intelligence to the Excise, a point he repeated in a letter of 23 December 1789: 'People may talk as they please of the ignominy of the Excise, but what will support my family and keep me independant of the world is to me a very important matter' (CL, 498). The deification of domesticity in the penultimate stanza encouraged excessive sentimentality in generations of Burnsians though, occurring in the context of a poem about 'strang necessity', it is capable of an ironical interpretation.
    Text H–H II, 128–31.

WOW, but your letter made me vauntie!
And are ye hale, and weel, and cantie?
I kend it still, your wee bit jauntie
            Wad bring ye to:
Lord send you ay as weel 's I want ye,
            And then ye 'll do!

The Ill-Thief blaw the Heron south,
And never drink be near his drouth!
He tauld mysel by word o' mouth,
                    He'd tak my letter:
I lippen'd to the chiel in trowth,
                    And bade nae better.

But aiblins honest Master Heron
Had at the time some dainty fair one
To ware his theologic care on
                    And holy study,
And, tired o' sauls to waste his lear on,
                    E'en tried the body.

But what d 'ye think, my trusty fier?
I'm turned a gauger —Peace be here!
Parnassian quines, I fear, I fear,
                    Ye 'll now disdain me,
And then my fifty pounds a year
                    Will little gain me!

Ye glaikit, gleesome, dainty damies,
Wha by Castalia's wimplin streamies
Lowp, sing, and lave your pretty limbies,
                    Ye ken, ye ken,
That strang necessity supreme is
                    'Mang sons o' men.

I hae a wife and twa wee laddies;
They maun hae brose and brats o' duddies:
Ye ken yoursels my heart right proud is—
                    I need na vaunt—
But I 'll sned besoms, thraw saugh woodies,
                    Before they want.

Lord help me thro' this warld o' care!
I 'm weary—sick o't late and air!
Not but I hae a richer share
                    Than monie ithers;
But why should ae man better fare,
                    And a' men brithers?

Come, firm Resolve, take thou the van,
Thou stalk o' carl-hemp in man!
And let us mind, faint heart ne'er wan
   A lady fair:
Wha does the utmost that he can
    Will whyles do mair.

But to conclude my silly rhyme
(I'm scant o' verse and scant o' time):
To make a happy fireside clime
    To weans and wife,
That's the true pathos and sublime
    Of human life.

My compliments to sister Beckie,
And eke the same to honest Lucky:
I wat she is a daintie chuckie
    As e'er tread clay:
And gratefully, my guid auld cockie,
    I 'm yours for ay.

AY WAUKIN, O

**First published, matched to a seventeenth-century tune, in
SMM (1790) and based on an old song ('O wat, wat – O wat
and weary!/Sleep I can get nane/For thinking on my deary')
Burns's lyric is a self-portrait of a lovesick insomniac.**
Text: H–H III, 45.

CHORUS
*Ay waukin, O
 Waukin still and weary:
Sleep I can get nane
 For thinking on my dearie.*

Simmer's a pleasant time:
 Flowers of every colour,
The water rins owre the heugh,
 And I long for my true lover.

When I sleep I dream,
   When I wauk I'm eerie,
Sleep I can get nane
   For thinkin on my dearie.

Lanely night comes on,
   A' the lave are sleepin,
I think on my bonie lad,
   And I bleer my een wi' greetin.

Chorus
Ay waukin, O
   Waukin still and weary:
Sleep I can get nane
   For thinking on my dearie.

JOHN ANDERSON MY JO

**Included in SMM (1790) and SC (1799). Burns said 'This song
is mine' (NSS, 48) but he based it on a bawdy monologue (included in MMC) in which a sexually energetic woman complains
of her husband's impotence.**
Text: H–H III, 63.

JOHN Anderson my jo, John,
   When we were first acquent,
Your locks were like the raven,
   Your bonie brow was brent;
But now your brow is beld, John,
   Your locks are like the snaw,
But blessings on your frosty pow,
   John Anderson my jo!

John Anderson my jo, John,
   We clamb the hill thegither,
And monie a cantie day, John,
   We've had wi' ane anither;
Now we maun totter down, John,
   And hand in hand we'll go,
And sleep thegither at the foot,
   John Anderson my jo!

TAM O' SHANTER. A TALE

Burns wrote his most celebrated poem at Ellisland in late autumn, 1790, having met Francis Grose in the summer and promised him a witch tale to accompany a drawing of Kirk Alloway in his *The Antiquities of Scotland*. In June 1790 Burns sent Grose three prose witch stories (see pp.311); on 1 December 1790 he sent Grose 'Tam o' Shanter' which he described as 'one of the Aloway-kirk Stories, done in Scots verse' (CL, 559). According to Lockhart's *Life of Burns* (1828) 'Tam o' Shanter' was the work of one day but the evidence suggests careful reworking: Burns thought the poem had 'a finishing polish that I despair of ever excelling' (CL, 194).

He named it as his 'own favourite' (CL, 578) of his own works and said 'I look on "Tam o' Shanter" to be my standard performance in the Poetical line' (CL, 194), an opinion endorsed by generations of critics beginning with A.F. Tytler who wrote to Burns, on 12 March 1791, 'when you describe the infernal orgies of the witches' sabbath and the hellish scenery in which they are exhibited, you display a power of imagination that Shakespeare himself could not have exceeded' (CH, 95). Sir Walter Scott (in the first issue of the *Quarterly Review*, Feb. 1809) also compared the Burns of 'Tam o' Shanter' with Shakespeare: 'No poet, with the exception of Shakespeare, ever possessed the power of exciting the most varied and discordant emotions with such rapid transitions.' (CH, 207.)

Burns confided to Mrs Dunlop, in 1789, that he wanted 'to write an epic poem of my own composition' (CL, 178). He never achieved that ambition but did write a masterly mock-epic in 'Tam o' Shanter'. On one level, the poem is a comical odyssey (Burns had read Pope's translations of Homer) following the homewards journey of a farmer to Kirkoswald, in the Carrick area of Ayrshire, from the county town of Ayr. Traditionally, the protagonists of the poem are supposedly modelled on characters Burns met when sent to school in Kirkoswald in the summer of 1775: Tam on Douglas Graham of Shanter farm; Kate on Graham's nagging wife Helen; Souter Johnie on John Davidson, a shoemaker who lived near Shanter farm; Kirkton Jean on Jean Kennedy who, with her sister Anne, kept an ale-house in Kirkoswald; Cutty-sark on Katie Steven, a local fortune-teller.

Above all, though, 'Tam o' Shanter' is an imaginative work

and it is clear that Burns has found the octosyllabic couplet the perfect form for a narrative that moves easily and swiftly from the natural to the supernatural, from the earthly to the other-worldly, thus giving Tam's odyssey a timeless dimension.

'Tam o' Shanter' first appeared in the *Edinburgh Magazine* (Mar. 1791) and the *Edinburgh Herald* (18 Mar. 1791) then as a footnote (pp.199–201) to the account of Kirk Alloway in the second volume of Grose's *The Antiquities of Scotland* (Apr. 1791). In these first printings, four lines completed the section ending 'Which even to name wad be unlawfu' '.

> Three lawyers' tongues, turn'd inside out,
> Wi' lies seam'd like a beggar's clout;
> Three priests' hearts, rotten, black as muck,
> Lay stinking, vile, in every neuk.

Writing to Alexander Fraser Tytler in April 1791, Burns agreed there were faults in the poem as first published: 'one of them, the hit at the lawyer and priest, I shall cut out' (CL, 578). So he did, omitting the four lines when he collected the poem in the second Edinburgh edition of 1793.

Text: H–H I, 278–286.

> *Of Brownyis and of Bogillis full is this Buke.*
> GAWIN DOUGLAS

> When chapman billies leave the street,
> And drouthy neebors neebors meet;
> As market-days are wearing late,
> An' folk begin to tak the gate;
> While we sit bousing at the nappy,
> An' getting fou and unco happy,
> We think na on the lang Scots miles,
> The mosses, waters, slaps, and styles,
> That lie between us and our hame,
> Whare sits our sulky, sullen dame,
> Gathering her brows like gathering storm,
> Nursing her wrath to keep it warm.

> This truth fand honest 'Tam o' Shanter,
> As he frae Ayr ae night did canter:
> (Auld Ayr, wham ne'er a town surpasses,
> For honest men and bonie lasses).

O Tam, had'st thou but been sae wise,
As taen thy ain wife Kate's advice!
She tauld thee weel thou was a skellum,
A blethering, blustering, drunken blellum;
That frae November till October,
Ae market-day thou was nae sober;
That ilka melder wi' the miller,
Thou sat as lang as thou had siller;
That ev'ry naig was ca'd a shoe on,
The smith and thee gat roaring fou on;
That at the Lord's house, even on Sunday,
Thou drank wi' Kirkton Jean till Monday.
She prophesied, that, late or soon,
Thou would be found deep drown'd in Doon,
Or catch'd wi' warlocks in the mirk
By Alloway's auld, haunted kirk.

Ah! gentle dames, it gars me greet,
To think how monie counsels sweet,
How monie lengthen'd, sage advices
The husband frae the wife despises!

But to our tale:—Ae market-night,
Tam had got planted unco right,
Fast by an ingle, bleezing finely,
Wi' reaming swats, that drank divinely;
And at his elbow, Souter Johnie,
His ancient, trusty, drouthy cronie:
Tam lo'ed him like a very brither;
They had been fou for weeks thegither.
The night drave on wi' sangs and clatter;
And ay the ale was growing better:
The landlady and Tam grew gracious
Wi' secret favours, sweet and precious:
The Souter tauld his queerest stories;
The landlord's laugh was ready chorus:
The storm without might rair and rustle,
Tam did na mind the storm a whistle.

Care, mad to see a man sae happy,
E'en drown'd himsel amang the nappy.

As bees flee hame wi' lades o' treasure,
The minutes wing'd their way wi' pleasure:
Kings may be blest but Tam was glorious,
O'er a' the ills o' life victorious!

But pleasures are like poppies spread:
You seize the flow'r, its bloom is shed;
Or like the snow falls in the river,
A moment white—then melts for ever;
Or like the borealis race,
That flit ere you can point their place;
Or like the rainbow's lovely form
Evanishing amid the storm.
Nae man can tether time or tide;
The hour approaches Tam maun ride:
That hour, o' night's black arch the key-stane,
That dreary hour Tam mounts his beast in;
And sic a night he taks the road in,
As ne'er poor sinner was abroad in.

The wind blew as 'twad blawn its last;
The rattling showers rose on the blast;
The speedy gleams the darkness swallow'd;
Loud, deep, and lang the thunder bellow'd:
That night, a child might understand,
The Deil had business on his hand.

Weel mounted on his gray mare Meg,
A better never lifted leg,
Tam skelpit on thro' dub and mire,
Despising wind, and rain, and fire;
Whiles holding fast his guid blue bonnet,
Whiles crooning o'er some auld Scots sonnet,
Whiles glow'ring round wi' prudent cares,
Lest bogles catch him unawares:
Kirk-Alloway was drawing nigh,
Whare ghaists and houlets nightly cry.

By this time he was cross the ford,
Whare in the snaw the chapman smoor'd;

And past the birks and meikle stane,
Whare drunken Charlie brak 's neck-bane;
And thro' the whins, and by the cairn,
Whare hunters fand the murder'd bairn;
And near the thorn, aboon the well,
Whare Mungo's mither hang'd hersel.
Before him Doon pours all his floods;
The doubling storm roars thro' the woods;
The lightnings flash from pole to pole;
Near and more near the thunders roll:
When, glimmering thro the groaning trees,
Kirk-Alloway seem'd in a bleeze,
Thro' ilka bore the beams were glancing,
And loud resounded mirth and dancing.

Inspiring bold John Barleycorn,
What dangers thou canst make us scorn!
Wi' tippenny, we fear nae evil;
Wi' usquabae, we'll face the Devil!
The swats sae ream'd in Tammie's noddle,
Fair play, he car'd na deils a boddle.
But Maggie stood, right sair astonish'd,
Till, by the heel and hand admonish'd,
She ventur'd forward on the light;
And, vow! Tam saw an unco sight!

Warlocks and witches in a dance:
Nae cotillion, brent new frae France,
But hornpipes, jigs, strathspeys, and reels,
Put life and mettle in their heels.
A winnock-bunker in the east,
There sat Auld Nick, in shape o' beast;
A tousie tyke, black, grim, and large,
To gie them music was his charge:
He screw'd the pipes and gart them skirl,
Till roof and rafters a' did dirl.
Coffins stood round, like open presses,
That shaw'd the dead in their last dresses;
And, by some devilish cantraip sleight,
Each in its cauld hand held a light:

By which heroic Tam was able
To note upon the haly table,
A murderer's banes, in gibbet-airns;
Twa span-lang, wee, unchristen'd bairns;
A thief new-cutted frae a rape—
Wi' his last gasp his gab did gape;
Five tomahawks wi' bluid red-rusted;
Five scymitars wi' murder crusted;
A garter which a babe had strangled;
A knife a father's throat had mangled—
Whom his ain son o' life bereft—
The grey-hairs yet stack to the heft;
Wi' mair of horrible and awefu',
Which even to name wad be unlawfu'.

    As Tammie glowr'd, amaz'd, and curious,
The mirth and fun grew fast and furious;
The piper loud and louder blew,
The dancers quick and quicker flew,
They reel'd, they set, they cross'd, they cleekit,
Till ilka carlin swat and reekit,
And coost her duddies to the wark,
And linket at it in her sark!

    Now Tam, O Tam! had thae been queans,
A' plump and strapping in their teens!
Their sarks, instead o' creeshie flannen,
Been snaw-white seventeen hunder linen!—
Thir breeks o' mine, my only pair,
That ance were plush, o' guid blue hair,
I wad hae gi'en them off my hurdies
For ae blink o' the bonie burdies!

    But wither'd beldams, auld and droll,
Rigwoodie hags wad spean a foal,
Louping and flinging on a crummock,
I wonder did na turn thy stomach!

    But Tam kend what was what fu' brawlie:
There was ae winsome wench and wawlie,

That night enlisted in the core,
Lang after kend on Carrick shore
(For monie a beast to dead she shot,
An' perish'd monie a bonie boat,
And shook baith meikle corn and bear,
And kept the country-side in fear).
Her cutty sark, o' Paisley harn,
That while a lassie she had worn,
In longitude tho' sorely scanty,
It was her best, and she was vauntie . . .
Ah! little kend thy reverend grannie,
That sark she coft for her wee Nannie,
Wi' twa pund Scots ('twas a' her riches),
Wad ever grac'd a dance of witches!

But here my Muse her wing maun cour,
Sic flights are far beyond her power:
To sing how Nannie lap and flang
(A souple jad she was and strang),
And how Tam stood like ane bewitch'd,
And thought his very een enrich'd;
Even Satan glowr'd, and fidg'd fu' fain,
And hotch'd and blew wi' might and main;
Till first ae caper, syne anither,
Tam tint his reason a' thegither,
And roars out: 'Weel done, Cutty-sark!'
And in an instant all was dark;
And scarcely had he Maggie rallied,
When out the hellish legion sallied.

As bees bizz out wi' angry fyke,
When plundering herds assail their byke;
As open pussie's mortal foes,
When, pop! she starts before their nose;
As eager runs the market-crowd,
When 'Catch the thief!' resounds aloud:
So Maggie runs, the witches follow,
Wi' monie an eldritch skriech and hollo.

Ah, Tam! Ah, Tam! thou 'll get thy fairin!
In hell they 'll roast thee like a herrin!

In vain thy Kate awaits thy comin!
Kate soon will be a woefu' woman!
Now, do thy speedy utmost, Meg,
And win the key-stane of the brig;
There, at them thou thy tail may toss,
A running stream they dare na cross!
But ere the key-stane she could make,
The fient a tail she had to shake;
For Nannie, far before the rest,
Hard upon noble Maggie prest,
And flew at Tam wi' furious ettle;
But little wist she Maggie's mettle!
Ae spring brought off her master hale,
But left behind her ain grey tail:
The carlin claught her by the rump,
And left poor Maggie scarce a stump.

Now, wha this tale o' truth shall read,
Ilk man, and mother's son, take heed:
Whene'er to drink you are inclin'd,
Or cutty sarks run in your mind,
Think! ye may buy the joys o'er dear:
Remember Tam o' Shanter's mare.

AE FOND KISS

On 6 December 1791, in Edinburgh, Burns met Mrs McLehose
for the last time. She had decided to join her now-prosperous
husband in Jamaica (a disastrous decision as it turned out)
and her parting gift to Burns was a lock of her hair which
he had set in a ring. On his return to Dumfries, Burns sent
'Ae Fond Kiss' (and two other songs) to Mrs McLehose on 27
December. Burns's song was influenced by Robert Dodsley's
'The Parting Kiss', included in *The Charmer* (1749), which begins: 'One kind kiss before we part,/Drop a tear, and bid
adieu:/Tho' we sever, my fond heart,/Till we meet, shall pant
for you.' A past master of the valedictory mode, Burns far
surpasses Dodsley. The song appeared in SMM (1792) matched
to the tune 'Rory Dall's port'.
  Text: H–H III, 105–6.

AE fond kiss, and then we sever!
Ae farewell, and then forever!
Deep in heart-wrung tears I'll pledge thee,
Warring sighs and groans I'll wage thee.
Who shall say that Fortune grieves him,
While the star of hope she leaves him?
Me, nae cheerfu' twinkle lights me,
Dark despair around benights me.

I'll ne'er blame my partial fancy:
Naething could resist my Nancy!
But to see her was to love her,
Love but her, and love for ever.
Had we never lov'd sae kindly,
Had we never lov'd sae blindly,
Never met—or never parted—
We had ne'er been broken-hearted.

Fare-thee-weel, thou first and fairest!
Fare-thee-weel, thou best and dearest!
Thine be ilka joy and treasure,
Peace, Enjoyment, Love and Pleasure!
Ae fond kiss, and then we sever!
Ae farewell, alas, for ever!
Deep in heart-wrung tears I'll pledge thee,
Warring sighs and groans I'll wage thee.

THE DEUK'S DANG O'ER MY DADDIE

**First published, with a lively tune, in SMM (1792) this lyrical
exchange on impotence ('downa-do') is based on a traditional
song 'The nine pint bicker's fa'n aff the bink' in which these
lines appear: 'The bairns they a' set up a shout,/The deuks
dang o'er my daddie, O'.**
    Text: H–H II, 139–40.

THE bairns gat out wi' an unco shout:—
    'The deuk 's dang o'er my daddie, O!'
'The fien-ma-care,' quo' the feirrie auld wife,
    'He was but a paidlin body, O!

He paidles out, and he paidles in,
  An' he paidles late and early, O!
This seven lang years I hae lien by his side,
  An' he is but a fusionless carlie, O!'

'O, haud your tongue, my feirrie auld wife,
  O, haud your tongue, now Nansie, O!
I've seen the day, and sae hae ye,
  Ye wad na been sae donsie, O.
I've seen the day ye butter'd my brose,
  And cuddl'd me late and early, O;
But downa-do's come o'er me now,
  And och, I find it sairly, O!'

THE DEIL'S AWA WI' TH'EXCISEMAN

**Matched to the tune 'Madam Cossy' in SMM (1792) this was
sent to John Leven, Supervisor of Excise at Edinburgh, in
March 1792, as 'a ballad which I composed & sung at one
of [Dumfries Collector John Mitchell's] Excise-court dinners'
(CL, 614). It acknowledges the popular dislike of the Exciseman
by making him a natural, or supernatural, partner of the devil;
by incorporating the title of the song in its last line, Burns
makes the diabolic dance a circular one.**
  Text: H–H III, 141–2.

CHORUS
The Deil's awa, the Deil's awa,
  The Deil's awa wi' th' Exciseman!
He's danc'd awa, he's danc'd awa,
  He's danc'd awa wi' th' Exciseman!

THE Deil cam fiddlin thro' the town,
  And danc'd awa wi' th' Exciseman,
And ilka wife cries:—'Auld Mahoun,
  I wish you luck o' the prize, man!

'We'll mak our maut, and we 'll brew our drink,
  We'll laugh, sing, and rejoice, man,
And monie braw thanks to the meikle black Deil,
  That danc'd awa wi' th' Exciseman.

There's threesome reels, there's foursome reels,
    There's hornpipes and strathspeys, man,
But the ae best dance ere cam to the land
    Was *The Deil's Awa wi' th' Exciseman*
                CHORUS
    The Deil's awa, the Deil's awa,
        The Deil's awa wi' th' Exciseman!
    He's danc'd awa, he's danc'd awa,
        He's danc'd awa wi' th' Exciseman!

WHY SHOULD NA POOR FOLK MOWE

**From Sanquhar, Burns sent this to Robert Cleghorn on 12
December 1792: 'I send you a song, just finished this moment'
(CL, 277). It was published in MMC.**

**The Duke of Brunswick, George III's brother-in-law, led
Austrians and Prussians against France but on 20 September
1792 the invaders were stopped at the battle of Valmy. Frederic
is Frederick William II, Prussian king 1786–97, who waged war
on the French Revolution; Auld Kate is Empress Catherine of
Russia who made her lover, Stanislaus Poniatowski, puppet
ruler in Poland in 1792.**

Text: CW, 476–7.

                CHORUS
And why shouldna poor folk mowe, mowe, mowe,
    And why shouldna poor folk mowe:
The great folk hae siller, and houses and lands,
    Poor bodies hae naething but mowe.

When Princes and Prelates and het-headed zealots
    All Europe hae set in a lowe,
The poor man lies down, nor envies a crown,
    And comforts himsel with a mowe.

When Brunswick's great Prince cam a cruising to France
    Republican billies to cowe,
Bauld Brunswick's great Prince wad hae shawn better sense,
    At hame with his Princess to mowe.

Out over the Rhine proud Prussia wad shine,
    To *spend* his best blood he did vow;
But Frederic had better ne'er forded the water,
    But *spent* as he docht in a mowe.

By sea and by shore! the Emperor swore,
    In Paris he'd kick up a row;
But Paris sae ready just leugh at the laddie
    And bade him gae tak him a mowe.

Auld Kate laid her claws on poor Stanislaus,
    And Poland has bent like a bow:
May the deil in her ass ram a huge prick o brass!
    And damn her in hell with a mowe!

But truce with commotions and new-fangled notions,
    A bumper I trust you'll allow:
Here's George our gude king and Charlotte his queen,
    And lang may they tak a gude mowe!

SCOTS, WHA HAE

'Independent of my enthusiasm as a Scotchman,' Burns declared in a letter (12 Jan. 1794), 'I have rarely met with any thing in History which interests my feelings as a Man, equally with the story of Bannockburn.' (CL, 268) In Robert Bruce's victory over Edward II on 24 June 1314 at Bannockburn, near Stirling, a relatively small Scottish army (5500 trained men as well as 2000 untrained volunteers) defeated a huge English army (20,000 men including heavy cavalry, archers and spear-wielding foot soldiers). On Sunday, 26 August 1787, during his Highland tour with William Nicol, Burns visited the battlefield.

Around 30 August 1793, Burns sent George Thomson this song, entitled 'Robert Bruce's march to BANNOCKBURN' and matched to the tune 'Hey, tutti taitie'. In a postscript, Burns said he was inspired by Bruce's 'glorious struggle for Freedom, associated with the glowing ideas of some other struggles of the same nature, *not quite so ancient*' (CL, 639). Audaciously, Burns had made Bruce sing a song of a freedom still being fought for in contemporary Scotland: on 1 February

1793, the French Republic had declared war on Britain and the British government increased its attempts to suppress the Friends of the People, a radical movement organized largely by the young lawyer, Thomas Muir of Huntershill, whose trial was fixed for 30 August, the date assigned to Burns's letter to Thomson. Had Burns openly declared his radical sympathies he might well have been treated like Muir, who was sentenced to fourteen years' transportation for seditiously inciting the Scottish people to oppose the government. Significantly, Burns agreed to the *Morning Chronicle* (8 May 1794) publishing his song but insisted 'let them insert it as a thing they have met with by accident, & unknown to me' (CL, 699). It was included in SC (1799); Thomson, preferring the tune 'Lewie Gordon' to 'Hey, tutti taitie', persuaded the poet to elongate the fourth line of each stanza. In SC (1802) Thomson reunited the original words with the tune for which they were intended.

Text: H–H III, 251–2.

> Scots, wha hae wi' Wallace bled,
> Scots, wham Bruce has aften led,
> Welcome to your gory bed
>   Or to victorie!
>
> Now's the day, and now's the hour:
> See the front o' battle lour,
> See approach proud Edward's power—
>   Chains and slaverie!
>
> Wha will be a traitor knave?
> Wha can fill a coward's grave?
> Wha sae base as be a slave?—
>   Let him turn, and flee!
>
> Wha for Scotland's King and Law
> Freedom's sword will strongly draw,
> Freeman stand or freeman fa',
>   Let him follow me!
>
> By Oppression's woes and pains,
> By your sons in servile chains,
> We will drain our dearest veins
>   But they shall be free!

Lay the proud usurpers low!
Tyrants fall in every foe!
Liberty's in every blow!
        Let us do, or die!

A RED RED ROSE

First published in Pietro Urbani's *Scots Songs* **(1794) to an original tune; the first three stanzas appeared in SMM (1796) to the Neil Gow tune 'Major Graham'; it then appeared in SC (1799), altered to fit William Marshall's tune 'Wishaw's Favourite'; it gained immense popularity when matched to the air 'Low down in the Broom' in Robert Archibald Smith's** *Scottish Minstrel* **(1821). Sending the lyric to Alexander Cunningham in November 1793, Burns calls it 'a simple old Scots song which I had pickt up in this country' (CL, 468); taking his cue from this, and the fact that almost every line can be traced back to a chapbook source, Kinsley thinks the song was collected, not composed by Burns. (Kinsley, 1455).**

Text: H–H III, 143–4.

O, my luve is like a red, red rose,
    That 's newly sprung in June.
O, my luve is like the melodie,
    That's sweetly play'd in tune.

As fair art thou, my bonie lass,
    So deep in luve am I,
And I will luve thee still, my dear,
    Till a' the seas gang dry.

Till a' the seas gang dry, my dear,
    And the rocks melt wi' the sun!
And I will luve thee still, my dear,
    While the sands o' life shall run.

And fare thee weel, my only luve,
    And fare thee weel a while!
And I will come again, my luve,
    .Tho' it were ten thousand mile!

THE REEL O' STUMPIE

Published in SMM (1796) then in MMC (with two additional quatrains) 'The Reel o' Stumpie' (the title of the tune a euphemism for sexual intercourse) is Burns's version of an old song. The first quatrain is the chorus.
Text: H–H III, 166.

> Wap and rowe, wap and rowe,
> Wap and rowe the feetie o't;
> I thought I was a maiden fair,
> Till I heard the greetie o't!

> My daddie was a fiddler fine,
> My minnie she made mantie, O,
> And I myself a thumpin quine,
> And danc'd the Reel o' Stumpie, O.

IT WAS A' FOR OUR RIGHTFU' KING

Published in SMM (1796) and based on the chapbook ballad 'Mally Stewart', this is one of the most poignant of Burns's Jacobite songs – sung by a cavalier exiled to Ireland for the Roman Catholic cause of James VII & II. As the cavalier could conceivably be reunited with a human love, Burns provides a context that makes the lost love Scotland (a reading encouraged by the third line of the second stanza).
Text: H–H III, 182–3.

> It was a' for our rightfu' king
> We left fair Scotland's strand;
> It was a' for our rightfu' king,
> We e'er saw Irish land,
>   My dear—
> We e'er saw Irish land.

Now a' is done that men can do,
    And a' is done in vain,
My Love and Native Land fareweel,
    For I maun cross the main,
            My dear—
    For I maun cross the main.

He turn'd him right and round about
    Upon the Irish shore,
And gae his bridle reins a shake,
    With adieu for evermore,
            My dear—
    And adieu for evermore!

The soger frae the wars returns,
    The sailor frae the main,
But I hae parted frae my love
    Never to meet again,
            My dear—
    Never to meet again.

When day is gane, and night is come,
    And a' folk bound to sleep,
I think on him that's far awa
    The lee-lang night, and weep,
            My dear—
    The lee-lang night and weep.

IS THERE FOR HONEST POVERTY

**Burns sent this to George Thomson in January 1795 as 'two
or three pretty good *prose* thoughts, inverted into rhyme' (CL,
669); the same month, in a letter to Mrs Dunlop, he referred
to the executions of Louis XVI and Marie Antoinette as 'the
deserved fate of . . . a perjured Blockhead & an unprincipled
Prostitute' (CL, 214). Clearly he was in a revolutionary mood
that month and this song combines hatred of a rank-ridden
past with faith in an egalitarian future. Printed in the *Glasgow***

Magazine (Aug. 1795) and the *Oracle* (2 June 1796) it was collected
by Currie (1800) and included in SC (1805), matched to the
tune 'Up and war them a' Willy'
  Text: H–H III, 271–3.

Is there for honest poverty
    That hings his head, an' a' that?
The coward slave, we pass him by—
    We dare be poor for a' that!
For a' that, an' a' that,
    Our toils obscure, an' a' that,
The rank is but the guinea's stamp,
    The man's the gowd for a' that.

What though on hamely fare we dine,
    Wear hoddin grey, an' a' that?
Gie fools their silks, and knaves their wine—
    A man's a man for a' that.
For a' that, an' a' that,
    Their tinsel show, an' a' that,
The honest man, tho' e'er sae poor,
    Is king o' men for a' that.

Ye see yon birkie ca'd 'a lord,'
    Wha struts, an' stares, an' a' that?
Tho' hundreds worship at his word,
    He's but a cuif for a' that.
For a' that, an' a' that,
    His ribband, star, an' a' that,
The man o' independent mind,
    He looks an' laughs at a' that.

A prince can mak a belted knight,
    A marquis, duke, an' a' that!
But an honest man's aboon his might—
    Guid faith, he mauna fa' that!
For a' that, an' a' that,
    Their dignities, an' a' that,
The pith o' sense an' pride o' worth
    Are higher rank than a' that.

Then let us pray that come it may
   (As come it will for a' that)
That Sense and Worth o'er a' the earth
   Shall bear the gree an' a' that!
For a' that, an' a' that,
   It's comin yet for a' that,
That man to man the world o'er
   Shall brithers be for a' that.

THE DUMFRIES VOLUNTEERS

On 31 January 1795 Burns was involved in the founding of the
Dumfries Volunteers, a force for the defence of the burgh
against France (at war with Britain since 1793). For the Volunteers he wrote this song (to the tune 'Push about the jorum')
which was published in the *Edinburgh Courant* (4 May 1795), the
Dumfries Journal (5 May) and the *Caledonian Mercury* (7 May). For
Snyder the song 'gave notice . . . that Burns was heartily on
the side of King and Country' (Snyder, 372). However, the final
stanza is open to ironic interpretation: the tyrant and throne
might be damned as well as the wretches and the last word of
the song is given, subversively, to the common people.
   Text: H–H III, 195–6.

Does haughty Gaul invasion threat?
   Then let the loons beware, Sir!
There's wooden walls upon our seas
   And volunteers on shore, Sir!
The Nith shall run to Corsincon,
   And Criffel sink in Solway,
Ere we permit a foreign foe
   On British ground to rally!

O, let us not, like snarling tykes,
   In wrangling be divided,
Till, slap! come in an unco loun,
   And wi' a rung decide it!
Be Britain still to Britain true,
   Amang oursels united!
For never but by British hands
   Maun British wrangs be righted!

The kettle o' the Kirk and State,
   Perhaps a clout may fail in 't;
But Deil a foreign tinkler loon
   Shall ever ca' a nail in 't!
Our fathers' blude the kettle bought,
   And wha wad dare to spoil it,
By Heav'ns! the sacrilegious dog
   Shall fuel be to boil it!

The wretch that would a tyrant own,
   And the wretch, his true-sworn brother,
Who would set the mob above the throne,
   May they be damn'd together!
Who will not sing *God save the King*
   Shall hang as high 's the steeple;
But while we sing *God save the King*,
   We'll ne'er forget the People!

O, WERT THOU IN THE CAULD BLAST

In the summer of 1796 Burns was emaciated through illness
and anguished over his financial position. As Jean was pregnant again, eighteen-year-old neighbour Jessy Lewars (sister
of Burns's fellow-Exciseman John Lewars) was brought in to
nurse the poet and help with the housework. Apparently the
song was inspired by hearing Jessy play:

> He called on her one morning and offered, if she
> would play him any tune of which she was fond, to
> write new verses to it. She sat down at her piano
> and played over several times the air of an old song
> beginning – 'The robin cam to the wren's nest'.
> (Ch–W IV, 267)

The result was probably Burns's penultimate song and certainly
his last great lyric. As Snyder says, 'it was a product of the same
formula that had occasioned the earliest of his boyish attempts
['O, once I lov'd a bonie lass']: a scrap of an old tune, and a
pretty girl' (Snyder, 386). It was collected by Currie in 1801.
   Text: H–H IV, 43.

O, wert thou in the cauld blast
  On yonder lea, on yonder lea,
My plaidie to the angry airt,
  I'd shelter three, I'd shelter thee.
Or did Misfortune's bitter storms
  Around thee blaw, around thee blaw,
Thy bield should be my bosom,
  To share it a', to share it a'.

Or were I in the wildest waste,
  Sae black and bare, sae black and bare,
The desert were a Paradise,
  If thou wert there, if thou wert there.
Or were I monarch of the globe,
  Wi' thee to reign, wi' thee to reign,
The brightest jewel in my crown
  Wad be my queen, wad be my queen.

PART TWO

PROSE

from FIRST COMMONPLACE BOOK

**Burns started his first Commonplace Book at Lochlea in April
1783, stopped it at Mossgiel in October 1785. The original
manuscript was bought in 1868 by John Adam, Town Cham-
berlain of Greenock, whose edited text was privately printed
in Edinburgh in 1872 as *Robert Burns' Common Place Book*. The
Adam edition was reprinted (Wakefield: S.R. Publishing, 1969)
with corrections by Raymond Lamont Brown and the following extracts adopt Brown's text. The Commonplace Book of
1783–5 contains several poems as well as prose comments on life
and the character of the author who, at the time of writing, was
an unpublished poet infatuated by thoughts of literary fame.**

Observations, Hints, Songs, Scraps of Poetry, &c., by Robt Burness:
a man who had little art in making money, and still less in keeping it;
but was, however, a man of some sense, a great deal of honesty, and
unbounded good-will to every creature – rational or irrational. As he
was but little indebted to scholastic education, and bred at a plough-tail,
his performances must be strongly tinctured with his unpolished, rustic
way of life; but, as I believe they are really his own, it may be of some
entertainment to a curious observer of human-nature to see how a
ploughman thinks and feels under the pressure of Love, Ambition,
Anxiety, Grief, with the like cares and passions, which, however
diversified by the modes and manners of life, operate pretty much
alike, I believe, in all the Species.

(April 1783)
Notwithstanding all that has been said against Love, respecting the folly
and weakness it leads a young unexperienced mind into; still I think
it, in a great measure, deserves the highest encomiums that have been
passed upon it. If any thing on earth deserves the name of rapture
or transport, it is the feelings of green eighteen in the company of
the mistress of his heart when she repays him with an equal return
of affection.

(August 1783)
For my own part I never had the least thought or inclination of turning

Poet till I got once heartily in Love, and then Rhyme & Song were, in a manner, the spontaneous language of my heart.

(September 1783)
I entirely agree with that judicious philosopher Mr Smith in his excellent Theory of Moral Sentiments, that Remorse is the most painful sentiment that can embitter the human bosom. Any ordinary pitch of fortitude may bear up tolerably well, under those calamities, in the procurement of which we ourselves have had no hand; but when our own follies or crimes have made us miserable and wretched, to bear it up with manly firmness, and at the same time have a proper penitential sense of our misconduct, – it is a glorious effort of self-command.

(March 1784)
I have often observed in the course of my experience of human life that every man, even the worst, have something good about them, though very often nothing else than a happy temperament of constitution inclining them to this or that virtue; on this likewise depend a great many, no man can say how many, of our vices; for this reason no man can say in what degree any person besides himself can be, with strict justice, called wicked. Let any of the strictest character for regularity of conduct among us, examine impartially how many of his virtues are owing to constitution and education; how many vices he has never been guilty of, not from any care or vigilance, but from want of opportunity, or some accidental circumstance intervening; how many of the weaknesses of mankind he has escaped because he was out of the line of such temptation; and what often, if not always, weighs more than all the rest; how much he is indebted to the world's good opinion, because the world does not know all; I say, any man who can thus think, will scan the failings, nay the faults and crimes of mankind around him, with a brother's eye.

(March 1784)
I have often coveted the acquaintance of that part of mankind commonly known by the ordinary phrase of blackguards, sometimes farther than was consistent with the safety of my character; those who, by thoughtless prodigality or headstrong passions, have been driven to ruin; though disgraced by follies, nay, sometimes 'stained with guilt and crimson'd o'er with crimes,' I have yet found among them, in not a few instances, some of the noblest virtues, magnanimity, generosity,

disinterested friendship, and even modesty, in the highest perfection.

(March 1784)
There was a certain period of my life that my spirit was broke by
repeated losses and disasters, which threatened and indeed affected the
utter ruin of my fortune. My body, too, was attacked by that most
dreadful distemper, a hypochondria, or confirmed melancholy; in this
wretched state, the recollection of which makes me yet shudder, I hung
my harp on the willow trees, except in some lucid intervals . . .

(April 1784)
As I am what the men of the world, if they knew of such a man,
would call a whimsical mortal; I have various sources of pleasure
and enjoyment which are, in a manner, peculiar to myself; or some
here and there such other out-of-the-way person. Such is the peculiar
pleasure I take in the season of winter, more than the rest of the year.
This, I believe, may be partly owing to my misfortunes giving my mind
a melancholy cast; but there is something even in the

> Mighty tempest and the hoary waste
> Abrupt and deep stretch'd o'er the buried earth,

which raises the mind to a serious sublimity, favourable to every thing
great and noble. There is scarcely any earthly object gives me more –
I don't know if I should call it pleasure, but something which exalts
me, something which enraptures me – than to walk in the sheltered
side of a wood or high plantation, in a cloudy, winter day, and hear
a stormy wind howling among the trees and raving o'er the plain.
It is my best season for devotion; my mind is rapt up in a kind
of enthusiasm to *Him* who, in the pompous language of Scripture,
'walks on the wings of the wind'.

(April 1784)
Shenstone observes finely that love-verses writ without any real passion
are the most nauseous of all conceits: and I have often thought that no
man can be a proper critic of Love composition, except he himself,
in one, or more instances, have been a warm votary of this passion.
As I have been all along, a miserable dupe to Love, and have been

led into a thousand weaknesses and follies by it, for that reason I put the more confidence in my critical skill in distinguishing foppery and conceit, from real passion and nature.

(April 1784)
I think the whole species of young men may be naturally enough divided in two grand classes, which I shall call the Grave, and the Merry; tho' by the bye these terms do not with propriety enough express my ideas. There are, indeed, some exceptions; some part of the species who, according to my ideas of these divisions, come under neither of them; such are those individuals whom Nature turns off her hand, oftentimes, very like blockheads, but generally, on a nearer inspection, have somethings surprisingly clever about them. They are more properly men of conceit than men of Genius; men whose heads are filled, and whose faculties are engrossed, by some whimsical notions in some art or science; so that they cannot think, nor speak with pleasure, on any other subject. Besides this pedantic species, nature has always produced some meer, insipid blockheads who may be said to live a vegetable life in this world.

The Grave, I shall cast into the usual division of those who are goaded on; by the love of money; and those whose darling wish, is, to make a figure in the world. The Merry, are the men of pleasure, of all denominations; the jovial lads who have too much fire and spirit to have any settled rule of action; but without much deliberation, follow the strong impulses of nature: the thoughtless; the careless; the indolent; and in particular he who, with a happy sweetness of natural temper, and a cheerful vacancy of thought, steals through life, generally indeed, in poverty and obscurity; but poverty and obscurity are only evils to him who can sit gravely down, and making a repining comparison, between his own situation and that of others; and lastly, to grace the quorum, such are generally the men whose heads are capable of all the towerings of genius, and whose hearts are warmed with the delicacy of feeling.

(August 1785)
However I am pleased with the works of our Scotch poets, particularly the excellent Ramsay, and the still more excellent Ferguson, yet I am hurt to see other places of Scotland, their towns, rivers, woods, haughs, &c., immortalized in such celebrated performances, whilst my dear native country, the ancient Baillerics of Carrick, Kyle, and Cunningham, famous both in ancient and modern times

for a gallant and warlike race of inhabitants, a country where civil, and particularly religious Liberty have ever found their first support, and their last asylum; a country, the birthplace of many famous Philosophers, Soldiers, and Statesmen, and the scene of many important events recorded in Scottish History, particularly a great many of the actions of the Glorious Wallace, the Saviour of his country; Yet, we have never had one Scotch Poet of any eminence, to make the fertile banks of Irvine, the romantic woodlands and sequestered scenes on Aire, and the heathy mountainous source, and winding sweep of Doon, emulate Tay, Forth, Ettrick, Tweed, &c., this is a complaint I would gladly remedy, but Alas! I am far unequal to the task both in native genius and education. Obscure I am, and obscure I must be, though no young Poet, nor young Soldier's heart ever beat more fondly for fame than mine.

(September 1785)
There is a certain irregularity in the Old Scotch Songs, a redundancy of syllables with respect to that exactness of accent and measure that the English Poetry requires, but which glides in, most melodiously with the respective tunes to which they are set. For instance, the fine old Song of 'The Mill Mill O,' to give it a plain prosaic reading it halts prodigiously out of measure; on the other hand, the song set to the same tune in Bremner's collection of Scotch Songs which begins 'To Fanny fair could I impart' &c. it is most exact measure, and yet, let them be both sung before a real Critic, one above the biasses of prejudice, but a thorough Judge of Nature, how flat and spiritless will the last appear, how trite, and lamely methodical, compared with the wild warbling cadence, the heart-moving melody of the first. This particularly is the case with all those airs which end with a hypermetrical syllable. There is a degree of wild irregularity in many of the compositions and fragments which are daily sung to them by my compeers, the common people – a certain happy arrangement of Old Scotch syllables, and yet, very frequently, nothing, not even *like* rhyme, or sameness of jingle at the ends of the lines. This has made me sometimes imagine that perhaps, it might be possible for a Scotch Poet, with a nice, judicious ear, to set compositions to many of our most favorite airs, particularly that class of them mentioned above, independent of rhyme altogether.

There is a noble sublimity, a heart-melting tenderness in some of these ancient fragments, which show them to be the work of a masterly hand, and it has often given me many a heartake to reflect that such

glorious old Bards – Bards, who, very probably, owed all their talents
to native genius yet have described the exploits of Heroes, the pangs
of Disappointment, and the meltings of Love with such fine strokes
of Nature, and, O mortifying to a Bard's vanity their very names are
'buried 'mongst the wreck of things which were.'

O ye illustrious names unknown! who could feel so strongly and
describe so well! the last, the meanest of the Muses train – one who,
though far inferiour to your flights, yet eyes your path, and with
trembling wing would sometimes soar after you – a poor Rustic Bard
unknown, pays this sympathetic pang to your memory! Some of you
tell us, with all the charms of verse, that you have been unfortunate
in the world, unfortunate in love; he too, has felt all the unfitness
of a Poetic heart for the struggle of a busy, bad world; he has felt
the loss of his little fortune, the loss of friends, and worse than all,
the loss of the woman he adored! Like you, all his consolation was
his Muse. She taught him in rustic measures to complain – Happy,
could he have done it with your strength of imagination, and flow
of verse! May the turf rest lightly on your bones! And may you now
enjoy that solace and rest which this world rarely gives to the heart
tuned to all the feelings of Poesy and Love!

(October 1785)
If ever any young man, on the vestibule of the world, chance to throw
his eye over these pages, let him pay a warm attention to the following
observations; as I assure him they are the fruit of a poor devil's dear
bought experience. I have, literally like that great poet and great gallant,
and by consequence, that great fool Solomon, – 'turned my eyes to
behold madness and folly' – nay I have, with all the ardor of a lively,
fanciful and whimsical imagination, accompanied with a warm, feeling,
poetic heart, shaken hands with their intoxicating friendship. In the first
place, let my Pupil, as he tenders his own peace, keep up a regular,
warm intercourse with the Deity.

PREFACE TO THE KILMARNOCK EDITION

**The Kilmarnock edition of *Poems, Chiefly in the Scottish Dia-
lect* appeared in late July 1786, probably on Monday 31 July.
Printed by John Wilson of Kilmarnock, the edition of 612
copies comprised 240 pages of text including a Preface and**

a five-page glossary. Stitched in blue paper covers, the book
sold at three shillings a copy, 350 copies having been subscribed
for prior to publication; by 28 August, Wilson had only thirteen
copies left. The Preface determined the tone of the response to
the poems; disarming sophisticated critics in advance, the im-
mensely well-read Burns stressed his educational limitations,
grim circumstances, artistic insecurity, inferiority to his Scots
predecessors Ramsay and Fergusson. The scene was set for
Henry Mackenzie (*Lounger*, 9 Dec. 1786) to acclaim Burns as
'this Heaven-taught ploughman' (CH, 70).

The following trifles are not the production of the Poet, who, with
all the advantages of learned art, and perhaps amid the elegancies
and idlenesses of upper life, looks down for a rural theme, with an
eye to Theocrites or Virgil. To the Author of this, these and other
celebrated names their countrymen are, in their original languages, 'A
fountain shut up, and a book sealed'. Unacquainted with the necessary
requisites for commencing Poet by rule, he sings the sentiments and
manners, he felt and saw in himself and his rustic compeers around
him, in his and their native language. Though a Rhymer from his
earliest years, at least from the earliest impulses of the softer passions,
it was not till very lately, that the applause, perhaps the partiality, of
Friendship, wakened his vanity so far as to make him think any thing
of his was worth showing; and none of the following works were ever
composed with a view to the press. To amuse himself with the little
creations of his own fancy, amid the toil and fatigues of a laborious
life; to transcribe the various feelings, the loves, the griefs, the hopes,
the fears, in his own breast; to find some kind of counterpoise to
the struggles of a world, always an alien scene, a task uncouth to the
poetical mind; these were his motives for courting the Muses, and in
these he found Poetry to be it's own reward.

Now that he appears in the public character of an Author, he
does it with fear and trembling. So dear is fame to the rhyming
tribe, that even he, an obscure, nameless Bard, shrinks aghast, at the
thought of being branded as 'An impertinent blockhead, obtruding
his nonsense on the world; and because he can make a shift to jingle
a few doggerel, Scotch rhymes together, looks upon himself as a Poet
of no small consequence forsooth.'

It is an observation of that celebrated Poet,[1] whose divine Elegies do
honor to our language, our nation, and our species, that 'Humility has

[1] Shenstone.

depressed many a genius to a hermit, but never raised one to fame.'
If any Critic catches at the word *genius*, the Author tells him, once
for all, that he certainly looks upon himself as possest of some poetic
abilities, otherwise his publishing in the manner he has done, would
be a manœuvre below the worst character, which, he hopes, his worst
enemy will ever give him: but to the genius of a Ramsay, or the
glorious dawnings of the poor, unfortunate Ferguson, he, with equal
unaffected sincerity, declares, that, even in his highest pulse of vanity,
he has not the most distant pretensions. These two justly admired
Scotch Poets he has often had in his eye in the following pieces;
but rather with a view to kindle at their flame, than for servile
imitation.

   To his Subscribers, the Author returns his most sincere thanks. Not
the mercenary bow over a counter, but the heart-throbbing gratitude
of the Bard, conscious how much he is indebted to Benevolence and
Friendship, for gratifying him, if he deserves it, in that dearest wish
of every poetic bosom – to be distinguished. He begs his readers,
particularly the Learned and the Polite, who may honor him with
a perusal, that they will make every allowance for Education and
Circumstances of Life: but, if after a fair, candid, and impartial criticism,
he shall stand convicted of Dulness and Nonsense, let him be done by,
as he would in that case do by others – let him be condemned, without
mercy, to contempt and oblivion.

DEDICATION TO THE FIRST EDINBURGH
EDITION

When Burns decided to bring out a second and enlarged edition
of *Poems, Chiefly in the Scottish Dialect* he found John Wilson,
the Kilmarnock printer of the first edition, hesitant about the
venture so decided on an Edinburgh production. On 7 December 1786, eight days after his first arrival in Edinburgh, Burns
wrote to Gavin Hamilton: 'Through [the Earl of Glencairn's]
influence it is inserted in the records of the Caledonian Hunt,
that they universally, one & all, subscribe for the 2d Edition.'
(CL, 66) This exclusive club of noblemen and country gentlemen subscribed for 100 copies and Burns duly dedicated the
first Edinburgh edition to them. Three thousand copies were
printed – 2900 taken by 1500 subscribers – and the volume,

selling at five shillings to subscribers and six shillings to other purchasers, was printed by William Smellie and published by William Creech (who acquired the copyright for 100 guineas) on 17 April 1787. The fanciful dedication to the Caledonian Hunt is a fulsome variation on the theme announced in the Preface to the Kilmarnock edition. Again Burns promotes himself as a poetic primitive but, since he is no longer unknown, he is more assertive: 'I was bred to the Plough, and am independent.' The highly polished prose was well calculated to seduce a responsive audience.

TO THE
NOBLEMEN AND GENTLEMEN
OF THE
CALEDONIAN HUNT.

My Lords, and Gentlemen,
A Scottish Bard, proud of the name, and whose highest ambition is to sing in his Country's service, where shall he so properly look for patronage as to the illustrious Names of his native Land; those who bear the honours and inherit the virtues of their Ancestors? – The Poetic Genius of my Country found me as the prophetic bard Elijah did Elisha – at the *plough*; and threw her inspiring *mantle* over me. She bade me sing the loves, the joys, the rural scenes and rural pleasures of my natal Soil, in my native tongue: I tuned my wild, artless notes, as she inspired. – She whispered me to come to this ancient metropolis of Caledonia, and lay my Songs under your honoured protection: I now obey her dictates.

Though much indebted to your goodness, I do not approach you, my Lords and Gentlemen, in the usual stile of dedication, to thank you for past favours; that path is so hackneyed by prostituted Learning, that honest Rusticity is ashamed of it. – Nor do I present this Address with the venal soul of a servile Author, looking for a continuation of those favours: I was bred to the Plough, and am independent. I come to claim the common Scottish name with you, my illustrious Countrymen; and to tell the world that I glory in the title. – I come to congratulate my Country, that the blood of her ancient heroes still runs uncontaminated; and that from your courage, knowledge, and public spirit, she may expect protection,

wealth, and liberty. – In the last place, I come to proffer my warmest
wishes to the Great Fountain of Honour, the Monarch of the Uni-
verse, for your welfare and happiness.

When you go forth to waken the Echoes, in the ancient and
favourite amusement of your Forefathers, may Pleasure ever be of
your party; and may Social-joy await your return! When harassed in
courts or camps with the justlings of bad men and bad measures, may
the honest consciousness of injured Worth attend your return to your
native Seats; and may Domestic Happiness, with a smiling welcome,
meet you at your gates! May Corruption shrink at your kindling
indignant glance; and may tyranny in the Ruler and licentiousness in
the People equally find you an inexorable foe!

I have the honour to be,
With the sincerest gratitude and highest
respect,

My Lords and Gentlemen,
Your most devoted humble servant,
ROBERT BURNS

Edinburgh,
Apr. 14. 1787

from SECOND COMMONPLACE BOOK

**Burns began his second Commonplace Book in Edinburgh on
9 April 1787, in a folio that cost him four shillings three pence.
It was his intention to preserve in it poems 'that must never
see the light' (one was the Jacobite song for the Duchess of
Albany, see p.208), comment on characters he encountered, tell
his 'own private story' but he virtually abandoned the plan after
leaving Edinburgh (which is why the second Commonplace
Book is often referred to as the Edinburgh Journal). First
printed in *Macmillan's Magazine* (vols.xxxix–xl, 1878–9), the
manuscript is in the Cottage Museum, Alloway.**

Text: Ch–W II, 83–4, 86–7, 344–5.

EDINR., *April ninth,* 1787

As I have seen a good deal of human life in Edinr., a great many
characters which are new to one bred up in the shades of life as I
have been, I am determined to take down my remarks on the spot.

Gray observes in a letter of his to Mr Palgrave, that 'Half a word fixed upon or near the spot, is worth a cart-load of recollection.' I don't know how it is with the world in general, but with me, making remarks is by no means a solitary pleasure. I want some one to laugh with me, some one to be grave with me; some one to please me and help my discrimination with his or her own remark, and at times, no doubt, to admire my acuteness and penetration. The World are so busied with selfish pursuits, ambition, vanity, interest or pleasure, that very few think it worth their while to make any observation on what passes around them; except where that observation is a sucker or branch of the darling plant they are rearing in their fancy. Nor am I sure, notwithstanding all the sentimental flights of Novel-writers and the sage philosophy of Moralists, if we are capable of so intimate and cordial a coalition of friendship as that one of us may pour out his bosom, his every thought and floating fancy, his very inmost soul, with unreserved confidence, to another, without hazard of losing part of that respect man demands from man; or, from the unavoidable imperfections attending human nature, of one day repenting his confidence.

For these reasons, I am determined to make these pages my Confidante. I will sketch every character that anyway strikes me, to the best of my observation, with unshrinking justice; I will insert anecdotes, and take down remarks, in the old law phrase, without feud or favor: where I hit on any thing clever, my own applause will, in some measure, feast my vanity; and (begging Patroclus' and Achates's pardon) I think a lock and key a security at least equal to the bosom of any friend whatever.

My own private story likewise, my amours, my rambles, the smiles and frowns of Fortune on my Bardship, my Poems and fragments that must never see the light, shall be occasionally inserted: in short, never did four shillings purchase so much friendship since Confidence went first to market, or Honesty was set to Sale.

To these seemingly invidious, but too just ideas of human friendship, I shall chearfully and truly make one exception – the connection between two persons of different sex, when their interests are united or absorbed by the sacred tie of Love—

> When thought meets thought ere from the lips it part,
> And each warm wish springs mutual from the heart.

There Confidence, confidence that exalts them the more in one another's opinion, confidence that endears them the more to

one another's heart, unreservedly and luxuriantly 'reigns and revels.'
But this is not my lot, and in my situation, if I am wise (which by the by I
have no great chance of being) my fate should be cast with the Psalmist's
sparrow, 'To watch alone on the house-tops.' Oh, the pity!!!

There are few of the sore evils under the sun give me more
uneasiness and chagrin than the comparison how a man of genius,
nay, avowed worth, is everywhere received, with the reception which
a meer ordinary character, decorated with the trappings and futile
distinctions of Fortune, meets. Imagine a man of abilities, his breast
glowing with honest pride, conscious that men are born equal, still
giving that 'honor to whom honor is due;' he meets at a Great man's
table a Squire Something, or a Sir Somebody; he knows the noble
landlord at heart gives the Bard or whatever he is a share of his good
wishes beyond any at table perhaps, yet how will it mortify him to see a
fellow whose abilities would scarcely have made an eight penny taylor,
and whose heart is not worth three farthings, meet with attention and
notice that are forgot to the Son of Genius and Poverty?
    The noble Glencairn has wounded me to the soul here, because I
dearly esteem, respect and love him. He showed so much attention,
engrossing attention, one day, to the only blockhead, as there was
none but his lordship, the Dunderpate and myself, that I was within
half a point of throwing down my gage of contemptuous defiance, but
he shook my hand and looked so benevolently good at parting – God
bless him, though I should never see him more, I shall love him untill
my dying day! I am pleased to think I am so capable of the throes of
gratitude, as I am miserably defficient in some other virtues. With Dr
Blair I am more at ease. I never respect him with humble veneration;
but when he kindly interests himself in my welfare, or, still more, when
he descends from his pinnacle and meets me on equal ground, my heart
overflows with what is called *liking*: when he neglects me for the meer
carcase of Greatness, or when his eye measures the difference of our
points of elevation, I say to myself with scarcely an emotion, what do
I care for him or his pomp either?
    It is not easy forming an exact judging judgement of any one, but
in my opinion Dr Blair is meerly an astonishing proof what industry
and application can do. Natural parts like his are frequently to be met
with; his vanity is proverbially known among his acquaintances; but
he is justly at the head of what may be called fine writing; and a Critic
of the first, the very first rank in Prose; even in Poesy a good Bard of
Nature's making can only take the pas of him. He has a heart, not of

the finest water, but far from being an ordinary one. In short, he is [a] truly worthy and most respectable character.

Mr Greenfield is of a superiour order. The bleedings of humanity, the generous resolve, a manly disregard of the paltry subjects of vanity, virgin modesty, the truest taste, and a very sound judgement, characterize him. His being the first Speaker I ever heard is perhaps half owing to industry. He certainly possesses no small share of poetic abilities; he is a steady, most disinterested friend, without the least affectation of seeming so; and as a companion, his good sense, his joyous hilarity, his sweetness of manners and modesty, are most engagingly charming.

The most perfect character I ever saw is Mr Stuart [Dugald Stewart]. An exalted judge of the human heart, and of composition. One of the very first public speakers; and equally capable of generosity as humanity. His principal discriminating feature is; from a mixture of benevolence, strength of mind and manly dignity, he not only at heart values, but in his deportment and address bears himself to all the Actors, high and low, in the drama of Life, simply as they merit in playing their parts. Wealth, honors, all that is extraneous of the man, have no more influence with him than they will have at the Last Day. His wit, in the hour of social hilarity, proceeds almost to good-natured waggishness; and in telling a story he particularly excels.

The next I shall mention, my worthy Bookseller, Mr C[reech] is a strange multiform character. His ruling passions of the left hand kind are extreme vanity, and something of the more harmless modifications of selfishness. The one, mixed, as it often is, with great goodness of heart, makes him rush into all public matters, and take every instance of unprotected merit by the hand, provided it is in his power to hand it into public notice; the other quality makes him, amid all the embarras in which his vanity entangles him, now and then to cast half a squint at his own interest. His parts as a man, his deportment as a gentleman, and his abilities as a scholar are much above mediocrity. Of all the Edinr. literati and wit he writes the most like a gentleman. He does not awe you with the profoundness of the philosopher, or strike your eye with the soarings of genius; but he pleases you with the handsome turn of his expression, and the polite ease of his paragraph. His social demeanour and powers, particularly at his own table, are the most engaging I have ever met with. On with whole he is, as I said before, a multiform, but an exceedingly respectable, worthy character.

ELLISLAND, *14th June* 1788. *Sunday*
This is now the third day I have been in this country. Lord, what is man! what a bustling little bundle of passions, appetites, ideas and

fancies! and what a capricious kind of existence he has here! If
legendary stories be true, there is indeed an Elsewhere, where, as
Thomson says, 'Virtue sole survives.'

> ——————————Tell us ye Dead;
> Will none of you in pity disclose the secret,
> What 'tis you are, and we must shortly be?
> ——————————————a little time
> Will make us learned as you are and as close.[1]

I am such a coward in Life, so tired of the Service, that I would almost
at any time with Milton's *Adam*—

> ——gladly lay me in my Mother's lap,
> And be at peace.

but a wife and children, in poetics, 'The fair Partner of my soul, and
the little dear Pledges of our mutual love,' these bind me to struggle
with the stream; till some chopping squall overset the silly vessel, or,
in the listless return of years, its own craziness drive it to a wreck.
Farewel, now, to those giddy Follies, those varnished Vices, which,
though half sanctified by the bewitching levity of Wit and Humour, are
at best but thriftless idling with the precious current of Existence; nay,
often poisoning the whole, that, like the Plains of Jericho, 'The water
is naught, and the ground barren,' and nothing short of a supernaturally
gifted Elisha can ever after heal the evils.

Wedlock, the circumstance that buckles me hardest to Care, if
Virtue and Religion were to be anything with me but mere names,
was what in a few seasons I must have resolved on; in the present case
it was unavoidably necessary. Humanity, Generosity, honest vanity of
character, Justice to my own happiness for after-life, so far as it could
depend, which it surely will a great deal, on internal peace, all these
joined their warmest suffrages, their most powerful solicitations, with
a rooted Attachment, to urge the step I have taken. Nor have I any
reason on her part to rue it. I can fancy *how*, but have never seen
where, I could have made it better. Come then, let me return to my
favourite Motto, that glorious passage in Young—

> On REASON build RESOLVE,
> That column of true majesty in man.

[1] Blair: *The Grave*

from JOURNAL OF THE BORDER TOUR

From 5 May to 1 June 1787 Burns made a tour of the Borders, most of it in the company of Robert Ainslie, a Borderer born at Berrywell, near Duns. Ainslie was a 21-year-old law student in the Edinburgh office of Samuel Mitchelson when the poet met him early in 1787; he seems to have returned to his studies around 24 May. For the tour Burns bought a mare in Edinburgh for over £4 sterling; he named the mare Jenny Geddes after the woman traditionally credited with throwing a stool at the Bishop of Edinburgh on Sunday, 23 July 1637, in St Giles Cathedral when the Bishop attempted to impose on Scotland a Liturgy authorised by Charles I.

The Journal was first published in Allan Cunningham's *The Works of Robert Burns* (1834); the original holograph manuscript (57 octavo pages) is held by the Murray family who own the publishing house of John Murray Ltd.

The following extracts use the text in *Robert Burns's Tour of the Borders* (Ipswich: The Boydell Press, 1972) edited by Raymond Lamont Brown.

[*Leaving Edinburgh around 6.30am on Saturday, 5 May 1787, Burns travelled towards Berrywell (in Berwickshire, otherwise known as 'the Merse') where he met Ainslie's father, mother, 19-year-old sister Rachel, 16-year-old brother Douglas. He talked with William Dudgeon, a Berwickshire poet and listened to a sermon by Revd Dr Robert Bowmaker in the parish church of Duns. Bowmaker's sermon on the infernal fate of sinners supposedly disturbed Rachel Ainslie so Burns produced and passed to her the following quatrain which was first published in R.H. Cromek's* Reliques of Robert Burns *(1808):*

> Fair maid, you need not take the hint,
>   Nor idle texts pursue;
> 'Twas only sinners that he meant,
>   Not angels such as you.]

May 6th
Left Edinr. – Lammermuir hills miserably dreary but at times very picturesque – Lanton edge a glorious view of the Merse – reach Berrywell – Old Mr Ainslie an uncommon character – his hobbies Agriculture

natural philosophy & politics – In the first he is unexceptionably the clearest-headed, best-informed man I ever met with; in the other two, very intelligent – As a Man of business he has uncommon merit, and by fairly deserving it has made a very decent independance – Mrs Ainslie an excellent, sensible, chearful, amiable old woman – Miss Ainslie an angel – her person a little of the embonpoint but handsome her face, particularly her eyes full of sweetness and good humour – she unites three qualities rarely to be found together, keen, solid penetration; sly, witting observation and remark; and the gentlest, most unaffected female Modesty – Douglas a clever, fine, promising young fellow – The family meeting with their brother, my compagnion [sic] de voyage, very charming, particularly the sister—

The whole family remarkably attached to their menials – Mrs A[inslie] – full of stories of the sagacity & sense of the little girl in the kitchen – Mr A[inslie] – high in the praises of an African, his house servant – All his people old in his service – Douglas's old Nurse came to Berry-well yesterday to [tell-deleted] remind them of its being Douglas's birth day—

A Mr Dudgeon, a Poet at times, a worthy, remarkable character – [a good deal of – deleted] natural penetration, a great deal of information, some genius, and extreme Modesty—

Sunday – went to church at Dunse – Dr Bowmaker a man of strong lungs and pretty judicious remark; but ill skilled in propriety, and altogether unconscious of his want of it—

[On Monday, 7 May, Burns and Ainslie went to Coldstream where they crossed the Tweed into England. Burns mentions only that he 'went over to England' but Ainslie published a colourful account of the incident in Chambers's Edinburgh Journal (28 Apr. 1832): 'When they arrived at Coldstream, where the dividing line between England and Scotland is the Tweed, Mr Ainslie suggested going across to the other side of the river by the Coldstream Bridge, that Burns might be enabled to say he had been in England. They did so, and were pacing slowly along on English ground, enjoying their walk, when Mr Ainslie was surprised to see the poet throw away his hat, and, thus uncovered, kneel down with uplifted hands, and apparently rapt in a fit of enthusiasm. Mr Ainslie kept silence, uncertain what was next to be done, when Burns, with extreme emotion, and an expression of countenance which his companion could never forget, prayed for and blessed Scotland most solemnly, by pronouncing aloud, in tones of the deepest devotion, the two concluding stanzas of the "Cotter's Saturday Night" . . . ' (Ch–W II, 103–4).

On 8 May Burns breakfasted at Kelso then proceeded to Jedburgh where he spent the night. The Jedburgh references are to James Fair, a lawyer *who married Catherine Lookup; Captain John Rutherford, once enslaved by Chippewah Indians; Mr Potts, possibly an English lawyer; the Revd Dr Thomas Somerville, minister at Jedburgh; Miss Hope of Cowdenknowes; and Isabella Lindsay, daughter of a Jedburgh doctor.]*

Wednesday (9 May)
   Breakfast with Mr Fair in Jedburgh a blind man but the first man of business as a Writer in town – a squabble between Mrs F[air], a craz'd talkative Slattern and a sister of hers an old maid, respecting a relief Minister – Miss gives Madam the lie, & Madam by way of revenge upbraids her that she laid snares to entangle the said minister, then a widower, in the net of matrimony – go about two miles out of Jedburgh to a roup of [grass] Parks – meet a polite soldier-like gentleman, a Captn. Rutherford who had been many years thro the wilds of America, a prisoner among the Indians – Charming, romantic situation, of Jedburgh, with gardens, orchards, &c. intermingled among the houses – fine old ruins, a once magnificent Cathedral [and strong castle – *deleted*] – All the towns here have the appearance of old, rude grandeur; but extremely idle – Jed a fine romantic little river—
   Dine with Captn. Rutherford. The Captn. a specious polite fellow, very fond of money in his farming way, but showed a particular respect to My Bardship – his lady exactly a proper matrimonial second part for him – Miss Rutherford a beautiful girl, but too far gone woman to expose so much of so fine a swelling bosom – her face tho' very fine rather inanimately heavy – return to Jedburgh – walk up Jed with some ladies to be shown Love-lane & Black-burn two fairy scenes – introduced to Mr Potts, Writer, a very clever fellow; & Mr Somerville the clergyman of the place, a man & a gentleman; but sadly addicted to punning – The walking Partie of ladies – Mrs F[air] & Miss Lookup her sister before-mentioned. N.B. these two appear still more comfortably ugly & stupid, and bore me most shockingly – [The – *deleted*] Two Miss Fairs, tolerably agreable but too much of the Mother's half-ell [features – *deleted*] mouth & hag-like features – Miss Hope, a tolerably pretty girl, fond of laughing & fun – Miss Lindsay a good-humor'd amiable girl; rather short et embonpoint, but handsome and extremely graceful – beautiful hazle eyes full of spirit & sparkling with delicious moisture – an engaging face & manner, un tout ensemble that speaks her of the first order of female minds – her sister, a bonie, strappan, rosy, sonsie lass – Shake myself loose, after several unsuccessful efforts, of Mrs F[ai]r & Miss L[ooku]p and somehow of other get hold of Miss Lindsay's arm – my heart thawed into melting pleasure after being so long frozen up in the Greenland bay of Indifference amid the noise and

nonsense of Edinr. – Miss seems very well pleased with my Bardship's distinguishing her, and after some slight qualms which I could easily mark, she sets the titter round at defiance, and kindly allows me to keep my hold; and when parted by the ceremony of my introduction to Mr Somerville she met me half to resume my [hold – *deleted*] situation – Nota Bene – The Poet within a point and a half of being damnably in love – I am afraid my bosom still nearly as much tinder as ever—

The old, cross-grained, whiggish, ugly, slanderous hag, Miss Lookup with all the poisonous spleen of a disappointed, ancient maid, stops me very unseasonably to [fall abusively foul – *deleted*] ease her hell-rankling bursting breast by falling [foul – *deleted*] abusively foul on the Miss Lindsays, particularly my Dulcinea; I hardly refrain from cursing her to her face – May she, for her pains, be curst with eternal desire and damn'd with endless disappointment! Hear me, O Heavens, and give ear, O Earth! may the burden of antiquated Virginity crush her down to the lowest regions of the bottomless Pit! for daring to mouth her calumnious slander on one of the finest pieces of the workmanship of Almighty Excellence. Sup at Mr F[*air's*] vexed that the Miss Lindsays are not of the supper party as they only are wanting – Mrs F[*air*] & Miss L[*ooku*]p still improve infernally on my hands—

[*Still in Jedburgh on Friday, 11 May, Burns met Esther Easton, the wife of a working gardener. The proof-print he mentions was the engraving John Beugo prepared for the first Edinburgh edition.*]

Breakfast next morning [*11 May*] with Mr Sommerville – the bruit of Miss Lindsay and my Bardship by means of the invention & malice of Miss L[*ooku*]p – Mr Sommerville sends to Dr Lindsay begging him & family to breakfast [but at all ev – *deleted*] if convenient, but at all events to send Miss L[*indsay*] accordingly Miss L[*indsay*] only comes – I find Miss L[*indsay*] would soon play the devil with me – I meet with some little flattering attentions from her—

Mrs S[*ommerville*] an excellent, motherl[*y*], agreable woman, and a fine famil[*y*] – Mr Ainslie & Mr S[*ommerville*] Junrs. with Mr Fair, Miss Lindsay and me, go to see Esther, a very remarkable woman for reciting Poetry of all kinds, and sometimes making Scotch doggerel herself – She can repeat by heart almost every thing she has ever read, particularly Pope's Homer from end to end – has studyed Euclid by herself, and in short is a woman of very extraordinary abilities – on conversing with her I find her fully to come up to the character given of her – She is very much flattered that I send for her, and that she sees a Poet who has put out a book as she says – She is, among other things, a great Florist – and is rather past the meridian of once celebrated beauty but alas!

J

tho very well married, before that period she was violently suspected for some of the tricks of the Cytherean Déesse—

I walk down Esther's garden with Miss L[indsay] and after some little chit-chat of the tender kind I presented her with a proof-print of my nob, which she accepted with something more tender than gratitude – She told me many little stories which Miss L[ooku]p had retailed concerning her and me, with prolonging pleasure – God bless her!

Was waited on by the Magistrates and presented with the freedom of the burgh—

Took farewell to Jedburgh with some melancholy, disagreable sensations – Jed, pure be they chrystal streams, and hallowed thy sylvan banks! Sweet Isabella Lindsay, may Peace dwell in thy bosom, uninterrupted, except by the tumultuous throbbings of rapturous Love! That love-kindling eye must beam on another, not me; that graceful form must bless another's arms, not mine!

[*After visiting various places (including Melrose, Selkirk, Berwick, Eyemouth, Dunbar) Burns was back at Berrywell on Thursday, 24 May. In the following extract Burns refers to Sir John Home, Coldingham farmer; Lumsden, Roxburghshire farmer; Robert Ker, Roxburghshire farmer; Thomas Hood, Berwickshire farmer.*]

Found Miss Ainslie, the amiable, the sensible, the good-humored, the sweet Miss Ainslie all alone at Berrywell – Heavenly Powers who know the weaknesses of human hearts support mine! what happiness must I see only to remind me that I cannot enjoy it!

Lammermuir hills from East Lothian to Dunse, very wild – Dine with the Farmer's club at Kelso. – Sir J[oh]n Hume & Mr Lumsden there but nothing worth remembering when the following circumstance is considered – I walk in to Dunse before dinner, & out to Berrywell in the evening with Miss Ainslie – how well-bred, how frank, how good she is! I could grasp her with rapture on a bed of straw, and rise with contentment to the most sweltering drudgery of stiffening Labor!

(*Thursday* – deleted) – Mr Kerr & I set out for to dine at Mr Hood's on our way to England—

Charming Rachel! [*Ainslie*] may thy bosom never be wrung by the evils of this life of sorrows, or by the villainy of this world's sons!

I am taken extremely ill with strong feverish symptoms, & take a servant of Mr Hood's to watch me all night – embittering Remorse scares my fancy at the gloomy forebodings of death – I am determined to live for the future in such a manner as not to be scared at the approach of Death – I am sure I could meet him with indifference, but for 'The Something beyond the grave' – Mr Hood agrees to accompany us to England if we will wait him till Sunday—

(Thursday – deleted)

Friday (25 May)

   I go with Mr Hood to see the roup [*ie, auction sale*] of an unfortunate Farmer's stock – rigid Economy & decent Industry, do you preserve me from being the principal Dramatis Persona in such a scene of horrors! Meet my good old friend Mr Ainslie who calls on Mr Hood in the evening to take farewel of my Bardship – this day I feel myself warm wt. sentiments of gratitude to the Great Preserver of men who has kindly restored me to health and strength once more – A pleasant walk with my young friend Douglas Ainslie, a sweet, modest, clever young fellow—

[*On Sunday, 27 May, Burns crossed the Tweed for a second sight of England. On 29 May he rode south to Newcastle but the manuscript makes no mention of this. However, Cunningham's printed text supplies an amorous envoi to the Border tour.*]

Thursday (31 May) – Reach Longtown to dine, and part there with my good friends Messrs Hood and Ker. – A hiring day in Longtown. – I am uncommonly happy to see so many young folks enjoying life. – I come to Carlisle. (Meet a strange enough romantic adventure by the way, in falling in with a girl and her married sister – the girl, after some overtures of gallantry on my side, sees me a little cut with the bottle, and offers to take me in for a Gretna-green affair [*ie, an elopement*]. I, not being quite such a gull as she imagines, make an appointment with her, by way of vive la bagatelle, to hold a conference on it when we reach town. – I meet her in town and give her a brush of caressing and a bottle of cyder; but finding herself un peu trompée in her man, she sheers off.)

from JOURNAL OF THE HIGHLAND TOUR

**From 25 August to 16 September 1787 Burns toured the High-
lands with William Nicol, a sadistic Edinburgh schoolmaster
(according to the *Memorials* of Lord Cockburn who suffered
at his hands). The two tourists travelled in a chaise and Burns
kept a Journal though most of it is merely a record of places
visited.**

**A facsimile of the manuscript, edited by J.C. Ewing,
was published as *Journal of a Tour in the Highlands* (1927);
Burns's thirty-five-page holograph manuscript is now in
the Alloway Monument Museum. The following extracts
use the text in *Robert Burns's Tours of the Highlands and
Stirlingshire 1787* (Ipswich: The Boydell Press, 1973) edited
by Raymond Lamont Brown.**

(Saturday, 25 August)
Linlithgow, the appearance of rude, decayed, idle grandeur – charm-
ingly rural, retired situation – the old royal palace a tolerably fine, but
melancholy, ruin – sweetly situated on a small elevation by the brink of
a Loch – shown the room where the beautiful injured Mary Queen of
Scots was born – a pretty good old Gothic church – the infamous stool
of repentance standing, in the old Romish way, on a lofty situation.

What a poor, pimping business is a Presbyterian place of worship,
dirty, narrow and squalid, stuck in a corner of old Popish grandeur
such as Linlithgow and, much more, Melrose! ceremony and show, if
judiciously thrown in, absolutely necessary for the bulk of mankind,
both in religious and civil matters.

(Sunday, 26 August)
Come on to Bannockburn – shown the old house where James 3d was
murdered – the field of Bannockburn – the hole where glorious Bruce
set his standard.

(Friday, 31 August)
[*At Dunkeld Burns met Neil Gow, celebrated Scottish fiddler and composer, who lived at Inver with his wife.*]
Neil Gow plays – a short, stout-built, honest highland figure, with his grayish hair shed on his honest social brow – an interesting face, marking strong sense, kind open-heartedness mixed with unmistrusting simplicity – visit his house – Marget Gow.

(Tuesday, 4 September)
Findhorn river – rocky banks – come on to Castle Cawdor – where Macbeth murdered King Duncan – Saw the bed in which King Duncan was stabbed—

(Friday, 7 September)
[*Burns was entertained at Castle Gordon by the Duke and Duchess of Gordon.*]
The Duke makes me happier than ever great man did – noble, princely, yet mild, condescending and affable, gay and kind – the Duchess charming, witty, kind and sensible – God bless them!

(Thursday, 13 September)
Leave Montrose – breakfast at Auchmithie, and sail along that wild rocky coast, and see the Caverns, particularly ye Garriepot – land and dine at Arbroath – stately ruins Arbroath Abbey – come to Dundee, through a fertile Country – Dundee a low-lying but pleasant town – old steeple – Tayfrith – Broughty Castle, a finely situated ruin, jutting into the Tay.

(Sunday, 16 September)
come through a cold barren Country to Queensferry – dine – cross the Ferry, and come to Edinburgh.

LETTERS

More than 700 letters by Burns have been preserved: written between 29 July 1780, when he was twenty-one; and 18 July 1796, a few days before his death. They range thematically from bawdy letters to friends such as Bob Ainslie, through diplomatic letters to potential patrons, to strategically guided missives to the likes of Mrs McLehose.

Burns was highly skilled at telling his correspondents exactly what they wanted to hear: compare the remarks on religion to Mrs McLehose (p.292) with comments on the same subject to Alexander Cunningham (p.316); or his defence of virtue in various letters to Mrs McLehose with his advice to his brother William on sexual matters (p.309). In his letters, as in his life, there was much roleplaying though when he was overcome by anguish he relinquished the roleplaying, most movingly in the desperate letters of his dying days.

Burns studied the fine art of letter-writing at an early age. At home, in the Alloway cottage, he was entertained by the Scottish oral skills of his mother and old Betty Davidson; at school, with John Murdoch from 1765–7, he was introduced to the formal English affectations of literary letters. Arthur Masson's *Collection of Prose and Verse, from the Best English Authors, for the Use of Schools* (2nd edn, 1767), a basic text taught by Murdoch, included examples of the *Letters Moral and Entertaining* of Mrs Rowe, taken from her *Friendship in Death: In Twenty Letters from the Dead to the Living To which are added, Letters Moral and Entertaining* (5th edtn, 1738). Mrs Rowe's letters, sentimental in content and style, make edifying comments on the prospect of life as a long preparation for death.

Burns learned, from Mrs Rowe, how to contain his feelings in an epistolary frame, how to structure his sentiments for maximum effect. One of Mrs Rowe's letters, anthologized by Masson, is cast as the death-bed confession of a Duke who expresses himself thus:

> Before you receive this, my final state will be determined by the judge of all the earth; in a few days at most, perhaps in a few hours, the inevitable sentence will be past, that shall raise me to the

heights of happiness, or sink me to the depths of
misery. While you read these lines, I shall be either
groaning under the agonies of absolute despair, or
triumphing in fullness of joy.

'Tis impossible for me to express the present
disposition of my soul, the vast uncertainty I am
struggling with; no words can paint the force and
vivacity of my apprehensions: Every doubt wears
the face of horror, and would perfectly overwhelm
me, but for some faint beams of hope, which dart
across the tremendous gloom. What tongue can
utter the anguish of a soul, suspended between the
extreams of infinite joy, or eternal misery. I am
throwing my last state for eternity, and tremble and
shudder for the important event.

Burns's letter of 27 December 1781 to his father (p.263) adopts
the Duke's terminal tone. Mrs Rowe is an important stylistic
source for Burns's achievement as a man of letters.

Another source is Richardson's epistolary novel *Pamela*
(1740–1). In the summer of 1772 Burns and his brother Gilbert
attended, week about, Dalrymple parish school. According
to Gilbert, it was then that 'a bookish acquaintance of my
father's procured us a reading of two volumes of Richardson's
Pamela, which was the first novel we read' (Currie I, 64).
Burns puts his reading of *Pamela* at a later date, in the Autobiographical Letter, but another reference suggests Gilbert's
chronology is accurate. Discussing fictional explorations of
human emotion, in a letter of 28 February 1791 to Dr John
Moore, Burns says of Richardson:

> unhappily, his Dramatis personae are beings of some
> other world; & however they may captivate the
> unexperienced, romantic fancy of a boy or girl, they
> will ever, in portion as we have made human nature
> our study, disgust our riper minds. (CL, 262)

Burns would hardly have come to such a conclusion unless
he had first encountered Richardson with 'the unexperienced,
romantic fancy of a boy', and been duly captivated.

Pamela is obsessed by her own virtue, indeed virtue is the

favourite word of a novel subtitled *Virtue Rewarded*. Her voice, in her letters, is the voice of virtue and Burns, too, enjoyed dwelling on the notion of virtue in his pointedly moral letters to ladies such as Mrs Dunlop and Mrs McLehose. When writing to Mrs McLehose, indeed, Burns sounds like a character from an epistolary novel like *Pamela*. Pamela always projects herself as the honest woman, protesting against the exploitation of her poverty. Burns frequently projects himself as the honest man, protesting against the exploitation of his poverty. Read *Pamela* then look at the letters of Burns and the influence of Richardson is obvious.

After his summer at Kirkoswald in 1775, Burns returned to Mount Oliphant farm 'very considerably improved', as he explained in the Autobiographical Letter: 'I had met with a collection of letters by the Wits of Queen Ann's reign, and I pored over them most devoutly'. This collection has not been identified but is thought to have included selections from the correspondence of Swift and Bolingbroke with Pope. If Burns could burden his letters with an Augustan solemnity he could also enliven them with Augustan wit. Both extremes are exhibited in the letter of 30 June 1787 to James Smith (p.286).

The bawdy letters, especially the 'horse litter' letter to Ainslie (p.298), reveal a different Burns. In these he casts off the sentimental conventions of his epistolary models to write with the erotic immediacy that came naturally to him. Writing letters to ladies like Mrs Dunlop and Mrs McLehose, Burns was performing the role of the Man of Feeling; writing to Ainslie, Burns was being himself, at least that part of himself functioning as a highly-sexed farmer with an astonishing range of amorous images. On reading the bawdy letters of Burns, Byron exclaimed: 'What an antithetical mind! – tenderness, roughness – delicacy, coarseness – sentiment, sensuality – soaring and grovelling, dirt and deity – all mixed up in that one compound of inspired clay!' (CH, 257–8)

Burns may have impulsively dashed off his bawdy letters but he wrote drafts of letters he considered artistically important; carefully polished his epistolary prose. Before he sent his Autobiographical Letter to Dr Moore, he showed the original copy to Mrs Dunlop who pronounced it finer than Richardson and Fielding, thus rightly reading it as a well-crafted literary work, not a carelessly confessional missive.

In his letters Burns could be sycophantic or scornful, superficial or serious, affected or earnest. He had several styles
at his command and the style he selected when writing a
letter was determined by his reading of the character of the
correspondent.

TO WILLIAM BURNES
(CL, 41–2)

Irvin, December 27th 1781

Honored Sir,

I have purposely delayed writing in the hope that I would have the pleasure of seeing you on Newyearday but work comes so hard upon us that I do not chuse to come as well for that, as also for some other little reasons which I shall tell you at meeting. – My health is much about what it was when you were here only my sleep is rather sounder and on the whole I am rather better than otherwise tho it is but by very slow degrees. – The weakness of my nerves has so debilitated my mind that I dare not, either review past events, or look forward into futurity; for the least anxiety, or perturbation in my breast, produces most unhappy effects on my whole frame. –

Sometimes, indeed, when for an hour or two, as is sometimes the case, my spirits are a little lightened, I glimmer a little into futurity; but my principal, and indeed my only pleasurable enjoyment is looking backwards & forwards in a moral & religious way – I am quite transported at the thought that ere long, perhaps very soon, I shall bid an eternal adieu to all the pains, & uneasiness & desquietudes of this weary life; for I assure you I am heartily tired of it, and, if I do not very much deceive myself I could contentedly & gladly resign it. –

> The Soul uneasy & confin'd from home,
> Rests & expatiates in a life to come.
> Pope[1]

It is for this reason I am more pleased with the 15th, 16th & 17th verses of the 7th Chapter of Revelation than any ten times as many verses in the whole Bible, & would not exchange the noble enthusiasm with which they inspire me, for all that this world has to offer – As for this world I despair of ever making a figure in it – I am not formed for the bustle of the busy nor the flutter of the Gay I shall never again be capable of it. – Indeed, I am altogether unconcern'd at the thoughts of it. I foresee that very probably Poverty & Obscurity await me & I am, in some measure prepared & daily preparing to meet & welcome them. – I have but just time & paper to return you my grateful thanks for the many Lessons of Virtue & Piety you have given me – Lessons which were but too much neglected when they were given but which, I hope have been remembered ere it is yet too late – Present my dutiful

respects to my Mother & my Compliments to Mr & Mrs Muir and
with wishing you all a merry Newyearday I shall conclude—

I am, Honored Sir, your dutiful son

Robert Burns

my meal is nearly out but I am going to borrow till I get more—
1 *Essay on Man*. Epistle 1, lines 97–8.

TO JOHN MURDOCH
(CL, 54–5)

Lochlee, 15th January 1783

Dear Sir,

As I have an opportunity of sending you a letter without putting you
to that experience which any production of mine would but ill repay;
I embrace it with pleasure to tell you that I have not forgotten, nor
never will forget, the many obligations I lie under to your kindness
and friendship. I do not doubt, Sir, but you will wish to know what
has been the result of all the pains of an indulgent father, and a masterly
teacher; and I wish I could gratify your curiosity with such a recital as
you would be pleased with; but that is what I am afraid will not be
the case. I have, indeed, kept pretty clear of vicious habits; & in this
respect, I hope, my conduct will not disgrace the education I have
gotten; but as a man of the world, I am most miserably deficient.
– One would have thought that, bred as I have been under a father
who has figured pretty well as un hommes des affaires, I might have
been, what the world calls, a pulsing, active fellow; but, to tell you
the truth, Sir, there is hardly any thing more my reverse – I seem
to be one sent into the world, to see, and observe; and I very easily
compound with the knave who tricks me of my money, if there be
any thing original about him which shews me human nature in a
different light from any thing I have seen before. In short, the joy of
my heart is to 'Study men, their manners, and their ways:'[1] and for
this darling subject, I chearfully sacrifice every other consideration:
I am quite indolent about those great concerns that set the bustling,
busy Sons of Care agog; and if I have to answer the present hour, I
am very easy with regard to any thing further. – Even the last, worst
shift of the unfortunate and the wretched, does not much terrify me:
I know that even then, my talent for what country folks call 'a sensible
crack,' when once it is sanctified by a hoary head, would procure me
so much esteem, that even then – I would learn to be happy. However,
I am under no apprehensions about that, for though indolent, yet so

far as an extremely delicate constitution permits, I am not lazy; and
in many things, especially in tavern matters, I am a strict eo-conomist;
not, indeed, for the sake of the money, but one of the principal parts
in my composition is a kind of pride of stomach; and I scorn to fear
the face of any man living: above every thing, I abhor as hell, the idea
of sneaking in a corner to avoid a dun – possibly some pitiful, sordid
wretch, who in my heart I despise and detest. 'Tis this, and this alone,
that endears eo-conomy to me. In the matter of books, indeed, I am
very profuse. – My favorite authors are of the sentimental kind,
such as Shenstone, particularly his Elegies, Thomson, Man of feeling, a book I prize next to the Bible, Man of the World, Sterne,
especially his Sentimental journey, McPherson's Ossian, &c. these are
the glorious models after which I endeavour to form my conduct,
and 'tis incongruous, 'tis absurd to suppose that the man whose
mind glows with sentiments lighted up at their sacred flame – the
man whose heart distends with benevolence to all the human race
– he 'who can soar above this little scene of things'[2] – can he
descend to mind the paltry concerns about which the terrae-filial
race fret, and fume, and vex themselves? O how the glorious triumph swells my heart! I forget that I am a poor, insignificant devil,
unnoticed and unknown, stalking up and down fairs and markets
when I happen to be in them, reading a page or two of mankind,
and 'catching the manners living as they rise,'[3] whilst the men of
business jostle me on every side, as an idle encumbrance in their
way. – But I dare say I have by this time tired your patience; so
I shall conclude with begging you to give Mrs Murdoch – not
my compliments – for that is a mere common place story; but my
warmest, kindest wishes for her welfare; and accept of the same yourself
from,

Dear Sir, your sincere friend, and oblidged humble Servant

Robert Burns

1 Pope: *January and May*, line 157
2 Thomson: *Autumn*, line 964
3 Pope: *Essay on Man*, Espistle I, line 14

TO JAMES BURNESS
(CL, 57–8)

Lochlee, 21st June 1783

Dear Sir,

My father received your favor of the 10th Current, and as he has been
for some months very poorly in health, & is in his own opinion,
& indeed in almost ev'ry body's else, in a dying condition; he has
only, with great difficulty, wrote a few farewel lines to each of his
brothers-in-law; for this melancholy reason I now hold the pen for
him to thank you for your kind letter, & to assure you Sir, that it shall
not be my fault if my father's correspondence in the North die with
him. – My brother writes to John Caird, & to him I must refer you for
the news of our family. I shall only trouble you with a few particulars
relative to the present wretched state of this country. Our markets are
exceedingly high; oatmeal 17 & 18d per peck, & not to be got even
at that price. We have indeed been pretty well supplied with quantities
of white pease from England & elsewhere, but that resource is likely to
fail us; & what will become of us then, particularly the very poorest
sort, Heaven only knows. – This country, till of late was flourishing
incredibly in the Manufactures of Silk, Lawn & Carpet Weaving, and
we are still carrying on a good deal in that way but much reduced
from what it was; we had also a fine trade in the Shoe way, but now
entirely ruined & hundreds driven to a starving condition on account
of it. – Farming is also at a very low ebb with us. Our lands, generally
speaking, are mountainous & barren; and our Landholders, full of ideas
of farming gathered from the English, and the Lothians and other rich
soils in Scotland; make no allowance for the odds of the quality of land,
and consequently stretch us much beyond what, in the event, we will be
found able to pay. We are also much at a loss for want of proper methods
in our improvements of farming: necessity compels us to leave our old
schemes; & few of us have opportunities of being well informed in
new ones. In short, my dear Sir, since the unfortunate beginning of
this American war, & its as unfortunate conclusion, this country has
been, & still is decaying very fast.

Even in higher life, a couple of our Ayrshire Noblemen, and the
major part of our Knights & squires, are all insolvent. A miserable job
of a Douglas, Heron, & Co.'s Bank, which no doubt you have heard
of, has undone numbers of them; and imitating English, and French,
and other foreign luxuries & fopperies, has ruined as many more. –
There is great trade of smuggling carried on along our coasts, which,

however destructive to the interests of the kingdom at large, certainly enriches this corner of it; but too often indeed at the expence of our Morals; however, it enables individuals to make, at least for a time, a splendid appearance; but Fortune, as is usual with her when she is uncommonly lavish of her favours, is generally even with them at the last; & happy were it for numbers of them if she would leave them no worse than when she found them—

My mother sends you a small present of a cheese, 'tis but a very little one as our last year's stock is sold off; but if you could fix on any correspondent in Edinburgh, or Glasgow, we would send you a proper one in the season. Mrs Black promises to take the cheese under his care so far, and then to send it to you by the Stirling carrier.

I shall conclude this long letter with assuring you that I shall be very happy to hear from you or any of our friends in your country when opportunity serves. –

My Father sends you, probably for the last time in this world, his warmest wishes for your welfare and happiness; and mother & the rest of the family desire to inclose their kind Compliments to you, Mrs Burness and the rest of your family along with

Dear Sir, Your affectionate Cousin,
Robt Burness

TO JAMES BURNESS
(CL, 59–60)

Mossgiel 3rd August 1784

My dear Sir,
I ought in gratitude to have acknowledged the receipt of your last kind letter before this time, but without troubling you with any apology I shall proceed to inform you that our family are all in health at present and we were very happy with the unexpected favor of John Caird's company for near two weeks; & I must say it of him he is one the the most agreable, facetious, warm-hearted lads I was ever acquainted with. –

We have been surprized with one of the most extraordinary Phenomena in the moral world, which, I dare say, has happened in the course of this last Century. – We have had a party of the Presbytry Relief as they call themselves, for some time in this country. A pretty thriving society of them has been in the Burgh of Irvine for some years past, till about two years ago, a Mrs Buchan from Glasgow came among them, & began to spread some fanatical notions of religion among them,

& in a short time made many converts among them & among others their Preacher, one Mr Whyte, who upon that account has continued however, to preach in private to this party, & was supported, both he, & their spiritual Mother as they affect to call old Buchan, by the contributions of the rest, several of whom were in good circumstances; till in spring last the Populace rose & mobbed the old leader Buchan, & put her out of the town; on which, all her followers voluntarily quitted the place likewise, & with such precipitation, that many of them never shut their doors behind them; one left a washing on the green, another a cow bellowing at the crib without meat or any body to mind her, & after several stages, they are fixed at present in the neighbourhood of Dumfries. – Their tenets are a strange jumble of enthusiastic jargon, among others, she pretends to give them the Holy Ghost by breathing on them, which she does with postures & practices that are scandalously indecent; they have likewise disposed of all their effects & hold a community of goods, & live nearly an idle life, carrying on a great farce of pretended devotion in barns, & woods, where they lodge and lye all together, & hold likewise a community of women, as it is another of their tenets that they can commit no moral sin. – I am personally acquainted with most of them, & I can assure you the above mentioned are facts. –

This My Dear Sir, is one of the many instances of the folly in leaving the guidance of sound reason, & common sense in matters of Religion. – Whenever we neglect or despise these sacred Monitors, the whimsical notions of a perturbed brain are taken for the immediate influences of the Deity, & the wildest fanaticism, & the most inconsistant absurdities will meet with abettors & converts. – Nay I have often thought, that the more-out-of-the-way & ridiculous their fancies are, if once they are sanctified under the sacred name of RELIGION, the unhappy, mistaken votaries are the more firmly glued to them. –

I expect to hear from you soon, & I beg you will remember me to all friends, & believe me to be,

My Dear Sir your affectionate Cousin
Robert Burness
Direct to me at Mossgiel, Parish of Machline, near Kilmarnock.

TO GAVIN HAMILTON
(CL, 65–6)

Mossgiel, Saturday morn: [15th April, 1786]

My proposals came to hand last night, and I know you would wish to have it in your power to do me a service as early as anybody, so I inclose you a sheet of them. – I must consult you, first opportunity, on the propriety of sending my *quondam* friend, Mr Aiken, a copy. – If he is now reconciled to my character as an honest man, I would do it with all my soul; but I would not be beholden to the noblest being ever God created, if he imagined me to be a rascal. – Apropos, old Mr Armour prevailed with him to mutilate that unlucky paper, yesterday. – Would you believe it? tho' I had not a hope, nor even a wish, to make her mine after her conduct; yet when he told me, the names were all cut out of the paper, my heart died within me, and he cut my very veins with the news. – Perdition seize her falsehood, and perjurious perfidy! but God bless her and forgive my poor, once-dear, misguided girl. – She is ill-advised. – Do not despise me, Sir: I am indeed a fool, but a *knave* is an infinitely worse character than any body, I hope, will dare to give

the unfortunate Robt Burns

TO JOHN ARNOT
(CL, 107–10)

[April 1786]

Sir,
I have long wished for some kind of claim to the honor of your acquaintance, & since it is out of my power to make that claim by the least service of mine to you, I shall do it by asking a friendly office of you to me. – I should be much hurt, Sir, if any one should view my poor Parnassian Pegasus in the light of a spur-galled Hack, & think that I wish to make a shilling or two by him. – I spurn the thought. –

> It may-do – maun do, Sir, wi' them wha
> Maun please the great folk for a wame-fou;
> For me, sae laigh I need na bow,
> For, Lord be thankit. I can plough:
> And when I downa yoke a naig,
> Then, Lord be thankit! I can beg – [1]

You will then, I hope Sir, forgive my troubling you with the Inclosed; & spare a poor, heart-crushed devil, a world of apologies: a business he is very unfit for at any time, but at present, widowed as he is of every woman-giving comfort, he is utterly incapable of. – Sad & grievous, of late, Sir, has been my tribulation, & many & piercing, my sorrows; & had it not been for the loss the world would have sustained in losing so great a Poet, I had, ere now, done as a much wiser man, the famous Achitophel of long-headed memory, did before me, when 'he went home & set his house in order.'² – I have lost, Sir, that dearest earthly treasure, that greatest blessing here below, that last, best gift which compleated Adam's happiness in the garden of bliss, I have lost – I have lost – my trembling hand refuses its office, the frightened ink recoils up the quill – Tell it not in Gath – I have lost – a – a – A WIFE!

> Fairest of God's creation, last & best!
> *How art thou lost*³ –

You have doubtless, Sir, heard my story, heard it all with all its exaggerations; but as my actions, & my motives for action, are peculiarly like myself, & that is peculiarly like nobody else, I shall just beg a leisure-moment & a spare-tear of you, untill I tell my own story my own way. –

I have been all my life, Sir, one of the rueful-looking, long-visaged sons of Disappointment. – A damned Star has always kept my zenith, & shed its baleful influence, in that emphatic curse of the Prophet – 'And behold, whatsoever he doth, it shall not prosper!'⁴ – I rarely hit where I aim; & if I want any thing, I am almost sure never to find it where I seek it. – For instance, if my pen-knife is needed, I pull out twenty things – a plough-wedge, a horse-nail, an old letter or a tattered rhyme, in short, every thing but my pen-knife; & that at last, after a painful fruitless search, will be found in the unsuspected corner of an unsuspected pocket, as if on purpose thrust out of the way. – Still, Sir, I had long had a wishing eye to that inestimable blessing, a wife. – My mouth watered deliciously, to see a young fellow, after a few idle, common-place stories from a gentleman in black, strip & go to bed with a young girl & no one durst say black was his eye; while I, for just doing the same thing, only wanting that ceremony, am made a Sunday's laughing stock, & abused like a pick-pocket. – I was well aware though, that if my ill-starred fortune got the least hint of my connubial wish, my schemes would go to nothing. – To prevent this, I determined to take my measures with such thought & forethought, such caution & precaution, that all the malignant planets in the Hemisphere should be unable to blight by designs. – Not content with, to use the words of the celebrated Westminster Divines, 'The outward & ordinary means,' I left no *stone* unturned; sounded every unfathomed *depth*; stopped up every *hole* & bore of an objection: but, how shall I tell it! notwithstanding all this turning of stones, stopping of bores, &c. – whilst I, with secret pleasure, marked my project *swelling* to the proper crisis, & was singing Te deum in my own fancy; or to change the metaphor, whilst I was vigorously pressing on the siege; had carried the counter-scarp, & made a practicable breach behind the curtin in the gorge of the very principal bastion; nay, having mastered the covered way, I had found means to slip a choice detachment into the very citadel; while I had nothing less in view than displaying my victorious banners on the top of the walls – 'Heaven & Earth, must I remember'! my damned Star wheeled about to the zenith by whose baleful rays Fortune took the alarm, & pouring in her forces on all quarters, front, flank & rear, I was utterly routed, my baggage lost, my military chest in the hands of the enemy; & your poor devil of a humble servant, commander in chief forsooth, was obliged to scamper away, without wither arms or honors of war, except his bare bayonet & cartridge-pouch; nor in all probability had he escaped even with them, had he not made a shift to hide them under the lap of his military cloak. –

In short, Pharaoh at the Red Sea, Darius at Arbela, Pompey at Pharsalia, Edward at Bannockburn, Charles at Pultaway[5], Burgoyne at Saratoga – no Prince, Potentate or Commander, of ancient or modern unfortunate memory, ever got a more shameful or more total defeat. –

O horrible! O horrible. Most horrible![6]

How I bore this, can only be conceived. – All powers of recital labor far, far behind. – There is a pretty large portion of bedlam in the composition of a Poet at any time; but on this occasion, I was nine parts & nine tenths, out of ten, stark staring mad. – At first, I was fixed in stuporific insensibility, silent, sullen, staring, like Lot's wife besaltified in the plains of Gomorrah. – But my second paroxysm chiefly beggars description. – The rifted northern ocean, when returning suns dissolve the chains of winter & loosening precipices of long accumulated ice tempest with hideous crash the foamy Deep – images like these may give some faint shadow of what was the situation of my bosom. – My chained faculties broke loose; my maddening passions, roused to tenfold fury, bore over their banks with impetuous, resistless force, carrying every check & principle before them. – Counsel, was an unheeded call to the passing hurricane; Reason, a screaming elk in the vortex of Moskoe strom; & Religion, a feebly-struggling beaver down the roaring of Niagara. – I reprobated the first moment of my existence; execrated Adam's folly-infatuated wish for that goodly-looking but poison-breathing gift, which had ruined him, & undone me; & called on the womb of uncreated night to close over me & all my sorrows. –

A storm naturally overblows itself. – My spent passions gradually sank into a lurid calm; & by degrees, I have subsided into the time-settled sorrow of the sable widower, who, wiping away the decent tear, lifts up his grief-worn eye to look – for another wife. –

> Such is the state of man; today he buds
> His tender leaves of hope; tomorrow blossoms,
> And bears his blushing honors thick upon him;
> The third day comes a frost, a killing frost,
> And nips his root, & then he falls as I do – [7]

Such, Sir, has been this fatal era of my life. – 'And it came to pass, that when I looked for sweet, behold bitter; & for light, behold darkness.' – [8]

But this is not all. – Already the holy beagles, the houghmagandie pack, begin to snuff the scent; & I expect every moment to see them cast off, & hear them after me in full cry: but as I am an old fox, I shall give them dodging & doubling for it; & by & bye, I intend to earth among the mountains of Jamaica. –

I am so struck, on a review, with the impertinent length of this letter, that I shall not increase it with one single word of an apology; but abruptly conclude with assuring you, that I am,

Sir, your, & Misery's most humble servant

1 A *Dedication to Gavin Hamilton*, lines 11–16.
2 Samuel 17:23
3 Milton: *Paradise Lost*, Bk, IX, lines 896 & 900.
4 Jeremiah 10:21, misquoted
5 Charles XII of Sweden, at Poltava, 1712.
6 Shakespeare: *Hamlet*, Act 1, sc. 5
7 Shakespeare: *Henry VIII*, ACT III, sc. 2, altered
8 Job 30:26, altered

TO DAVID BRICE
(CL, 111-12)

Mossgiel, 12th June 1786

Dear Brice –

I received your message by G. Paterson, and as I am not very throng at present, I just write to let you know that there is such a worthless, rhyming reprobate, as your humble servant still in the land of the living, tho' I can scarcely say, in the place of hope. – I have no news to tell you that will give me any pleasure to mention, or you, to hear. – Poor, ill-advised, ungrateful Armour came home on Friday last. – You have heard all the particulars of that affair; and a black affair it is. – What she thinks of her conduct now, I don't know; one thing I know, she has made me compleatly miserable. – Never man lov'd, or rather ador'd, a woman more than I did her and, to confess a truth between you and me, I do still love her to distraction after all, tho' I won't tell her so, tho I see her which I don't want to do. – My poor dear, unfortunate Jean! how happy have I been in her arms! – It is not the losing her that makes me so unhappy; but for *her* sake I feel most severely. – I foresee she is on the road to, I am afraid, *eternal* ruin; and those who made so much noise, and showed so much grief, at the thought of her being *my wife*, may, some day, see her connected in such a manner as may give them more real cause of vexation. – I am sure I do not wish it: may Almighty God forgive her ingratitude and perjury to me, as I from my very soul forgive her! and may His grace be with her, to bless her in all her future life! – I can have no nearer idea of the place of eternal punishment than what I have felt in my own breast on her account. – I have tryed often to forget her: I have run into all kinds of dissipation and riot, Mason-meetings, drinking matches, and other mischief, to drive her out of my head, but all in vain: and now for a grand cure, the Ship is on her way home that is to take me out to Jamaica, and then, farewel, dear old Scotland, and farewel dear, ungrateful Jean, for never, never will I see you more!

You will have heard that I am going to commence Poet in print; and tomorrow, my works go to the press. – I expect it will be a Volume about two hundred pages. – It is just the last foolish action I intend to do; and then turn a wise man as fast as possible. –

I shall expect a letter from you first leisure moment; and believe me to be,

Dear Bryce, your friend & wellwisher
Robt Burns

TO JOHN RICHMOND
(CL, 77-8)

Old Rome Foord, 30th July 1786

My Dear Richmond,

My hour is now come. – You and I will never meet in Britain more. – I have orders within three weeks at farthest to repair aboard the Nancy, Captain Smith, from Clyde, to Jamaica, and to call at Antigua. – This, except to our friend Smith, whom God long preserve, is a secret about Mauchlin. – Would you believe it? Armour has got a warrant to throw me in jail till I find security for an enormous sum. – This they keep an entire secret, but I got it by a channel they little dream of; and I am wandering from one friend's house to another, and like a true son of the Gospel 'have no where to lay my head.'[1] – I know you will pour an execration on her head, but spare the poor, ill-advised Girl for my sake: tho', may all the Furies that rend the injured, enraged Lover's bosom, await the old Harridan, her Mother, untill her latest hour! May Hell string the arm of Death to throw the fatal dart, and all the winds of warring elements rouse the infernal flames to welcome her approach! For Heaven's sake burn this letter, and never show it to a living creature. – I write it in a moment of rage, reflecting on my miserable situation, – exil'd, abandon'd, forlorn –

I can write no more – let me hear from you by the return of Connel.[2] – I will write you ere I go.

I am, Dear Sir, yours here & hereafter
Robt Burns

1 Matthew 8:20, paraphrased.
2 James Connel, carrier of Mauchline.

TO MRS DUNLOP
(CL, 131-2)

Mossgiel, 15th November 1786

Madam,

I am truly sorry I was not at home yesterday when I was so much honored with your order for my Copies, and incomparably more so by the handsome compliments you are pleased to pay my poetic abilities. – I am fully persuaded that there is not any class of Mankind so feelingly alive to the titillations of applause as the Sons of Parnassus; nor is it easy to conceive how the heart of the poor Bard dances with rapture, when Judges honor him with their approbation. –

Had you been thoroughly acquainted with me, Madam, you could not have touched my darling heart-chord more sweetly, than by noticing my attempts to celebrate your illustrious Ancestor, the SAVIOUR OF HIS COUNTRY –

> Great Patriot hero! ill-requited Chief![1]

The first books I met with in my early years, which I perused with pleasure, were, the lives of Hannibal, and Sir William Wallace. – For several of my earlier years, I had few other Authors; and many a solitary hour have I stole out, after the laborious vocations of the day, to shed a tear over their glorious but unfortunate Story. – In those boyish days, I remember in particular, being much struck with that part of Wallace's history where these lines occur –

> Syne to the Leglen wood when it was late
> To make a silent and a safe retreat –[2]

I chose a fine summer Sunday, the only day of the week in my power and walked half a dozen miles to pay my respects to the 'Leglen wood', with as much devout enthusiasm as ever Pilgrim did to Lorreto; and as I explored every den and dell where I could suppose my heroic Countryman to have sheltered, I recollect (for even than I was a Rhymer) that my heart glowed with a wish to be able to make a Song on him equal to his merits –

I have only been able to send you five Copies: they are all I can command. – I am thinking to go to Edinburgh in a week or two at farthest, to throw off a second Impression of my book: but on my return, I shall certainly do myself the honor to wait on you, and thank you in person for the oblidging notice you have been pleased to take of.

Madam,
your much indebted
and very humble servant
Robert Burns

1 Thomson: *Autumn*, line 899.

2 William Hamilton of Gilbertfield's recension of Blind Harry's *History of Sir William Wallace*, Bk II, chap. I, lines 11–12, misquoted. Leglen Wood, two miles east of Ayr on the river Ayr, was a hiding-place of William Wallace.

TO JOHN BALLANTINE
(CL, 99–100)

Edinburgh, 13th December 1786

My honored Friend,

I would not write you till I could have it in my power to give you some account of myself & my matters, which by the bye is often no easy task. – I arrived here on Tuesday was se'ennight, and have suffered ever since I came to town with a miserable headach & stomach complaint; but am now a good deal better. – I have found a worthy, warm friend in Mr Dalrymple of Orangefield who introduced me to lord Glencairn, a man whose worth and brotherly kindness to me I shall remember when time will be no more. – By this interest it is passed in the Caledonian Hunt, & entered in their books, that they are all to take each a Copy of the second Edition, for which they are to pay one guinea. – I have been introduced to a good many of the noblesse, but my avowed Patrons & Patronesses are, the Duchess of Gordon – the Countess of Glencairn, with my lord & lady Betty – the Dean of Faculty –[1] Sir John Whiteford. – I have likewise warm friends among the Literati, Professors Stewart, Blair, Greenfield, and Mr McKenzie the Man of feeling. – An unknown hand left ten guineas for the Ayrshire Bard in Mr Sibbald's hand, which I got. I since have discovered my generous unknown friend to be Patrick Miller Esq. brother to the Justice Clerk; and drank a glass of claret with him by invitation at his own house yesternight. – I am nearly agreed with Creech to print my book; and, I suppose, I will begin on monday. – I will send a subscription bill or two next post; when I intend writing my first, kind Patron Mr Aiken. I saw his Son today, and he is very well. –

Dugald Stewart and some of my learned friends put me in the periodical paper called The Lounger, a copy of which I here inclose you. – I was, Sir, when I was first honored with your notice, too obscure, now I tremble lest I should be ruined by being dragged suddenly into the glare of polite & learned observation. – I shall certainly, my ever-honored Patron, write you an account of my every step; & better health and more spirits may enable me to make it something better than this stupid, matter-of-fact epistle. –

I have the honor to be, good Sir,
Your ever grateful humble servant
Robert Burns

If any of my friends write me, my direction is

Care of Mr Creech, Bookseller

1 Hon. Henry Erskine.

TO REVD WILLIAM GREENFIELD
(CW, 221)

December 1786

Reverend Sir

On raking the recesses of my memory the other day, I stumbled on two songs[1] which I here inclose you as a kind of curiosity to a Professor of the Belle lettres de la Nature; which, allow me to say, I look upon as an additional merit of yours; a kind of bye Professorship, not always to be found among the systematic Fathers and Brothers of scientific Criticism. – They were the works of Bards such as I lately was; and such as, I believe, I had better still have been. –

Never did Saul's armour sit so heavy on David when going to encounter Goliah,[2] as does the encumbering robe of public notice with which the friendship and patronage of some 'names dear to fame' have invested me. – I do not say this in the ridiculous idea of seeming self-abasement, and affected modesty. – I have long studied myself, and I think I know pretty exactly what ground I occupy, both as a Man, & a Poet; and however the world, or a friend, may sometimes differ from me in that particular, I stand for it, in silent resolve, with all the tenaciousness of Property. – I am willing to believe that my abilities deserved a better fate than the veriest shades of life; but to be dragged forth, with all my imperfections on my head, to the full glare of learned and polite observation, is what, I am afraid, I shall have bitter reason to repent. –

I mention this to you, once for all, merely, in the Confessor style, to disburthen my conscience, and that – 'When proud Fortune's ebbing tide recedes'[3] – you may bear me witness, when my buble of fame was at the highest, I stood, unintoxicated, with the inebriating cup in my hand, looking forward, with rueful resolve, to the hastening time when the stroke of envious Calumny, with all the eagerness of vengeful triumph, should dash it to the ground. –

I am ever, &c.

1 By obscure Ayrshire authors.
2 See 1 Samuel 17:38–9.
3 Shenstone: *Elegy VII*, stanza 19.

TO JOHN BALLANTINE
(CL, 100–1)

Edinburgh, 14th January 1787

My honored Friend,
It gives me a secret comfort to observe in myself that I am not yet so far gone as Willie Gaw's Skate, 'Past redemption;' for I have still this favorable symptom of grace, that when my Conscience, as in the case of this letter, tells me I am leaving something undone that I ought to do, it teases me eternally till I do it. –

I am still 'dark as was Chaos'[1] in respect to Futurity. – My generous friend, Mr Peter Miller, brother to the Justice Clerk, has been talking with me about a lease of some farm or other in an estate called Dasswinton which he has lately bought near Dumfries. – Some life-rented, embittering Recollections whisper me that I will be happier any where than in my old neighborhood, but Mr Miller is no Judge of land; and though I dare say he means to favour me, yet he may give me, in his opinion, an advantageous bargain that may ruin me. – I am to take a tour by Dumfries as I return and have promised to meet Mr Miller on his lands some time in May. –

I went to a Mason-lodge yesternight where the Most Worshipful Grand Master Charters, and all the Grand lodge of Scotland visited. – The meeting was most numerous and elegant; all the different Lodges about town were present, in all their pomp. – The Grand Master who presided with great solemnity, and honor to himself as a Gentleman and Mason, among other general toasts gave, 'Caledonia, & Caledonia's Bard, brother B——,' which rung through the whole Assembly with multiplied honors and repeated acclamations. – As I had no idea such a thing would happen, I was downright thunderstruck, and trembling in every nerve made the best return in my power. – Just as I finished, some of the Grand Officers said so loud as I could hear, with a most comforting accent, 'Very well indeed!' which set me something to rights again. –

I have just now had a visit from my Landlady who, is a staid, sober, piously-disposed, sculdudery-abhoring Widow, coming on her grand climacterick. – She is at present in sore tribulation respecting some 'Daughters of Belial' who are on the floor immediately above. – My Landlady who as I said is a flesh-disciplining, godly Matron, firmly believes her husband is in Heaven; and having been very happy with him on earth, she vigorously and perseveringly practices some of the most distinguishing Christian virtues, such as, attending Church, railing against vice, &c. that she may be qualified to meet her dear quondam Bedfellow in that happy place where the Unclean & the ungodly shall never enter. – This, no doubt, requires some strong exertions of Self-denial, in a hale, well-kept Widow of forty-five; and as our floors are low and ill-plaistered, we can easily distinguish our laughter-loving, night-rejoicing neighbors – when they are eating, when they are drinking, when they are singing, when they are &c., my worthy Landlady tosses sleepless & unquiet, 'looking for rest but finding none,'[2] the whole night. – Just now she told me, though by the by she is sometimes dubious that I am, in her own phrase, 'but a rough an' roun' Christian' that 'We should not be uneasy and envious because the Wicked enjoy the good things of this life; for these base jades who, in her own words, lie up gandygoing with their filfthy fellows, drinking the best of wines, and singing abominable songs, they shall one day lie in hell, weeping and wailing and gnashing their teeth over a cup of God's wrath!'

I have today corrected my 152d page. – My best good wishes to Mr Aiken. —

I am ever
Dear Sir,
your much indebted humble servant
Robert Burns

1 Blair: *The Grave*, line 14.
2 Luke 11:24.

TO MRS DUNLOP
(CL, 132–3)

Edinburgh, 15th January 1787

Madam,
Yours of the 9th current, which I am this moment honoured with, is a deep reproach to me for ungrateful neglect. I will tell you the real truth, for I am miserably awkward at a fib: I wished to have written Dr

Moore before I wrote to you; but though, every day since I received
yours of Dec. 30, the idea, the wish to write to him, has constantly
pressed on my thoughts, yet I could not for my soul set about it.
I know his fame and character, and I am one of 'the sons of little
men.' To write him a mere matter-of-fact affair, like a merchant's
order, would be disgracing the little character I have; and to write
the author of *The View of Society and Manners*, a letter of sentiment –
I declare every artery runs cold at the thought. I shall try, however,
to write to him tomorrow or next day. His kind interposition in my
behalf I have already experienced, as a gentleman waited on me the
other day, on the part of Lord Eglinton, with ten guineas, by way of
subscription for two copies of my next edition.

The word you object to in the mention I have made of my
glorious countryman and your immortal ancestor, is indeed borrowed
from Thomson; but it does not strike me as an improper epithet. I
distrusted my own judgment on your finding fault with it, and applied
for the opinion of some of the Literati here, who honour me with
their critical strictures, and they all allow it to be proper. The song
you ask, I cannot recollect, and I have not a copy of it. I have not
composed any thing on the great Wallace, except what you have seen
in print, and the inclosed,[1] which I will print in this edition. You will
see I have mentioned some others of the name. When I composed
my *Vision* long ago, I had attempted a description of Koyle, of which
the additional stanzas are a part, as it originally stood. My heart glows
with a wish to be able to do justice to the merits of the *Saviour of his
Country*, which, sooner or later, I shall at least attempt.

You are afraid I shall grow intoxicated with my prosperity as a poet.
Alas! Madam, I know myself and the world too well. I do not mean
any airs of affected modesty; I am willing to believe that my abilities
deserved some notice; but in a most enlightened, informed age and
nation, when poetry is and has been the study of men of the first natural
genius, aided with all the powers of polite learning, polite books, and
polite company – to be dragged forth to the full glare of learned
and polite observation, with all my imperfections of awkward rusticity
and crude unpolished ideas on my head – I assure you, Madam, I do not
dissemble when I tell you I tremble for the consequences. The novelty
of a poet in my obscure situation, without any of those advantages
which are reckoned necessary for that character, at least at this time
of day, has raised a partial tide of public notice, which has borne me to
a height where I am absolutely feelingly certain my abilities are inadequate to support me; and too surely do I see that time when the same
tide will leave me, and recede, perhaps, as far below the mark of

truth. I do not say this in the ridiculous affectation of self-abasement and modesty. I have studied myself, and know what ground I occupy; and, however a friend or the world may differ from me in that particular, I stand for my own opinion, in silent resolve, with all the tenaciousness of property. I mention this to you, once for all, to disburthen my mind, and I do not wish to hear or say more about it – But

> When proud fortune's ebbing tide recedes,[2]

you will bear me witness, that, when my bubble of fame was at the highest, I stood, unintoxicated, with the inebriating cup in my hand, looking forward with rueful resolve to the hastening time when the blow of Calumny should dash it to the ground, with all the eagerness of vengeful triumph.

Your patronising me, and interesting yourself in my fame and character as a poet, I rejoice in; it exalts me in my own idea; and whether you can or cannot aid me in my subscription, is a trifle. Has a paltry subscription-bill any charms to the heart of a bard, compared with the patronage of the descendant of the immortal Wallace?

1 Enlarged version of *The Vision* in first Edinburgh edition. Burns had previously honoured Wallace in *To William Simson, Ochiltree* and *The Cotter's Saturday Night* in the Kilmarnock edition.
2 Shenstone: *Elegy VII*, stanza 19.

TO DR JOHN MOORE
(CL, 246–7)

Edinburgh, January 1787

Sir,
my worthy honored Patroness Mrs Dunlop has been so kind as send me extracts of letters she has had from you, where you do the rustic Bard the honor of noticing him and his works. – Those who have felt the anxieties of Authorship can only know what pleasure it gives to be noticed, in such a manner, by Judges of the first character. –

Your criticisms, Sir, I receive with reverence; only I am sorry they mostly came too late: a peccant passage or two that I would certainly have altered were gone to the Press. –

The hope to be admired for Ages is, in by far the greater part of what are even Authors of repute, an unsubstantial dream. – For my part, my first ambition was, and still my strongest wish is, to please my Compeers, the rustic Inmates of the Hamlet, while ever-changing lanugage and manners will allow me to be relished and understood. –

I am very willing to admit that I have some poetical abilities; and as few, if any Writers, either moral or poetical, are intimately acquainted with the classes of Mankind among whom I have chiefly mingled, I may have seen men and manners in a different phasis, which may assist originality of thought. – Still I know very well, the novelty of my character has by far the greatest share in the learned and polite notice I have lately got; and in a language where Pope and Churchill have raised the laugh, and Shenstone and Gray drawn the tear; where Thomson and Beattie have painted the landskip, and Littleton and Collins described the heart; I am not vain enough to hope for distinguished Poetic fame. –

I have the honor to be, &c.

TO THE HON. THE BAILIES OF THE CANONGATE
(CL, 265)

Edinburgh, 6th February 1787

Gentlemen,

I am sorry to be told that the remains of Robert Ferguson the so justly celebrated Poet, a man whose talents for ages to come will do honor, to our Caledonian name, lie in your church yard among the ignoble Dead unnoticed and unknown. – Some memorial to direct the steps of the Lovers of Scottish Song, when they wish to shed a tear over the 'Narrow house' of the Bard who is now no more, is surely a tribute due to Ferguson's memory: a tribute I wish to have the honor of paying. – I petition you then, Gentlemen, for your permission to lay a simple stone over his revered ashes, to remain an unalienable property to his deathless fame. –

I have the honor to be Gentlemen,
your very humble servant
Robert Burns

TO MRS DUNLOP
(CL, 134-5)

Edinburgh, 22nd March 1787

Madam,

When I was honoured with yours of the 26th February, I likewise received one from Dr Moore, where he informed me that he had upon the way to Scotland his medical treatise, and his sketch of Society and manners; the first he desired me to transmit to you, the last he has done me the honor to present me with. – I delayed writing you till the books should arrive, which they did yesterday; and the first Carrier for your country-side I shall send yours. –

I read your letter, Madam, with watery eyes. – A little, very little while ago, I had scarce a friend but the stubborn pride of my own bosom; now I am distinguished, patronised, befriended by YOU. – Your friendly advices, I will not give them the cold name of criticisms, I receive with reverence. – I have made some small alterations in what I before had printed. – I have the advice of some very judicious friends among the Literati here, but with them I sometimes find it necessary to claim the priviledge of thinking for myself. – The noble Earl of Glencairn, to whom I owe more than to any man of earth, does me the honor of giving me his strictures: his hints, with respect to impropriety or indelicacy, I follow implicitly. –

You kindly interest yourself, my honored Patroness, in my future views and prospects; then I can give you no light. It is all –

> Dark as was Chaos ere the infant sun
> Was roll'd together, or had try'd his beams
> Athwart the gloom profound –[1]

The appellation of a Scotch Bard is by far my highest pride; to continue to deserve it is my most exalted ambition. – Scottish scenes, and Scottish story are the themes I could wish to sing. – I have no greater, no dearer aim than to have it in my power, unplagu'd with the routine of business, for which Heaven knows I am unfit enough, to make leisurely pilgrimages through Caledonia; to sit on the fields of her battles; to wander on the romantic banks of her rivers; and to muse by the stately tower or venerable ruins, once the honored abodes of her heroes. –

But these are all Utopian ideas: I have dallied long enough with life: 'tis time to be in earnest. – I have a fond, aged Mother to care for; and some other bosom-ties, perhaps equally tender. – Where the

Individual only suffers by the consequences of his own thoughtlessness, indolence or folly, he may be excusable; nay shining abilities, and some of the nobler virtues may half sanctify the character; but where God and Nature have entrusted the welfare of others to his care, those whose weal or woe must depend upon his, where the trust is sacred and the ties are dear, that man must be far gone in unfeeling selfishness, or strangely lost to reflection and thought, whom these connections will not rouse to active attention and serious resolve –

I guess that I shall clear between two and three hundred pounds by my Authorship; with that sum I intend, so far as I may be said to have any intention, to return to my old acquaintance, the plough, and, if I can meet with a lease by which I can live, to commence Farmer. – I do not intend to give up Poesy: being bred to labor secures me independance, and the Muses are my chief, sometimes have been my only enjoyment. – If my practice second my resolution, I shall have principally at heart the serious business of life; but while following my plough or building up my shocks, I shall cast a leisure glance to that dear, that only feature of my character which gave me the notice of Caledonia, and the patronage of a Wallace. –

Thus, honored Madam, I have given you the Bard, his situation and his views, native as they are in his own bosom. – An integritive character, honest pride, and my poetic fame, will, I hope, ever ensure my welcome with those whose esteem I value: the trappings and luxuries of upper stations, I have seen a little of them in Edinburgh – I can live without them. – I shall never blush for my own poverty, nor the poverty of my Country. –

> I am, with the sincerest throe of gratitude,
> Madam your much indebted, humble servant
> Robert Burns

P.S. I have today corrected the last proof sheet of my poems and have now only the Glossary and subscribers names to print. Printing this last is much against my will, but some of my friends whom I do not chuse to thwart will have it so. – I have both a second and a third Edition going on as the second was begun with too small a number of copies. – The whole I have printed is three thousand. – Would the profits of that afford it, with rapture I would take your hint of a military life, as the most congenial to my feelings and situation of any other, but, 'What is wanting cannot be numbered.'

> R.B.

1 Blair: *The Grave*, lines 14–16.

TO WILLIAM NICOL
(CL, 342-3)

Carlisle 1st June 1787 — or
I believe the 39th o' May rather

Kind, honest-hearted Willie,

I'm sitten down here, after seven and forty miles ridin, e'en as forjesket and forniaw'd as a forfoughten cock, to gie you some notion o' my landlowper-like stravaguin sin the sorrowfu' hour that I sheuk hands and parted wi' auld Reekie. —

My auld, ga'd Gleyde o' a meere has huch-yall'd up hill and down brae, in Scotland and England, as teugh and birnie as a vera devil wi' me. — It's true, she's as poor's a Sang-maker and as hard's a kirk, and tipper-taipers when she taks the gate first like a Lady's gentlewoman in a minuet or a hen on a het girdle, but she's a yauld, poutherie Girran for a' that; and has a stomach like Willie Stalker's meere that wad hae digeested tumbler-wheels, for she'll whip me aff her five stimparts o' the best aits at a down-sittin and ne'er fash her thumb. — When ance her ring-banes and spavies, her crucks and cramps, are fairly soupl'd, she beets to, beets to, and ay the hindmost hour the tightest. — I could wager her price to a thretty pennies that, for twa or three wooks ridin at fifty mile a day, the deil-sticket a five gallopers acqueesh Clyde and Whithorn could cast saut in her tail. —

I hae daunder'd owre a' the kintra frae Dumbar to Selcraig, and hae forgather'd wi' monie a guid fallow and monie a weel-far'd hizzie. — I met wi' twa dink quines in particular, ane o' them a sonsie, fine fodgel lass, baith braw and bonie; the tither was a clean-shankit, straught, tight, weel-far'd winch, as blythe's a lintwhite on a flowrie thorn, and as sweet and modest's a new blawn plumrose in a hazle shaw. — They were baith bred to mainers by the beuk, and onie ane o' them has as muckle smeddum and rumblegumtion as the half o' some Presbytries that you and I baith ken. — They play'd sik a deevil o' a shavie that I daur say if my harigals were turn'd out, ye wad see twa nicks i' the heart o' me like the mark o' a kail-whittle in a castock. —

I was gaun to write you a lang pystle, but, Gude forgive me, I gat myself sae notouriously bitchify'd the day after kail-time that I can hardly stoiter but and ben. —

My best respecks to the guidwife and a' our common friens, especiall Mr & Mrs Cruikshank[1] and the honest Guidman o' Jock's Lodge. —

I'll be in Dumfries the morn gif the beast be to the fore and the branks bide hale.—

> Gude be wi' you, Willie! Amen—
> Robt Burns

1 William Cruickshank

TO JAMES SMITH
(CL, 119–21)

[30th June 1787]

On our return, at a Highland gentleman's hospitable mansion, we fell in with a merry party, and danced 'till the ladies left us, at three in the morning. Our dancing was none of the French or English insipid formal movements; the ladies sung Scotch songs like angels, at intervals; then we flew at *Bab at the Bowster, Tullochgorum, Loch Erroch side,* &c. like midges sporting in the mottie sun, or craws prognosticating a storm in a hairst day. – When the dear lasses left us, we ranged round the bowl till the good-fellow hour of six; except a few minutes that we went out to pay our devotions to the glorious lamp of day peering over the towering top of Benlomond. We all kneeled; our worthy land-lord's son held the bowl; each man a full glass in his hand; and I, as priest, repeated some rhyming nonsense, like Thomas a Rhymer's prophecies I suppose. – After a small refreshment of the gifts of Somnus, we proceeded to spend the day on Lochlomond, and reached Dumbarton in the evening. We dined at another good fellow's house, and consequently push'd the bottle; when we went out to mount our horses, we found ourselves 'No vera fou but gaylie yet.'[1] My Two friends and I rode soberly down the Loch side, till by came a Highlandman at the gallop, on a tolerably good horse, but which had never known the ornaments of iron or leather. We scorned to be out-galloped by a Highlandman, so off we started, whip and spur. My companions, though seemingly gayly mounted, fell sadly astern; but my old mare, Jenny Geddes, one of the Rosinante[2] family, she strained past the Highlandman in spite of all his efforts, with the hair-halter: just as I was passing him, Donald wheeled his horse, as if to cross before me to mar my progress, when down came his horse, and threw his rider's breekless arse in a clipt hedge; and down came Jenny Geddes over all, and my bardship between her and the Highlandman's horse. Jenny Geddes trode over me with such cautious reverence, that matters were not so bad as might well have been expected; so I came off with a few cuts and bruises, and a thorough resolution to be a pattern of sobriety for the future.

I have yet fixed on nothing with respect to the serious business of life. I am, just as usual, a rhyming, mason-making, raking, aimless, idle fellow. However, I shall somewhere have a farm soon. I was going to say, a wife too; but that must never be my blessed lot. I am but a younger son of the house of Parnassus, and, like other younger sons of great families, I may intrigue, if I choose to run all risks, but must not marry.

I am afraid I have almost ruined one source, the principal one indeed, of my former happiness; that eternal propensity I always had to fall in love. My heart no more glows with feverish rapture. I have no paradisical evening interviews stolen from the restless cares and prying inhabitants of this weary world. I have only ★★★★. This last is one of your distant acquaintances, has a fine figure, and elegant manners; and in the train of some great folks whom you know, has seen the politest quarters in Europe. I do like her a good deal; but what piques me is her conduct at the commencement of our acquaintance. I frequently visited her when I was in ——, and after passing regularly the intermediate degrees between the distant formal bow and the familiar grasp round the waist, I ventured in my careless way to talk of friendship in rather ambiguous terms; and after her return to ——, I wrote to her in the same style. Miss, construing my words farther I suppose than even I intended, flew off in a tangent of female dignity and reserve, like a mounting lark in an April morning, and wrote me an answer which measured me out very completely what an immense way I had to travel before I could reach the climate of her favour. But I am an old hawk at the sport; and wrote her such a cool, deliberate, prudent reply as brought my bird from her aerial towerings, pop, down at my foot like corporal Trim's hat.

As for the rest of my acts, and my wars, and all my wise sayings, and why my mare was called Jenny Geddes, they shall be recorded in a few weeks hence at Linlithgow, in the chronicles of your memory, by

Robert Burns

1 David Herd: *Ancient and Modern Scottish Songs*, II, 121. 'We're gayly yet'
2 Jenny Geddes, who is reputed to have thrown her footstool at Bishop Lindsay in St Giles Cathedral (1637). Rosinante was Don Quixote's horse.

TO ARCHIBALD LAWRIE
(CL, 128–9)

Edinburgh, 14th August 1787

My dear Sir,

Here am I – that is all I can tell you of that unaccountable BEING –
Myself. – What I am doing, no mortal can tell; what I am thinking,
I myself cannot tell; what I am usually saying, is not worth telling.
– The clock is just striking, one, two, three, four, —, —, —, —,
—, —, —, twelve, forenoon; and here I sit, in the Attic story, alias,
the garret, with a friend on the right hand of my standish – a friend
whose kindness I shall largely experience at the close of this line –
there – thank you – A Friend, my dear Mr Lowrie, whose kindness
often makes me blush; A Friend who has more of the milk of human
kindness than all the human race put together, and what is highly to
his honor, peculiarly a friend to the friendless as often as they come
in his way, in short, Sir, he is, without the least alloy, a universal
Philanthropist; and his much beloved name is A BOTTLE OF GOOD
OLD PORT! In a week, if whim and weather serve, I shall set out for
the North, a tour to the Highlands. –

I ate some Newhaven broth, in other words, boiled mussles with
Mr Farquhar's family t'other day – Now I see you prick up your
ears – They are all well and Madamoiselle is particularly well. –
She begs her respects to you all; along with which, please present
those of your humble servant. –

I can no more. – I have so high a veneration or rather idolatrization
for the cleric character, that even a little *futurum esse vel fuisse*
Priestling in his *Penna, pennae, pennae, &c.* throws an awe over my
mind in his presence, and shortens my sentences into single ideas. –

Farewell, and believe me to be ever,
My dear Sir,
yours
Robt Burns

TO AGNES McLEHOSE
(CL, 372)

Saturday even:
St James Square No 2
[8th December 1787]

I can say with truth, Madam, that I never met with a person in my life whom I more anxiously wished to meet again than yourself. – Tonight I was to have had that very great pleasure – I was intoxicated with the idea – but an unlucky fall from a coach has so bruised one of my knees that I can't stir my leg off the cushion. So, if I don't see you again, I shall not rest in my grave for chagrin. – I was vexed to the soul I had not seen you sooner; I determined to cultivate your friendship with the enthusiasm of Religion, but thus has Fortune ever served me. – I cannot bear the idea of leaving Edinburgh without seeing you – I know not how to account for it – I am strangely taken with some people; nor am I often mistaken. You are a stranger to me; but I am an odd being: some yet unnamed feelings; things not principles, but better than whims, carry me farther than boasted reason ever did a Philosopher. –

Farewel! every happiness be yours!

Robt Burns

TO AGNES McLEHOSE
(CL, 374-5)

Friday eve
[28th December 1787]

I beg your pardon, my dear 'Clarinda', for the fragment scrawl I sent you yesterday. – I really don't know what I wrote. A gentleman for whose character, abilities and critical knowledge I have the highest veneration, called in, just as I had begun the second sentence, and I would not make the Porter wait. – I read to my much-respected friend several of my own bagatelles and among others your lines which I had copied out. – He began some criticisms on them as on the other pieces, when I informed him they were the work of a young lady in this town; which I assure you made him stare. – My learned friend seriously protested that he did not believe any young woman in Edinburgh was capable of such lines; and if you know any thing of Professor Gregory you will neither doubt of his abilities nor his sincerity. – I do love you if possible still better for having so fine a taste and turn for Poesy. – I have again gone wrong in my usual unguarded way, but you may erase the word, and put esteem, respect, or any other tame Dutch expression you please in its place. – I believe there is no holding converse or carrying on correspondence, with an amiable woman, much less a *gloriously amiable, fine woman*, without some mixture of that delicious Passion, whose most devoted Slave I have more than once had the honor of being: but why be hurt or offended on that account? Can no honest man have a prepossession for a fine woman, but he must run his head against an intrigue? Take a little of the tender witchcraft of Love, and add it to the generous, the honorable sentiments of manly Friendship; and I know but *one* more delightful morsel, which few, few in any rank ever taste. – Such a composition is like adding cream to strawberries – it not only gives the fruit a more elegant richness, but has a peculiar deliciousness of its own. –

I inclose you a few lines I composed on a late melancholy occasion. – I will not give above five or six copies of it at all, and I would be hurt if any friend should give any copies without my consent. –[1]

You cannot imagine, Clarinda, (I like the idea of Arcadian names in a commerce of this kind) how much store I have set by the hopes of your future friendship. – I don't know if you have a just idea of my character, but I wish you to see me *as I am*. – I am, as most people of my trade are, a strange will o' wisp being; the victim too frequently of much imprudence and many follies. – My great constituent elements are Pride and Passion: the first I have endeavoured to humanize into integrity and honour; the last makes me a Devotee to the warmest degree of enthusiasm, in Love, Religion, or Friendship; either of them or all together as I happen to be inspired. – 'Tis true, I never saw you but once; but how much acquaintance did I form with you in that once! Don't think I flatter you, or have a design upon you, Clarinda; I have too much pride for the one, and too little cold contrivance for the other; but of all God's creatures I ever could approach in the beaten way of acquaintance, you struck me with the deepest, the strongest, the most permanent impression. – I say the most permanent, because I know myself well, and how far I can promise either on my prepossessions or powers. – Why are you unhappy? and why are so many of our fellow creatures, unworthy to belong to the same species with you, blest with all they can wish? You have a hand all benevolent to give, why were you denied the pleasure? You have a heart form'd, gloriously form'd, for all the most refined luxuries of love; why was that heart ever wrung? O Clarinda! shall we not meet in a state, some yet unknown state of Being, where the lavish hand of Plenty shall minister to the highest wish of Benevolence; and where the chill north-wind of Prudence shall never blow over the flowery fields of Enjoyment? if we do not, Man was made in vain! I deserv'd most of the unhappy hours that have linger'd over my head; they were the wages of my labour; but what unprovoked Demon, malignant as Hell, stole upon the confidence of unmistrusting busy Fate, and dash'd your cup of life with undeserved sorrow? –

Let me know how long your stay will be out of town: I shall count the hours till you inform me of your return. – Cursed etiquette forbids your seeing me just now; and so soon as I can walk, I must bid Edinburgh adieu. – Lord, why was I born to see misery which I cannot relieve, and to meet with friends whom I can't enjoy! I look back with the pang of unvailing avarice on my loss in now knowing you sooner: all last winter; these three months past; what luxury of intercourse have I not lost! Perhaps tho' 'twas better for my peace. – You see I am either above, or incapable of Dissimulation. – I believe it is want of that particular genius. – I despise Design because I want either coolness or wisdom to be capable of it. – I may take a fort by storm, but never by Siege. –

> I am interrupted – Adieu! my dear Clarinda!
>
> Sylvander

1 Probably *On the Death of Lord President Dundas*

TO AGNES McLEHOSE
(CL, 378)

Saturday noon [5th January 1788]

Some days, some nights, nay some *hours*, like the 'ten righteous persons in Sodom,'[1] save the rest of the vapid, tiresome, miserable months and years of life. – One of these *hours*, my dear Clarinda blesst me with yesternight –

> —One well spent hour.
> In such a tender circumstance for Friends,
> Is better than an age of common time!
> Thomson[2]

My favorite feature in Milton's Satan is, his manly fortitude in supporting what cannot be remedied – in short, the wild broken fragments of a noble, exalted mind in ruins. – I meant no more by saying he was a favorite hero of mine. –

I mention'd to you my letter to Dr Moore, giving an account of my life: it is truth, every word of it; and will give you the just idea

of a man whom you have honor'd with your friendship. – I am afraid
you will hardly be able to make sense of so torn a piece. – Your verses
I shall muse on – deliciously – as I gaze on your image in my mind's
eye, in my heart's core: they will be in time enough for a week to
come. – I am truly happy your head-ach is better – O, how can
Pain or Evil be so daringly, unfeelingly, cruelly savage as to wound
so noble a mind, so lovely a form! –

My little fellow is all my Namesake. – Write me soon. – My every,
strongest good wishes attend you, Clarinda

                                                        Sylvander
I know not what I have wrote – I am pestered with people around
me –

1 Genesis 18:32, paraphrased.
2 *Alfred: A Masque*, Act I, sc. 6, altered.

TO AGNES McLEHOSE
(CL, 378–80)

Tuesday night
[8th January 1788]

I am delighted, charming Clarinda, with your honest enthusiasm for
Religion. Those of either sex, but particularly the female, who are
lukewarm in that most important of all things, 'O my soul, come
not thou into their secrets!'[1] – I feel myself deeply interested in
your good opinion, and will lay before you the outlines of my
belief. He, who is our Author and Preserver, and will one day
be our Judge, must be, (not for his sake in the way of duty, but
from the native impulse of our hearts,) the object of our reverential
awe and grateful adoration: He is almighty and all-bounteous, we are
weak and dependent; hence, prayer and every other sort of devotion.
– 'He is not willing that any should perish, but that all should come
to everlasting life;'[2] consequently, it must be in every one's power
to embrace His offer of 'everlasting life;' otherwise He could not,
in justice, condemn those who did not. A mind pervaded, actuated
and governed by purity, truth and charity, though it does not *merit*
heaven, yet is an absolutely necessary pre-requisite, without which
heaven can neither be obtained nor enjoyed; and, by Divine promise,
such a mind shall never fail of attaining 'everlasting life;' hence,
the impure, the deceiving, and the uncharitable, extrude themselves
from eternal bliss, by their unfitness for enjoying it. The Supreme

Being has put the immediate administration of all this, for wise and
good ends known to himself, into the hands of Jesus Christ, a great
Personage, whose relation to Him we cannot comprehend, but whose
relation to us is a Guide and Saviour; and who, except for our own
obstinacy and misconduct, will bring us all, through various ways and
by various means, to bliss at last.

These are my tenets, my lovely friend; and which, I think, cannot be well disputed. My creed is pretty nearly expressed in the
last clause of Jamie Dean's grace, an honest weaver in Ayrshire;
'Lord grant that we may lead a gude life! for a gude life maks a
gude end, at least it helps weel!'

I am flattered by the entertainment you tell me you have found in
my packet. You see me as I have been, you know me as I am, and
may guess at what I am likely to be. I too may say, 'Talk not of Love,
&c.' for indeed he has 'plung'd me deep in woe!'[3] Not that I ever saw
a woman who pleased unexceptionably, as my Clarinda elegantly says,
'In the companion, the friend, and the mistress.'[4] *One* indeed I could
except – *One*, before passion threw its mists over my discernment I
knew it, *the* first of women! Her name is indelibly written in my heart's
core – but I dare not look in on it – a degree of agony would be the
consequence. – Oh, thou perfidious, cruel, mischief-making demon,
who president o'er that frantic passion – thou mayst, thou dost poison
my peace, but shall not taint my honour – I would not for a single
moment give an asylum to the most distant imagination, that would
shadow the faintest outline of a selfish gratification, at the expence of
her whose happiness is twisted with the threads of my existence – May
she be happy as she deserves! And if my tenderest, faithfulest friendship
can add to her bliss – I shall at least have one solid mine of enjoyment
in my bosom! *Don't guess at these ravings!*

I watched at our front window to-day, but was disappointed. It has
been a day of disappointments. I am just risen from a two-hours bout
after supper, with silly or sordid souls, who could relish nothing in
common with me – but the Port. 'One' – 'Tis now 'witching time of
night;'[5] and whatever is out of joint[6] in the foregoing scrawl, impute
it to enchantments and spells; for I can't look over it, but will seal it
up directly, as I don't care for tomorrow's criticisms on it.

You are by this time fast asleep, Clarinda; may good angels attend
and guard you as constantly and faithfully as my good wishes do!

> Beauty, which whether waking or asleep,
> Shot forth peculiar graces –[7]

John Milton, I wish thy soul better rest than I expect on my pillow to-night! O for a little of the cart-horse part of human nature! Good night, my dearest Clarinda!

Sylvander

1 Genesis 49:6.
2 John 3:16, misquoted.
3 From a poem by Mrs McLehose.
4 From Mrs McLehose's letter to Burns of the previous night.
5 Shakespeare: *Hamlet*, Act I, sc. 5.
6 See Shakespeare: *Hamlet*, Act III, sc. 2.
7 Milton: *Paradise Lost*, Bk. V, lines 14–15.

TO AGNES McLEHOSE
(CL, 383–4)

Tuesday Evening [15th January 1788]

That you have faults, my Clarinda, I never doubted; but I knew not where they existed, and Saturday night made me more in the dark than ever. O, Clarinda, why will you wound my soul by hinting that last night must have lessened my opinion of you! True; I was 'behind the scenes with you' but what did I see? A bosom glowing with honour and benevolence; a mind ennobled by genius, informed and refined by education and reflection, and exalted by native religion, genuine as in the climes of heaven; a heart formed for all the glorious meltings of friendship, love and pity. These I saw. – I saw the noblest immortal soul, creation ever shewed me.

I looked long, my dear Clarinda, for your letter; and am vexed that you are complaining. I have not caught you so far wrong as in your idea, that the commerce you have with *one* friend hurts you, if you cannot tell every tittle of it to *another*. Why have so injurious a suspicion of a good God, Clarinda, as to think that Friendship and Love, on the sacred, inviolate principles of Truth, Honour and Religion, can be any thing else than an object of His divine approbation?

I have mentioned, in some of my former scrawls, Saturday evening next. Do, allow me to wait on you that evening. Oh, my angel! how soon must we part! and when can we meet again! I look forward on the horrid interval with tearful eyes! What have I lost by not knowing you sooner. I fear, I fear my acquaintance with you is too short, to make that *lasting* impression on your heart I could wish.

Sylvander

TO AGNES McLEHOSE
(CL, 386-8)

Sunday night – [20th January 1788]

The impertinence of fools has joined with a return of an old indisposition, to make me good for nothing today. – The paper has lain before me all this evening, to write to my dear Clarinda, but –

Fools rush'd on fools, as waves succeed to waves – [1]

I cursed them in my soul: they sacreligiously disturbed my meditations on her who holds my heart. – What a creature is man! A little alarm last night and today that I am mortal, has made such a revolution on my spirits! There is no Philosophy, no Divinity, comes half so home to the mind. – I have no idea of courage that braves Heaven. – 'Tis the wild ravings of an imaginary hero in Bedlam. –

I can no more, Clarinda; I can scarce hold up my head: but I am happy you don't know it, you would be so uneasy. –

Sylvander

Monday morning –

I am, my lovely friend, much better this morning, on the whole; but I have a horrid languor on my spirits. –

Sick of the world, and all its joy,
   My soul in pining sadness mourns:
Dark scenes of woe my mind employ,
   The past and present in their turns – [2]

Have you ever met with a saying of the Great and likewise Good Mr Locke, Author of the famous essay on the human understanding. – He wrote a letter to a friend, directing it, 'not to be delivered till after my decease;' it ended thus – 'I know you loved me when living, and will preserve my memory now I am dead. – All the use to be made of it is; that this life affords no solid satisfaction, but in the consciousness of having done well, and the hopes of another life. – Adieu! I leave my best wishes with you. – J. Locke – '[3]

Clarinda, may I reckon on your friendship for life? I think I may. – Thou Almighty Preserver of Men! Thy friendship, which hitherto I have too much neglected, to secure it shall, all the future days and nights of my life, be my steady care! – The idea of my Clarinda follows –

Hide it my heart, within that close disguise,
Where mix'd with God's her lov'd idea lies – [4]

But I fear that inconstancy, the consequent imperfection of human weakness. – Shall I meet with a friendship that defies years of Absence and the chances and changes of Fortune? Perhaps 'such things are'; *One* honest man I have great hopes from, that way: but who, except a Romance-writer, would think on a *love* that could promise for life, in spite of distance, absence, chance and change; and that too, with slender hopes of Fruition? – For my own part, I can say to myself in both requisitions, 'Thou art the man!'[5] I dare, in cool resolve I dare, declare myself that Friend, and that Lover. – If Womankind is capable of such things, Clarinda is. – I trust that she is; and feel I shall be miserable, if she is not. – There is not one Virtue which gives worth, or one Sentiment which does honor to the Sex, that she does not possess superiour to any woman I ever saw: her exalted mind, aided a little perhaps by her situation, is, I think, capable of that nobly-romantic Love-enthusiasm. –

May I see you on Wedensday evening, my dear angel? The next Wedensday again will, I conjecture, be a hated day to us both. – I tremble for censorious remark, for your sake; but in extraordinary cases, may not usual and useful Precaution be a little dispensed with? Three evenings, three swift-winged evenings, with pinions of down, are all the past – I dare not calculate the future. – I shall call at Miss Nimmo's tomorrow-evening; 'twill be a farewell call. –

I have wrote out my last sheet of paper, so I am reduc'd to my last half-sheet – What a strange, mysterious faculty is that thing called Imagination? We have no ideas almost at all, of another world; but I have often amused myself with visionary schemes of what happiness might be enjoyed by small alterations, alterations that we can fully enter to, in this present state of existence – For instance; suppose you and I just as we are at present; the same reasoning Powers, sentiments and even desires; the same fond curiousity for knowledge and remarking observation in our minds; & imagine our bodies free from pain and the necessary supplies for the wants of nature, at all times and easily within our reach: imagine farther that we were set free from the laws of gravitation which binds us to this globe, and could at pleasure fly, without inconvenience, through all the yet unconjecture'd bounds of Creation – what a life of bliss would we lead, in our mutual pursuit of virtue and knowledge, and our mutual enjoyment of friendship and love! –

I see you laughing at my fairy fancies, and calling me a voluptuous Mahometan; but I am certain I would be a happy creature, beyond any thing we call bliss here below: nay, it would be a paradise congenial to you too. – Don't you see us hand in hand, or rather my arm about your lovely waist, making our remarks on Sirius, the nearest of the fixed stars; or surveying a Comet flaming inoxious by us, as we just now would mark the passing pomp of a travelling Monarch: or, in a shady bower of Mercury or Venus, dedicating the hour to love; in mutual converse, relying honor and revelling endearment – while the most exalted strains of Poesy and Harmony would be the ready, spontaneous language of our souls! Devotion is the favorite employment of your heart; so is it of mine: what incentives then to, and powers for, Reverence, Gratitude, Faith and Hope in all the fervours of Adoration and Praise to that Being whose unsearchable Wisdom, Power and Goodness so pervaded, so inspired every Sense and Feeling! – By this time, I dare say, you will be blessing the neglect of the maid that leaves me destitute of Paper. –

Sylvander

1 Not identified.
2 Not identified.
3 Letter to Anthony Collins of 23rd August 1704.
4 Pope: *Eloisa to Abelard*, lines 11–12 altered to fit the opposite sex.
5 2 Samuel 12:7.

TO AGNES McLEHOSE
(CL, 399–400)

[Mossgiel, 23rd February 1788]

I have just now, My ever dearest Madam, delivered your kind present to my sweet, little Bobbie; who I find a very fine fellow. – Your letter was waiting me. – Your interview with Mr K—[1] opens a wound, ill-closed, in my breast: not that I think his friendship of so much consequence to you, but because you set such a value on it. – Now for a little news that will please you. – I, this morning as I came home, called for a certain woman. – I am disgusted with her; I cannot endure her! I, while my heart smote me for the prophanity, tried to compare her with my Clarinda: 'twas setting the expiring glimmer of a farthing taper beside the cloudless glory of the meridian sun. – Here was tasteless inspidity, vulgarity of soul, and mercenary fawning; there, polished good sense, heaven-born genius, and the most generous, the most delicate, the most tender Passion. – I have done with her, and she with me. –

[*One line of MS cut away here*] I set off tomorrow for Dumfriesshire. – 'Tis merely out of Compliment to Mr Miller, for I know the

Excise² must be my lot. – I will write you from Dumfries, if these horrid postages don't frighten me. –

> Whatever place, whatever land I see,
> My heart, untravell'd, fondly turns to thee:
> Still to 'Clarinda' turns with ceaseless pain:
> And drags, at each remove, a lengthen'd chain!³

I just stay to write you a few lines before I go to call on my friend, Mr Gavin Hamilton. – I hate myself as an unworthy sinner, because these interviews of old, dear friends make me for half a moment almost forget Clarinda. –

Remember tomorrow evening at eight o'clock: I shall be with the Father of mercies, at that hour, on your account. – Farewell! if the post goes not tonight, I'll finish the other page tomorrow morning. –

Sylvander

1 Kemp.
2 Heavily scored through.
3 Goldsmith: *The Traveller*, lines 7ff., paraphrased.

TO ROBERT AINSLIE
(CL, 331–2)

Mauchline, 3rd March, 1788

My dear Friend,

I am just returned from Mr Miller's farm. My old friend whom I took with me was highly pleased with the bargain, and advised me to accept of it. He is the most intelligent sensible farmer in the county, and his advice has staggered me a good deal. I have the two plans before me: I shall endeavour to balance them to the best of my judgment, and fix on the most eligible. On the whole, if I find Mr Miller in the same favourable disposition as when I saw him last, I shall in all probability turn farmer.

I have been through sore tribulation and under much buffeting of the Wicked One since I came to this country. Jean I found banished, like a martyr – forlorn destitute and friendless: All for the good old cause. I have reconciled her to her fate, and I have reconciled her to her mother. I have reconciled her to her mother. I have taken her a room. I have taken her to my arms. I have given her a mahogany bed. I have given her a guinea, and I have f—d her till she rejoiced with joy unspeakable and full of glory. But, as I always am on every occasion, I have been prudent and cautious to an astonishing degree. I swore her privately and solemnly never to attempt any claim on me as a husband, even though anybody should persuade her she had such a claim (which she had not), neither during my life nor after my death. She did all this like a good girl, and I took the opportunity of some dry horse litter, and gave her such a thundering scalade that electrified the very marrow of her bones. Oh, what a peacemaker is a guid weel-willy pintle! It is the mediator, the guarantee, the umpire, the bond of union, the solemn league and covenant, the plenipotentiary, the Aaron's rod, the Jacob's staff, the prophet Elisha's pot of oil, the Ahasuerus' Sceptre, the sword of mercy, the philosopher's stone, the Horn of Plenty, and Tree of Life between Man and Woman.

I shall be in Edinburgh the middle of next week. My farming ideas I shall keep private till I see. I got a letter from Clarinda yesterday, and she tells me she has got no letter of mine but one. Tell her that I wrote to her from Glasgow, from Kilmarnock, from Mauchline, and yesterday from Cumnock, as I returned from Dumfries. Indeed she is the only person in Edinburgh I have written to till this day today. How are your soul and body putting up? – A little like man and wife, I suppose.

Your faithful friend,
R.B.

TO ROBERT MUIR
(CL, 89–90)

Mossgiel 7th March 1788

I have partly changed my ideas, my dear Friend, since I saw you. – I took old Glenconner[1] with me to Mr Miller's farm, and he was so pleased with it, that I have wrote an offer to Mr Miller, which if he accepts, I shall sit down a plain farmer, the happiest of lives when a Man can live by it. – In this case I shall not stay in Edinburgh above a week. – I set out on Monday, and would have come by Kilmarnock but there are several small sums owing me for my first Edition, about Galston and Newmills; and I shall set off so early as to dispatch my business and reach Glasgow by night. – When I return, I shall devote a forenoon or two to make some kind of acknowledgement for all the kindness I owe your friendship. – Now that I hope to settle with some credit and comfort at home, there was not any friendship or friendly correspondence that promised me more pleasure than yours – I hope I will not be disappointed. – I trust the Spring will renew your shattered frame and make your friends happy. – You and I have often agreed that life is no great blessing on the whole. – The close of life indeed, to a reasoning eye, is 'Dark as was chaos, ere the infant sun

> Was roll'd together, or had try'd his beams
> Athwart the gloom profound – [2]

But an honest man has nothing to fear. – If we lie down in the grave, the whole man a piece of broke machinery, to moulder with the clods of the valley, – be it so; at least there is an end of pain, care, woes and wants: if that part of us called Mind, does survive the apparent destruction of the man – away with old-wife prejudices and tales! Every age and every nation has had a different set of stories; and as the many are always weak, of consequence they have often, perhaps always been deceived: a man, conscious of having acted an honest part among his fellow creatures; even granting that he may have been the sport, at times, of passions and instincts; he goes to a great unknown Being who could have no other end in giving him existence but to make him happy; who gave him those passions and instincts, and well knows their force. –

These my worthy friend, are my ideas; and I know they are not far different from yours. – It becomes a man of sense to think of himself; particularly in a case where all men are equally interested, and where indeed all men are equally in the dark. –

These Copies of mine you have on hand; please send ten of them to M. John Ballantine of the bank in Ayr; for the remainder, I'll write you about them from Glasgow. –

Adieu, my dear Sir! God send us a chearful meeting!

Robt Burns

1 John Tennant of Glenconner.
2 Blair: *The Grave*, lines 15–16.

TO JAMES SMITH
(CL, 121–2)

Mauchline 28th April 1788

Beware of your Strasburg[1], my good Sir! Look on this as the opening of a correspondence, like the opening of a twenty four gun battery! –

There is no understanding a man properly, without knowing something of his previous ideas (that is to say if the Man has any ideas for I know many who in the Animal-muster pass for Men that are the scanty Masters of only one idea on any given subject, and by far the greatest part of your acquaintances and mine can barely boast of Ideas 1.25, 1.5, 1.75, or some such fractional matter) so to let you a little into the secrets of my Pericranium, there is, you must know, a certain clean-limb'd, handsome bewitching young Hussy of your acquaintance to whom I have lately and privately given a matrimonial title to my Corpus. –

> Bode a robe, and wear it;
> Bode a pock, and bear it,

says the wise old Scots Adage! I hate to presage ill-luck; and as my girl in some late random trials has been *doubly* kinder to me than even the best of women usually are to their Partners of our Sex, in similar circumstances; I reckon on twelve times a brace of children against I celebrate my twelfth wedding-day: these twenty four will give me twenty four Gossipings, twenty four christenings (I mean, one equal to two) and I hope by the blessing of the God of my fathers to make them twenty four dutiful children to their Parents, twenty four useful Members of Society, and twenty four approven servants of their God; not to mention twenty four times a hundred and eighty two Mason-meetings on the business that I hope to have with their Mother into the bargain. –

'Light's heartsome,' quo' the wife when she was stealing sheep: you see what a lamp I have hung up to lighten your paths, when you are idle enough to explore the combinations and relations of my ideas. – 'Tis now as plain as a pike-staff why a twenty four gun battery was a Metaphor I would readily employ. –

Now for business. – I intend to present Mrs Burns with a printed shawl, an article of which I dare say you have variety, 'tis my first present to her since I have *irrevocably* called her mine, and I have a kind of whimsical wish to get her the said first present from an old and much valued friend of hers & mine, a trusty Trojan on whose friendship I count myself possessed of a life-rent lease; Connel goes to Edinburgh next week, it will oblidge me unspeakably if you will transmit by him the shawl, or you may send it by [*two or three words missing*] in Ronald's quarters which I believe will be best. – The quality, let it be of the best; the Pattern I leave to your taste. – The money I'll pay to your sister, or transmit to any Correspondent of yours in Edinburgh or Glasgow. Look on this letter as a 'beginning of sorrows': I'll write you till your eyes ache with reading nonsense. –

.

Mrs Burns ('tis only her private designation) begs her best Compliments to you. –

I am, My dear Sir,
ever most truly
yours Robt Burns

¹Its pentagonal citadel, built in 1682–4, was a byword for an impregnable fortress.

TO MRS DUNLOP
(CL, 145)

Mauchline, 4th May 1788

Madam,

I laid in a stock of apologies in my last which I intend shall serve me for the Season; so in this, and my future letters, I shall be brief or diffuse, witty or dull, as Time, genius, spirits, and the other auxiliaries of Composition, befriend me, without any kind of preface or preamble till the said stock of apologies are exhausted. –

Dryden's Virgil has delighted me. – I don't know whether the critics will agree with me, but the Georgics are to me by far the best of Virgil. – It is indeed a species of writing entirely new to me; and has filled my head with a thousand fancies of emulation: but alas! when I read the Georgics, and then survey my own powers, 'tis like the idea of a Shetland Pony drawn up by the side of a thorough bred Hunter, to start for the Plate. –

I own I am disappointed in the Eneid. – Faultless correctness may please, and does highly please the lettered Critic; but to that aweful character I have not the most distant pretentions. – I don't know whether I do not hazard my pretentions to be a Critic of any kind, when I say that I think Virgil, in many instances, a *servile* Copier of Homer. – If I had the Odyssey by me, I could parallel many passages where Virgil has evidently copied, but by no means improved Homer. – Nor can I think there is any thing of this owing to the Translators; for, from every thing I have seen of Dryden, I think him, in genius and fluency of language, Pope's master. – I have not perused Tasso enough, to form an opinion: in some future letter, you shall have my ideas of him; tho' I am conscious my criticisms must be very inaccurate and imperfect as *there* I have ever felt & lamented my want of Learning most. –

I send you the inclosed Bagatelles by way of a sin-offering for past offences. –

My old Direction, at Mauchline, will find me for two or three
weeks to come. –

I have the honor to be,
Madam, your oblidged humble servant,
Robt Burns

TO MRS DUNLOP
(CL, 148–50)

Mauchline 10th [July], 1788
[*Edinburgh Bishop mark* JY 17]

My much honored Friend,
Yours of the 24th June is before me. – I found it, as well as another
valued friend – MY WIFE – waiting to welcome me to Ayrshire: I met
both with the sincerest pleasure. –

When I write you, Madam, I do not sit down to answer every
paragraph of yours, by echoing every sentiment – like, The faithful
Commons of Great Britain, in parliament assembled, answering a
speech from the best of Kings! I just write in the fulness of my
heart, and may perhaps be guilty of neglecting some of your
kind enquiries – but not from your very odd reason that I do
not read your letters. – All your epistles, for several months,
have cost me nothing – except a deep-felt sentiment of respectful veneration, or a swelling throb of native Gratitude. –

Mrs Burns, Madam, is the identical woman who was the mother
of twice twins to me in seventeen months. – When she first found
herself – 'As women wish to be who love their lords,'[1] as I lov'd her
near to distraction, I took some previous steps to a private marriage.
– Her Parents got the hint; and in detestation of my guilt of being a
poor devil, not only forbade me her company & their house, but on
my rumored West Indian voyage, got a warrant to incarcerate me in
jail till I should find security in my about-to-be Paternal relation. –
You know my lucky reverse of fortune. – On my eclatant return to
Mauchline, I was made very welcome to visit my girl. – The usual
consequences began to betray her; and as I was at that time laid up
a cripple in Edinburgh, she was turned, literally out of doors, and I
wrote to a friend to shelter her, till my return. – I was not under
the least verbal obligation to her, but her happiness or misery were
in my hands, and who could trifle with such a deposite? – To the
least temptation to Jealousy or Infidelity, I am an equal stranger. –
My preservative from the first, is the most thorough consciousness

of her sentiments of honour, and her attachment to me; my antidote against the last, is my long & deep-rooted affection for her. – In housewife matters, of aptness to learn and activity to execute she is eminently mistress; and during my absence in Nithsdale, she is regularly & constantly apprentice to my Mother & Sisters in their dairy & other rural business. – In short, I can easily *fancy* a more agreable companion for my journey of Life, but, upon my honor, I have never *seen* the individual Instance! – You are right that a Bachelor state would have ensured me more friends; but, from a cause you will easily guess, conscious Peace in the enjoyment of my own mind, and unmistrusting Confidence in approaching my God, would seldom have been of the number. The Muses must not be offended when I tell them, the concerns of my wife & family will, in my mind, always take the Pas; but I assure them, their Ladyships shall ever come next in place. – Should my farm, which it possibly may, turn out a ruinous bargain, I have a certainty of an employment, poor as it may *comparatively* be, whose emoluments are luxury to any thing my first twenty five years of Life could promise. – I don't know if ever I mentioned to you my most favorite Quotation –

> – On Reason build Resolve,
> That column of true majesty in Man![2]

Circumstanced as I am, I could never have got a female partner for life who could have entered into my favorite studies, relished my favorite Authors, &c. without entailing on me at the same time, expensive living, fantastic caprice, apish affectation, with the other blessed, Boarding-school acquirements which (pardonnez moi, Madame!) are some times to be found among females of the upper ranks, but almost universally pervade the Misses of the Would-be-gentry. – In this kind of literary, sentimental correspondence, FRIENDSHIP must be my social channel; at the same time I declare to God, You are almost the [only] friend of this Kind I have. – So far from tiring of your correspondence, Madam, it would be one of the greatest misfortunes that could befall me, were I to lose it. – I really tremble at the idea that days & years are making you older, and that the all-conquering hand of Time may deprive me of a FRIEND whose WORTH I shall ever gratefully revere, and whose loss (should I be so unfortunate) I shall ever inconsolably deplore. –

I like your way in your Church-yard lucubrations. – Thoughts that are the spontaneous result of accidental situations, either respecting health, place, or company, have often a strength, and always an

Originality, that would in vain be looked for in faded circumstances and studied paragraphs. – For me, I have often thought of keeping a letter, *in progression*, by me, to send you when the sheet was wrote out. – Now I talk of sheets, I must tell you, my reason for writing to you on paper of this kind is my pruriency of writing to you at LARGE. – A page of Post is on such a dissocial narrow-minded scale, that I cannot abide it; & double letters, at least in my miscellaneous, reverie manner, are a monstrous tax, in a close Correspondence. –

> I have the honor to be, Madam,
> your oblidged & most obedient humble servant,
> Robt Burns

1 Home: *Douglas*, Act I, sc. 1.
2 Young: *Night Thoughts*, Night I, lines 30–1.

TO JOHN TENNANT JUN.
(CL, 73)

Ellisland, 22nd December 1788

My dear Sir,
I yesterday tried my cask of whisky for the first time, and I assure you it does you great credit. – It will bear five waters, strong; or six, ordinary Toddy. – The Whisky of this country is a most rascally liquor; and by consequence, only drunk by the most rascally part of the inhabitants. – I am persuaded, if you once got a footing here, you might do a great deal of business; both in the way of consumpt, and should you commence Distiller again, this is the native barley-country. –

I am ignorant if, in your present way of dealing, you would think it worth while to extend your business so far as this country-side – I write you this on the account of an accident which I must take the merit of having partly designed too. – A neighbour of mine, a John Currie, miller in Carse-mill, a man who is in a word, 'a good man,' a 'very' good man, even for 500£ bargain, he and his wife were in the country Publick-house & sell a great deal of foreign spirits but all along thought that Whisky would have degraded their house. – They were perfectly astonished at my whisky, both for its taste & strength, and by their desire I write you to know if you could supply them with liquor of an equal quality, and at what price. – Please write me by first Post, & direct to me, at Ellisland near Dumfries. – If you could take a jaunt this way yourself, I have a spare spoon, knife and fork, very much at your

service. – My compliments to Mrs Tennant, and all the good folks
in Glenconner & Barquharrie. –

I am most truly, My dear Sir, yours
Robt Burns

TO JAMES BURNESS
(CL, 62–3)

Ellisland, 9th February, 1789

My dear Sir,

Why I did not write to you long ago is what, even on the rack I could
not answer. – If you can in your mind form an idea of indolence,
dissipation, hurry, cares, changes of country, entering on untried scenes
of life – all combined; you will save me the trouble of a blushing
apology. – It could not be want of regard for a man for whom I had a
high esteem before I knew him – an esteem which has much increased
since I did know him; and this caveat entered, I shall plead guilty to
any other indictment with which you shall please to charge me. –

After I parted from you, for many months, my life was one continued scene of dissipation. – Here, at last, I am become stationary,
and have taken a farm, and – a wife. The farm lies beautifully situated
on the banks of the Nith, a large river that runs by Dumfries & falls into
the Solway Firth. – I have gotten a lease of my farm as long as I pleased;
but how it may turn out is just a guess, as it is yet to improve and inclose,
&c.; however I have good hopes of my bargain on the whole. –

My Wife is my Jean, with whose story you are partly acquainted.
– I found I had a much-loved fellow-creature's happiness or misery
among my hands, and I durst not trifle with so sacred a deposite.
– Indeed I have not any reason to repent the step I have taken,
as I have attached myself to a very good wife, & have shaken myself loose of a very bad failing. –

I have found my book a very profitable business; and with the
profits of it, have begun life pretty decently. – Should Fortune not
favour me in farming, as I have no great faith in her fickly Ladyship,
I have provided myself in another resource, which, however some
folks may affect to despise it, is still a comfortable shift in the day of
misfortune. – In the heyday of my fame, a gentleman whose name at
least I dare say you know, as his estate lies somewhere near Dundee,
Mr Graham of Fintry, one of the Commissioners of Excise, offered
me the commission of an Excise-Officer. – I thought it prudent to

accept the offer, and accordingly I took my Instructions, and have my Commission by me. – Whether I may ever do duty, or be a penny better for it, is what I do not know; but I have this comfortable assurance, that come whatever fate will, I can on my simple petition to the Excise board, get into employ. –

We have lost poor uncle Robert this winter. – He has long been weak and with very little alteration in him, he expired January 3rd. – His son William, has been with me this winter, & goes in May to bind himself to be a Mason with my fatherinlaw who is a pretty considerable architect in Ayrshire. – His other Son, the eldest, John, comes to me, I expect in summer. – They are both remarkable stout young fellows, & promise to do well. – His only daughter Fanny has been with me ever since her father's death and I purpose keeping her in my family till she be quite woman grown, & be fit for better service. – She is one of the cleverest girls, and has one of the most amiable dispositions that I have ever seen. –

All friends in this country and Ayrshire are well. – Remember me to all friends in the North. – My wife joins in Compliments to your bedfellow & family. – I would write your brother-in-law, but have lost his Address. – For goodness sake don't take example by me, but write me soon. – I am ever, My dear cousin,

yours most sincerely. –
Robt Burns

TO AGNES McLEHOSE
(CL, 405–6)

9th March 1789

Madam

The letter you wrote me to Heron's carried its own answer in its bosom: you forbade me to write you, unless I was willing to plead, Guilty, to a certain Indictment that you were pleased to bring against me. – As I am convinced of my own innocence, and though conscious of high imprudence & egregious folly, can lay my hand on my breast and attest the rectitude of my heart; you will pardon me, Madam, if I do not carry my complaisance so far, as humbly to acquiesce in the name of, Villain, merely out of compliment even to YOUR opinion; much as I esteem your judgement, and warmly as I regard your worth. – I have already told you, and I again aver it, that at the Period of time alluded to, I was not under the smallest moral tie to Mrs B——; nor did I, nor could I then know, all the powerful circumstances that omnipotent

Necessity was busy lying in wait for me. – When you call over the scenes that have passed between us, you will survey the conduct of an honest man, struggling successfully with temptations the most powerful that ever beset humanity, and preserving untainted honor in situations where the austerest Virtue would have forgiven a fall – Situations that I will dare to say, not a single individual of all his kind, even with half his sensibility and passion, could have encountered without ruin; and I leave you to guess, Madam, how such a man is likely to digest an accusation of perfidious treachery!

Was I to blame, Madam, in being the distracted victim of Charms which, I affirm it, no man ever approached with impunity? – Had I seen the least glimmering of hope that these Charms could ever have been mine – or even had not iron Necessity – but these are unavailing words. –

I would have called on you when I was in town, indeed I could not have resisted it, but that Mr A[inslie] told me that you were determined to avoid your windows while I was in town, lest even a glance of me should occur in the Street. –

When I have regained your good opinion, perhaps I may venture to solicit your friendship: but be that as it may, the first of her Sex I ever knew, shall always be the object of my warmest good wishes. –

TO WILLIAM BURNS
(CL, 516)

Ellisland, 5th May, 1789

My dear William,
I am happy to hear by yours from Newcastle, that you are getting some employ. Remember

> On reason build Resolve,
> That column of true majesty in man. – [1]

I had a visit of your old landlord. In the midst of a drunken frolic in Dumfries, he took itto in his head to come and see me; and I took all the pains in my power to please and entertain the old veteran. He is high in your praises, and I would advise you to cultivate his friendship, as he is, in his way, a worthy, and to you may be a useful man.

Anderson I hope will have your shoes ready to send by the waggon tomorrow. I forgot to mention the circumstance of making them pumps; but I suppose good calf shoes will be no great mistake. Wattie[2] has paid me for the thongs.

What would you think of making a little inquiry how husbandry matters go, as you travel, and if one thing fail, you might perhaps try another?

Your falling in love is indeed a phenomenon. To a fellow of your turn it cannot be hurtful. I am, you know, a veteran in these campaigns, so let me advise you always to pay your particular assiduities and try for intimacy as soon as you feel the first symptoms of the passion: this is not only best, as making the most of the little entertainment which the sportabilities of distant addresses always gives, but is the best preservative for one's peace. I need not caution you against guilty amours – they are bad and ruinous everywhere, but in England they are the very devil. I shall be in Ayrshire about a fortnight. Your sisters send their compliments. God bless you.

                                                        Robert Burns

1 Young: *Night Thoughts*, Night I, lines 30–1.
2 Walter Auld.

TO ROBERT AINSLIE
(CL, 337–8)

Ellisland, 8th June 1789

My dear Friend,
I am perfectly ashamed of myself when I look at the date of your last. It is not that I forget the friend of my heart and the companion of my peregrinations; but I have been condemned to drudgery beyond sufferance, though not, thank God, beyond redemption. I have had a collection of poems by a lady put into my hands to prepare them for the press; which horrid task, with sowing my corn with my own hand, a parcel of masons, wrights, plaisterers, &c. to attend to, roaming on business through Ayrshire – all this was against me, and the very first dreadful article was of itself too much for me.

13th. I have not had a moment to spare from incessant toil since the 8th. Life, my dear Sir, is a serious matter. You know by experience that a man's individual self is a good deal, but believe me, a wife and family of children, whenever you have the honor to be a husband and a father, will shew you that your present most anxious hours of solicitude are spent on trifles. The welfare of those who are very dear to us, whose only support, hope and stay we are – this, to a generous mind, is another sort of more important object of care than any concerns whatever which center merely in the individual. On the

other hand, let no young, unmarried, rakehelly dog among you, make
a song of his pretended liberty and freedom from care. If the relations
we stand in to king, country, kindred, and friends, be any thing but
the visionary fancies of dreaming metaphysicians; if religion, virtue,
magnanimity, generosity, humanity and justice be aught but empty
sounds; then the man who may be said to live only for others, for
the beloved, honorable female whose tender faithful embrace endears
life, and for the helpless little innocents who are to be the men and
women, the worshippers of his God, the subjects of his king, and the
support, nay the very vital existence of his COUNTRY, in the ensuing
age; – compare such a man with any fellow whatever, who, whether
he bustle and push in business among laborers, clerks, statesmen; or
whether he roar and rant, and drink and sing in taverns – a fellow
over whose grave no-one will breathe a single heigh-ho, except from
the cobweb-tie of what is called good fellowship – who has no view
nor aim but what terminates in himself – if there be any grovelling
earthborn wretch of our species, a renegado to common sense, who
would fain believe that the noble creature, man, is no better than a
sort of fungus, generated out of nothing, nobody knows how, and
soon dissipating in nothing, nobody knows where; such a stupid beast,
such a crawling reptile might balance the foregoing unexaggerated
comparison, but no-one else would have the patience.

Forgive me, my dear Sir, for this long silence. *To make you amends*, I
shall send you soon, and more encouraging still, without any postage,
one or two rhymes of my later manufacture.

TO WILLIAM BURNS
(CL, 518)

Ellisland, 10th February 1790

My dear William

I would have written you sooner but I have mislaid Mr Murdoch's[1]
letter, and cannot for my life lay my hand on it; so I cannot write him
for want of a Direction. – If I find it afterwards, I will write him &
inclose it to you in London. – Now that you are setting out for that
place, put on manly resolve, & determine to persevere; & in that case
you will less or more be sure of success. – One or two things allow
me to particularize to you. – London swarms with worthless wretches
who prey on their fellow-creatures' thoughtlessness or inexperience. –
Be cautious in forming connections with comrades and companions. –
You can be pretty good company to yourself, & you cannot be too shy

of letting any body know you farther than to know you as a Sadler. – Another caution; I give you great credit for your sobriety with respect to that universal vice, Bad Women. – It is an impulse the hardest to be restrained, but if once a man accustoms himself to gratifications of that impulse, it is then nearly or altogether impossible to restrain it. – Whoring is a most ruinous expensive species of dissipation; is spending a poor fellow's money with which he ought clothe & support himself nothing? Whoring has ninety nine chances in a hundred to bring on a man the most nauseous & excrutiating diseases to which Human nature is liable; are disease & an impaired constitution trifling considerations? All this is independant of the criminality of it. –

I have gotten the Excise Division in the middle of which I live. – Poor little Frank is this morning at the height in the Small-pox. – I got him inoculated, & I hope he is in a good way. –

Write me before you leave Newcastle, & as soon as you reach London. – In a word, if ever you be, as perhaps you may be, in a strait for a little ready cash, you know my direction. – I shall not see you beat, while you fight like a Man. –

Farewell! God bless you!
Robt Burns

1 John Murdoch, Robert's former schoolmaster, then teaching French in London.

TO CAPTAIN FRANCIS GROSE
(CL, 557–9)

[?June 1790]

Among the many Witch Stories I have heard relating to Aloway Kirk, I distinctly remember only two or three.

Upon a stormy night, amid whirling squalls of wind and bitter blasts of hail, in short, on such a night as the devil would chuse to take the air in, a farmer or farmer's servant was plodding and plashing homeward with his plough-irons on his shoulder, having been getting some repairs on them at a neighbouring smithy. His way lay by the Kirk of Aloway, and being rather on the anxious look-out in approaching a place so well known to be a favourite haunt of the devil and the devil's friends and emissaries, he was struck aghast by discovering through the horrors of the storm and stormy night, a light, which on his nearer approach, plainly shewed itself to proceed from the haunted edifice. Whether he had been fortified from above on his devout supplication, as is customary with people when they suspect the immediate presence of Satan; or whether, according to another custom, he had got courageously drunk at the smithy, I will not pretend to determine; but so it was that he ventured to go up to, nay into the very kirk. As good luck would have it, his temerity came off unpunished. The members of the infernal junto were all out on some midnight business or other, and he saw nothing but a kind of kettle or caldron, depending from the roof, over the fire, simmering some heads of unchristened children, limbs of executed malefactors, &c. for the business of the night. It was, in for a penny, in for a pound, with the honest ploughman: so without ceremony he unhooked the caldron from off the fire, and pouring out the damnable ingredients, inverted it on his head, and carried it fairly home, where it remained long in the family a living evidence of the truth of the story.

Another story which I can prove to be equally authentic was as follows.

On a market day in the town of Ayr, a farmer from Carrick, and consequently whose way lay by the very gate of Aloway kirk-yard, in order to cross the river Doon at the old bridge, which is about two or three hundred yards further on than the said gate, had been detained by his business, 'till by the time he reached Aloway, it was the wizard hour, between night and morning. Though he was terrified, with a blaze streaming from the kirk, yet as it is a well-known fact that to turn back on these occasions is running by far the greatest risk of mischief, he prudently advanced on his road. When he had reached the gate of the kirk-yard, he was surprised and entertained, through the ribs and arches of an old gothic window which still faces the highway, to see a dance of witches merrily footing it round their old sooty blackguard master, who was keeping them alive with the powers of his bag-pipe. The farmer stopping his horse to observe them a little, could plainly descry the faces of many old women of his acquaintance and neighbourhood. How the gentleman was dressed, tradition does not say; but the ladies were all in their smocks: and one of them happening unluckily to have a smock which was considerably too short to answer all the purpose of that piece of dress, our farmer was so tickled that he involuntarily burst out, with a loud laugh, 'Well luppen Maggy wi' the short sark!' and recollecting himself, instantly spurred his horse to the top of his speed. I need not mention the universally known fact, that no diabolical power can pursue you beyond the middle of a running stream. Lucky it was for the poor farmer that the river Doon was so near, for notwithstanding the speed of his horse, which was a good one, against he reached the middle of the arch of the bridge, and consequently the middle of the stream, the pursuing, vengeful, hags, were so close at his heels, that one of them actually sprung to seize him; but it was too late, nothing was on her side of the stream but the horse's tail, which immediately gave way to her infernal grip, as if blasted by a stroke of lightning; but the farmer was beyond her reach. However, the unsightly, tailless condition of the vigorous steed was to the last hour of the noble creature's life, an awful warning to the Carrick farmers, not to stay too late in Ayr markets.

The last relation I shall give, though equally true, is not so well identified as the two former, with regard to the scene: but as the best authorities give it for Aloway, I shall relate it.

On a summer's evening, about the time that Nature puts on her sables to mourn the expiry of the chearful day, a shepherd boy belonging to a farmer in the immediate neighbourhood of Aloway Kirk, had just folded his charge, and was returning home. As he passed the kirk, in the adjoining field, he fell in with a crew of men and women, who were busy pulling stems of the plant ragwort. He observed that as each person pulled a ragwort, he or she got astride of it and called out, 'Up horsie!' on which the ragwort flew off, like Pegasus, through the air with its rider. The foolish boy likewise pulled his ragwort, and cried with the rest 'Up horsie!' and, strange to tell, away he flew with the company. The first stage at which the cavalcade stopt, was a merchant's wine cellar in Bourdeaux, where, without saying by your leave, they quaffed away at the best the cellar could afford, until the morning, foe to the imps and works of darkness, threatened to throw light on the matter, and frightened them from their carousals.

The poor shepherd lad, being equally a stranger to the scene and the liquor, heedlessly got himself drunk and when the rest took horse, he fell asleep, and was found so next day by some of the people belonging to the merchant. Somebody that understood Scotch, asking him what he was, he said he was such-a-one's herd in Aloway; and by some means or other getting home again, he lived long to tell the world the wondrous tale.

I am, &c, &c.
Rob Burns

TO PETER HILL
(CL, 321)

Dumfries, 5th February 1792

My dear Friend,

I send you by the bearer, Mr Clarke, a particular friend of mine, six pounds & a shilling, which you will dispose of as follows. – £5-10, per account I owe to Mr Robt Burn, Architect, for erecting the stone over poor Ferguson. – He was two years in erecting it, after I commissioned him for it; & I have been two years paying him, after he sent me his account; so he & I are quits. – He had the hardiesse to ask me interest on the sum; but considering that the money was due by one Poet, for putting a tomb-stone over another, he may, with grateful surprise, thank Heaven that ever he saw a farthing of it.

With the remainder of the money, pay yourself the 'Office of a Messenger'[1] that I bought of you, & send me by Mr Clarke a note of its price. – Send me likewise the fifth volume of the Observer by Mr Clarke; & if any money remain, let it stand to account.

My best Compliments to Mrs Hill. – I sent you a Maukin by last week's Fly, which I hope you received. –

Yours most sincerely,
Robt Burns

1 Robert Thomson: *The Duty and Office of a Messenger at Arms*, Edinburgh (1790).

TO ALEXANDER CUNNINGHAM
(CL 465–7)

Dumfries, 10th September 1792

No! I will not attempt an apology. – Amid all my hurry of business, grinding the faces of the Publican & the Sinner on the merciless wheels of the Excise; making ballads, & then drinking, & singing them; & over & above all, the correcting the Presswork of two different Publications; still, still I might have stolen five minutes to dedicate to one of the first of my Friends & Fellow-creatures. – I might have done, as I do at present, snatched an hour near 'witching time of night'[1] – & scrawled a page or two. – I might have congratulated my Friend on his marriage; or, I might have thanked the Caledonian Archers for the honor they have done me: (though, to do myself justice, I

intended to have done both in RHYME, else I had done both long
ere now. –) Well then, here is to your good health! for you must
know, I have set a nipperkin of TODDY by me, just by way of SPELL
to keep away the meikle horned Deil, or any of his subaltern Imps
who may be on their nightly rounds. –

But what shall I write you? – 'The Voice said, Cry! and I said, What
shall I cry?'[2] – O, thou Spirit! whatever thou art, or wherever thou
makest thyself visible! Be thou a Bogle by the eerie side of an auld
thorn, in the dreary glen through which the herd-callan maun bicker
in his gloamin route frae the fauld! – Be thou a BROWNIE, set, at dead of
night, to thy task by the blazing ingle, or in the solitary barn where the
repercussions of thy iron flail half affright thyself, as thou performest the
work of twenty of the sons of men, ere the cock-crowing summon thee
to thy ample cog of substantial BROSE! – Be thou a KELPIE, haunting the
ford, or ferry, in the starless night, mixing thy laughing yell with the
howling of the storm & the roaring of the flood, as thou viewest the
perils & miseries of Man on the foundering horse, or in the tumbling
boat! – Or, lastly, be thou a GHOST, paying thy nocturnal visits to the
hoary ruins of decayed Grandeur; or performing thy mystic rites in the
shadow of the time-worn Church while the Moon looks, without a
cloud, on the silent, ghastly dwellings of the dead around thee; or
taking thy stand by the bed-side of the Villain, or the Murderer,
pourtraying on his dreaming fancy, pictures, dreadful as the horrors
of unveiled Hell, & terrible as the wrath of incensed Deity ! ! !
Come, thou Spirit, but not in these horrid forms; come with the
milder, gentle, easy inspirations which thou breathest round the wig
of a prating ADVOCATE, or the tête of a tea-bibbing Gossip, while their
tongues run at the light-horse gallop of clishmaclaiver for ever & ever
– come, & assist a poor devil who is quite jaded in the attempt to share
half an idea among half a hundred words; to fill up four quarto pages,
while he has not got one single sentence of recollection, information,
or remark, worth putting pen to paper for! –

I feel, I feel the presence of Supernatural assistance! Circled in the
embrace of my elbow-chair, my breast labors, like the bloated Sybil
on her three-footed stool, & like her too, labors with Nonsense. –
Nonsense, auspicious name! – Tutor, Friend & Finger-post in the
mystic mazes of Law; the cadaverous paths of Physic; & particularly
in the sightless soarings of SCHOOL DIVINITY, who, leaving Common
Sense confounded at his strength of pinion, Reason delirious with
eyeing his giddy flight, & Truth creeping back into the bottom of
her well, cursing the hour that ever she offered her scorned alliance to
the wizard Power of Theologic Vision – raves abroad on all the winds,

'On Earth, Discord! A gloomy Heaven above opening her jealous gates to the nineteen thousandth part of the tithe of mankind! And below, an inescapable & inexorable Hell, expanding its leviathan jaws for the vast residue of Mortals! ! !' O, doctrine! comfortable & healing to the weary, wounded soul of man! – Ye sons & daughters of affliction, ye pauvres Miserables, to whom day brings no pleasure, & night yields no rest, be comforted! ' 'Tis but *one* to nineteen hundred thousand, that your situation will mend in this world;' so, alas, the Experience of the Poor & the Needy too truly affirms; & 'tis nineteen hundred thousand to *one*, by the dogmas of Theology, that you will be damned eternally in the World to come!

But of all Nonsense, Religious Nonsense is the most nonsensical; so enough, & more than enough of it – Only, by the bye, will you, or can you tell me, my dear Cunningham, why a religioso turn of mind has always a tendency to narrow & illiberalize the heart? They are orderly; they may be just; nay, I have known them merciful: but still your children of Sanctity move among their fellow-creatures with a nostril snuffing putrescence, & a foot spurning filth, in short, with that conceited dignity which your titled Douglases, Hamiltons, Gordons, or any other of your Scots Lordlings of seven centuries standing, display when they accidentally mix among the many-aproned Sons of Mechanical life. – I remember, in my Plough-boy days, I could not conceive it possible that a noble Lord could be a Fool, or that a godly Man could be a Knave. – How ignorant are Plough-boys! – Nay, I have since discovered that a *godly woman* may be a—! – But hold – Here's t'ye again – This Rum is damn'd generous Antigua, so a very unfit menstruum for scandal. –

Apropos, how do you like, I mean *really* like, the Married Life? – Ah, my Friend! Matrimony is quite a different thing from what your love-sick youths & sighing girls take it to be! – But Marriage, we are told, is appointed by God & I shall never quarrel with any of HIS Institutions. – I am a Husband of older standing than you, & I shall give you *my* ideas of the Conjugal State. – (En passant, you know I am no Latin, is not 'Conjugal' derived from 'Jugum' a yoke?) Well then, the scale of Good-wife-ship I divide into ten parts. – Good Nature, four; Good-Sense, two; Wit, one; Personal Charms, viz. a sweet face, eloquent eyes, fine limbs, graceful carriage, (I would add a fine waist too, but that is so soon spoilt you know) all these, one: as for the other qualities belonging to, or attending on, a Wife, such as, fortune, connections education, (I mean, education extraordinary) family-blood, &c. divide the two remaining degrees among them as you please; only, remember that all these minor properties must be expressed by *fractions*; for there is not any one of them, in the aforesaid scale, entitled to the dignity of an *integer*. –

As for the rest of my fancies & reveries – How I lately met with Miss Lesley Bailie, the most beautiful, elegant woman in the world – How I accompanied her & her Father's Family fifteen miles on their journey, out of pure devotion to admire the loveliness of the works of God in such an unequalled display of them – How, in galloping home at night, I made a ballad on her of which these two Stanzas make a part –

> Thou, bonie Lesley, art a queen,
>   Thy subjects we before thee;
> Thou, bonie Lesley, art divine,
>   The hearts o' men adore thee. –
>
> The very Deil, he could na scathe
>   Whatever wad belang thee!
> He'd look into thy bonie face,
>   And say, 'I canna wrang thee – '[3]

Behold all these things are written in the Chronicles of my imaginations, & shall be read by thee, my dear Friend, & by thy beloved Spouse, my other dear Friend, at a more convenient season. –

Now, to thee, & to thy before-designed *bosom*-companion, be given the precious things brought forth by the Sun, & the precious things brought forth by the Moon, & the benignest influences of the Stars, & the living streams which flow from the fountains of Life & by the tree of Life, for ever & ever! AMEN! ! !

                                                      Robt Burns

1 Shakespeare: *Hamlet*, Act III, sc. 2.
2 Isaiah 30:6.
3 Original version, extensively revised when published.

TO GEORGE THOMSON
(CL, 617–18)

Dumfries 16th September 1792

Sir

I have just this moment got your letter. – As the request you make to me will positively add to my enjoyments in complying with it, I shall enter into your undertaking with all the small portion of abilities I have, strained to their utmost exertion by the impulse of Enthusiasm.

– Only, don't hurry me: 'Deil tak the hindmost' is by no means the Crie de guerre of my Muse. – Will you, as I am inferiour to none of you in enthusiastic attachment to the Poetry & Music of old Caledonia, &, since you request it, have chearfully promised my mite of assistance, will you let me have a list of your airs with the first line of the verses you intend for them, that I may have an opportunity of suggesting any alteration that may occur to me – you know 'tis in the way of my trade – still leaving you, Gentlemen, the undoubted right of Publishers, to approve, or reject, at your pleasure in your own Publication? – I say, the first line of the verses, because if they are verses that have appeared in any of our Collections of songs, I know them & can have recourse to them. Apropos, if you are for *English* verses, there is, on my part, an end of the matter. – Whether in the simplicity of the *Ballad*, or the pathos of the *Song*, I can only hope to please myself in being allowed at least a sprinkling of our native tongue. – English verses, particularly the works of Scotsmen, that have merit, are certainly very eligible. – Tweedside; Galashiels, viz. Ah! the poor shepherd's mournful fate &c. Gilderoy, viz. Ah, Chloris, could I now but sit, except, excuse my vanity, you should for Gilderoy prefer my own song, 'From thee, Eliza, I must go' &c. all these you cannot mend; but such insipid stuff, as, 'To Fanny fair could I impart' &c. usually set to The Mill Mill O, 'tis a disgrace to the Collections in which it has already appeared, & would doubly disgrace a Collection that will have the very superiour merit of yours. – But more of this in the farther prosecution of the Business, if I am to be called on for my strictures & amendments – I say, amendments: for I will not *alter* except where I myself at least think that I *amend*. –

As to any remuneration, you may think my Songs either *above*, or *below* price; for they shall absolutely be the one or the other. – In the honest enthusiasm with which I embark in your undertaking, to talk of money, wages, fee, hire, &c. would be downright Sodomy of Soul! – A proof of each of the Songs that I compose or amend, I shall receive as a favor. – In the rustic phrase of the Season, 'Gude speed the wark!'

I am, Sir, your very humble servant

Robt Burns

P.S. I have some particular reasons for wishing my interferance to be known as little as possible. –

R.B.

TO CAPTAIN WILLIAM JOHNSTON
(CL, 681)

Dumfries, 13th November 1792

Sir,

I have just read your Prospectus of the Edinburgh Gazetteer. – If you go on in your Paper with the same spirit, it will, beyond all comparison, be the first Composition of the kind in Europe. – I beg leave to insert my name as a Subscriber; & if you have already published any papers, please send me them from the beginning. – Point out your own way of settling payments in this place, or I shall settle with you through the medium of my friend, Peter Hill, Bookseller, Edinburgh. –

Go on, Sir! Lay bare, with undaunted heart & steady hand, that horrid mass of corruption called Politics & State-Craft! Dare to draw in their native colors these

Calm, thinking VILLAINS whom no faith can fix[1] –

whatever be the shiboleth of their pretended Party. –

The address, to me at Dumfries, will find,

Sir, your very humble Servant
Robt Burns

1 Pope: *The Temple of Fame*, line 410.

TO ROBERT GRAHAM OF FINTRY
(CL, 436–8)

Dumfries 5th January 1793

Sir,

I am this moment honored with your letter: with what feelings I received this other instance of your goodness, I shall not pretend to describe. –

Now, to the charges which Malice & Misrepresentation have brought against me. –

It has been said, it seems, that I not only belong to, but head a disaffected party in this place. – I know of no party in this place, either Republican or Reform, except an old party of Borough-Reform, with which I never had any thing to do. – Individuals, both Republican & Reform, we have, though not many of either; but if they have associated, it is more than I have the least knowledge of: & if there exists such

an association, it must consist of such obscure nameless beings, as pre-
cludes any possibility of my being known to them, or they to me. –

I was in the playhouse one night, when Ça ira was called for. – I
was in the middle of the pit, & from the Pit the clamour arose. –
One or two individuals with whom I occasionally associate were of
the party, but I neither knew of the Plot, nor joined in the Plot; nor
ever opened my lips to hiss, or huzza, that, or any other Political tune
whatever. – I looked on myself as far too obscure a man to have any
weight in quelling a Riot; at the same time, as a character of higher
respectability, than to yell in the howlings of a rabble. – This was the
conduct of all the first Characters in this place & these Characters
know, & will avow, that such was my conduct. –

I never uttered any invectives against the king. – His private worth,
it is altogether impossible that such a man as I, can appreciate; and in
his Public capacity, I always revered, & ever will, with the soundest
loyalty, revere, the Monarch of Great-britain, as, to speak in Masonic,
the sacred KEYSTONE OF OUR ROYAL ARCH CONSTITUTION. –

As to REFORM PRINCIPLES, I look upon the British Constitution,
as settled at the Revolution, to be the most glorious Constitution
on earth, or that perhaps the wit of man can frame; at the same
time, I think, & you know what High and distinguished Characters
have for some time thought so, that we have a good deal deviated
from the original principles of that Constitution; particularly, that an
alarming System of Corruption has pervaded the connection between
the Executive Power and the House of Commons. – This is the
Truth, the Whole truth, of my Reform opinions; opinions which,
before I was aware of the complection of these innovating times, I
too unguardedly (now I see it) sported with: but henceforth, I seal
up my lips. – However, I never dictated to, corresponded with, or
had the least connection with, any political association except, that
when the Magistrates & principal inhabitants of this town, met to
declare their attachment to the Constitution, & their abhorrence of
Riot, which declaration you would see in the Papers, I, as I thought
my duty as a Subject at large, & a Citizen in particular, called upon
me, subscribed the same declaratory Creed. –

Of Johnston, the publisher of the Edinburgh Gazetteer, I know
nothing. – One evening in company with four or five friends, we
met with his prospectus which we thought manly & independant;
& I wrote to him, ordering his paper for us. – If you think that
I act improperly in allowing his Paper to come addressed to me, I
shall immediately countermand it. – I never, so judge me, God!
wrote a line of prose for the Gazetteer in my life. – An occasional

address, spoken by Miss Fontenelle on her benefit night here, which I called, the Rights of Woman, I sent to the Gazetteer; as also, some extempore stanzas on the Commemoration of Thomson: both these I will subjoin for your perusal.[1] – You will see that they have nothing whatever to do with Politics. – At the time when I sent Johnston one of these poems, but which one, I do not remember, I inclosed at the request of my warm & worthy friend, Robert Riddel Esq: of Glenriddel, a prose Essay, signed Cato, written by him, & addressed to the delegates for the County Reform, of which he was one for this County. – With the merits, or demerits, of that Essay I have nothing to do, farther than transmitting it in the same Frank, which Frank he had procured me. –

As to France, I was her enthusiastic votary in the beginning of the business. – When she came to shew her old avidity for conquest, in annexing Savoy, &c. to her dominions, & invading the rights of Holland, I altered my sentiments. – A tippling·Ballad[2] which I made on the Prince of Brunswick's breaking up his camp, & sung one convivial evening, I shall likewise send you, sealed up, as it is not every body's reading. – This last is not worth your perusal; but lest Mrs FAME should, as she has already done, use, & even abuse, her old priviledge of lying, you shall be the master of every thing, le pour et le contre, of my political writings & conduct. –

This, my honored Patron, is all. – To this statement I challenge disquisition. – Mistaken Prejudice, or unguarded Passion, may mislead, & often have misled me; but when called on to answer for my mistakes, though, I will say it, no man can feel keener compunction for his errors, yet, I trust, no man can be more superiour to evasion or disguise. –

I shall do myself the honor to thank Mrs Graham for her goodness, in a separate letter. –

If, Sir, I have been so fortunate as to do away these misapprehensions of my conduct & character, I shall with the confidence which you were wont to allow me, apply to your goodness on every opening in the way of business, where I think I with propriety may offer myself. – An instance that occurs just now; Mr Mcfarlane, Supervisor of the Galloway District is & has been for some time, very ill. – I spoke to Mr Mitchel as to his wishes to forward my application for the job, but though he expressed & ever does express every kindness for me, he hesitates, in hopes that the disease may be of short continuance. – However, as it seems to be a paralytic affection, I fear that it may be some time ere he can take charge of so extended a District. – There is a great deal of fatigue, & very little business in the District; two things suitable enough to my hardy constitution, & inexperience in that line of life. —

I have the honor to be, Sir,
your ever grateful, as highly obliged humble servant
Robt Burns

1 Burns enclosed *The Rights of Woman* and *Extempore — on some Commemorations of Thomson.*
2 See p.227.

TO JOHN FRANCIS ERSKINE,
(CL, 689–91)

[In the year 17⁹²⁄₃3, when Royalist & Jacobin had set all Britain by the ears, because I unguardedly, rather under the temptation of being witty than disaffected, had declared my sentiments in favor of Parliamentary Reform, in the manner of that time, I was accused to the Board of Excise of being a Republican; & was very near being turned adrift in the wide world on that account. — Mr Erskine of Mar, *a gentleman indeed*, wrote to my friend Glenriddell to know if I was really out of place on account of my Political principles; & if so, he proposed a Subscription among the friends of Liberty for me, which he offered to head, that I might be no pecuniary loser by my political Integrity. — This was the more generous, as I had not the honor of being known to Mr Erskine. I wrote him as follows. —]¹

[Dumfries, 13th April 1793]

Sir,
degenerate as Human Nature is said to be, & in many instances, worthless & unprincipled it certainly is; still there are bright examples to the contrary; examples, that even in the eye of Superiour Beings must shed a lustre on the name of Man. — Such an example have I now before me, when you, Sir, came forward to patronise & befriend a distant, obscure stranger; merely because Poverty had made him helpless, & his British hardihood of mind had provoked the arbitrary wantonness of Power. — My much esteemed friend, Mr Riddell of Glenriddell, has just read me a paragraph of a letter he had from you. — Accept, Sir, of the silent throb of gratitude; for words would but mock the emotions of my soul. —

You have been misinformed, as to my final dismission from the Excise: I still am in the service. — Indeed, but for the exertions of a gentleman who must be known to you, Mr Graham of Fintry, a gentleman who has ever been my warm & generous friend, I had, without so much as a hearing, or the smallest previous intimation, been turned adrift, with my helpless family, to all the horrors of Want. – Had I had any other resource, probably I might have saved them the trouble of a dismissal; but the little money I gained by my Publication, is almost every guinea embarked, to save from ruin an only brother; who, though one of the worthiest, is by no means one of the most fortunate of men. –

In my defence to their accusations, I said, that whatever might be my sentiments of Republics, ancient or modern as to Britain, I abjured the idea. – That a Constitution which, in its original principles, experience had proved to be every way fitted for our happiness in society, it would be insanity to sacrifice to an untried, visionary theory. – That, in consideration of my being situated in a department, however humble, immediately in the hands of the people in power, I had forborne taking any active part, either personally, or as an author, in the present business of Reform. – But that, where I must declare my sentiments, I would say that there existed a system of corruption between the Executive Power & the Representative part of the Legislature, which boded no good to our glorious Constitution; & which every patriotic Briton must wish to see amended. – Some such Sentiments as these I stated in a letter to my generous Patron, Mr Graham, which he laid before the Board at large, where it seems my last remark gave great offence; & one of our Supervisors general, a Mr Corbet, was instructed to enquire, on the spot, into my conduct, & to document me – 'that *my* business was to *act*, not to think; & that whatever might be Men or Measures, it was my business to be silent & obedient' – Mr Corbet was likewise my steady friend; so, between Mr Graham & him, I have been partly forgiven: only, I understand that all hopes of my getting officially forward are blasted. –

Now, Sir, to the business in which I would more immediately interest you. – The partiality of my Countrymen has brought me forward as a man of genius, & has given me a Character to support. – In the Poet, I have avowed manly & independant sentiments, which I trust will be found in the Man. – Reasons of no less weight than the support of a wife & children have pointed out as the eligible, & indeed the only eligible line of life for me, my present occupation. – Still, my honest fame is my dearest concern, & a thousand times have I trembled at the idea of the degrading epithets that Malice, or Misrepresentation may affix to my name. I have often, in blasting anticipation, listened to some future hackney Magazine Scribbler, with the heavy malice of savage stupidity, exulting in his hireling paragraphs that 'Burns, notwithstanding the fanfaronade of independance to be found in his works, & after having been held forth to Public View & Public Estimation as a man of some genius, yet, quite destitute of resources within himself to support this borrowed dignity, he dwindled into a paltry Exciseman; & slunk out the rest of his insignificant existence in the meanest of pursuits & among the vilest of mankind.' –

In your illustrious hands, Sir, permit me to lodge my strong disavowal & defiance of these slanderous falsehoods. – BURNS was a poor man, from birth; & an Exciseman, by necessity: but – I will say it! – the sterling of his honest worth, no poverty could debase; & his independant British mind, Oppression might bend, but could not subdue! – Have not I, to me, a more precious stake in my Country's welfare, than the richest Dukedom in it? – I have a large family of children, & the probability of more. – I have three sons, whom, I see already, have brought with them into the world souls ill qualified to inhabit the bodies of Slaves. – Can I look tamely on, & see any machination to wrest from them, the birthright of my boys, the little independant Britons in whose veins runs my own blood? – No! I will not! – should my heart stream around my attempt to defend it! –

Does any man tell me, that my feeble efforts can be of no service; & that it does not belong to my humble station to meddle with the concerns of a People? – I tell him, that it is on such individuals as I, that for the hand of support and the eye of intelligence, a Nation has to rest. – The uninformed mob may swell a Nation's bulk, & the titled, tinsel Courtly throng may be its feathered ornament, but the number of those who are elevated enough in life, to reason & reflect; & yet low enough to keep clear of the venal contagion of a Court; these are a Nation's strength. –

One small request more: when you have honored this letter with a perusal, please commit it to the flames. – BURNS, in whose behalf you have so generously interested yourself, I have here, in his native colours, drawn *as he is*; but should any of the people in whose hands is the very bread he eats, get the least knowledge of the picture, it would ruin the poor Bard for ever. –

My Poems having just come out in another edition, I beg leave to present you with a copy; as a small mark of that high esteem & ardent gratitude with which I have the honor to be –

Sir,
Your deeply indebted,
And ever devoted humble servant

1 Burns's introduction to the letter in the Glenriddell Manuscript.

TO MRS RIDDELL
(CL, 697–8)

[This so-called 'letter from Hell' has caused problems for writers on Burns. No manuscript is extant and when Currie reprinted it in his second edition of 1801 he addressed it 'To Mrs R★★★★★. *Supposes himself to be writing from the dead to the living.*' (Currie II, 445.) It is immediately obvious from the letter that Burns had made some dreadful social and sexual blunder in his cups and wished to atone for it. Robert Chambers, in *The Life and Works of Burns* (1852) identified the recipient of the letter as Maria Riddell, thus placing the unspecified incident at Woodley Park, the home (four miles south-west of Dumfries) of Walter and Maria Riddell. In the Henley-Henderson centenary edition of 1896, the editors confidently put a date and description to the affair: 'Then, at a party at Woodley Park, in January 1794, he [Burns] and the men got drunk in the dining-room. The talk ran on the Rape of the Sabines' (H–H II, 420). When the men approached the women in the drawing-room, Burns supposedly laid 'rude hands on his hostess' (Ibid). Later commentators, however, showed that Walter Riddell was out of Scotland, in the West Indies, from (around) June 1793–April 1794: therefore the reference to 'Your husband' could not have meant Walter Riddell, if the incident indeed occurred during his absence, ergo the recipient was another 'Mrs R★★★★★', namely, Elizabeth Riddell who lived with her husband Robert at Friars' Carse, just north of Ellisland. Most authorities now assume the 'letter from Hell' was written in early January 1794 to Elizabeth Riddell. However, Currie may have tinkered with the text – he altered the Autobiographical Letter, changing 'a certain fashionable failing' to 'illicit love' (Currie I, 51) – and was capable of rephrasing Burns's original (possibly 'Your sister Elizabeth's husband' or simply 'Your sister's husband', by sister meaning sister-in-law since such usage was common in Burns's time) to read 'Your husband' in order to obscure the identify of Maria Riddell. On reading the letter, Maria wrote to Currie: 'That letter of [Burns] from the other world I am puzzled to guess how you came by. I had somehow mislaid it, and it certainly was not among those I delivered for your perusal.' (*Burns Chronicle*, 1946, p.10). If the mystery remains, the fact remains that Burns offended both Riddell wives, Elizabeth and Maria breaking with him after the incident.]

[?January 1794]

Madam,

I daresay this is the first epistle you ever received from this nether world. I write you from the regions of Hell, amid the horrors of the damned. The time and manner of my leaving your earth I do not exactly know, as I took my departure in the heat of a fever of intoxication, contracted at your too hospitable mansion; but, on my arrival here, I was fairly tried, and sentenced to endure the purgatorial tortures of this infernal confine for the space of ninety-nine years, eleven months, and twenty-nine days, and all on account of the impropriety of my conduct yesternight under your roof. Here am I, laid on a bed of pityless furze, with my aching head reclined on a pillow of ever-piercing thorn, while an infernal tormentor, wrinkled and old, and cruel, his name I think is *Recollection*, with a whip of scorpions, forbids peace or rest to approach me, and keeps anguish eternally awake. Still, Madam, if I could in any measure be reinstated in the good opinion of the fair circle whom my conduct last night so much injured, I think it would be an alleviation to my torments. For this reason I trouble you with this letter. To the men of the company I will make no apology. – Your husband, who insisted on my drinking more than I chose, has no right to blame me and the other gentlemen were partakers of my guilt. But to you, Madam, I have much to apologize. Your good opinion I valued as one of the greatest acquisitions I had made on earth, and I was truly a beast to forfeit it. There was a Miss I——, too, a woman of fine sense, gentle and unassuming manners – do make, on my part, a miserable damned wretch's best apology to her. A Mrs G——, a charming woman, did me the honour to be prejudiced in my favour; this makes me hope that I have not outraged her beyond all forgiveness. – To all the other ladies please present my humblest contrition for my conduct, and my petition for their gracious pardon. O, all ye powers of decency and decorum! whisper to them that my errors, though great, were involuntary – that an intoxicated man is the vilest of beasts – that it was not in my nature to be brutal to any one – that to be rude to a woman, when in my senses, was impossible with me – but –

Regret! Remorse! Shame![1] ye three hell-hounds that ever dog my steps and bay at my heels, spare me! spare me!
Forgive the offences, and pity the perdition of, Madam,

Your humble slave,

---

1 *Man was Made to Mourn*, line 52.

TO SAMUEL CLARK JUN.
(CL, 702)

Sunday morning –
[?1794]

Dear Sir

I was, I know, drunk last night, but I am sober this morning. – From the expressions Captain Dods made use of to me, had I had nobody's welfare to care for but my own, we should certainly have come, according to the manners of the world, to the necessity of murdering one another about the business. – The words were such as generally, I believe, end in a brace of pistols; but I am still pleased to think that I did not ruin the peace welfare of a wife & a family of children in a drunken squabble. – Farther, you know that the report of certain Political opinions being mine, has already once before brought me to the brink of destruction. – I dread lest last night's business may be misrepresented in the same way – You, I beg, will take care to prevent it. – I tax your wish for Mr Burns's welfare with the task of waiting as soon as possible, on every gentleman who was present, & state this to him, & as you please shew him this letter. – What after all was the obnoxious toast? – 'May our success in the present war be equal to the "justice of our cause" – A toast that the most outrageous frenzy of loyalty cannot object to. – I request & beg that this morning you will wait on the parties present at the foolish dispute. – The least delay may be of unlucky consequence to me. – I shall only add, that I am truly sorry that a man who stood so high in my estimation as Mr Dods, should use me in the manner in which I conceive he has done. –

I am, Dear Sir, yours sincerely
Robt Burns

TO GILBERT BURNS
(CL, 358)

10th July [1796]

Dear Brother

It will be no very pleasing news to you to be told that I am dangerously ill, & not likely to get better. – An inveterate rheumatism has reduced me to such a state of debility, & my appetite is gone, so that I can scarce stand on my legs. – I have been a week at sea-bathing, & I will continue

there or in a friend's house in the country all the summer. – God help
my wife & children, if I am taken from their head! – They will be poor
indeed. – I have contracted one or two serious debts, partly from my
illness these many months & partly from too much thoughtlessness as
to expense when I came to town that will cut in too much on the
little I leave them in your hands. – Remember me to my Mother. –

Yours
R Burns

TO JAMES BURNESS
(CL, 63–4)

12th July 1796

My dearest cousin,
When you offered me money-assistance little did I think I should want
it so soon. – A rascal of a Haberdasher to whom I owe a considerable
bill taking it into his head that I am dying, has commenced a process
against me & will infallibly put my emaciated body into jail. – Will
you be so good as to accommodate me, & that by return of post,
with ten pound. – O, James! did you know the pride of my heart,
you would feel doubly for me! Alas! I am not used to beg! The worst
of it is, my health was coming about finely; you know & my Physician
assures me that melancholy & low spirits are half my disease, guess then
my horrors since this business began. – If I had it settled, I would be
I think quite well in a manner. – How shall I use the language to you,
O do not disappoint me! but strong Necessity's curse command. –

I have been thinking over & over my brother's affairs & I fear
I must cut him up; but on this I will correspond at another time,
particularly as I shall want your advice. –

Forgive me for once more mentioning by return of Post. – Save
me from the horrors of jail!

My compliments to my friend James, & to all the rest. I do not
know what I have written, – The subject is so horrible, I dare not
look it over again. –

Farewel
R Burns

TO GEORGE THOMSON
(CL, 679-80)

12th July [1796]

After all my boasted independance, curst necessity compels me to
implore you for five pounds. – A cruel scoundrel of a Haberdasher
to whom I owe an account, taking it into his head that I am dying,
has commenced a process & will infallibly put me into jail.[1] – Do,
for God's sake, send me that sum, & that by return of post. – Forgive
me this earnestness, but the horrors of a jail have made me half
distracted. – I do not ask all this gratuitously; for upon returning
health, I hereby promise & engage to furnish you with five pounds'
worth of the neatest song genius you have seen. – I tryed my hand
on Rothiemurchie this morning. – The measure is so difficult that it
is impossible to infuse much genius into the lines – they are on the
other side. – Forgive, forgive me!

Yours
R Burns
Turn

Song, tune, Rothiemurchie
Chorus
Fairest maid on Devon banks[2]

1 Annotated by Thomson: 'This idea is exaggerated – he could not have
been in any such danger at Dumfries nor could he be in such necessity to implore aid from *Edinr*.' Thomson wrote to Burns on 14th July
enclosing a draft for the sum requested.
2 Annotated: 'These I presume are the last verses which came from the great
Bard's pen, as he died very soon after. G.T.'

TO JEAN ARMOUR BURNS
(CL, 479)

Brow, Thursday.
[14th July 1796]

My dearest Love,
I delayed writing until I could tell you what effect sea-bathing was
likely to produce. It would be injustice to deny that it has eased
my pains, and, I think, has strengthened me, but my appetite is still
extremely bad. No flesh nor fish can I swallow; porridge and milk

are the only thing I can taste. I am very happy to hear, by Miss Jess Lewars, that you are all well. My very best and kindest compliments to her, and to all the children. I will see you on Sunday.

Your affectionate husband,
R. B.

TO JAMES ARMOUR
(CL, 722)

Dumfries, 18th July 1796

My dear Sir,

Do, for heaven's sake, send Mrs Armour here immediately. My wife is hourly expecting to be put to bed. Good God! what a situation for her to be in, poor girl, without a friend! I returned from sea-bathing quarters to-day, and my medical friends would almost persuade me that I am better, but I think and feel that my strength is so gone that the disorder will prove fatal to me.

Your son-in-law,
R.B.

EPILOGUE

MARRIAGE OF ROBIN REDBREAST AND THE WREN

MARRIAGE OF ROBIN REDBREAST AND THE WREN

Including this tale in his *Popular Rhymes of Scotland* (1826), Robert Chambers noted it was taken down from the recitation of Mrs Isabella Begg (1771–1858), sister of Burns: 'The poet was in the habit of telling it to the younger members of his father's household, and Mrs Begg's impression is, that he *made* it for their amusement.' The reference to Burns's father places the story as a product of the Lochlea period, 1777–84, but Isabella was also part of Burns's household at Mossgiel.

There was an auld gray Poussie Baudrons, and she gaed awa' down by a water-side, and there she saw a wee Robin Redbreast happin on a brier; and Poussie Baudrons says, 'Where's tu gaun, wee Robin?' And wee Robin says, 'I'm gaun awa' to the king to sing him a sang this guid Yule morning.' And Poussie Baudrons says, 'Come here, wee Robin, and I'll let you see a bonny white ring round my neck.' But wee Robin says, 'Na, na! gray Poussie Baudrons; na, na! Ye worry't the wee mousie; but ye'se no worry me.' So wee Robin flew awa' till he came to a fail-fauld dike, and there he saw a gray greedy gled sitting. And gray greedy gled says, 'Where's tu gaun, wee Robin?' And wee Robin says, 'I'm gaun awa' to the king to sing him a sang this guid Yule morning.' And gray greedy gled says, 'Come here, wee Robin, and I'll let ye see a bonny feather in my wing.' But wee Robin says, 'Na, na! gray greedy gled; na, na! Ye pookit a' the wee lintie; but ye'se no pook me.' So wee Robin flew awa' till he came to the cleuch o' a craig, and there he saw slee Tod Lowrie sitting. And slee Tod Lowrie says, 'Where's tu gaun, wee Robin?' And wee Robin says, 'I'm gaun awa' to the king to sing him a sang this guid Yule morning.' And slee Tod Lowrie says, 'Come here, wee Robin, and I'll let ye see a bonny spot on the tap o' my tail.' But wee Robin says, 'Na, na! slee Tod Lowrie; na, na! Ye worry't the wee lammie; but ye'se no worry me.' So wee Robin flew awa' till he came to a bonny burn-side, and there he saw a wee callant sitting. And the wee callant says, 'Where's tu gaun, wee Robin?' And wee Robin says, 'I'm gaun awa' to the king to sing him a sang this guid Yule morning.' And the wee callant says, 'Come here, wee Robin, and I'll gie ye a wheen grand moolins out o' my pooch.' But wee Robin says, 'Na, na! wee callant; na, na! Ye speldert the gowdspink; but ye'se no spelder me.' So wee Robin flew awa' till he came to the king, and there he sat on a winnock sole, and

sang the king a bonny sang. And the king says to the queen, 'What'll
we gie to wee Robin for singing us this bonny sang?' And the queen
says to the king, 'I think we'll gie him the wee wran to be his wife.'
So wee Robin and the wee wran were married, and the king, and the
queen, and a' the court danced at the waddin'; syne he flew awa' hame
to his ain water-side, and happit on a brier.

GLOSSARY

The glossary gives the English equivalents of Scots words used by Burns in works included in this anthology. Those with a specialist interest in Scots are referred to *The Scottish National Dictionary* (10 vols., Edinburgh and Aberdeen, 1929–76) edited by William Grant and David D. Murison. Useful one-volume dictionaries are *Chambers' Scots Dictionary* (Edinburgh, 1911), compiled by Alexander Warrack; and *The Concise Scots Dictionary* (Aberdeen, 1985) edited by Mairi Robinson.

a': *all*
aboon: *above*
abread: *abroad*
acquent: *aquainted*
acquesh: *between*
a'-day: *day-long*
ae: *one*
aff: *off*
aften: *often*
agley: *askew*
aiblins: *maybe*
ain: *own*
air: *early*
airn: *iron*
airt: *direction*
aith: *oath*
aits: *oats*
amaist: *almost*
amang: *among*
an': *and*
ance: *once*
ane: *one*
anither: *another*
asklent: *askew*
aspar: *with legs apart*
Auld Reekie: *Edinburgh (old smoky)*
aumous dish: *alms dish*
ava: *at all*
awa: *away*
awnie: *bearded*
ay: *always*
ayont: *beyond*

bade: *asked*
bainie: *bony*
bairn: *child*
baith: *both*
bakes: *biscuits*
bane: *bone*
barley-brie: *whisky*
barmie: *fermenting with ideas*
batts: *colic*
bauckie-bird: *bat*
bauld: *bold*
bear: *barley*
beet: *fan*
beets to: *accelerates*
beld: *bald*
belyve: *by-and-by*
ben: *indoors, within*
bensmost: *inmost*
bestead: *provided*
beuk: *book*
bicker (n): *beaker*
bicker (v): *stagger*
bide: *endure, remain*
bield: *shelter*
bienly: *finely*
biggin: *cottage*
billie: *friend*
birk: *birch*
birkie: *fellow*
birnie: *rough*
bitchify'd: *intoxicated*
black-bonnet: *kirk elder*
blate: *shy*
blather: *bladder*

blaw: *blow*
blellum: *babbler*
blether: *bladder, chatter*
blinkers: *spies*
blue-boram: *pox*
boddle: *copper coin, equivalent to sixth of English penny*
bonie: *pretty*
bore: *crevice*
bowse: *booze*
braid: *broad*
braid-claith: *broad cloth*
brak: *break*
branks: *halter, bridle*
brash: *illness*
brats: *scraps*
braw: *splendid*
breeks: *britches*
brent: *straight*
brig: *bridge*
brock: *badger*
brose: *oatmeal mixed with boiling water*
brose, butter'd my: *satisfied me sexually*
brugh: *burgh*
brunstane: *brimstone*
buirdly: *stalwart*
bum-clock: *humming beetle*
burdie: *lady, girl (bird)*
Burnewin: *blacksmith*
butching: *butchering*
buttock-hire: *ecclesiastical fine for fornication*
byke: *crowd, hive*

ca': *call, drive*
cadger: *hawker*
caff: *chaff*
calf-ward: *small enclosure for calves*
callant: *boy*
caller: *fresh, cool*

callet: *girlfriend*
cantraip: *magic*
carl-hemp: *seed-bearing hemp*
carlie: *old man*
carlin: *old woman*
cartes: *cards*
castock: *cabbage stem*
Catch-the-Plack: *money-grubbing*
caup: *wooden bowl*
causey: *causeway*
cavie: *(hen-) coop*
change-house: *ale-house*
chap: *liquid measure, half a Scots pint*
chapman: *pedlar*
chaup: *stroke*
chiel: *fellow*
chuck: *dear*
cit: *citizen*
clachan: *village*
claes: *clothes*
claith: *cloth*
claithing: *clothes*
clash: *chatter*
clatter: *gossip*
claught: *seized*
clean-shankit: *clean-limbed*
cleek: *clutch*
cleekit: *linked arms*
cleuch: *ravine*
clinkin: *sitting swiftly*
Clinkumbell: *bell-ringer*
clish-ma-claver: *nonsense*
cloot: *hoof*
clout: *patch*
coft: *bought*
cog: *wooden drinking vessel made of staves and girded with metal bands*
coor: *cover*
coost: *cast*
corbie: *raven*

core: *crowd*
coulter: *ploughshare*
countra: *country*
cowpit: *stumbled*
cozie: *snug*
crack: *conversation*
cragie: *throat*
craig: *crag*
crambo-jingle: *rhyming*
cranks: *creakings*
cranreuch: *hoar-frost*
crap: *crop*
craw: *crow*
creel: *wicker basket*
creeshie: *greasy, filthy*
croon: *hum*
crouse: *merry*
crowdie: *porridge*
crowdie-time: *breakfast time*
crowl: *crawl*
cruck: *limp*
crumnock: *stick with crooked head*
crump: *crisp*
curmurring: *commotion*
cuif: *dolt*
cutty: *short*

daffin: *fun*
dail: *plank*
daimen-icker: *occasional ear of corn*
damn'd haet: *damn all*
dang: *pushed, knocked*
darg: *work*
daunder'd: *strolled*
daunton: *subdue*
daur: *dare*
dawd: *lump*
Deil: *Devil*
deil-sticket: *devil-botched*
delver: *gardener*
deuk: *duck*

dight: *wipe*
dink: *trim*
dinna: *do not*
dint: *affection*
dirl: *ring*
ditty: *ground of indictment*
dizzen: *dozen*
docht: *dared*
dochter: *daughter*
doited, doitit: *muddled*
donsie: *restive, bad-tempered*
douce: *sedate, sober*
dow: *can*
downa-do: *impotence (cannot do)*
doylt: *stupid*
doytin: *dolting*
drap: *drop*
dreeping: *dripping*
driddle: *saunter*
droddum: *backside*
drouth: *thirst*
drucken: *drunken*
drumlie: *muddy*
dub: *puddle*
duddie: *ragged*
duddies: *rags*
dusht: *pushed by a ram*
dyke: *low dry-stone wall*

e'e: *eye*
een: *eyes*
e'en: *even*
eerie: *apprehensive*
eild: *old age*
eldricht: *unearthly, haunted*
ell: *unit of measurement (37.059 inches)*
eneugh, enow: *enough*
ettle: *purpose, aim*
eydent: *diligent*

fa': *befall*

fae: *foe*
faem: *foam*
fail: *turf*
fain: *fond*
fairin: *reward, deserts*
fairy: *tiny*
fand: *found*
farl: *quarter of the circular oaten bannock*
fash: *brother, trouble*
Fasten-e'en: *Shrove Tuesday*
fatt'rills: *ribbon ends*
fauld dyke: *wall of a sheep fold*
faut: *fault*
fawsont: *seemly*
feck: *majority*
feckless: *worthless, weak*
feerie: *sturdy*
feetie: *little feet*
fell: *pungent*
fend: *support*
ferlie, ferly: *marvel, wonder*
fidgin-fain: *tingling wild*
fient-ma-care: *devil-may-care*
fient a: *the devil a*
fient haet: *devil have it*
fissle: *tingle*
flainen: *flannel*
fleesh: *fleece*
fley'd: *frightened*
flichterin': *fluttering*
flinging-tree: *flail*
fodgel: *plump, buxom*
foggage: *coarse grass*
forfairn: *worn out*
forfoughten: *exhausted*
forgie: *forgive*
forjesket: *fatigued*
forniaw'd: *fatigued*
fou, fow, fu': *full, drunk*
foughten: *troubled*
frae: *from*

freath: *froth*
fud: *backside, tail*
furm: *form, bench*
fusionless: *weak*
fyke: *fidget*
fyl'd: *fouled*

gab (n): *mouth*
gab (v): *chatter*
ga'd: *galled*
gae: *go*
gaet: *way*
gane: *gone*
gang: *go*
gar: *make*
gash: *respectable*
gat: *got*
gate: *road*
gaud: *went*
gauger: *exciseman*
gaun: *going*
gawsie: *jolly, ample*
gear: *possessions*
Geordie: *guinea*
get: *issue*
ghaist: *ghost*
gie: *give*
gif: *if*
gimmer-pet: *pet yearling ewe*
girdle: *griddle*
girn: *snarl*
girran: *garron*
glaikit: *idiotic*
gleyde: *common kite*
gloaming: *twilight, dusk*
glunch: *growl*
goavan's: *staring . . . as if*
goom: *gum*
gos: *goshawk*
gowan: *daisy*
gowd: *gold*
gowdspink: *goldfinch*

grain: *groan*
graith: *harness*
gree: *prize, social degree*
greet: *weep*
greetie: *cry*
gree't: *agreed*
grozet: *gooseberry*
gruntle: *snout*
grushie: *growing*
Gude: *God*
guid: *good*
guid-een: *good evening*
guid-willie waught: *cup of kindness*
gully: *large knife*
gumlie: *muddy*

ha': *hall*
hae: *have*
haet: *have it*
haffet: *side-lock of hair*
ha'-folk: *servants*
hafflins: *halfway, partly*
hainch: *haunch*
hairum-scairum: *wild*
hald: *holding*
hale: *whole*
hallin: *clay or mud partition*
Hallow-mass: *festival of All Saints*
haly: *holy*
hame: *home*
han: *hand*
hansel: *good-luck gift*
hap: *hop, wrap*
happer: *hopper (of a mill)*
harigals: *entrails*
harkit: *listened*
harn: *coarse linen*
hash: *oaf*
haud: *hold*
hauffet: *temple*
haughs: *hollows*

havins: *manners*
hawkie: *white-faced cow*
healsome: *wholesome*
heapit: *heaped*
herryment: *waste*
het: *hot*
heugh: *crag, steep bank*
hing: *hang*
hirplin: *hopping, limping*
hizzie: *wench*
hoast: *cough*
hoddin (n): *coarse grey homespun cloth of mixed black and white wool*
hoddin (pple): *jogging along*
hoolie: *halt*
horn: *horn vessel, horn spoon*
Hornie: *Devil*
host: *cough*
hotch: *jerk*
houghmagandie: *fornication*
houlet: *owl*
hov'd: *swollen*
howdie: *midwife*
howe: *hollow*
howk: *dig*
hunkers: *haunches*
hurchin: *urchin*
hurchyall'd: *tottered*
hurdies: *buttocks*
hurl: *crash*

ilk: *each*
ilka: *every*
Ill-Thief: *Devil*
ingine: *genius*
ingle: *fire burning on a hearth*
ingle-cheek: *fireside*
ither: *other*

jad: *jade*
jauk: *trifle*
jaup: *splash*

jo: *sweetheart*
Johnie Ged's hole: *the grave*
jorum: *drinking vessel, punch bowl*
jouk: *dodge, duck*
jow: *swing*

kail: *cabbage*
kail-blade: *cabbage leaf*
kail-runt: *cabbage stalk*
kail-whittle: *knife for cutting cabbage*
kail-yard: *cabbage patch*
kain: *payment in kind*
kebars: *rafters*
kebbuck: *cheese*
keek: *peep*
kelpie: *horse-shaped water monster*
ken: *know*
kend: *known*
kennin: *trifle*
ken't: *knew*
ket: *fleece*
kiaugh: *anxiety*
Kilbaigie: *Clackmannanshire whisky distillery*
kin': *kind*
king's hood: *second stomach in a ruminant, paunch, scrotum*
kintra: *country*
kirk: *church*
kirk-hammer: *clapper*
kirn: *harvest-home*
kirsen: *christen*
kittle (n): *difficult*
kittle (adj): *tickle*
knappin-hammer: *stone-breaking hammer*
knoited: *knocked*
kye: *cattle*

lalland: *lowland*
Lammas: *1 August*

lammie: *lamb*
landlowper: *roving vagabond*
lane: *lone*
lang: *long*
lave: *the rest, remainder, others*
lav'rock: *lark*
lear: *learning*
lee-lang: *live-long*
leeze . . . on: *blessing*
leister: *pronged spear, trident*
leugh: *laughed*
leuk: *look*
limmer: *jade, mistress, whore*
linket: *skipped*
lint: *flax*
lintie: *linnet*
lintwhite: *linnet*
lippen: *trust*
loan: *grassy strip through arable land*
loof: *palm*
loon, loun: *rogue, fellow*
lowe: *flame*
lowin: *flaming*
lowp: *jump*
lowse: *loose*
lug: *ear*
lugget caup: *two-handled wooden drinking dish*
luggie: *two-handled wooden drinking dish*
luntin: *smoking*
lyart: *grey, withered, grizzled*

mae: *more*
Mahoun: *Devil*
mailin: *leased arable land*
mair: *more*
mak: *make*
mantie: *gown*
mantling: *foaming*
maukin: *hare*

maun: *must*
mauna: *must not*
maut: *malt*
maw: *mow*
meere: *mare*
meikle: *big*
melder: *meal-grinding*
mell: *meddle*
melvie: *to soil with meal*
menseless: *senseless*
messin: *cur*
minnie: *mother*
mishanter: *mishap*
mislear'd: *outwitted, mischievous*
mither: *mother*
monie: *many*
moolin: *crumb*
moop: *nibble*
mottle: *dusty*
moudiewort: *mole*
mowe: *copulate*
muckle: *much, great*
muslin-kail: *beefless broth*

na': *not*
naig: *small horse, pony*
nane: *none*
nappy: *ale*
near-hand: *well nigh*
neebor: *neighbour*
needfu': *needful*
neist: *next*
neuk: *corner*
nick: *cut*
nieve: *fist*
niffer: *exchange*
nit: *nut*
no: *not*
noddle: *brain, head*
nowt: *cattle, oxen*

o' boot: *gratis*

onie: *any*
orra: *spare*
o't: *of it*
out-owre: *above*
owre: *over*

pack: *confidential*
paidle: *paddle*
paidl'd: *paddled*
paitrick: *partridge*
painch: *paunch*
pang: *crams*
parritch: *porridge*
pat: *put*
pattle: *small long-handled spade for cleaning plough*
pawkie: *cunning, sly*
pechan: *stomach*
penny-fee: *wages*
penny wheep: *small beer*
philibeg: *kilt*
pin: *skewer*
pint-stowp: *pint-measure*
pit: *put*
plack: *small coin (four pennies Scots)*
plaister: *plaster*
plea: *law-case*
pleugh, plew: *plough*
pliver: *plover*
plumrose: *primrose*
poind: *seize*
pooch: *pocket*
pook: *pluck*
poortith: *poverty*
pou: *pull*
pouk: *poke*
poutherie: *powdery*
poussie: *hare*
Poussie Baudrons: *affectionate name for a cat*
pow: *head*

pownie: *pony*

prent: *print*

presses: *cupboards*

prief: *proof*

priggin: *haggling*

proveses: *provosts*

pussie: *hare*

pyke: *pick*

pystle: *epistle*

quat: *leave, quit*

quier: *choir*

quine: *young woman*

raible: *gabble*

rairin: *roaring*

ram–stam: *headstrong, reckless*

randie: *riotous*

rape: *rope*

rash: *rush*

ratton: *rat*

raucle: *sturdy*

ream: *froth, foam*

reave: *plunder*

red: *advise*

reek: *smoke*

reekin: *smoking, steaming*

remead: *remedy*

rief: *plunder*

rig: *ridge*

riggin: *roof*

rigwoodie: *back-band for a cart horse*

rin: *run*

ripp: *handful of unthreshed corn*

rive: *split*

roose: *praise*

roosty: *rusty*

row, rowe: *roll*

rowth: *abundance*

rowtin: *lowing*

rozet: *rosin*

rumblegumtion: *common sense*

run: *downright*

rung: *cudgel*

runkl'd: *wrinkled*

ryke: *reach*

sae: *so*

sair (v): *serve*

sair (adj): *sore, hard*

saft: *soft*

sark: *shirt, shift*

saugh woodies: *ropes of twisted sallow-withes*

saul: *soul*

saut: *salt*

saw: *sow*

sax: *six*

scar: *scare*

scraichin: *screaming*

scrievin: *gliding along*

scrimpit: *short*

scunner: *disgust*

session: *court*

shavie: *prank, trick*

shaw (n): *small wood in a hollow*

shaw (v): *show*

sheugh: *ditch*

sheuk: *shook*

shool: *shovel*

shoon: *shoes*

shot: *sort*

shouther: *shoulder*

sic, sik: *such*

sicker: *steady, secure*

simmer: *summer*

sin: *since*

skaith: *damage, harm*

skellum: *rascal*

skelpin: *rushing*

skinking: *watery*

skirl: *squeal*

sklent: *side-look*

skyte: *lash*
slade: *crept*
slae: *blackthorn*
slap: *gap in a dyke*
slee: *sly*
sleekit: *sleek, sly*
sloken: *slake*
sma': *small*
smeddum: *fine powder used as insecticide*
smeek: *smoke*
smiddie: *smithy*
smoor'd: *smothered*
smytrie: *litter*
snakin': *sneering*
snaw-broo: *half-melted snow*
sned: *crop, cut off, prune*
snell: *bitter*
sneshin mill: *snuff box*
snick: *latch*
snirtle: *snigger*
snowkit: *snuffed*
sodger: *soldier*
sole: *sill*
sonnet: *song*
sonsie: *pleasant*
souple: *soft, supple*
souter: *cobbler*
sowpe: *drink, mouthful*
sowther: *solder, patch*
spair: *spare*
spak: *spoke*
spavie: *spavin*
spean: *wean*
speat: *spate*
speel: *climb*
speet: *skewer*
spelder: *tear apart*
spence: *parlour*
spier: *ask*
spleuchan: *tobacco pouch, purse, scrotum, vagina*

splore: *carousal*
sprattle: *scramble*
spunk: *spark, spirit*
spunkie: *will o' the wisp*
squattle: *squat*
stacher: *stagger*
stan': *stand, halt*
stane: *stone*
stang: *sting*
stank: *pool*
stap: *stop*
staumrel: *stammering, silly*
staw (v): *sicken*
staw (v pa.t.): *stole*
stechin: *cramming*
steek: *stitch*
steer: *stir, agitate*
stell: *still*
stent: *impost, duty*
stibble: *stubble*
stimpart: *fourth part of a peck, in dry measure*
stirk: *young bullock*
stoiter: *lurch*
stotter: *stagger*
stoure: *battle*
stowp: *cup*
strae: *straw*
strak: *struck*
straught: *straight*
stravaugin: *roaming*
streekit: *stretched*
stroan't: *pissed*
studdie: *anvil*
sturt: *fret*
sucker: *sugar*
sugh: *rushing sound of wind*
suthron: *English (southern)*
swankie: *fine fellow*
swat: *sweated*
swats: *new small beer*
swatch: *sample*

swith: *away*
swither: *state of agitation*
swoor: *swore*
syne: *since, then*

tae: *toe*
taen: *taken*
tak: *take*
tald: *told*
tap: *top*
tapsalteerie: *topsy-turvy*
tassie: *drinking-cup*
tawted: *matted*
tent (n): *care*
tent (v): *tend*
tentie: *careful*
teugh: *tough*
thack: *thatch*
thae: *those*
thairm: *fiddle-string*
thegither: *together*
thirl'd: *thrilled*
thole: *endure*
thowe: *thaw*
thrang (n): *crowd*
thrang (adj): *busy*
thrang (adv): *busily*
thrave: *two stooks of corn, hence measure of straw*
thraw: *twist, turn*
thretty: *thirty*
thrissle: *thistle*
till't: *to it*
timmer: *timber, trees*
tipper-taiper: *teeter*
tinkler: *tinker*
tinkler-hizzie: *tinker wench*
tint: *lost*
tippence: *twopence*
tippeny: *twopenny beer*
tips: *tups*
tither: *other*

tittlin: *whispering*
tod: *fox*
Tod Lowrie: *fox*
toom: *empty*
toop: *tup*
tother: *other*
tousie: *shaggy*
tow: *rope*
towsing: *roughly handling*
towmond: *twelve-month*
toy: *close-fitting cap*
tozie: *tipsy, cosy*
trowth: *trust*
'twad: *would have*
tumbler-wheels: *cart-wheels*
twal: *twelve*
twin: *separate from*
tyke: *cur*

unco: *odd, strange*
unkend: *unknown, unnoticed*
upstan't: *stood*
usquabae: *whisky*

vauntie: *proud*
vera, verra: *very*
virls: *rings*

wa': *wall*
wabster: *weaver*
wad: *wager*
wad: *would*
waddin': *wedding*
wae: *woe*
waesucks: *alas*
wale: *choice*
walie: *ample, fine*
wame: *stomach, belly*
wanchancie: *dangerous*
wanrestfu': *restless*
wap: *wrap*
warl': *world*

warlock-beef: *charter conveying magical powers*
warl'y: *worldly*
warn: *warn*
warsle: *struggle*
wat: *wot*
water-brose: *brose made with water*
water-fit: *river's mouth*
wauken: *waken*
waukin: *awake, sleepless*
waukit: *calloused*
waur: *worse, worst*
wawlie: *handsome*
weary fa': *plague upon*
wean: *child*
weanies: *infants*
weason: *gullet*
weed: *clothes*
weel: *well*
weel-far'd: *well-favoured*
weel-hain'd: *well-saved*
wha: *who*
whae: *who*
whalpit: *whelped*
whang: *thick slice of cheese*
whase: *whose*
wheen: *quantity*
whid: *fib*
whiddin: *scudding*
whigmaleerie: *whimsical ornament*
whin: *gorse*
whipper-in: *huntsman responsible for keeping hounds in pack*
whist: *peace*

whirlygigums: *flourishes*
whitter: *draught of liquor*
whittle: *blade*
whunstane: *whin-rock*
whup: *peace*
whyles: *sometimes*
wi': *with*
willyart: *awkward*
wimplin: *winding*
winch: *wench*
winnock-bunker: *window seat*
win's: *winds*
winna: *will not*
woo': *wool*
woodie: *gallows*
wook: *week*
wrack: *torment*
wran: *wren*
Writer [to the Signet]: *lawyer*
wud: *wild, angry*
wyliecoat: *flannel vest*
wyte: *reproach*

yauld: *vigorous*
yealing: *contemporary in age*
yerk: *stir up*
yestreen: *yesterday evening*
yill: *ale*
yill-caup: *ale-cup*
yokin: *set-to*
yon: *that*
younkers: *young folk*
yowe: *ewe*
yowie: *ewe-lamb*

DAPHNE: A PORTRAIT OF DAPHNE DU MAURIER
by Judith Cook

'Last night I dreamed I went to Manderley.' So begins one of the most remarkable novels ever written – *Rebecca*. Extraordinary because it captured the imagination of millions of readers throughout the world and is still, today, a bestseller. Its author was Daphne du Maurier.

Daphne du Maurier came from an extraordinary family. It was when the du Mauriers bought a holiday home in Cornwall that Daphne's career began. Cornwall was to be her great love, inspiring a passion in her quite unmatched by her love for her husband, 'Boy' Browning, or her children. It was Cornwall that fed her writing and it was her house, Menabilly, that sparked her creative imagination. Here Daphne wrote the novels which made her famous – novels such as *Jamaica Inn*, *Frenchman's Creek* and *My Cousin Rachel*.

Judith Cook's portrait of Daphne du Maurier is an illuminating insight into the life of a complex and introverted woman whose books continue to captivate generations of readers, entranced by her superb sense of place and atmosphere, and above all by her unique gift for storytelling.

0 552 99422 7

THE MARQUIS DE SADE
by Donald Thomas

Few people know anything about the Marquis de Sade (1740–1814), the man whose name is synonymous with perverse cruelty and sexual depravity. Was he a monster? Or was he simply a product of his time and class?

An aristocrat in an age of decadence, Sade attracted scandal in the grand manner. Accusations of orgies in black-draped rooms, whippings, poisonings and more extreme sexual crimes, led to twenty-seven years of imprisonment under royal and revolutionary regimes. Yet he became a judge in the revolutionary government who opposed the guillotine, saved enemies from prison and campaigned fearlessly against state terror and injustice. His writings, which resulted in his detention till death in the Charenton asylum and which even today provoke violent condemnation, are considered by many to be the work of a visionary whose ideas foreshadowed twentieth-century thinking.

Following the storm of controversy surrounding the re-publication of Sade's novels, *Justine* and *Juliette,* Donald Thomas's timely biography presents a portrait of a complex and contradictory man, unravelling his life against the turbulent backdrop of revolutionary France, and assessing his legacy in the context of our own time.

0 552 99499 5

A SELECTION OF TITLES AVAILABLE FROM CORGI AND BLACK SWAN

THE PRICES SHOWN BELOW WERE CORRECT AT THE TIME OF GOING TO PRESS. HOWEVER TRANSWORLD PUBLISHERS RESERVE THE RIGHT TO SHOW NEW RETAIL PRICES ON COVERS WHICH MAY DIFFER FROM THOSE PREVIOUSLY ADVERTISED IN THE TEXT OR ELSEWHERE.

☐ 99065 5	THE PAST IS MYSELF	Christabel Bielenberg	£5.99
☐ 99469 3	THE ROAD AHEAD	Christabel Bielenberg	£5.99
☐ 99422 7	DAPHNE: A PORTRAIT OF DAPHNE DU MAURIER	Judith Cook	£5.99
☐ 13126 1	CATHERINE COOKSON COUNTRY	Catherine Cookson	£9.99
☐ 13407 4	LET ME MAKE MYSELF PLAIN	Catherine Cookson	£3.99
☐ 13928 9	DAUGHTER OF PERSIA	Sattareh Farman-Farmaian	£5.99
☐ 99479 0	PERFUME FROM PROVENCE	Lady Fortescue	£5.99
☐ 99557 6	SUNSET HOUSE	Lady Fortescue	£5.99
☐ 99558 4	THERE'S ROSEMARY, THERE'S RUE	Lady Fortescue	£5.99
☐ 99418 9	A HOME BY THE HOOGHLY	Eugenie Fraser	£4.99
☐ 12833 3	THE HOUSE BY THE DVINA	Eugenie Fraser	£5.99
☐ 99438 3	A PLACE FOR US	Nicholas Gage	£5.99
☐ 99425 1	A HOUSE WITH FOUR ROOMS	Rumer Godden	£5.99
☐ 99347 6	A TIME TO DANCE, NO TIME TO WEEP	Rumer Godden	£4.99
☐ 99505 5	TRUTH TO TELL	Ludovic Kennedy	£7.99
☐ 13892 4	FIFTY YEARS IN THE SYSTEM	Jimmy Laing	£5.99
☐ 13550 X	DIANA'S STORY	Deric Longden	£3.99
☐ 13769 3	LOST FOR WORDS	Deric Longden	£3.99
☐ 13822 3	THE CAT WHO CAME IN FROM THE COLD	Deric Longden	£3.99
☐ 13356 6	NOT WITHOUT MY DAUGHTER	Betty Mahmoody	£4.99
☐ 99463 4	DOROTHY: MEMOIRS OF A NURSE	Dorothy Moriarty	£4.99
☐ 99509 6	MARTHA JANE AND ME	Mavis Nicholson	£5.99
☐ 13946 7	NICOLA	Nicola Owen	£4.99
☐ 13983 1	DIETRICH	Donald Spoto	£5.99
☐ 13950 5	JESUS THE MAN	Barbara Thiering	£5.99
☐ 99499 5	THE MARQUIS DE SADE	Donald Thomas	£6.99

All Corgi/Bantam Books are available at your bookshop or newsagent, or can be ordered from the following address:

Corgi/Bantam Books
Cash Sales Department
P.O. Box 11, Falmouth, Cornwall TR10 9EN

UK and B.F.P.O. customers please send a cheque or postal order (no currency) and allow £1.00 for postage and packing for the first book plus 50p for the second book and 30p for each additional book to a maximum charge of £3.00 (7 books plus).

Overseas customers, including Eire, please allow £2.00 for postage and packing for the first book plus £1.00 for the second book and 50p for each subsequent title ordered.

NAME (Block letters) ....

ADDRESS ....